The Last Great War

What was it that the British people believed they were fighting for in 1914–1918? This compelling history of the British home front during the First World War offers an entirely new account of how British society understood and endured the war. Drawing on official archives, memoirs, diaries and letters, Adrian Gregory sheds new light on the public reaction to the war, examining the role of propaganda and rumour in fostering patriotism and hatred of the enemy. He shows the importance of the ethic of volunteerism and the rhetoric of sacrifice in debates over where the burdens of war should fall as well as the influence of religious ideas on wartime culture. As the war drew to a climax and tensions about the distribution of sacrifices threatened to tear society apart, Gregory shows how victory and the processes of commemoration helped create a fiction of a society united in grief.

ADRIAN GREGORY is Lecturer in Modern History at Pembroke College, University of Oxford. His previous publications include *The Silence of Memory: Armistice Day 1919–1946* (1994) and, as editor, *A War to Unite Us All: Ireland and the Great War* (2002).

The Last Great War

British Society and the First World War

Adrian Gregory

DAMAGED

CAMBRIDGE
UNIVERSITY PRESS

CAMBRIDGE UNIVERSITY PRESS
Cambridge, New York, Melbourne, Madrid, Cape Town, Singapore,
São Paulo, Delhi, Dubai, Tokyo

Cambridge University Press
The Edinburgh Building, Cambridge CB2 8RU, UK

Published in the United States of America
by Cambridge University Press, New York

www.cambridge.org
Information on this title: www.cambridge.org/9780521728836

First published 2008
Reprinted 2010

Printed in the United Kingdom at the University Press, Cambridge

A catalogue record for this publication is available from the British Library

Library of Congress Cataloguing in Publication Data
Gregory, Adrian.
The last Great War : British society and the First World War / Adrian Gregory.
    p.   cm.
ISBN 978-0-521-45037-9
1. World War, 1914-1918 – Great Britain.   2. World War, 1914-1918 – Social
aspects – Great Britain.   3. Great Britain – History – George V, 1910-1936.
I. Title.
D524.7.G7 G74   2009
940.3'41–dc22
                                                            2008041687

ISBN 978-0-521-45037-9 hardback
ISBN 978-0-521-72883-6 paperback

Contents

Illustrations   *page* vi
Acknowledgements   vii

Introduction: The war that did not end all wars   1

1   Going to war   9

2   Defining the enemy: Atrocities and propaganda
    1914–1915   40

3   From spectatorship to participation; From volunteering
    to compulsion 1914–1916   70

4   Economies of sacrifice   112

5   Redemption through war: Religion and the languages
    of sacrifice   152

6   The conditional sacrifices of labour 1915–1918   187

7   Struggling to victory 1917–1918   213

8   The last war?   249

    Conclusion   277

    Notes   297
    Index   341

Illustrations

1. Recruiting *page* 30
2. Belgian refugees arrive in London 50
3. Physical drill for volunteers 74
4. A voluntary canteen for soldiers 97
5. Post for the Army 132
6. Policewomen and soldiers on leave 134
7. Digging for victory 143
8. Allotment holders pledge allegiance 145
9. The Roman Catholic Archbishop of Westminster addresses a War Loan rally 164
10. Petition for a day of prayer 183
11. Work gates at Woolwich Arsenal 193
12. Labour Conference 1918 201
13. A voluntary public kitchen 204
14. Recruiting the Women's Army Auxiliary Corps 246
15. Flag day in aid of Indian soldiers 247
16. American troops in London 247
17. A war widow and her child presented to the King 256
18. Rehabilitation of blinded soldiers 265

All photographs are used with the permission of the Trustees of the Imperial War Museum, London.

Acknowledgements

It would be impossible to acknowledge all the individual debts incurred in the course of writing this book. So, to avoid boring the reader, I shall make a series of collective acknowledgements. It began when I was a research fellow at King's College, Cambridge; my thanks to the Fellows and students of that college and the participants in various history seminars there.

I wish to thank all my comrades and colleagues in the Fellowship of Pembroke College, Oxford, the Historial de la Grande Guerre, the Capital Cities at War project, the International Society of First World War historians and the Modern History Faculty of the University of Oxford. I also wish to thank the Humanities Board of the University of Oxford for a term of matching leave which helped me get a chapter written.

A negative acknowledgement goes to whoever thought the Research Assessment Exercise was a good idea. Books are done when they are done, and the history of centrally imposed production quotas is hardly an impressive one, for reasons most second-year history or economics undergraduates could explain.

My undergraduate and graduate students probably delayed this book by at least three years. In my view this was probably a 'Good Thing'.

I will limit myself to thanking a very small number of individuals, most also included in the acknowledgements above: Dr Peter Claus and Dr Andrea Smith for physical and moral support in the final stages; Professor Hew Strachan who helped more than he may realise in saving me from despair of ever finishing; the usual filial debt to Professor Jay Winter and apologies for the Oedipal moments; Professor Niall Ferguson, Professor Susan Grayzel and Dr Jeffrey Verhey for the stimulation; Dr Pierre Purseigle, Dr Jon Lawrence and Dr Senia Paseta for innumerable debts; Professor Miri Rubin and Dr Stephen Tuck for sharing the college load; and Dr Tracey Sowerby for this, and her model professionalism which reminded me of why I started.

None of the above should be blamed for any errors or deficiencies. In some cases I know I have ignored their good advice out of sheer perversity.

I would like to thank Michael Watson, Helen Waterhouse and Jodie Barnes for their support and patience. Elizabeth King-Sloan and Christine Bland kindly gave me permission to quote from family letters deposited at the Imperial War Museum. I have attempted without success to contact family members in other cases. I would therefore like to acknowledge my gratitude to all the writers who have deposited their letters for posterity without whom the historian would be helpless.

Every effort has been made to secure necessary permissions to reproduce copyright material in this work, though in some cases it has proved impossible to trace copyright holders. If any omissions are brought to our notice, we will be happy to include appropriate acknowledgements on reprinting.

Finally, how do I thank Dr Sarah Cohen who has had to live with all of this? And more.

Next year in?

Introduction: The war that did not end all wars

Popular memory and historical understanding

The British still seem to take the First World War personally. It would be difficult to imagine a contemporary British historian of the Napoleonic Wars writing a preface about how their great-great-great-grandfather died of typhoid at Walcheren or lost an arm at Badajoz, but it seems almost instinctive to evoke a grandfather at Loos or a great-uncle on the Somme. Moral indignation is not without benefits for a historian; the crimes and follies of mankind do require something other than cold detachment. But history demands perspective, and intense personal involvement can and does lead to distortion.

Hindsight has been the other curse of writing about the war. Of course, it would be absurd to banish hindsight from our historical judgement. It is one of our assets. We know how things turned out and can therefore attempt to explain why they turned out as they did. But hindsight carries risks when applied to understanding the thoughts and actions of people in the past.

We must remember that hindsight is unavailable to those who are living through the experience, and it cannot inform their decisions. We might choose to condemn the First World War as a human tragedy and an error of colossal proportions, but in doing so we must be aware that there is something essentially anachronistic about this. It can lead to unjustifiable wishful thinking based on little more than romantic nostalgia.

It can certainly be argued that Britain gained nothing and lost much as a result of the First World War. The principal results of the war were more than 700,000 young men dead, a similar number injured, many permanently, and a massive increase of national indebtedness. By comparison, the compensations were distinctly limited. There were a few colonial gains, disguised as mandates, which had negligible real value, and, objectively, may have been a burden for the British. There was a modest improvement in working-class living standards and security, and a very

1

limited emancipation of women. The latter two phenomena were largely accidental and the last is debatable.

Even if these 'gains' are acknowledged, the 'opportunity costs' were staggering. War efforts are by definition wasteful and, according to political inclination, it is not difficult to propose better uses of the energy expended: massive investment in the economic modernisation of Britain and the empire, reduction in taxes to stimulate growth or even social programmes on a near utopian scale. Had there been no war, then Britain, *in principle*, could have built new universities in every major city, hundreds of advanced hospitals, thousands of schools, increased pension provision and childcare, and still experienced a lower tax burden in 1919 than it did. Furthermore 700,000 mostly young lives would have been spared.

No one in 1914 knew or could have known the alternatives outlined here. The alternative they believed they faced was quite different. Their choice was between war and the German domination of Europe. Rightly or wrongly, and to varying degrees, the vast majority of the British people, soldiers and civilians alike, came to believe in 1914 that such domination by Germany would be a disaster. Most still believed it in 1918 and many would continue to believe it for their entire lives.

Happy is the country with no history of defeat. Comparison is instructive regarding this point. In human terms the First World War was a disaster for France that dwarfed the British experience. In absolute numbers, French losses were almost double the British, while in proportion to the population they were more than double. The fighting of the war on French soil led to unprecedented material destruction. Yet the *long-term* cultural trauma of the First World War has not been as great in France. There *is* something worse than bloody and expensive victory, and that is defeat. In French memories, the First World War is bracketed between the debacle of 1870 and the debacle of 1940. The almost unimaginable human suffering of Verdun is modified and mollified by the fact that, in 1918, 'France' had survived. No such compensation was offered in 1870, or 1940. In the words of the singer Georges Brassens, 'Qu'est-ce que c'est la guerre que je préfère, c'est la guerre de "14–18".'[1]

The First World War itself proves this point; that defeat is the worst 'trauma'. The country most overwhelmed by a sense of the futility of the war after 1918 was Germany. There was no compensation at all for the German experience of Verdun or the Somme. Two million young Germans had died for nothing. Nothing and worse than nothing. It was a reality too painful to admit. The only 'benefit' the German people received from the war was democracy, and that democracy was tainted as the product of defeat. This was trauma on an epic scale. The only escape was fantasy. To make sacrifice worthwhile, victory had to be claimed on some other level, a triumph of the spirit. To make that interpretation work, an explanation had to be found for the mundane and observable reality of defeat. The 'November Criminals' became the alibi of nationalists. They argued against all the evidence that Germany had won the war, but had been betrayed. Conservative Germany did not renounce the war; it renounced the defeat.[2]

By a slow and hesitant process, the British came to renounce the war. They are still renouncing it. The verdict of popular culture is more or less unanimous. The First World War was stupid, tragic and futile. The stupidity of the war has been a theme of growing strength since the 1920s. From Robert Graves, through *Oh! What a Lovely War* to *Blackadder Goes Forth*, the criminal idiocy of the British High Command has become an article of faith.[3]

Stupidity leads to tragedy. These incompetents butchered the flower of British manhood incessantly for four years without remorse or even, in many cases, awareness. Youth was truly doomed. Under the direction of madmen, they marched like lambs to the slaughterhouse. The enormous success of Pat Barker's *Regeneration* trilogy testifies to the power of this view. It would have been far more of a shock to the expectations of the reading public if she had allowed her main protagonist, Billy Prior, to live through the war. Indeed, one could argue that the reason Barker shifts her lens away from Siegfried Sassoon, who is the focus of the first book, to the fictional (and implausible) 'Prior' and the historical figure of Wilfred Owen, is the rather annoying fact that Sassoon *survives* the war and that this is not tragic enough.

Even the comic mode is infected by the tragic; how else could *Blackadder Goes Forth* end except with the death of the main characters?[4] This has become the definitive image of the First World War for a generation. Such was the impact of this scene that it found a place in the top thirty most famous 'moments' ever televised in Britain.

Stupidity plus tragedy equals futility. Even academics can get in on the act here. Niall Ferguson is not a historian to accept the conventional wisdom; he is self-consciously revisionist and deeply provocative. But the final paragraph of *The Pity of War* puts him squarely in the predominant popular tradition:

The title of this book, then, is at once a sincere allusion to Wilfred Owen's twice used phrase and an echo of the understated idiom of the ordinary private soldier of the trenches. The First World War was at once piteous, in the poet's sense, and 'a pity'. It was something worse than a tragedy, which is ultimately something we are taught by the theatre to regard as unavoidable. It was the greatest *error* of modern history.[5]

Everything in this statement reflects what the mass of people in Britain already think about the First World War. For the British, the war is, at worst, an apocalyptic fall from grace, at best, the definitive *bad* war. In 1996, on Remembrance Day, it was described by former Education Secretary Kenneth Baker as the greatest disaster of the twentieth century.[6] The public rhetoric of Remembrance Day brackets the First and Second World War together, the poppy is worn in remembrance of the dead of *both* wars, and we are told incessantly that the dead of both wars sacrificed their lives to preserve our freedom. But the British public doesn't believe this. It believes that the dead of the Second World War did this, but that the dead of the First World War died in vain. In schools the First World War is taught more as tragic poetry than as history. It is likely that not one in a hundred people in Britain could name a single British battlefield victory of the First World War whilst many people could name at least three victories from the Second: the Battle of Britain, El Alamein and D-Day.

Likewise, the disasters of British arms in the First War are well known: the first day of the Somme, Passchendaele and Gallipoli are the memorable parts of the First World War. By contrast, the litany of British catastrophes that makes up a large part of the Second World War is swept under the carpet. The fall of Singapore, a disaster that dwarfed anything Britain suffered in 1914–1918, has been expunged from popular memory, except in as far as the victims of Japanese camps can keep it alive. As an indictment of the stupidity of the 'military mind', Britain's performance in the Second World War would be difficult to match: from Norway in 1940, through France in the same year, the Western Desert, Greece and Crete in 1941, Hong Kong, Burma, Dieppe, Tobruk and Singapore in 1942, much of the Italian campaign, and good deal of the Bomber Offensive from 1943 onwards, the repeated botched offensives in Normandy, and finally Arnhem in 1944, the latter characteristically 'spun' as a worthwhile near miss. If 'died in vain' means men being killed without contributing anything much to the final victory, then there should be some serious questions asked about 1939–1945. The British do not ask those questions because they have 1914–1918 instead. The extent to which the memory of the First World War has been reshaped as a negative counterpoint to a mythologised version of the Second World War cannot be overestimated. The late John Grigg, in a brilliant short essay, had the audacity to argue that by almost any measure a genuine historical comparison of British participation in the two world wars ought to lead to a more favourable assessment of the First World War. Grigg's thoughtful contribution has been almost entirely ignored.[7]

The British have been and still are deeply ambivalent about war. The liberal and Christian heritage tells them that war is wrong; utterly wrong and utterly evil. But the same heritage tells them that they must be prepared to defend the values of that heritage to the death. If they recognise 'pure evil', they should oppose it and, so, war can be the lesser evil. The Nazis, in retrospect, were easy to fight. It takes an extraordinary act of pacifism will to claim that Nazism was really a lesser evil than 'war'. As a result, the war of 1939–1945 is sanitised and romanticised in order to lessen the lesser evil. It is an inconvenient truth that the Second World War, like the First, was cripplingly expensive, bloody and frequently mismanaged. It was, in short, a war; and all wars are like that. There are of course some revisionists who argue that Britain had no direct interest in defeating Nazism; that left alone Hitler's Reich would have collided with Stalin's Soviet Union and that these two evil empires would have bled each other white. Leaving aside the questionable morality of this, and the idea that depravity across the Channel is no concern of the islanders, the practical fact that the emergent victor of that conflict would have become unstoppably powerful makes this argument unappealing. Both morality and long-term self-interest appear to argue that Britain was right to go to war against Nazism in 1939.

What the British have forgotten is that in 1914, throughout the First World War, and for some time afterwards the majority of the British people believed precisely the same thing about the Kaiser's Germany. In retrospect this may appear deluded, but the First World War was not fought in retrospect and to understand it we must stop re-fighting it that way.[8]

The war they were fighting was the 'war to end all wars'. H. G. Wells popularised this term in August 1914. For Wells it was also 'the last war'. This was a term that would come retrospectively to encompass an irony due to the ambiguities of the English language. Whilst the war was being fought it was the last war meaning 'final', a war to end war itself. By the 1930s as the prospect of a Second World War loomed the idea of the 'last war' began to mutate into meaning the 'previous' war. The working title for this book was 'The Last War' but I was convinced by editors that this would be taken by most people to mean the 'Second World War'. This nicely illustrates the gap in understanding that both writer and reader must overcome in order to penetrate the minds of those who actually experienced what we *now* call the 'First World War'.

Remembering the home front

There is a disproportionate fascination amongst the public with the mud and blood of Flanders. The proportion of books written about the lives of the vast majority of the population on the home front is small by comparison, once again a contrast with both the academic and popular history writing of the Second World War. Although Wells apparently also coined the term 'The People's War' in 1914, we tend to reserve this perspective to 1939–1945. There is a thriving literature on women's history and the issue of the change (or lack of change) in gender roles and recently a burgeoning literature on the issue of the memory of war. But the central question of how and why the British people endured the upheaval of war remains to a large extent unanswered.

Answering this question involves walking a narrow line between new cultural history and old social history. The construction of contemporary reality through culture – its practices, unspoken assumptions and linguistic conventions – needs to be brought into connection with quotidian experience – hunger, cold, injury, grief, boredom and exhaustion – which are certainly framed and understood through discourses, but which have a reality beyond the purely linguistic, albeit one which is more or less impossible to recover unmediated. It also needs to be remembered that understandings of the world are also about real and existing power relations between people, and that these have practical dimensions. Finally it should be remembered that languages and discourses are not as deterministic as some post-modern scholars would assert, and that language is a tool to be used and not simply parroted. This reinforces my view that occasionally it is important to allow contemporary voices to be heard through extensive quotation, to bring home a sense of the individual voice making use of the general language framework for their own purposes. So, in short, this book contains quite a lot of numbers and quite a lot of doggerel! As perhaps some compensation I have largely avoided using oral history collections. As a central contention of this work is that it is important to view the mentalities of the First World War without reference to the Second, there are serious problems with people trying to reconstruct their attitudes in 1914–1918 in interviews after 1945.

This book is intended to provide an interpretation of the course of the war for the civilian population of Britain. It begins with an attempt to understand why the population consented to war. It attempts to get away from the generalisation of war enthusiasm, an idea which has clouded our understanding since the inter-war period. But it does not deny that in a broader sense the majority reaction to war was patriotic and in some respects idealistic. It then proceeds to consider the role of propaganda.

Again, the intention is to move away from the assumption that the British sustained the war effort because they had been manipulated and fooled. This is not to deny that a culture of hatred towards the enemy developed during the first year of the war, but the suggestion is that this process was more organic and less artificial than is commonly supposed. The third chapter considers one of the guiding ideas of the first two years of the war: that of volunteerism and voluntary action. While it considers the well-documented story of volunteering for the Army, it seeks to extend this by considering the broader dimensions of the voluntary phenomenon. It also considers the limits of this, the degree to which voluntarism came into conflict with ideas of fairness, and argues that this concern in itself drove the population to accept increasing compulsion. This leads to the next chapter which begins to analyse the importance of the idea of sacrifice and its role in balancing the demands made on social groups. This in turn leads to a consideration of religion in wartime and the role of ideas drawn from traditional religion in underpinning the popular understanding of war. The next two chapters follow the growing sense of crisis on the home front as the strains of war eroded idealistic concepts of sacrifice and gave way to increased resentment and increasing internal enmity. This manifested in particular as sharpened class and ethnic antagonism. Finally it turns to the aftermath of victory. The argument is that the language of sacrifice was remade in order to stress universal grief as the common experience of war and that this is to some extent a mythology designed to cover up the social tensions that the war had created. The future understanding of the war would be shaped by this idea of universal bereavement.

The book is intended as an argument and an interpretative synthesis, and not as a textbook. It does not outline the high political narrative of the war, although it is intended to provide some thoughts on how a new political structure based on mass voting emerged after 1918. It is also not structured to engage directly with some of the existing paradigms of debate; for example, whether the war was radical or conservative in its effect on British society. I return to this point in the conclusion, but in some respects I find such a stark dichotomy conceals more than it reveals.

Much excellent recent work has been shaped around the idea that wars are intensely gendered and gendering events. I certainly have no quarrel with this, but it is not the only interesting thing about civilian life during the war and, precisely because other historians have done it so well, it has not been the central focus of this work, although such work has certainly influenced parts of the argument. Finally the neglect of military history, strictly defined, in this work should not be construed as disrespect for the extraordinary contributions of historians of the British armed forces, who have produced an increasingly sophisticated social history of men at war; indeed quite the contrary. In fact, central to this work is an argument that the mass experience of Army life and of combat, and the human consequences of military operations were *the* main pillars of civilian existence during the First World War. The great conceptual revolution of modern historical writing about the war has been the escape from the idea of the utter isolation of civilian life from 'the trenches'. That there is an existential gap between those who have been under fire and those who haven't seems a reasonable proposition, but the 'myth of war experience' as applied specifically to 1914–1918 has distorted our understandings of the contemporary linkages and dynamics of the nation at war. Which leads to a final apology. The nation that fought the war was the United Kingdom of Great Britain and Ireland. The break-up of that United Kingdom, in large part as a result of the war, is central to any overall history of the 'British' war. I have written on this subject elsewhere, but I have not found a way to integrate *that* story without massively over-burdening this book.

Above all it is hoped that the book will open some paths for future scholars to explore. It is likely that some arguments will need to be modified or even abandoned under future research scrutiny. I am all too aware of barely scratching the surface of the available material, but if this work generates further sympathetic consideration of those who lived through these dramatic times, sometimes maligned and frequently the victims of the condescension of posterity, I will be very satisfied.

1   Going to war*

> It is the achievement of Bloch and Norman Angell to have shown that even a successful conflict between modern states can bring no material gain. We can now look forward with something like confidence to the time when war between civilised nations will be considered as antiquated as the duel, and when the peacemakers shall be called the children of God.
>
> G. P. Gooch, *The History of Our Time: 1885–1913*[1]

> The fourth of August 1914 caused no great burst of patriotic fervour amongst us. Little groups, men and women together (unusual, this) stood talking earnestly in the shop or at the street corner, stunned a little by the enormity of events. But soon public concern yielded to private self interest.
>
> Robert Roberts, *The Classic Slum: Salford Life in the First Quarter of the Century*[2]

Jingoism and war enthusiasm: the myth of 1914

The predominant interpretation of the war is clear on one point: the British people went to war because they wanted to. According to Arthur Marwick, 'British society in 1914 was strongly jingoistic and showed marked enthusiasm for the outbreak of war.'[3] Images of cheering crowds outside Buckingham Palace, of long lines outside recruiting offices, of soldiers marching away singing 'Tipperary' dominate folk memory.[4]

The major sources for the idea of mass enthusiasm had obvious reasons for promulgating the idea. For wartime pacifists the war was irrational, and therefore support for the war was irrational. The first clear reference to 'enthusiasm' was a speech by Arthur Ponsonby in the House of Commons on Monday, 3 August 1914, referring to 'bands of half drunken youths waving flags ... the war fever has begun'.[5]

---

* This chapter was written before I was able to see the doctoral thesis by Catriona Pennell, presented for examination at Trinity College Dublin in 2008, on public reactions to the outbreak of war in the United Kingdom. Fortunately her impressive and imaginative research on a vast range of sources, public and private, largely supports the conclusions presented in this chapter.

It flattered the self-proclaimed heroic image of the pacifists to perceive themselves as isolated and far-sighted individuals who were 'above the melee'. The classic text in this regard is Bertrand Russell's *Autobiography*. Russell describes how he 'spent the evening walking the streets, especially in the neighbourhood of Trafalgar Square, noticing cheering crowds, and making myself sensitive to the emotions of passers-by. During this and the following days, I discovered to my amazement that average men and women were delighted at the prospect of war.'[6]

It certainly seems strange of Russell to claim to have been 'amazed' in 1914 at 'average' people's delight in war, when the idea of 'jingoism' had been firmly established in Liberal circles at the time of the Boer War.[7] Russell was undoubtedly brave in his stance in 1914, but it is quite clear that what really disturbed him was not so much 'mass enthusiasm' as his isolation in Liberal political circles after the invasion of Belgium. This sense of betrayal was best exemplified by Russell's friend and fellow opponent of the war, Ottoline Morrell, who vowed to 'cut' those of her friends who had defected to the 'jingo' cause.[8]

This image of 'war fever' received support from the memoirs of politicians. The decision for war in 1914 was taken by a very small number of men, but the idea that it was resoundingly endorsed by the population as a whole became a useful fiction in spreading the blame and avoiding awkward questions of personal culpability.

David Lloyd George gave a classic retrospective description of 'war enthusiasm':

The theory which is propagated today by pacifist orators ... that the Great War was engineered by elder and middle aged statesmen who sent young men to face its horrors, is an invention ... I shall never forget the warlike crowds that thronged Whitehall and poured into Downing Street, whilst the Cabinet was deliberating on the alternative of peace or war ... multitudes of young people concentrated in Westminster demonstrating for war against Germany.[9]

This passage must be regarded with enormous caution. When Lloyd George implied that the people impelled the declaration of war, he was justifying his own decision for war. The description of 'war enthusiasm' is clearly a defence against the accusation that 'old men' sacrificed the young. But the fact remains that the 'crowds' did not declare war on Germany, the Cabinet did; and Lloyd George personally played an important role in persuading Liberal Britain to accept war.[10]

Any consideration of the events of 1914 should start by acknowledging that the very idea of a uniform enthusiastic reaction from the 'masses' owes more to contemporary beliefs of the excitability of mass society, widespread amongst Liberals and Conservatives alike, than it does to empirical evidence. The evidence for mass enthusiasm at the time is surprisingly weak. Part of the problem is methodological: the domestic surveillance capacities of the British state were small compared with Continental counterparts, and there was little attempt to establish the popular mood at the outbreak of war. Thus the kind of evidence that has been brought to bear on this question by revisionist historians on the Continent is largely unavailable in the British case.[11] One point that such studies make strongly is that chronology matters, and this ought to be emphasised in the British case as well. Responses before the outbreak of war differed from responses afterwards, and public opinion continued to evolve. It will not do to take rowdy manifestations at midnight on 4 August 1914, the resigned editorials accepting war in the Liberal press over the next few days, or the rush to the colours at the end of the month as evidence of attitudes before the outbreak of war. Furthermore, discussion of responses to the war in Britain have been remarkably blind to major divisions in Edwardian society, particularly along regional (or national), class and gender lines. Any reconsideration must break down generalisations about 'the British' and examine particular groups more closely. A reassessment might usefully begin with an extreme case: that of Wales.

Wales in early August 1914

Wales might well have been expected to act as a focus for anti-war sentiment in 1914. Dominated in the south by trade unions with a well-developed sense of working-class consciousness, and in the rural centre and north by nonconformist Liberalism, Wales had been a major area of 'pro-Boer' opposition to the war in South Africa, and had provided anti-war sentiment at the turn of the century with its most charismatic leader in David Lloyd George. Yet it is assumed that in 1914, anti-war sentiment, whether of the socialist or Christian variety, was swept aside by patriotic fervour. Kenneth Morgan, the standard authority on modern Wales, states, 'the overwhelming mass of the Welsh people cast aside their political and industrial divisions and threw themselves into the war with gusto'.[12] This is far from true.

In fact the first major response to the war in the Principality came from the South Wales Miners' Federation (SWMF), which ostentatiously refused to accede to a Government request on 3 August 1914 to cut short the annual holiday. This decision was reaffirmed on 5 August 1914, the day after Britain entered the war. The pro-war *Merthyr Express* stated on 22 August 1914 that, despite appeals to return to work, only 100 of the 11,000 South Wales miners on holiday had actually done so. This was not an explicit anti-war stance, but it does indicate that generalisations about war fever over-riding civilian concerns need to be reconsidered. Welsh miners were in no mood to be rushed into giving up hard-won peacetime concessions.

Nor was rural Wales swept fervently into the imperial cause. The Welsh-language press was full of foreboding: *Seren Cymru*, the Baptist weekly paper, predicted on 7 August, 'the Napoleonic wars will seem as nothing but playing compared to the coming conflict'. The same day, the Methodist paper, *Y Goleuad*, saw 'civilization breaking down'. *Y Dinesydd Cymreig* predicted on 12 August that 'the remains of this war will be left behind for generations, in hate, jealousy, misery and poverty'.[13]

Wales did come around quite quickly to accepting the war. But it did so for local and specific reasons. Welsh Liberals were motivated principally by loyalty to what they very much saw as *their* Government, which had recently delivered their overwhelming priority: Welsh Church disestablishment.

The story in the coal fields was more complex. On 9 August, the Government and owners requested that the miners should work an extra hour per day. This was widely resisted until the end of the month, and as late as 30 August a mass meeting of miners at Merthyr Tydfil overturned a union recommendation on this score. It was only on 1 September, when a special conference of the SWMF itself resolved to back the extra hour, that the dispute was settled. But the context is significant: the conference in return demanded higher pay for soldiers and better separation allowances. Rather than converting to an abstract patriotic stance, it could also be suggested that the SWMF was widening its remit to protect those of its members who had enlisted. It is also the case that by the end of August the military context had changed dramatically. Britain as a whole appeared to be facing defeat, and the decision of the SWMF to 'rally' corresponded with a general upsurge in defensive patriotism.[14]

The most infamous example of 'jingoism' in South Wales was the heckling of the pacifist Independent Labour Party (ILP) leader James Keir Hardie at Aberdare on 6 August 1914. On balance it appears that this was a carefully organised effort on the part of local partisan opponents and was overplayed in the press, although there can be no doubt that Hardie was shocked and dismayed. What is less often noted is that in meetings at the end of October in Merthyr and Aberdare, Hardie was able to speak to cheering crowds and gain unanimous votes of confidence. This may be in part because Hardie had compromised with the developing mood of defensive patriotism, stating that he would pro-vide any assistance to a young man who chose to volunteer, and that 'The lads who have gone forth ... should not be disheartened by any discord at home.'[15] But it does imply that Hardie was not the isolated and tragic figure usually portrayed.

It might be possible to dismiss lukewarm Welsh reactions to the outbreak of war as the response of an atypical periphery of the United
Kingdom. But the response to war at the undoubted centre of both nation
and empire was also less overwhelmingly enthusiastic than is generally
assumed.

London in early August 1914

Cyril Pearce, in documenting the mood of Huddersfield at the outbreak of
war, has understandably complained about metropolitan bias in descriptions of popular opinion in Britain. 'Bank holiday crowds' gathered around
Buckingham Palace ought not be taken as representative of the nation as a
whole, and are no more and probably a lot less representative than
'provincial' trade unionists and nonconformist congregations signing
neutrality petitions.[16] This is a valid point, but it needs to be extended.
The motivations and composition of London crowds should be considered more seriously before generalising about 'carnivalesque enthusiasm'
in an immense and diverse metropolis.

It is instructive to compare the description of the crowds in central
London, cited above, written retrospectively by Lloyd George, with a
contemporary account:

thousands of holiday makers who in other circumstances would have been only too
happy to get out of town made their way to Whitehall in the hope of catching a
glimpse of Ministers as they arrived. Quiet and orderly, this typical English crowd,
obviously comprising all classes of people bore itself well. There was no feverish
excitement. Downing Street itself was kept clear by Police – a duty easily managed
by a handful of men, so correct was the behaviour of the crowd ... As usual on a
fine August Bank Holiday, St James Park and Green Park were invaded by good
humoured crowds, bent on enjoying themselves to the utmost ... suddenly the
sound of military music was heard from the direction of Wellington Barracks.
Immediately there was a stampede. Fathers packed up their children, mothers
gathered the bottles of milk, bags of cake and fruit and there was a general rush in
the direction of the Palace.[17]

This description appears in an evening paper of Tory persuasion unlikely
to downplay pro-war enthusiasm. It was written immediately after the
events described. Not only does it contradict Lloyd George in detail; it
places the crowd in a very different context, as essentially a normal August
Bank Holiday crowd.[18] These people are interested spectators rather than
a jingoistic mob baying for war. Jeffrey Verhey, in his study of Germany at
the outbreak of war, writes of 'audience' crowds, and this seems a good
description of the central London phenomenon. These crowds frequently
act as an interested audience for the great events going on. A Liberal critic

of the war, Irene Cooper Willis, writing in 1918 before the image of war enthusiasm had become an article of pacifist faith, makes a similar point, the deliberations over war perceived as another Bank Holiday diversion:

Yet, outside of the House of Commons and the *bank holiday crowd* who greeted the declaration of war and demonstrated their patriotism in front of Buckingham Palace on the night of August 4, there was no jubilation. There was more tension than excitement during the last two days of peace in London; one remembers on that fateful Monday, the *holiday makers* drifted about Parliament Square and Downing Street, scanning the latest newspaper posters and watching for a sight of the ministers.[19]

As in Germany, close examination of the 'pro-war' crowds in the metropolis during the war crisis causes their numbers to dwindle. Estimates of numbers are very imprecise. I have been unable to find a police estimate of numbers in the Metropolitan Police files (in itself a point of some significance, suggesting a real lack of concern). Reliable estimates of numbers are hard to find, even in the press. The *Evening Standard* estimated the crowd outside Buckingham Palace on 3 August as 6,000, the *Star* at 10,000. Given the fluid nature of crowd assembly on that day, this order of magnitude is about as useful a guide as we can get. One measure might be the receipts of the London County Council's tramways for the August Bank Holiday. The record receipts for that Monday, 3 August as reported in the *South London Observer* were £9,622 as opposed to £8,451 for the Bank Holiday in 1913. The newspaper attributed this to the 'many thousands of people who journeyed by tramcar to Westminster and Victoria to witness the exciting scenes in the neighbourhood of the Houses of Parliament'.[20] So perhaps up to 10,000 more than usual in central London. These numbers should be seen in the perspective of a city of almost 7 million inhabitants. To grasp what this implies, a crowd of 8,000 (halfway between the estimates quoted above) would imply the presence of little over 1 in 1,000 of the metropolitan population. A useful 'control' on these numbers is the estimated 100,000 Londoners who flocked to central London upon the news of the Armistice in 1918, and continued to do so for several subsequent days.[21]

Away from the centre of London, in the areas in which the vast majority of Londoners actually spent their holiday, the mood was noticeably different. Hampstead Heath, the pre-eminent gathering spot, saw a holiday which according to the local paper was:

a dismal affair ... the true holiday spirit as only was to be expected was absent. Many attempts were made to infuse gaiety into the proceedings, but even when these attempts were partially successful, incongruity was afforded by the harsh and discordant voices of news vendors shouting out the latest war news ... Nowhere was there the slightest sign of 'Mafficking' and it was obvious to the observer that the idea of war was distasteful to all.[22]

The London correspondent of the *Manchester Guardian* went a lot further: 'What seemed almost unanimous was that no one seemed to want war. There were no war songs or war talk except by way of a joke or forecast. The "we don't want war" that we heard so often should be made into a song to counter the jingo one.'[23] Other newspapers noted a determination to get on with the holiday: 'On the Bank Holiday the general population of Woolwich seemed bent on enjoyment. Here and there knots of men anxiously discussed the situation, but the tramcars and omnibuses bound for Borstal Woods, Bexley and Eltham were packed all day long.'[24] Some suggested that the crisis had added to enjoyment:

The North Londoner didn't forget all about what people call the European situation ... but remembrance of it did not weigh heavily upon him ... If anything the war lent a zest to the holiday making ... here is a scrap heard on top of a bus going from Finsbury park to Finchley. 'Pretty go this here war.' 'Bust up all round seemingly.' 'What do you reckon England will do?' ... 'Why stick up for her friends as soon as they're set upon – France in particular.' Quite a little burst of applause greeted the speaker's conclusion.[25]

Whilst this might suggest that there was a rather pro-interventionist popular attitude, it is worth noting that the major *organised* manifestations of public opinion were pro-neutrality and anti-war. The biggest socialist manifestation, the famous Trafalgar Square demonstration on Sunday, 2 August, polarised press reporting. There was clearly heckling from middle-class youths present, but what followed seems to have generated quite different accounts depending on the political bias of the reporting.

According to the Conservative press, the meeting was disrupted, red flags were torn down, blows were exchanged between socialists and their opponents, Henry Mayers Hyndman was heckled into inaudibility and Ben Tillett was challenged to a fist fight.[26] Naturally the socialist *Daily Herald* differed on this point and considered the meeting generally a success and dismissed the hecklers as 'a few rowdy clerks'. With no great commitment on either side, the *Daily Chronicle* also dismissed the hecklers as 'a negligible contingent of youths in front of the Southern plinth'. These hecklers, 'clerks by appearance', shouted 'patriotic songs until a heavy shower of rain dampened their enthusiasm and the mounted and foot police who had arrived to avert trouble found themselves with nothing to do'. The *Daily Chronicle* stated that, with the exception of these youths, the crowd gathered in the Square was completely unanimous in passing a resolution that 'deplored the impotency to which the democracy of Germany had been reduced and in calling on the British government in the first place to prevent the spread of the war and in the second place to see that the country is not dragged in to the conflict'. Not all was unanimity. The paper also noted that the 'Red Flag' was carried around the Square to the annoyance of the many present who were neither 'Socialist nor Jingoes'.[27]

Class and gender helped shape responses. The most vocally patriotic element of crowds appear to have been middle-class male youths. The *Daily Herald* report on the Trafalgar Square meeting stated that both the protesters and the 'patriacs' who heckled them were young men, but that the latter were middle class. It went as far as to claim that the sympathies of the police were with the protesters and that one constable had expressed contempt for the 'sanguinary little nuts'. Reporting on 'maffickers' at Buckingham Palace on the evening of the same day, it describes them as 'a hundred helots of the drapery counter' who were joined by a 'hundred serfs of the counting house'. These clerks and shop assistants were spurred on by an 'elegant young gentleman'.[28] Whilst class prejudice is evident in this description, it broadly corresponds with the observations of other newspapers. Photographic evidence shows more 'boaters' than 'cloth caps' amongst the more pro-intervention gatherings. This is not to say that pro-interventionist attitudes were confined to that group: by 2 August a wider body of predominantly Conservative middle-class opinion had become convinced of the necessity for intervention, but they tended to display their convictions more quietly. Nevertheless this pro-interventionist sentiment was almost certainly a minority opinion as late as 2 August, and possibly until the actual declaration of war on 4 August.

The public mood up to the outbreak of war

The Trafalgar Square resolutions were typical of a great deal of comment in the press throughout the country immediately prior to the outbreak of war. This was not confined to the most vehement Liberal newspapers: the *Daily News* edited by A. G. Gardiner, and the *Manchester Guardian* edited by C. P. Scott, both of which ran strong anti-war campaigns until 4 August.[29] Much of the provincial press, both Liberal and Unionist, had initially expressed a firm preference for neutrality. The Liberal *Huddersfield Daily Examiner*, in a typical editorial on 27 July, commented on the nation's 'fixed resolve' not to be drawn into any European conflict in any circumstances 'short of direct attack'. This was one of the unspoken assumptions of provincial Liberalism.[30]

On 28 July the *Cambridge Daily News* stated that 'British interests in the current dispute are quite negligible', and on 29 July it suggested that 'The ordinary man has heard too much of European conflagrations to believe it

until he sees the flames as well as the smoke.' A cartoon in the edition of
John Bull on 1 August showed Russia and Germany squaring off; underneath was the doggerel:

> Will Czar and Kaiser join the fray?
> Should Hague talk be all forgot,
> May 'Peace with honour' be our lot.

The headline read, 'The Great Fight'; this did not refer to Europe, but
rather to the Ahearn–Carpentier boxing match sponsored by *John Bull*,
scheduled for 17 August.[31]

On 27 July, the Conservative *Yorkshire Post* editorialised, 'Is it conceivable that Europe can be on the eve of a conflict between the tremendous
forces represented by all those great military nations? Happily we see no
reason why Great Britain should be drawn in.'[32] The *Oxford Chronicle* on
31 July editorialised that Britain's first duty was to localise the conflict and
that 'our second duty is to preserve our own neutrality'.[33] Although it
came to be widely believed in Liberal circles that the Unionist press was
trying to engineer a war, the Unionist press in the country as a whole was
not universally belligerent. Certainly Northcliffe's papers, *The Times* and
the *Daily Mail*, took a strong anti-German line from early in the crisis, but
their belligerence was as unrepresentative as the strongly pacificistic tendencies of the *Daily News* and the *Manchester Guardian*. In certain respects
the 'jingo' and the 'cocoa'[34] press cancelled each other out, or, more
likely, simply confirmed what their readerships already believed. Away
from the extremes, the press could be quite flexible and even surprising; a
full-page advertisement placed by the Neutrality League, appealing to
'Britons' to 'keep your country out of this wicked and stupid war'
appeared in the *Yorkshire Post* on 4 August.[35] The fact that the appeal of
the Neutrality League appeared in the press on the day that the war broke
out indicates sharply the main barrier to the organisation of widespread
anti-war feeling, the sheer speed of the crisis and its ultimate resolution in
British intervention.[36] A letter to the press from Eleanor Rathbone illustrates the sense of helplessness which the fairly widespread anti-war
opinion felt in the face of unfolding events, 'Sir, Before this letter can
appear in print the die may have been finally cast for war. But if it is not
so … ought not those Liverpool citizens who feel strongly on the question
of Britain's neutrality to take some steps such as are being taken in other
towns to make their convictions known?'[37]

In the event a large amount of anti-war sentiment was expressed
through various means. Letters to the newspapers expressed a great deal
of pro-neutrality opinion, much of it strongly anti-Russian and often with
an extremely powerful vision of war as a catastrophe for civilisation.

Norman Angell's views on the likely consequences of a European war were well known in Britain in 1914.[38] The immediate effects of the war crisis appeared to justify Angell's vision of the disastrous collapse of credit and trade that war would entail. On 30 July, the *Liverpool Daily Post* outlined the grim prospects for trade: 'The fears and apprehensions of the citizens were reflected in melancholy vigour in the business done on various marts and exchanges. The Liverpool stock exchange is practically paralysed … The effect of a great European war on Liverpool would be disastrous.'[39] On the eve of the war a trade union official in Norwich 'outlined a terrible picture of the consequences of war with food at famine prices and ordered government at an end'.[40] The *Leicester Daily Post* commented on the same day: 'Risen and rising prices for the necessities of life and their multiplying evils already constitute the stormy petrels of European conflict.'[41] The *Daily Chronicle* suggested that the rapid rise in food prices had sobered opinion:

> For me there exists no dread of war
> No fear of Armageddon
> I ask not 'Who is Russia for?
> Will Germany be led on
> to take a hand?' I only see
> In Europe's posture poetry.
>
> But what is this? A rise in bread
> A threatened spurt in bacon
> My stocks and shares resembling lead
> My credit being shaken
> Nay then, poetic outlook hence
> Give place to sober common sense.

The popular Sunday paper *The News of the World* commented with succinct irony to its mostly working-class readership, 'Just at the moment Britain may be called the dear homeland for everything is going up.'[42] An anonymous London woman noted in her diary on 2 August that reports were spreading 'that if we go to war there will be bread riots in London and food riots in Belfast'.[43]

Sombre realism was widespread: in Leeds on 2 August, 'there was an impending sense of disaster … a black outlook'. Radnor Hodgson wrote to the *Yorkshire Post*, 'War is death and destruction. All who participate in war, of course, intend to put the death and destruction on his enemies; but history shows that the crushing punishment has often fallen on those who thought they could impose it on others. War is not a game to be trifled with.'[44]

Reading the newspapers on either side of the outbreak of war suggests very strongly that the public were not as innocent about the consequences of war as is often imagined. Even those who were pro-intervention appear quite clear-headed about the perils of war. The idea that 'the war would be over by Christmas' is almost entirely absent in diaries and newspapers in August, except in the apocalyptic sense that civilisation was on the verge of complete and imminent collapse.[45] The idea of a quick victory did emerge later in 1914. On 15 September 1914, *The Star* reported that insurance brokers had just started to offer 'peace insurance'. For a premium of £80 a policy holder would receive a payment of £100 if the war hadn't ended by 1 January 1915, and for a premium of £22 a payment of £100 if it hadn't ended by 15 September 1915. But, once again, timing matters. This story appears *after* the crisis of late August and *after* the apparently decisive victory on the Marne, as well as exaggerated accounts of Russian success which led to a brief flurry of speculation about a 'race' to Berlin. It also appeared just *before* failure at Antwerp and the onset of trench warfare. Likewise, on 14 September, the ubiquitous Horatio Bottomley at a packed meeting predicted a short war: 'the war is not going to be of long duration, as has been prophesied from this platform and elsewhere (cheers) ... there is not enough food, there is not enough liquid capita nor credit'. In Bottomley's opinion the war would be bloody but brief: 'a war of this magnitude' could not last 'anything like the period which various states-men are indulging in prophesying'. Bottomley strongly implies that up to this point the belief in a short war had been a dissident view.[46] There is reason to suspect that the belief that the war would be over by Christmas was primarily the product of a brief flurry of optimism in mid-September. It is likely that 'memories' of the phrase at the start of the war represent a foreshortening of the period.[47] In August a 'short war' illusion did exist: there was a strong sense amongst the economically literate, usually Liberals, that the combatant nations would be forced to the negotiating table by the collapse of international trade at some vague time in the near future; indeed it was this view that Bottomley had picked up, which is ironic given that he was a critic of 'Norman Angelism', although it is typical of his eclectic crowd-pleasing tendencies. But the idea of a Sunday stroll to Berlin was not apparent even in this vision. This is unsurprising, as it had taken Britain three years to defeat a couple of small Boer Republics. That war had been prolonged by guerilla fighting, but even the conventional campaign had taken almost a year. The point was made explicitly by 'GWW' in the *Abingdon Free Press*: 'Those who remember the havoc caused by the South African War – and who does not! – cannot be expected to look upon a war as just a "bit of excite-ment".'[48] Because of South Africa, the British were probably the least ignorant people in Western Europe about modern land warfare. This is a relative judgement since the ignorance of others was almost total, but the

British were not conditioned by the memory of quick victory in 1870 in the way that part of the German population was. Whilst very few people anticipated a four-year war, most people probably imagined it lasting a year or so. Indeed they continued to do so for most of the war: the end was always going to come within the next year. At Talbot House, behind the lines on the Western Front, soldiers debated on New Year's Day in 1916, 1917 and 1918 the motion 'This house believes the war will end this year.' Each year the motion passed, although it nearly failed in 1918. Infamously, in October 1917, *John Bull* for the first time published a headline claiming the war would be over by Christmas.

Whatever the views about the duration of the war at the outset, the likely severity of the conflict was widely accepted. After the outbreak of war, the *Hackney Spectator* stated on its front page, 'we go to war in silence, every man, aye every child knows that war means red ruin'.[49]

This very real sense of concern about the risks of war did not in itself create widespread opposition. Such opposition needed a focal point. In the event there was quite a lot of opposition publicly expressed, but the speed of events prevented it coalescing into a clear anti-war movement. Instead opposition was dispersed between different groups and associational interests.

To begin with a small but visible minority, Jewish responses before the outbreak of the war appear to have been strongly anti-interventionist:

Dr Samuel Daiches, Professor of Hebrew at the Jewish College, London, speaking at a meeting held in Hope Hall, Liverpool yesterday ... alluded in a significant manner to the war outlook. He said there were nearly half a million Jews in the armies of Europe ready to fight and kill each other, not for national independence or the good of humanity, but in order to help Christian nations call down a curse upon their own heads and to make Europe a heap of ashes.[50]

Anti-Russian sentiment was naturally strong in this community, many of whom had left the 'Pogrom Lands' of Eastern Europe. The perception that Jews were in some respects anti-Entente and pro-German would later cause trouble for the community.

If we pass from a minority to the nominal majority in England, the picture is quite different. The Church of England generally followed a predictable line of concern tempered by national loyalty on Sunday, 2 August. This did not stop individual clerics speaking out. The most prominent was the Bishop of Lincoln in a sermon at Cleethorpes. He predicted that 'a continental war could be nothing short of disastrous when one thought of the militarism of Europe, of the hell of battlefields, of the miseries of the wounded, of ruined peasants'. He was reported as saying, 'we had no quarrel with Germany and to go to war without a reason was tempting providence. Moreover it would inflict upon our industrial community one of the most terrible curses possible to inflict. He asked them all to pray to God to keep our people from war.'[51] At a less exalted level, the rector of St Mary's Newmarket painted an apocalyptic picture of what a war would entail:

All the horrors of war in ancient times would be nothing to the horrors of war today … All the resources of science had been called upon to perfect weapons of destruction for mankind … no town in England was now safe. At night it might be turned into a smouldering ruin and its inhabitants into blackened corpses.[52]

In the parish of Bowerchalke in Wiltshire, the Reverend Collet wrote in his parish magazine:

THE CONTINENTAL WAR – which has unfortunately broken out and may possibly affect our country is very greatly to be deplored. Whatever the cause of it may be, the inevitable consequence cannot fail to be bloodshed and misery for many. It is true that a nation's honour must be upheld but surely that might be accomplished without loss of life.[53]

Whilst it is possible to find outspoken Anglican clergy opposing the idea of war, the majority simply prayed for peace and for divine guidance for the government. Anti-war opinion was expressed much more vigorously in sermons and in resolutions within the nonconformist chapels. The Muswell Hill Brotherhood unanimously passed a resolution calling for the Government to maintain 'the honourable position of pacificators'.[54] In Leicester, two Primitive Methodist chapels, the United Free Church and the Baptists sent petitions to Edward Grey calling for neutrality. The *Banbury Advertiser* reported that special prayers for the limitation of conflict were offered at most places of worship, and that the Grimsbury Brotherhood had passed a resolution that viewed 'with horror the terrible outrage to humanity and the menacing challenge to Christianity involved in a European war'.[55] The nonconformist reponse to the actual outbreak of war was perhaps more sorrow than anger. The sermon at the Unitarian Chapel in Banbury the next weekend regretted that 'the moral development of the people of Europe had not kept pace with their intellectual growth'.[56] In the end, nonconformist chapels accepted rather than opposed war. This wasn't a foregone conclusion. A study of Baptist attitudes demonstrates strong and determined opposition up until the last moment. The weekend before war broke out, organised nonconformist opposition to the war was on the point of becoming quite significant. On Saturday, 1 August, William Robertson Nicoll presented Lloyd George with a letter stating that the Free Churches would strongly oppose any war. On Monday, 3 August, George Riddell visited Nicoll and persuaded him that the Government had to stand by its responsibilities towards France. This information was passed on to Lloyd George by Charles Masterman in order to stiffen his resolve.[57]

Socialist and trade-union opposition was also widespread. An advertisement by thirteen trade unions, on 1 August in the *Daily Herald*, called for protests the next day. On the morning of Sunday, 2 August, a trade-union official in Norwich 'outlined a terrible picture of the consequences of war with food at famine prices and ordered government at an end'. On the same day an ILP meeting was held in Leicester, where Councillor Hallam stated that 'War would not make the capitalists or workers any better off. Was England to range herself on the side of Russian diplomatists.' Likewise the *Daily Herald* had for once shelved its antagonism and called for the 'great middle-class' to join the trade unions in preventing this 'criminal folly'.[58] This cut both ways: in Huddersfield, the Liberal *Daily Examiner*, which had a track record of hostility to socialism, looked to trade-union and socialist demonstrations to support its argument that the population as a whole opposed war.[59]

George Cook, addressing a crowd at the Birmingham Bull Ring that evening, Sunday, 2 August, expressed his opposition to being drawn into a quarrel between Austria and Serbia in less conciliatory terms: 'the workers already had on hand an industrial battle for better economic conditions which was far more important than entering into a war with their brothers on the continent'.[60] Charles Hobson of the Sheffield branch of the International Metal Trades Federation wrote to his local paper expressing his trade union's opposition to the war, and the British Socialist Party (BSP) in the same town passed a resolution against it.[61] On 2 August, a young Ernest Bevin addressed a trade-union meeting on Bristol's Clifton Downs which called for a general strike against war.[62] Huddersfield saw a broad-based mobilisation of Labour on the same day. Two meetings were held in St George's Square: the morning meeting called by the ILP; and an evening meeting originally called by the Trades Council in support of striking engineers, which became an anti-war rally. Both meetings involved speakers from the ILP, BSP and trade unions. The meetings filled the Square and passed resolutions condemning the 'insane conflict'. The Huddersfield resolutions stopped short of endorsing the almost Leninist position of the local socialist paper, which called for revolution in the event of war, but there was undoubtedly a powerful bedrock of neutralist sentiment.[63]

In Islington, under the auspices of the local BSP and the ILP, two anti-war meetings were held at Highbury Corner where it was decided to form a procession to march to Trafalgar Square and join the peace demonstration. This was followed by a further meeting in the evening where resolutions against the war were passed. In the East End, the Poplar

Trade Council held a mass protest meeting outside the dock gates.[64] It has been estimated that across the nation 100,000 people took part in socialist and Labour anti-war demonstrations on 2 August.[65]

But once again there was some movement towards a reluctant accept-ance of war, should it come. At a Labour Fete held on Bank Holiday Monday at Abbey Wood, Will Crooks pledged loyalty to the Government in the following terms:

> I cannot help myself, we have fought for peace to the last moment, but if war has got to come, you and I must shoulder the burden … our next order is to look after the food for the people, not at famine prices, but at reasonable prices that the poor can afford, then we have to look after the women and children. Do not forget that our obligations are beginning now. We have got to see the job through and present a united front to the enemy.[66]

It was reported that Crooks was 'loudly cheered'. The question inevitably arises as to which sentiment provoked the cheers: standing by the Government, or the condemnation of 'famine prices'. It is quite probable that both sentiments did. *John Bull* commented cynically on Will Crooks's speech that it might be thought that the armament workers of Woolwich had a vested interest in patriotism. To some extent the Labour movement fulfilled its obligations to internationalism on the weekend before the war, but it baulked at the ultimate gesture. On 29 July the *Daily Herald* had loyally called for a pan-European general strike against the war. As it became clear that the Second International branches on the continent were incapable of delivering this, the British socialists were unwilling to act unilaterally. After the outbreak of war there were some bitter recrimi-nations at the failure of German and French socialists. The *Daily Herald* actually renewed the international strike call on 5 August, but the moment had clearly passed.[67]

A similar paralysis and sense of recrimination can be observed in organised feminism. Initially there was an unprecedentedly broad response in favour of neutrality. The International Women's Suffrage Association, the National Union of Women's Suffrage Societies (NUWSS), the Women's Labour League and the Women's Co-operative Guild combined forces and resources to book a hall for a protest meeting at Kingsway Hall on 4 August. They were joined by the National Federation of Women Workers and the Women's Freedom League. Such was the perceived urgency of the situation that it was seriously considered that prominent anti-suffrage women should also be invited, although this was vigorously opposed and came to nothing. Conspicuous by their absence were the leadership of the Suffragettes, the Women's Social and Political Union, whose potentially violent and maverick attitudes were widely distrusted – rightly, as it turned out. The meeting went ahead on the evening that the ultimatum to Germany inexorably expired. It has been described as a 'sad meeting'. There were 2,000 women inside the hall and hundreds more had to be turned away. A sense of hopelessness descended. More for the sake of form than in any real hope, a pro-neutrality resolution was passed and a petition was taken to Downing Street, arriving just before the declaration of war.[68]

As an organisation the NUWSS rallied to the cause immediately, although individual members would remain steadfast in their opposition to war. On the day that war began, the NUWSS executives were sorting out and answering 200 letters from local branches requesting advice on how they should respond to the crisis. Nothing illustrates better the speed with which the crisis overwhelmed opposition: branches which had essentially asked for advice on how to oppose a war received instead advice on how best to serve the war effort.[69]

Generalisations about public attitude are very difficult to make. There was a widespread sentiment of sympathy with France and a sense of a moral obligation. At the same time there was a prevalent dislike of Russia[70] and a downright contempt for Serbia, best exemplified in the *John Bull* headline 'To Hell with Servia'.[71] Anti-German prejudice was expressed during the crisis, but so was pro-German sentiment.[72]

The possible effects of war were not romanticised, but duty and sacrifice were accepted. It is completely untenable to suggest that the politicians were forced into war by the public. Yet the *Daily Herald* claim that war had been declared 'without the consent of the British people, and against the feeling of the overwhelming mass of the nation' was no more convincing.[73] The public was undecided. The conclusion that the British public was divided and ambivalent about the prospect of war during the crisis might lack the narrative drama of the idea of enthusiasm, but has the benefit of reflecting the typical reaction of the British and other publics to better-documented war crises of the twentieth century.

It is in this respect that the German invasion of Belgium becomes significant. The invasion of Belgium does not initially appear to have changed many minds outside the Cabinet. Attitudes had tended to polarise around responses to a German attack on France; pro-interventionist sentiment was largely fixed before 2 August and anti-interventionist sentiment did not change. The importance of the attack on Belgium was *within* the Cabinet. It provided an excuse and a cover for Liberals who had already decided that Germany had to be resisted. By far the most important of these was Lloyd George. It was the decision of Liberal politicians and, to a lesser extent, Liberal newspaper editors to back the war effort, that guaranteed that anti-war sentiment remained marginalised after the outbreak of war.

Up until the outbreak of the war, opinion was clearly divided. Is it possible to generalise about the social lines of division? Evidence from Germany in particular suggests an extremely strong class division in attitudes, which is much as one would expect in the Second Reich. Pre-war Britain was far less organised than Germany around a politically embodied binary class division.

The impressionistic nature of the evidence from Great Britain forces a degree of caution. It seems safe to say that the middle classes were more in favour of intervention than the working class; that the metropolis was more pro-intervention than the provinces and constituent nations (although Scotland seemed more prone to patriotic fervour than the others); that the young were more pro-intervention than the old; Anglicans more pro-intervention than nonconformists, with Roman Catholics something of an enigma (the 'patriotic' stance of John Redmond seems to have had some influence on 'Irish' feeling in Britain); and finally, again with a great deal of caution, that men were more favourable to intervention than women.[74] The distinction between 'pro-intervention' and 'pro-war' might sound semantic, but it is crucial. The British public was not considering the idea of going to war in abstract terms, but in terms of entry into a very specific war. It was possible to believe, even before 2 August, that war in principle was an inglorious evil, and at the same time believe that Britain had a moral commitment to France, implying that Germany had to be opposed even at the price of war.

Mobilisation and the outbreak of war

The actual declaration of war, when it finally came, does seem to have generated something like enthusiasm in some circles. It is very difficult to be certain how this enthusiasm was distributed. Both retrospective and contemporary accounts seem principally to reflect the general attitude of the writer.

Mary Stocks, travelling by train from Birmingham across western England to Dorset on 5 August, whilst mobilisation was in full swing, recorded in her commonplace book that she had seen crowds at every station, but that they were unhappy, bewildered and apprehensive. Stocks saw no flags waved.[75]

The civic history of Portsmouth is very explicit in that the declaration of war was greeted with shock and horror: 'Surely it could never be that a great nation, professing its belief in God, would doom Europe to the devastating horrors of war.' The author evokes a dramatic scene of the countdown to the expiration of the British ultimatum: 'Ten Minutes to Eleven – no word, Two Minutes – no hope!' Finally at eleven o'clock, 'GOD HELP US! IT

WAS WAR!' Other civic histories present a very different story: 'Chester presented a fine study in the early hours. Never were such scenes witnessed in our city for never had a war been so enthusiastically accepted as just and unavoidable.'[76] It is not impossible that there was an objective difference between Portsmouth and Chester, because Portsmouth was going to be much more quickly involved at a familial level by the mobilisation of naval reservists. Yet on balance it is more likely that different writers emphasised different parts of the same mixed picture, that in most places there was both stunned silence and cheering, both dismay and enthusiasm. What is important is that the balance does seem to have shifted to some extent towards the latter. In Bridport in Dorset, the development of opinion seems to have followed a classic pattern. Until the weekend, ignorance and indifference. Then over the weekend, a 'period of terrible anxiety, when war and peace were hanging in the balance', but at the same time, 'uneventful life carried on' and 'summer holiday makers came to the West Bay as usual'. Finally, 'when the declaration of war was made known at the *Bridport News*, all was changed. Hundreds of people daily besieged the offices for the latest news.'[77] The public was now clearly engaged with the fact that a war was happening. What that meant was less clear. The historian of Attleborough admits, 'it is difficult to write down accurately what were our precise feelings at that time'. But among the reactions was a degree of excitement.[78]

The *Daily Chronicle* reported that up to this point there had been no 'Mafficking', but that the declaration of war had produced enthusiastic demonstrations akin to 1899:

Earlier in the evening a procession starting with 30 people outside Buckingham Palace marched through the City to Mansion House, increasing in numbers until 3,000 were taking part in it. Many carried Union Jacks, others displayed the French Tricolour and the Green Flag of Ireland waved triumphantly over several sections of the demonstration ... All the way from West to East and East to West, soldiers in Scarlet or Khaki, and sailors with their kitbags slung over their shoulders were greeted warmly. Outside the Palace an immense crowd had been assembled all evening. As the hours advanced it grew in numbers until it reached about 12,000. All sorts and conditions of men and women were there. Lord Lonsdale in evening dress was seen rubbing shoulders with one of the costers to whom he is a good friend and patron. Mothers brought their babies in arms with them and many quiet young children were held up by their parents that they might see the King and Queen. The enthusiasm was long sustained ... In contrast with the exuberance of the demonstrations outside the Mansion House was the quiet demeanour of the people who had gathered in the neighbourhood of Parliament Square.

Because the *Daily Chronicle* was a morning newspaper, the reporting more or less breaks off at midnight, but *The Globe*, an evening paper, picks up the story as the crowds became more exuberant still:

The receipt of the news was the climax to the evening's demonstration and for the next two hours stirring scenes were witnessed. Gaily decorated motor-cars crowded inside and out, passed round and round the Victoria memorial in processional order men and women standing on the tops of taxi-cabs and waving flags continuously ... when the police began to clear the vicinity of the palace people proceeded up the mall and demonstrated in other parts of the city until well into the morning ... There were scenes of great enthusiasm in Trafalgar Square and Piccadilly Circus when the news of the declaration of war spread. A great roar of defiance was the answer of a vast crowd in the Square at the news.[79]

All of this corresponds much more closely to the stereotype of war enthusiasm. This was the scene into which a depressed Bertrand Russell walked, and which made such an impact upon him. Such scenes, in central London and elsewhere over the next few days, do seem to confirm the idea of an outbreak of irrationality, a 'war fever'.

Such a view must be heavily qualified. The crowds remained a minority phenomenon, although it is not necessary to accept the *Daily Herald* view that 'the usual body of idlers which can always be found on the streets of a great city have now concentrated in the area of Whitehall'.[80]

The key aspect of 'enthusiasm' was the desire to give mobilising troops a good sendoff. This could be seen either side of the actual declaration of war. On 2 August 1914, a girl working in a photographic shop in Orkney noted in her diary: 'All the Thule territorials ordered to assemble ... most of the towns people went down to the drill hall to see what was up.'[81] The *East London Advertiser* mentions on 22 August that 'the war spirit has reached a very high pitch', linking this to 'the mobilisation of our citizen soldiers and the departure of reservists to rejoin their regiments'.[82] In Preston, the mayor would later note that the outbreak of war was greeted with excitement, but it was the departure of the town's reservists which was greeted with 'wild enthusiasm'.[83] The *Eastern Daily Press* reported on the scenes surrounding the departure of Territorial soldiers from Norwich:

The men as they were making the final preparations for leaving were in the highest of spirits. They sang their favourite melodies with vigour and shook hands cordially with friends who came to have a last word with them ... Girls rushed forward with merry laughter just to tap their military friends on the back and receive a warm glance of recognition as a reward. Umbrellas were waved in the air, handkerchiefs were flourished and all was done to make the Territorials feel that they were carrying away with them the best hopes of the ancient city.[84]

It is in the nature of the case that public manifestations of solidarity and enthusiasm attract notice. What is less easy to estimate is how many people privately reacted with shock and resignation. A suggestion of more private reactions can be found in reportage from the *Woolwich Herald* of the departure of troops on 6 August from the local barracks:

A young private came to the station with his mother. He looked a mere lad, but he at least did not intend a fuss ... A bombadier accompanied by his mother arrived. The woman was as pale as death, and the son was comforting her with the words 'I will soon be back'. 'That is what your father told me when he went to South Africa' was the woman's reply. 'You are all that I have in the world – and who knows?' Here she broke off.[85]

The problem with public actions is that they tend to conform to a 'script' of expected behaviour and, furthermore, are then written up in terms of journalistic cliché. Thus men must be cheery and stoical; women distressed and weeping, but ultimately comforted. The interesting thing about this account is that it does not entirely conform, some men are themselves emotional about parting and some women are not comforted. Equally indicative is the co-existence of real distress with patriotic manifestations; the report also states: 'Both yesterday and on Wednesday the streets and barracks were full of men ... people in the streets were singing patriotic songs.' The two might be related: patriotic songs and the like could be 'whistling in the dark', a cover for real anxiety. The *Daily Herald* believed that 'often the sorrow of parting is drowned in drinking and a devil may care attitude is adopted to cover underlying sorrow'.[86] The civic history of Leeds points to the release of tension that the actual declaration of war involved, 'with no light heart, and yet with some sense of relief, Leeds entered on the task that patriotic sentiment prescribed'.[87]

The outbreak of war did not bring an end to the economic dislocation caused by the war crisis. Hoarding continued and now took on distinctly unpatriotic implications: in Chester, 'a selfish minority occupied the fatal hours in besieging provision stores', and in Swindon, 'an ugly feature of the general perturbation caused by the outbreak of war was the selfish haste of some people to lay in a large stock of provisions'. The author of the Swindon civic history also condemns 'the equally selfish actions of some wholesalers and traders in raising the price of commodities'.[88] Government pronouncements, growing confidence, public condemnation and the fact that those who wanted to hoard supplies had mostly got what they wanted, meant that such behaviour temporarily died out in mid-August, although it would recur throughout the war. Prices fell slightly in late August, but a threshold had been passed. In Swindon a loaf which had cost 4½d in July, cost 6d in September. Serious inflation was set to be a prominent and permanent feature of the war.

Rising prices provoked a variety of reactions. In Hitchin, a shop was attacked and looted. In Benwell, near Newcastle, flour dealers' shops were wrecked. It seems likely that price rises were contributory to the intermittent attacks on German butchers and bakers in the first week of the war. A report on an attack on a German baker in Islington shows that there was resentment when he raised his bread prices, but that the catalyst for the riot was the false claim that he had deliberately raised the rents of some tenants – the families of reservists who had been called up.[89]

The police file on a riot in Dunstable, Bedfordshire, indicates that crowd action there was equally closely targeted. The retailer picked out for attack, which consisted of stones being thrown at his windows for two and a half hours, had supposedly remarked that 'he could do without the trade of the poorer classes'. He had also allegedly approached other shopkeepers to get them to raise their prices as well. An anonymous letter included with the report stated 'that the general opinion was that he had brought this disturbance upon himself entirely by his unwise action'. It further commented that there was a real danger that the riot would spread to the premises of other traders and people, 'who had foolishly laid in large stocks of provisions'. The police report agrees with this assessment and furthermore states that the shopkeeper's compensation claim had been deliberately inflated.[90]

The *Daily Herald* turned to attacking those responsible for price rises, but appeared unclear as to precisely who was to blame. Initially it was 'the greedy rich who grab food supplies', then small shopkeepers. One writer singled out 'the greed of the grocer' and claimed that the larger stores had held prices down, whilst another in the same issue claimed that small shopkeepers had behaved honourably and that it was the retail chains and big stores who were to blame.[91]

Herald League speakers addressed the large crowds who gathered at Tower Hill to listen to 'Jingo Speakers'. These socialists supposedly received a sympathetic hearing from the crowds in their condemnation of capitalism as a cause of the war and in their attacks on 'profiteering'. But the *Daily Herald* makes the crucial admission that these speeches were not 'anti-war'.[92]

Actual opposition, while not unknown, was thin on the ground. On 6 August, *The Labour Leader* carried the slogan 'Down with War!' on its front page, and on 11 August the National Council of the ILP reiterated the solidarity of the Second International. The majority of ILP branches endorsed this stance. On 9 August, the ILP, the BSP and the Peace Society held a joint demonstration in Glasgow demanding an Armistice. This supposedly attracted a crowd of 5,000. On the same day a peace meeting was held by nonconformist ministers and socialists in Todmorden which 'was generally disapproved of'. At this stage the first instinct of most of the war's opponents was to keep a low profile. Even within the ILP, the London Divisional Council admitted that 'We cannot at this moment take steps to stop the war.'[93] It took a month or so for Liberal and socialist opponents of the war to coalesce and organise what would become the Union of Democratic Control. The truth was that those who had opposed the war before 4 August were now deeply divided. There were various reasons for supporting the war or staying silent. Some had changed their minds and had accepted the British moral case for war. Some retained doubts about the moral case but hoped that the war could be invested with moral purpose. Some accepted the war as a pragmatic reality and looked to ameliorate its effects. These three groups probably made up a very substantial section of the population. Even within the little band of opponents there were differences. There were even some, such as James Ramsay MacDonald, who basically accepted the 'moral' validity of Britain entering war, while continuing to oppose it.[94]

Recruiting

The standard evidence for an enthusiastic response to the outbreak of war is the 'rush to the colours' that created Kitchener's Army. This is taken to stand both for the 'group psychology' of war enthusiasm and the transformative effect on individuals seeking the romantic excitement of war: 'the pride of Piccadilly – and other streets poured into the recruiting offices'. Yet when the chronology of recruitment is examined this phenomenon appears in a different light.[95]

1. Recruiting. IWM (Q 53219).

Large numbers did join up in the first few weeks of August. Between 4 and 8 August 8,193 men enlisted, and by 22 August numbers had grown to over 100,000. Of those who enlisted a substantial number probably *were* motivated by enthusiasm and a desire to fight. Not everyone was impressed – one Labour party figure supposedly scathingly referred to the first recruits being 'aristocrats and loafers'. The Mayor of Preston denied this, but then partly undermined himself by saying, 'this was true of the first few days only'.[96] War broke out during the 'long vacation'; throughout the country large numbers of university students enlisted in preference to returning when term began, and many of those who were due to matriculate never showed up.

Idealism as a chance to escape academic drudgery was not inexplicable in young men. The rush to the colours of clerks and shop assistants was similarly understandable. Dead-end jobs with poor and diminishing promotion prospects held little attraction compared with chivalric daydreams. Raymond Asquith, in a somewhat condescending manner, captured this in his poem, *The Volunteer*:

> Here lies a clerk, who half his life has spent
> Toiling at ledgers in a city grey,
> Thinking that his days would drift away
> With no lance broken in life's tournament.[97]

This should not lead us to overlook that there were other and perhaps more powerful reasons for enlistment at the outbreak of the war. Some traditional accounts of enlistment in 1914 have tended to overlook that the first impact of the war, and indeed the war crisis before that, was mass unemployment. Economic distress had always been the British Army's best recruiting agent, and the slump at the start of the war was in the short term one of the most severe bouts of economic distress in Britain in the twentieth century. Trade union reports to the Board of Trade indicated that unemployment among trade union members rose from 2.8% at the end of July to 7.1% at the end of August. Between July and September male employment fell 10%. This does not begin to express the whole impact of the war on the economy: much of the rest of the workforce was working on short time by mid-August 1914.

The burden of economic hardship fell on all classes, but perhaps most severely on sections of the workforce which were already the principal recruiting ground for the Army: the urban unskilled. It was reported from Birmingham that 78% of the volunteers in August came from the same classes which had joined the peacetime Army. The disproportionate numbers of the very early volunteers who enlisted in London is further evidence that the bulk of this enlistment was an intensified version of pre-war recruitment.[98] Even in these circumstances, the number of men out of work massively outnumbered those who volunteered. Although hardship alone does not explain mass enlistment, in his exhaustive study of the issue over the whole first year of the war, David Silbey concludes that 'growing industries' in the first year of the war did send significantly fewer men to the army than 'shrinking industries', and that statistical and anecdotal evidence support each other on this point.[99]

The beginnings of a real mass-recruitment movement came later in the month. The key moment was the publication of the Mons Despatch in *The Times* on 25 August.[100] Presenting the battle as a heroic defeat, it ended with an appeal for more men to join up. On 30 August, Louisa Harris of Yeovil noted in her diary, 'War news – most appalling – no one can foresee how it will end. Our losses have been heavy at the front and the demand for recruits is most urgent. It is now a question not only of honour, but self preservation.'[101] Violet Bonham Carter, daughter of then Prime Minister Herbert Henry Asquith, recounted the grim mood at a recruiting meeting held in Winchcombe, Gloucestershire, on Saturday, 28 August: previously 'people here have hardly heard of the war', but now 'the whole thing is like living a nightmare'. In a letter dated the next Monday she gave her opinion: 'I do really think some of the boys should enlist. Father will be asked why he doesn't begin recruiting at home.'[102] Other families had similar reactions that weekend and the response was instantaneous. On the next four days more than 10,000 men enlisted. Daily enlistment therefore exceeded the total enlistment for the first *week* of the war. By 31 August, daily enlistment topped 20,000, and on 3 September 33,304 men joined the army, the highest enlistment for any day of the war. In the week from 30 August to 5 September, 174,901 men joined the colours. The clarification of separation allowances was also a powerful enabling tool. It is important to note that many men were unwilling to join until they were assured of their family's well-being. This indicates that they were not swept away by enthusiasm, but were more calculating in their decisions.

All this is not merely a technical detail of chronology. If, as these figures suggest, the main rush to the colours occurred not immediately after the outbreak of war, but nearly a month later, it has important implications in understanding the major motivations for enlistment. Far from signing up in a burst of enthusiasm at the outbreak of war, the largest single component of volunteers enlisted at exactly the moment when the war turned serious. Most men did not join the British Army expecting a picnic stroll to Berlin, but in the expectation of a desperate fight for national defence.[103] On 28 August, the *Hackney Spectator* editorialised specifically: 'The idea of a cakewalk to Berlin, if entertained, has gone … Hardly a family in England will not have lost a dear one, or more, before the finish, but we cannot help that.' In Hove on 30 August, Arthur Conan Doyle addressed a recruiting meeting: 'The enemy is almost in sight of our shores ... there is a possibility of disaster.'[104]

Andrew Clark reports on the 30 August that his daughter had attended a service in a neighbouring church in Fairstead: 'The Rector, Thomas Sandgrove, preached a horrifying sermon on the horrible scenes of the battlefield and exhorted all young men to join the army.'[105] This doesn't sound like a case of soft-selling.

Ambivalence and ambiguity

Simplistic generalisations about war enthusiasm not only iron out the complexities of society; they also gloss over the complexities of individual response. Those really determined to do so were able to ignore the war. For example, Miss E. Barkworth in Devon barely mentions it in her diary and spent August going to the beach and reading Dickens. This reaction was more widespread than one might think.[106] The most extreme case of 'war indifference' might be the man discovered living on Hackney Marshes in October 1917, who claimed that he did not know that there was a war on.[107] Of course it is possible that he might have been lying.

Indifference was widespread, but not typical: most people did notice the war. The diaries of two middle-class women are indicative of the very mixed feelings, including apparently contradictory responses, that could occur in an individual across the course of a dramatic week. Mrs Eustace Miles, a restaurateur, kept a diary at the time, that was later published. On 1 August she wrote, 'We are having a quiet weekend at W on Sea ... There seems nothing wrong (outwardly) with the world, yet the air is full of whispers of coming trouble: and rumours of war are becoming more and more alarming and more and more persistent.' On 4 August she noted: 'Since writing these words we already seem to be in a new world. The awful declaration of war has been made and everything plunged into chaos. We are back in London. In the short time that we have been away everything seems to have changed ... awful as it is – it is very thrilling.'

The same mixture of foreboding and excitement appears the next day:

Of course at first we are all feeling terribly shaken and hardly anyone sleeps. The streets are full of people all night long, and the steady tramp of Territorials as they march to Headquarters seems never to cease. There are small and subtle changes too. I notice people in the streets are now singing the 'Marseillaise' and 'God Save the King' and 'Rule Britannia'; the very children are marching instead of walking and carrying bits of stick as bayonets and using old pieces of pails as drums ...

We are having to part with some of our most valued employees, who have been with us for years. It seems to bring the tragedy of war into our midst. It is like parting with members of our own family.[108]

In an unpublished diary, Mrs Ada Reece, the wife of an Army doctor, shows another mixture of reactions. On 2 August she wrote: 'we are on the eve of a Great European War in which we must engage against our will and the ultimate consequences of which none can foresee. But all are agreed that it will be more terrible than any previous war with all the horrible engines of destruction that science has been perfecting through a hundred years of peace.' Despite this she was firmly convinced that war was necessary, for the next day she wrote: 'We must fight, I wrote yesterday, it had never occurred to me that it was possible to do otherwise ... Of course we were not in a part which would be crowded on a Bank holiday, but the people seemed unusually quiet.'

Historians might separate out anxiety and enthusiasm, but for individuals the two could be closely linked:

I spent all the morning marketing. The CSSA was crowded, the rush to buy food by well to do people last Saturday has been very unfortunate, stocks are exhausted ... those of us who are calmer are forced to buy now before the greedy seize all. I gave an order for a large quantity of sugar which has already risen by ½ d per lb, some chocolate etc.

On Wednesday 5th we awoke to the glorious news that Great Britain declared war on Germany last night ... Glorious, I say although we undertake hostilities very gravely and reluctantly, but the suspense of the last few days has been great and some papers have been urging that Britain should remain neutral.

War might be glorious, but Reece was not unaware that it also brought misery:

Helene and I started out with Peggy, and walked from Queen's Road to Marble Arch and then by omnibus to Holborn. The buses are crowded, they say 400 chassis have been requisitioned by Government. There were many Khaki uniforms about and horses being led away by soldiers ... Mother came up in a very sad mood, had seen the London Scottish marching out and wept over them – full of fear for Dick and Harold.[109]

These literate testimonies might be treated as untypical in their complexity, but it is likely that the same mixture of emotions and motivations was widespread.

Establishing this ambiguity is more difficult from actions than from diaries, but there are some intriguing cases where public enthusiasm can be seen in relation to private anxiety. A press account of police court proceedings from Norwich shows how apparent jingoism was a mask for deeper concern:

Clara Mason, married woman, yesterday was charged with being drunk and disorderly ... Defendant said she was insulted by some person on St Andrews Plain. She was singing 'God Save the King' when he told her to shut up. Defendant said 'I shall not, my husband is fighting for such as you.' She then became very excited and did not know what happened afterwards ...

Police-constable Taylor said defendant picked up several pieces of brick and threw them at witness. One piece struck him in the head.

Defendant bursting into tears said – My Husband is at the front and all I wanted was to fight Germans. I have been worrying this past month about my Husband and lost my head a bit ... He is at the front and I have not been right since. I cannot eat anything. A friend of mine gave me a drink and it got hold of me.[110]

What should we make of this ambivalence? An earlier account of Britain in 1914 provides some useful insight. Caroline Playne wrote *The Pre-War Mind* in 1928. It was a passionate and pacifistic attempt to explain what had happened in 1914. Playne had hated the war and still found it almost inexplicable. Yet extensive reading of contemporary reporting had convinced her that *prior* to the outbreak of the war there 'was no sudden fit of passionate insanity which annihilated all reasonable action'. Instead, 'Soul possessing, permeating neurosis' had paralysed the public response and had caused a flight into irrational fantasy of anti-German liberal crusading *subsequent* to the outbreak of war.[111] The attempt to psycho-analyse the national mood, and the underlying assumption that support for the war in any form was clear evidence of irrationality, undermine some of the specifics of Playne's argument. But it is not without merit. The declaration of war did release some of the growing anxiety and tension, and the speed of the crisis did paralyse opposition. Finally, the urge to do *something*, whether it be to search for alleged German spies, contribute to relief funds or personally volunteer, was clearly prevalent in the first week of the war.

Perhaps an impressionistic view of the mood immediately after the outbreak of the war, published in a local North London newspaper, comes closest to capturing the anxiety, excitement and fear of the moment, and the multitude of reactions:

THEY SAY:
That the war greets you everywhere in Islington.
That you turn a corner and blunder into a man obsessed with his newspaper.
That you meet a friend and his first words are, 'What do you think of it?'
That from right, left and in front, news-vendors throw out nothing but war.
That you enter a tramcar and still find the subject being waged with fervour.
That finally, at the end of the day you go home to bed and dream about it.

That the closing of the banks was a move most businessmen were
unprepared for.
That a local tradesman remarked, 'It has fairly put the lid on.'
That a number of military reserve men in the local police have been
called to the colours.
That the response of the North London, 'Braves' to the country's call has
surprised the authorities.
That great crowds invaded the picture palaces of Islington last night to
see the war movements on the screen.
That when the great clap of thunder burst over North London at 11.30
yesterday
many people thought that a German bomb had been dropped from an
aeroplane.
That there has been a stampede of Germans from Finsbury Park.
That the appearance of uniformed Territorials in the streets caused
considerable excitement in Stoke Newington.
That the rise in the price of commodities is giving grave anxiety in the
poorer parts of Finsbury.[112]

This captures the way that British people entered the war.

Conclusions

Please God, your trampling vanities will jar
A sleeping giant, and such petty things
As crowns and Caesars shall at last make way
Before mankind's Republic, ending war.

Justin McCarthy, 'Armageddon'[113]

G. K. Chesterton wrote several open letters which were published in the
Daily Herald in the first week of the war. Whilst the newspaper remained
firmly anti-war, it did allow space for an argument that the war had to be
fought. In the first of these letters, Chesterton made no secret of his
emotional response: 'I think this war is a disgusting thing.' Nevertheless,
in an over-extended metaphor, he explained his rationale for supporting
it: 'How do we settle our personal quarrels? We settle them by deciding
who is right and punishing whoever is wrong.' He wrote that if the local
vicar decided to punch the nonconformist minister without provocation,
the public response would not be to form a ring around them to prevent
the vicar from 'hammering the nose of the local Rabbi, the Roman
Catholic priest, the Atheist cobbler and all the other ornaments of the
town'. Instead 'we arrest the vicar on a charge of assault'.[114]

The decision to support the war was about more than the violation of
Belgian neutrality: it was about acceptable behaviour in the international
sphere; about the maintenance of an idea of proper and lawful behaviour

among nations. Chesterton was confident that the socialist readers of the *Daily Herald* subscribed to the same basic principles, and he was right in his confidence.

The historian and political scientist Martin Ceadel proposes five basic attitudes to war. The two extremes are easily defined: militarism which views war as a social good in itself, and pacifism which views war simply as evil and to be opposed under all circumstances. The problems arise with the three middle positions. 'Pacificism', an old term Ceadel revives, sees war as an evil to be avoided if at all possible. It should also be actively opposed where possible, and action should be taken to prevent wars. 'Defencism' sees war as an evil which is acceptable as a lesser evil to protect oneself or one's vital interests. 'Crusading' is a position that sees war as a moral duty when it is clear that war is a lesser evil than the alternative, in terms of the threat that an opponent poses to core values. It also seeks to impose those core values on others by force.[115]

The problem with these three 'distinct' positions is that they tend in practice to overlap. In 1914 Britain, militarists and pacifists were rare birds. The arguments at the outbreak of war were conducted between 'defencists' and 'pacificists'. Was German action a real threat to Britain or not? Most people carried a little of each within themselves. In the end the defencists won. They won because German actions apparently confirmed the defencist position. The most striking development was the speed of conversion of the majority of pacificists to defencism and even to 'crusading'. The violation of Belgian neutrality convinced a number of very active pacificists, that *their* core values of peace and negotiation were threatened by 'Prussian Militarism'. Gilbert Murray, one of the most prominent voices in favour of neutrality and negotiation, informed C. P. Scott in the early hours of the morning of 4 August that he felt 'it very difficult to oppose Government action when the German Government has plainly run amok'.[116] Lord Weardale, in a letter to Christian Lange on 7 August 1914, stated:

If Germanic ambitions pursued with such ruthless disregard of treaties, solemn obligations or humanitarian considerations should, as I hope fail, the Throne of the Hapsburgs and the Hohenzollerns will be swept away. Europe will have learnt a lesson and those who have a primary share in the misery will rightly be the first to suffer.[117]

Weardale had been the head of the Inter-Parliamentary Union and, as such, a leading voice in the pre-war British peace movement. Truly, hell hath no fury like a pacificist spurned.

The *Evening News* commented in pessimistic verse on 29 July, the day of the Austrian invasion of Serbia:

Fact versus Theory

> War is a ghastly game
> and nobody wants to play it;
> War is the whole world's shame,
> But there is a power to stay it.
> Use common sense and war is dead!
> So the confident pacifist said.
>
> Arbitration's the thing
> For stopping war and foment
> and a big financial ring
> could stifle war in a moment ...
>
> War though it doesn't 'pay'
> (Think of the gold it's fed on!)
> Bringing us near to-day
> To the horror of Armageddon.
> The vile old Adam that lurks in man
> Has been too much for the pacifist's plan.[118]

This is the cynical comment of a Conservative newspaper on Liberal pacifist illusions, but it is not without a note of regret. It would be a mistake to characterise the public entry into the war as more in sorrow than in anger. It rapidly became both. Indeed, a large part of the dynamic of hatred that developed in 1914 was precisely because this was a war that the majority of people hadn't wanted. The 'vile old Adam' was quickly characterised as a specifically German weakness. In many respects the 'scaremonger' Germanophobes of pre-1914 proved more moderate in their reactions because they had expected nothing better. The pre-war defenders of Germany and of peace often became the ideological driving force behind the war.

Barbara Hammond wrote on 22 October 1914 to Arthur Ponsonby, declining his invitation to join the Union of Democratic Control: 'When a criminal assaults an inoffensive person your first duty is to stop him, not to discuss the question of how far society is to blame for his action by letting him grow up in a bad environment.'[119] More bluntly, Arnold Bennett wrote in a piece published in the press on 1 October 1914: 'Stupid bullies should be treated according to their mentality ... Many a savage brute has been permanently convinced of the advantages of civilization by a knock down blow.'[120] A 10 August letter to *The Times* from the classical archae-ologist, Professor Ramsay, who had been a signatory of the neutrality appeal of leading British academics on 3 August, shows how, in the space of a week, opinion could alter radically after the outbreak of war: 'The admiration which I feel for Germany as a civilising power in its own fashion (different from ours) is changed to dislike when she misuses her deserved influence in the world of thought to trample on law and right and to force the horrors of war on a neutral state.'[121]

We will understand the First World War a great deal better if we jettison the teleology of the war as an inevitable outcome of mass jingoism and anti-German antagonism. Instead we should try to get the causality right: although these phenomena were not absent, they did not cause the war. It was the other way around: it was *the war* that massively increased anti-Germanism and popular patriotism. The following chapter will address this issue.

2   Defining the enemy: Atrocities and propaganda 1914–1915

Lies and half-truths about the war

In a wartime history of Hyde in Cheshire, there are a number of anecdotes about the experiences of local inhabitants. When the *Lusitania* was torpedoed, two local people were drowned. Vernon Livermore, a ship's bugler from Hyde, survived. Nothing particularly remarkable about that, except that it turns out that he had also been a ship's bugler on the *Titanic*. The history doesn't record whether 'Jonah' Livermore went to sea again, or indeed whether any shipping line would employ him.[1]

Livermore wasn't the only link between the two doomed ships. The sinking of the *Lusitania* evoked memories of the *Titanic*, barely three years earlier. But whereas the latter was generally seen as an act, perhaps even a judgement, of God; the *Lusitania* sinking was understood as the work of the devil.

The torpedoing of the liner was the final evidence required to complete the 'demonising' of the enemy in the public mind. But it was also an act of war that involved the deliberate killing of over a thousand civilians. Every step on the way to the demonisation of Germany was prompted by real events, albeit events interpreted in a highly partisan framework. Any discussion of atrocity propaganda must bear in mind the reality of atrocities. That there was exaggeration and invention is undeniable, but the inhabitants of Hyde knew civilians who had died on the *Lusitania*, the inhabitants of West Hartlepool knew civilians killed by the German navy and the inhabitants of Folkestone knew civilians killed by bombing. By later standards of total war these casualties were few enough, but the shock at the time was genuine and great.

In both academic and popular writing, British 'propagandists' were presented in the inter-war period as devious liars.[2] The process of inventing this image of a clique of cynics manipulatively demonising the enemy began during the war itself. German propaganda harped incessantly on the hidden hand of Lord Northcliffe, the liar in chief, libelling the German emperor, armed forces and people.[3] Pacifist opinion in Britain and isolationist opinion in the United States picked up and reflected these charges. By the end of the 1920s they had become almost an orthodoxy.

The classic statement of this image is Arthur Ponsonby's work, *Falsehood in Wartime*, first published in 1928 and described on the cover as, 'an amazing collection of carefully documented lies circulated in Great Britain, France Germany, Italy and America during the Great War'. In reality, the book is overwhelmingly dominated by British 'material'. Although thoughtful recent historians of propaganda[4] particularly Philip Taylor, have expressed some doubts about Ponsonby's 'misconceptions', *Falsehood in Wartime* remains a major source of the historiographical and popular tradition about British propaganda. It is time to discard it. Far from being carefully documented, *Falsehood in Wartime* is fabricated from contentious interpretation and down-right invention. Ponsonby was a wartime and post-war pacifist, a sworn enemy of Northcliffe, deeply sympathetic to Germany in general and the Kaiser in particular. Bluntly, *Falsehood in Wartime* is not an exposure of the truth about propaganda lies, it *is* a propaganda lie.

To exemplify 'contentious interpretation', I will begin with one of the most notorious atrocity stories of the war. The German 'corpse-rendering factory' was an obscene invention, the idea that dead German (and perhaps Allied) soldiers were being rendered down to glycerine to aid armaments production remains the chief example of 'black propaganda', the outright lie, during the whole war. Ponsonby devotes a chapter to the tale. He states at the outset that it was invented in 1917 and was not finally disposed of until 1925. Ponsonby cites the first British press notice of the story as being on 16 April 1917, apparently quoting from *Berlin Lokalanzieger*. A letter in *The Times* on 26 April 1917 suggests that the story had appeared in the *North China Herald* on 3 March. German sources quickly denied the story, claiming that the British had deliberately mistranslated the German word *Kadaver* as human body, when it referred to the dead bodies of horses. When the issue was debated in Parliament, the British Government took a position of neither confirming nor denying it.

According to Ponsonby, not until 1925 'did the truth emerge'. At a speech by Brigadier General Charteris at a dinner of the National Arts Club in New York, he admitted that he had begun the story as 'propaganda for China' by switching the captions on two photographs which he dispatched to Shanghai. He intended to support the story with a fake German soldier's diary which 'was now in the war museum in London'.[5] This was reported immediately in the American press. The 'admission' caused a storm, including questions in Parliament. Charteris himself categorically denied the story, and Ponsonby quotes the Charteris denial, published in *The Times* on 4 November 1925. But Ponsonby makes his dismissal of Charteris's denial crystal-clear.[6]

Brigadier General Charteris was Chief of Intelligence for the British Expeditionary Force in 1917. He was certainly capable of twisting the truth, and was probably capable of doing that of which he was accused. But the story that he was the originator of the lie about the German corpse-rendering factory is clearly false. Overlooked by all those who have accepted the idea of Charteris as inventor of this story is the fact that it clearly existed at least six months before Charteris is supposed to have invented it.

Hidden in plain sight, the evidence has been there all along. In a poem by Siegfried Sassoon, 'The Tombstone Maker', written in October 1916 and published in the spring of 1917, is a clear reference to the story. It is very revealing about the true nature of atrocity stories:

> I told him with a sympathetic grin,
> That Germans boil dead soldiers down for fat;
> And he was horrified. "What shameful sin!
> O Sir, that Christian souls should come to that!"[7]

Sassoon's poem, one of his satires mocking civilian ignorance, is an invented conversation with a village tombstone-maker. The intent is clearly satirical, but it should be made clear that whatever it is that Sassoon is satirising, the date of the poem makes it clear that he is not satirising a story which was 'invented' in 1917. It is mischievously tempting to suggest that the real inventor of what Ponsonby calls 'one of the most revolting lies of the war' was not the 'Brass Hat' Charteris, but Sassoon, the famous 'truth-teller', anti-propagandist and anti-war poet. Unfortunately this too would be a distortion. A prototype version of the story appears in an unpublished civilian diary held at the Imperial War Museum. In an entry dated 12 July 1916, Harold Cousins wrote:

A story on the authority of a Jena Professor is to the effect that the dead bodies of soldiers are being used to provide nourishment in the form of rissoles, etc. It is certain that these bodies are not buried in the field, but sent back in bundles of five to be cremated – or otherwise dealt with.[8]

Doubtless these stories appeared in many other places as well.[9] The corpse-rendering factory was not the invention of a diabolical propagandist; it was a popular folktale, an 'urban myth', which had circulated for months before it received any official notice.[10] This is an important clue as to the real origin of 'atrocity' stories and will be expanded later.

A more blatant example of Ponsonby's method can be found in his much-repeated story of the 'Bells of Antwerp'. The version published in Ponsonby, under the title 'The Manufacture of News', is this:

The Fall of Antwerp
When the fall of Antwerp got known, the church bells were rung (meaning in Germany). (*Kölnische Zeitung*)

According to the *Kolnische Zeitung*, the clergy of Antwerp were compelled to ring the church bells when the fortress was taken. (*Le Matin*)

According to what *Le Matin* has heard from Cologne, the Belgian priests who refused to ring the church bells when Antwerp was taken have been driven away from their places. (*The Times*)

According to what *The Times* has heard from Cologne, the Belgian priests who refused to ring the church bells when Antwerp was taken have been sentenced to hard labour. (*Corriera della Sera*)

According to information from *Corriera della Sera* from Cologne via London, it is confirmed that the barbaric conquerors of Antwerp, punished the unfortunate Belgian priests for their heroic refusal to ring church bells by hanging them as living clappers to the bells with their heads down. (*Le Matin*)

It is the archetypal atrocity story. It has been widely reprinted, probably as a consequence of its repetition, word for word, in Robert Graves's best-selling autobiography, *Goodbye to All That*.[11] Graves clearly copied from Ponsonby, but where did Ponsonby get it from? Did he, as implied, scan through the pages of the Entente press? In which case, why didn't he cite dates?

The story of the Antwerp bells is truly one of the greatest pieces of lying propaganda of all time, but the brilliance rests in the fact that it is *German* propaganda. The story first appeared in the *Norddeutsche Allgemeine Zeitung* on 4 July 1915. Ponsonby copied the story word for word. A check of *The Times* and *Le Matin* clearly demonstrates that these stories never appeared. Ponsonby first published this story in English 1916, and the *Norddeutsche Allgemeine Zeitung* then repeated the story with Ponsonby as their source![12]

Ponsonby, in his willingness to believe the worst of the press on his own side, had been taken for a ride. It is typical of the methodology of *Falsehood in Wartime*. Material from American isolationist sources, the British pacifist press and even from Germany is taken as truth, British official pronouncements and the British press are assumed to be lying. His book is not an inquiry into propaganda; it *is* propaganda, of the most passionate sort:

Exposure may therefore be useful, even when the struggle is over, in order to show up the fraud, hypocrisy and humbug on which all war rests, and the blatant and vulgar devices which have been used for so long to prevent poor ignorant people from realising the true meaning of war.
    It must be admitted that many people were conscious and willing dupes. But many more were unconscious and sincere in their patriotic zeal. Finding now the elaborate and carefully staged deceptions practised upon them, they feel a resentment which has not only served to open their eyes, but may induce them to keep their eyes open when next the bugle sounds.[13]

That there was an enormous amount of falsehood perpetrated in wartime Britain is unquestionably true, and that some of it had official or semi-official sanction is fair comment. But Ponsonby's emphasis on 'carefully staged deceptions' was a deliberate attempt to discredit the war against Germany which he had opposed throughout, an attempt to rewrite history on behalf of the losers.

Propaganda: the 'black legend'

The minimisation and rationalisation of German military and naval behaviour has always been crucial to the process of blackening British wartime 'propaganda', at the same time, what British 'propagandists' actually wrote and said is exaggerated and distorted to the point of caricature. We have become so used to the idea of the British press being full of images of Belgian babies impaled on bayonets, that it comes as something of a shock to actually read the British wartime press and to find that, whilst images of Hunnish barbarity are certainly not absent, they are in fact far less prominent than generally believed and that most of them are very different from those imagined.[14]

It is helpful at the outset to examine the 'atrocities' committed by the German armed forces as understood at the time. The image of Germany waging a campaign of 'frightfulness'[15] was firmly established in the British popular mind during the first eighteen months of the war. Was this invention? In *retrospect* the archetypal German atrocity was the murder of Belgian civilians in the first six weeks of the war. Leaving aside non-combatants killed in bombardments and crossfire (in itself a rather generous interpretation in the context of an unprovoked invasion), somewhere in the region of 4,000 Belgian civilians were killed deliberately. The vast majority of these were men, and most were probably broadly of military age. Some clergy were murdered; so were some women and children. One example should suffice. On 8 August 1914, the German 165 Infantry regiment took seventy-two inhabitants of the village of Meten out into a meadow and executed them collectively. The group included eight women and four girls under the age of 13.[16]

These murders were of two types: cold-blooded executions of large numbers of hostages and more spontaneous massacres carried out by units that went on the rampage. In both cases, the rationale was that they were retaliation for the activities of the *Franc-Tireurs* – Belgian guerrillas waging an illegal sniping campaign against German troops. The *Franc-Tireur* defence was dubious at best. There is little reliable evidence for civilians taking up arms against the Germans at this time.[17] Most of the 'retaliations' were for casualties suffered in firefights against uniformed opponents and, in more than a few cases, 'friendly fire' from other German units. Equally to the point, had there actually been civilian resistance, German actions would still have been manifestly illegal under the Hague Convention on several counts. The taking and shooting of hostages was explicitly outlawed, as was the doctrine of collective responsibility of civilians. Furthermore, civilians were entitled to take up arms in defence of their country in the event of invasion: until such time as they had clearly fallen under the law of the occupying power, such civilians were entitled to prisoner-of-war status if captured. Justificatory statements, such as that by Philip Knightley, that 'they were shot as guerrilla fighters, as hostages or simply because they got in the way of a victorious advancing army in which not every soldier was a saint', are both morally disingenuous and factually misleading.[18]

These massacres, which were widely reported at the time in the American press,[19] genuinely shocked much of the world. There was a fair amount of hypocrisy in this. Similar standards had been widely applied in colonial campaigns by imperial powers. American forces in the Philippines had, in recent memory, done much worse. The British, of course, had been widely reviled for their 'counter-insurgency' tactics in South Africa, not least by liberal critics at home, many of whom would be prominently involved in justifying German war crimes later.[20] British policies in South Africa were, at the very least, extremely dubious in terms of human rights, at worst, a genuine war crime. But using them to justify German behaviour in Belgium was and is both morally blind and factually wrong. Faced with a genuine, not an imagined, guerrilla war, it is worth noting that the British generally treated these guerrillas as prisoners of war. The deaths in concentration camps were unforgivable, but this was not a deliberate policy of atrocity; rather one of criminal incompetence and neglect, exacerbated by racist attitudes. Some 28,000 Afrikaners and 16,000 black Africans died as a result of these policies. This cannot and should not be justified. But it should be used for an accurate comparison. The same causes, malnutrition and disease, resulting from brutal military occupation policies, were responsible for the deaths of somewhere in the order of *250,000* Belgian civilians during the First World War. This is in *addition* to those deliberately murdered in autumn 1914. Further illustrative of the difference between German norms and British is the response to the Easter Rising in Dublin. The mere suspicion of armed resistance in Belgium in 1914 led to thousands of executions, even amongst those the German Army knew had not taken up arms. By contrast after a week of street-fighting against almost a thousand armed rebels, who were unquestionably liable to execution both under the Hague Convention and ordinary criminal law, the British confined themselves to executing sixteen ringleaders. Whilst it is clearly the case that public opinion, in both Ireland and the United States, influenced this 'clemency', the crucial difference is that the British cared about this public opinion. It is not difficult to imagine how a similar uprising in Strasbourg or Poznań would have been treated: local nationalists, well aware of this, weren't foolish enough to test the Germans. There is one fully analogous case in British behaviour in the first quarter of the twentieth century, the Amritsar massacre of 1919. The brutal massacre of innocent civilians by fearful British military authorities 'to send a message' was the one act genuinely similar in motivation and scale to German military behaviour in Belgium. So to understand the reactions to the behaviour of the German Army it is perhaps easiest to point out that it committed half a dozen 'Amritsars' in the space of six weeks.

Such deliberate atrocities in Belgium received intermittent coverage in the first eighteen months of the war, and did provoke indignation. But to understand the core of the developing British perception of German methods of warfare, it is important to remember that Belgium was secondary in the perception of German barbarity. What really shocked the British press and public were 'atrocities' closer to home. A maritime insular power, it was German activity at sea and the killing of British civilians that provoked the greatest outcries. The indiscriminate use of naval mines, the bombardment of British coastal towns, the emergence of submarine warfare and the beginnings of air bombardment of civilians: these were the central British definitions of 'frightfulness'. The climax of British indignation came between the middle of April 1915 and the middle of May. In fast succession, the use by the German Army of chlorine gas at the battle of Ypres, the sinking of the *Lusitania*, air raids by Zeppelins on British towns and the publication of the Bryce Report into German atrocities in Belgium, established the image of Germany as having thrown aside civilised norms entirely. The most widespread outbreaks of anti-German rioting in British cities occurred at this time.

It was also a bad period on the battlefield: casualties were mounting up at the Gallipoli landings, at Ypres and in the abortive assault on Aubers ridge. Significant numbers of wartime volunteers were now being killed, in addition to pre-war regulars. There were doubts about the competence of the military and civil direction of the war. Just as it had at the end of August 1914, the war was turning very serious. Just as late August and early September 1914 had seen a marked increase in 'atrocity' coverage, so did this period, a product of the intensification of the war and an intensification in the scale of *actual* atrocities.

The latter half of 1915 saw atrocity stories and coverage begin to fade in prominence. In part this was because the news was increasingly stale, in part because, in the name of 'retaliation', the Allied war effort was beginning to lose any distinctive moral high ground. But by this time the image of Germany was set. However, the creation of this image was a much more complex process than is generally acknowledged. One way of examining it is to look at the central demon of German (and Ponsonby's) perceptions of British propaganda, the best-selling daily newspaper in Britain, Northcliffe's *Daily Mail*.

The *Daily Mail*: reporting atrocities

The effect of Harmsworth journalism, in particular, was that all through the war, it played on the nerves of the nation. (Caroline Playne, *Society at War*[21])

The press ... gave great prominence to atrocity stories. In the absence of factual information ... atrocity stories gave much needed copy ... These stories were sensational news. No effort was made to spare readers the gory details – they were indeed violent appeals to hate and the animal lust for blood. (Cate Haste, *Keep the Home Fires Burning*[22])

My first memory of Lord Northcliffe in the Great War is one that carries me to a mean hospital in the Belgian town of Furnes, where he sat by the bedside of a poor old woman of eighty years age who had been wounded by the splinter of a shell. He was greatly moved ... "What has she done" he asked me pointing to the pitiful white haired sufferer – "What has she done that War should punish her?" That question was characteristic of him. (Max Pemberton, *Lord Northcliffe: A Memoir* (London, n.d.), p. 148)

The *Daily Mail* was the publishing phenomenon of its time.[23] Founded in 1896 by the ambitious newspaper entrepreneur Alfred Harmsworth, who would be ennobled as Lord Northcliffe, it was the prototype of the modern British press: cheap, daily and having mass circulation. It was the first newspaper to achieve a regular daily circulation of over a million copies. It was undoubtedly the most influential single newspaper with the mass public in 1914, although it should be remembered that the daily-newspaper-reading public was largely a middle-class one.

The *Daily Mail* was synonymous with Germanophobia. In the pre-war period it had run the infamous 'Made in Germany' campaign against German industrial 'dumping' and had in 1906 serialised William Le Queux's infamous 'Invasion of 1910'. The latter was to be of some importance. The descriptions of German retaliatory shootings and indiscriminate bombardments of civilians helped set a script for 'expected' German behaviour in 1914. It also proved fairly accurate in grasping the style in which the German Army actually did wage war in Belgium in 1914.

Once the war had broken out, the *Daily Mail*, along with the rest of the papers, printed atrocity stories. Early reports are distinctly bland to a modern reader, but would have had an emotional impact on contemporary English readers. On 6 August 1914, the *Daily Mail* comments editorially on the destruction of a Belgian village and describes it as 'a monstrous crime against the laws of nations'. It also describes the laying of naval mines in shallow water as 'a disloyal and cruel form of war'.[24] In a post-nuclear age, the idea of free-floating naval mines as a noteworthy 'atrocity' seems rather over-stated, but for a maritime nation in 1914 it was very serious. The intensity of condemnation slowly steps up: on page 3 of the newspaper on 10 August there is a sub-heading, 'Belgian reports of German Outrages'. Two days later comes the first editorial on 'German Brutality'. This editorial is revealing:

> They are also reported in many places to have mistreated civilians on whom they have waged unprovoked war with appalling brutality. Our Special Correspondent in Belgium, Mr Jeffries says he cannot bring himself to believe these stories and hopes they will not be confirmed, but the grim account, which we reproduce today from the *Temps* proves that the Germans have shot unarmed Frenchmen for the sole crime of crying 'Vive La France'.[25]

A week into the war the paper was prepared to print its own correspondent's scepticism about atrocities and at the same time to accept a contradictory account, ostensibly taken from the French press. The editorial continues:

> In Belgium the Germans have treated the villages where any resistance has been offered to their attack with something like savagery. Peasants have been shot; houses have been wantonly burnt; hostages have been seized and maltreated, or forced to march in front of the German troops, where they would be most exposed to Belgian fire.
>
> Such are the methods of this people which claims the privileges of culture and civilization. The wanton attack upon little Belgium has already covered the reputation of Germany with the broadest discredit. In the North Sea the Germans have proceeded to show their system of maritime warfare is as cruel and callous as their system of war on land. By scattering mines in the highways of international traffic they have imperilled the shipping of neutral powers and brought the most terrible risks upon innocent non-combatants – women and children.

The point to note about this editorial comment is that not one word of it is actually untrue.[26] Everything described here had happened by 12 August. Yet there is rhetorical slippage: mining international sea-ways did seriously endanger non-combatants, but overwhelmingly adult male ones. By this date the number of women and children at sea was probably minimal.

The 'doubting' Jeffries also provides some accounts of small scale 'atrocities' on the same day: an old man bayoneted to death, a farm servant 'rather the worse for drink' shot for failing to stop when ordered. There is a small drip of 'German brutality' stories on the inner pages over the following week.[27] The temperature increases with an opinion piece by Hamilton Fyfe on 21 August 1914, entitled 'The Barbarity of German Troops – Sins against Civilisation'. It begins: 'In wartime all stories told by one side against the other (even if it is one's own side) must be read and listened to with caution. Therefore I have been sceptical about the tales of horror which appear in the French newspapers accusing the Germans of murder and brutality.' Now Fyfe claims that he can no longer ignore the 'evidence':

Unfortunately there is no doubt any longer that the Germans have been making war in a way that is very far indeed from being civilized. To call it 'savage' or 'barbarous' would be doing a monstrous injustice to uncivilized races … Do not think I mean to apply it to all German soldiers or even most of them … But that a large number of them have acted not like men but like devils is now beyond dispute.

Fyfe follows this with four paragraphs of French atrocity stories. There are two ways of reading this. One is to assume the worst of the writer: the nuance, scepticism and attempted balance are just so much rhetoric to soften the reader up for the real business of libelling the enemy. The other is to accept that it is possible that Fyfe is trying to tell the truth as he sees it. It is a mark of how effective the 'black legend' has been that the latter seems the more radical suggestion. Yet it is the one which fits the evidence best. By 21 August both the reality of German war crimes and the much exaggerated rumours of them amongst refugees were becoming too insistent for even a sceptical journalist to ignore. The well-documented became mixed with the apocryphal: an editorial the next day referred to the 'Agony of Belgium', which had been spared 'no extremity of human suffering'. The editorial claims that Belgian officers had been manacled to the stirrup leathers of an Uhlan's horse – which seems unlikely – and that the inhabitants of Brussels had been fined £8,000,000 as 'punishment' for Belgian resistance – which was true.[28] Editors, columnists and journalists were aware both that something terrible was happening and that it was being distorted in the telling. The problem, without direct access, was distinguishing the reliable stories, as one writer put it: 'Daily, I hear stories of Prussian horrors that curdle the blood, and when all the substratum of exaggeration and distortion is removed there remains the yet unforgettable tale of the Limburg priest.'[29] Recounting these examples in fact gives a rather exaggerated impression. The striking thing about the first three weeks of the war is that atrocities in Belgium take up remarkably little space in the *Daily Mail*: just a couple of editorials and some columns of reportage on inside pages.[30] It wasn't until 26 August that atrocities really receive 'headline' treatment. This was in response to the first report of the 'official' Belgian Committee of Inquiry. In reporting the Belgian 'findings'

2. Belgian refugees arrive in London. IWM (Q 53305).

we can see classic atrocity stories making their first appearance in the *Daily Mail*. A Mrs Deglimme is carried 'half naked' to a place two miles away and shot at by German troops (she survived). An old man is mutilated, hung upside down and burnt alive. 'Young girls have been violated and little children outraged, at Oramnel where several inhabitants suffered mutilations too horrible to describe.' Torture and rape for the first time are prominently reported along with the story of Aerschot, where 'in a single street six male inhabitants who crossed their threshold were seized and shot under the eyes of their wives and children'.[31] The paper is simply publicising and taking at face value an 'official' report. But the prominence is a good deal greater than earlier stories.

In the week that followed there is a great deal more coverage. The sack of Louvain is first reported on 29 August under the heading 'The War Lords' awful vengeance; A Belgian City in Ashes', and on 1 September an eyewitness report 'What I saw in Louvain' is given thirteen paragraphs, the longest 'atrocity story' up to that date. Stories about Louvain are prominent for the next week. An editorial on 8 September is entitled 'The horror of Louvain' and represents a further rhetorical escalation:

They drove the women and children into the fields, perpetrating on them atrocities which cannot be detailed in cold prose. No language of condemnation can be too strong for such iniquity. But those who know the repulsive torture chambers of Nuremberg and Regensburg and the merciless treatment of animals in the Fatherland will not be surprised by these cruelties.[32]

The accusation of cruelty to animals later in the paragraph is a wonderfully English touch.[33]

For the press, Louvain (Leuven), was the definitive atrocity of 1914 in Belgium. It is important to understand why. The key reason was access. After the destruction inflicted upon the town by the Germans, it was briefly recaptured. This was a rare occasion on which the press had something other than refugee rumour to work with.

But there is a good deal more to it than this. After all, in terms of human casualties – 209 civilians murdered in four days – Louvain did not stand out from the experiences of a dozen other Belgian towns in August and September. What gave Louvain a particular resonance was the physical destruction visited on the city's buildings and the framework in which this was interpreted.

It is easy for historians, who are used to dealing with text, to overlook the significance of pictures. Yet the photographic component of news coverage was the more shocking and important part in the minds of the *Daily Mail* readers. These photographic images in August and September are overwhelmingly of destroyed buildings. Whilst there are few news stories of German atrocities, there are a great number of pictures.[34] The destruction of buildings, rather than the killing of civilians, was the initial stimulus for the concept of 'Hunnish barbarity'.

For middle-class Britons the sanctity of home and public property was one of the 'unspoken assumptions' of 1914. Militant suffragettes understood this perfectly in their campaigns of window-breaking and picture-slashing.[35] The destruction of property made a deep and lasting impression. On 18 November 1914, almost three months after the destruction, a story describes 'The Heavy Hand of the Hun' and states, 'The horror of Louvain is indescribable, one might think one was in Pompey [sic].'[36] It is interesting to note that the term 'Hun' begins to appear rather late in the *Daily Mail*.[37] The earliest use is on 25 August: 'we are going about placidly as if we lived in ordinary times, as if the Huns were not battering at the gate'.[38] The combination of Louvain and Kipling's poem began to spread the usage. But it certainly does not predominate over 'German' at any point in 1914. Furthermore the context of usage is revealing. The Hun is the enemy of civilisation and specifically the destroyer of the physical manifestations of civilisation. A modern writer might have used the term 'vandal', as indeed the French press appears to have done. This in turn leads us to the specific importance of Louvain.[39] Unlike the anonymous mining towns that bore the brunt of German destruction, Louvain was a cultural gem. Amongst the buildings burnt down were the Old Market, the fourteenth-century Cloth Hall and the eighteenth-century University Library (with the loss of 250,000 books and 800 incunabulae and 950 manuscripts). Severe damage was done to the fifteenth-century church of St Peter's.[40] It was as if an invading army had arrived in Oxford and burnt down Duke Humfrey's Library, New College and Christ Church Cathedral. Norman Maclean, a Scottish clergyman, made exactly that analogy, adding St Andrews for local relevance. It is unsurprising that academics in Oxford and Cambridge in particular reacted with fury. Indeed it has been suggested that Louvain was the 'Sarajevo' of European intellectuals.[41] The British and French condemnation of events at Louvain and Rheims led in turn to the infamous manifesto of ninety-three German academics defending Germany's actions in October 1914, and the indignant response to this of British academics.[42]

The damage inflicted on Rheims Cathedral became reinforcing evidence for this interpretation of a 'Hunnish' threat to the physical manifestations of European civilisation. Rheims became confirming evidence of a trend. In an unusual use of a banner headline, the *Daily Mail* promised the story:

HOW RHEIMS CATHEDRAL WAS SHELLED: FULL STORY OF THE KAISER'S AWFULLEST CRIME

The back-page photographs were similarly emblazoned:

'WORSE THAN LOUVAIN' GERMANS DESTROY RHEIMS CATHEDRAL.

In fact the shell damage to the Cathedral was both much exaggerated and at least arguably justifiable under the Hague Convention, in a way that Louvain clearly was not.[43] Editorially the newspaper commented: 'The record of German violence and vandalism is aggravated today by the sad news of the destruction of Rheims Cathedral by enemy shells. These apostles of "culture", more barbarous than the Huns of Attila have not spared one of the supreme architectural glories of the world.'[44]

Once again it is worth noting the *precise* context of the word 'Huns', a word still not much used in the newspaper, as the destroyers of a civilised monument. Andrew Clark, in his clipping collection, 'English Words in Wartime', first notes the compound 'Hun-like methods' in *The Scotsman* on 8 September 1914, whereas his first notice of 'Hun' as a noun is from the same newspaper on 17 September.[45] It may seem odd to a modern reader that damage to property seems to take precedence in the *Daily Mail* over crimes against persons. But it does tell us something about the newspaper's style. Property damage was more easily verifiable and more easily represented. It was also, perhaps, easier to believe and relate to.

In discussing atrocity stories, or, one might argue, the attempted reportage of war crimes at such length, it is difficult to avoid falling into the trap of giving them undue prominence. In the first four months of the war they were a tiny fraction of the content of the *Daily Mail*. In August 1914 they made up *at most* 5% of the newspaper's written content. Counting pictures of destroyed buildings, important for the reasons mentioned above, they made up a significantly higher proportion of the visual content. In September, both the number and prominence of such stories rose considerably, perhaps 10% of the paper's written content and for the first time significant 'headline' stories. In October, atrocity stories fell back to a much lower level, and by November there were very few. The overwhelming bulk of the *Daily Mail* coverage was of ordinary military affairs, much of it recycled and desperately unreliable official bulletins.[46] Ordinary 'home news' was also still very prominent.

Of the atrocity stories that were printed, much more than half the content was broadly accurate in its references to the mass executions of Belgian civilians and material damage to Belgian towns. The worst cases of falsehood and exaggeration came from the reprinting of Belgian 'official reports', themselves tainted by an uncritical, but perhaps understandable, acceptance of refugee testimony.[47]

Even in these cases, much of what was reprinted was not far off the mark. For example, in a story on 21 November 1914, under the headline '400 peasants shot in Cold Blood Massacre by Huns in Belgium',[48] it is reported that 'the town of Dinant was sacked and destroyed by the German Army and its population decimated on August 22, 23, 24 and 25', and that in that area more than 700 of the inhabitants had been killed.[49] Given that, for obvious reasons, the German Army was not allowing access to the area, the striking thing about this story, which was based on second-hand testimony, is that it is remarkably accurate.[50]

But it would be wrong to deny that a small fraction of stories did not conform to the supposed classic model. On 18 September 1914 under the headline 'More German atrocities and houses burnt', the bulk of the story is about the incendiarism; but it is followed by, 'Of what happened in the village during the next hour, it is difficult even now to get a clear account. Eleven men were killed, women were ravished and every house save two was burnt.'[51] The really lurid component is the following, 'A friend of mine, a responsible public official, found among the ruins of the houses the foot of a little child hacked off at the ankle, a foot with its toes drawn up and its instep arched tightly with final agony.' This was illustrated with a photograph apparently of a man holding a child's foot. So at least one story of an abused and mutilated child did appear in the *Daily Mail* in 1914. What we do not know for certain is whether this story, almost certainly fictional, created more impact than the larger number of broadly accurate atrocity stories.

The most lurid atrocity stories appear in January 1915 with the reprinting of segments of the French Government report. Under the heading 'The Book of Outrages: Murder, Rape and Fire by Bavarians', the paper recounts the following:

> M. Adnot was shot and Mme. X had a breast and right arm cut off. The little girl of eleven had her foot cut off. The boy of five had his throat cut. Mme. X and the eleven year old child had been outraged before death ... The case of Mme. Masson of Embesnil is notable for the calm courage and noble conduct of this young woman who, at the time of her death, was about to become a mother.[52]

It is in this report we have the first mention of raped nuns, followed the next day by a Belgian report of priests shot and hanged. But it should be noted how late this coverage is and of course 'justified' as being material from an official report. During 1914 the *Daily Mail* had generally avoided dwelling on sexual and sadistic themes. This was to some extent a conscious policy. Northcliffe was well aware of sneers at his paper's 'sensationalism' and was keen to present the *Daily Mail* as a respectable paper. In a report of a Belgian's testimony on 3 November 1914, it is explicitly stated, 'Some of the writer's facts are unfit for publication.'[53] Other parts of the press were less inhibited. In March 1915 the popular cartoon weekly, *The Passing Show*, published an article by Arnold White claiming that there were a thousand Belgian women in London, including nuns and 16-year-olds who were expecting children after being raped by drunken German officers.[54]

As with the issue of 'scepticism', reticence can be read two ways. Either it is a cynical invitation for the reader to fill in the details from his or her own imagination, or it is a genuine attempt to remain respectable. One suspects in this case a little of both. What is certain is that the readers did imagine the details, as will be demonstrated below.

Before leaving Belgium entirely it is worth mentioning the testimony of one of the *Daily Mail* journalists who was actually reporting from Belgium at the time. J. M. N. Jeffries, in his 1930 autobiography, asserts that he and the other journalists working for the newspaper upheld fully their professional standards and reported as conscientiously as they could under very trying circumstances. He also states that they were under no editorial pressure to seek out lurid atrocities: his editor had written to him stating that such stories were coming from 'many sources', and 'wanted to know if there was any truth in them'. He replied that he had not witnessed any atrocities personally, but that he had sent stories when he believed that the eyewitness evidence was reliable. At the end of the passage he refers implicitly to Ponsonby and others: 'I write this in our defence, but I know I write it in vain. Any article I shall ever read upon propaganda and upon war hysteria will assume that the "popular press" gushed lies determinedly and without stint.'[55] Jeffries' defensive tone is understandable and could be dismissed as self-justifying, but his account of the content and tone of his newspaper is entirely consistent with what appeared in print in 1914 and far more accurate than what he describes as 'the manifold critics of the press', who assumed that 'tales of atrocities were lightly transmitted'.[56]

Home fires

If Louvain was the 'intellectuals' Sarajevo', for the mass of the population the definitive moment which proved beyond question the barbarity of their opponents was the bombardment of Hartlepool and Scarborough. In her diary, Ethel Bilsborough had intermittently noted press stories regarding destruction in Belgium, but it is the German Navy's bombardment of the east coast that seizes her imagination: 'killing many civilians and several women, children and babies – which is apparently their idea of chivalry. Over 100 lives were lost – or rather massacred.' She then goes on to link this destruction with Belgium: 'It is horrible to think that such things can take place in these enlightened days, but then the Germans are proving every day that they have no sense of right or justice, morality or honour.' She clipped two pictures from the newspapers and adds her own comment to one: 'House in Scarborough where dead babies were found after the bombardment.'[57]

Destroying architectural treasures, burning homes and killing civilians in Belgium was clearly reprehensible, but destroying homes and killing men, women and children in *Britain* was far worse for readers to contemplate. Furthermore, the press had full access in a way that it simply did not in Belgium. No incident in Belgium ever received similar coverage. On 17 December 1914, the day after the raid, three full pages of the *Daily Mail* were dedicated to its effects. The coverage dominated the press for three days and produced a distinct spike in circulation for all the newspapers: the *Evening News* noted on 19 December that *The Times* had sold out by 9.15 a.m. in London, and that vendors were charging inflated prices.[58]

Regarding Scarborough, the *Daily Mail* headlined, 'Damage to Churches, an Hotel and Private Houses', interestingly above and in larger type than the list of casualties. But: 'Unfortunately there has been loss of life. The names of 17 dead have been issued by the police, but there are also some wounded. A considerable proportion of these are after the German's own heart – women and children.'[59] The editorial comment was: 'Yesterday for the first time in two centuries, British towns were shelled by a foreign foe and British blood was spilt on British soil. What was the German object in attacking unfortified coast resorts and a commercial harbour?'[60]

The east coast raids allowed much more vivid and first-hand reporting. There were the coroner's inquests on dead men, women and children; there were eyewitness accounts from survivors; there were photographs of destroyed houses and buildings.

Perhaps most vivid of all was the chance to print photographs of the victims. On its picture page the *Daily Mail* used family photographs of children killed and wounded by the bombardment to illustrate the story.

This atrocity was not only verifiable, but it related directly to the civilian population and could be given the full paraphernalia of a human-interest story. In Hartlepool, for example, a German shell hit the Dixon house. The father was away in Kitchener's Army, but his wife was maimed, three of their six children were killed and two more injured.[61] In the space of a week the raid got more coverage than the Belgian atrocities had had in the previous two months.

Scarborough was peculiarly evocative as a seaside resort familiar to a great deal of the urban population of northern England. This was somewhat resented by 'the Hartlepools', which had suffered far greater casualties.[62] 'Remember Scarborough' became a useful slogan in the north. A poem by Jessie Pope,[63] which was blatant recruiting propaganda, nevertheless probably captures a genuinely widespread reaction to the newspaper coverage:

> Young Brown's repast was growing chill.
> Though he had only just begun it.
> He glared and said,
> 'The Castle Hill ... That's done it'
>
> War hadn't touched him up to date;
> He'd cheered his pals who went in batches,
> Yet still paid six pence on the gate,
> At football matches.
>
> But Scarborough! He loved the place.
> The happy haunt of summer revels,
> Bombarded! Blood rushed to his face,
> 'The Devils!'
>
> Those Yorkshire women lying dead!
> The news grew blurred – he tried to skim it,

Then rose, 'This is; he calmly said,
'The limit.'

To the recruiting shop down town
He strode – he almost seemed to run it.
'I want to dot them one', said Brown,
'That's done it.'[64]

Here was undisputed proof of German depravity. Winston Churchill, in an early example of his facility for the telling phrase, referred to the German Navy as 'the baby killers of Scarborough'.[65]

On 18 December 1914, in an editorial entitled 'The mark of the Hun', the *Daily Mail* commented:

One of the proofs that we have taken the lesson of the raid to heart will be when we abandon the debating habit of flinging the Articles of the Hague Convention in the face of the enemy. All paper restrictions on the conduct of warfare went into the wastepaper basket the moment war was declared.

After the raid, the paper's coverage was no less about the shock of individual actions but the description a pathology.

The *Daily Mail*: constructing the Hun

'Die Kultur'
You seek excuse in 'Die Kultur'
For every stratagem and lure
Outlaw device and deed of shame
with which you play the soldiers game;
For Hunnish Code and Mongol lust;
For violated pledge and trust;
For women raped and children slain
For Malines, Termonde, Rheims, Louvain
By every act and thought abjure
The very spirit of 'kultur'

Poem by Herbert Kaufman, *Daily Mail*, 26 September 1914

Even in March 1915 it was still possible to find in the reporting of the *Daily Mail* some laudable examples of German behaviour. Under the heading, 'Boats towed by obliging Pirate', the commander of U32 is praised for his treatment of the crew of the captured merchant ship *Delmira*. He is reported to have given them time to take to their boats and:

offered them a bottle of wine, which they refused. He told them that he would take them in tow and said, 'where can I take you'. They asked to be towed to the English coast. 'Well' he said, 'I cannot go too near that, because I have to consider the risk of losing my boat. I'll tow you until I can put you aboard some ship.'[66]

The point of this story, and earlier stories in 1914 when the *Kapitan* of the surface raider *Emden* is singled out for praise, is to demonstrate that the British could accept a traditional version of commerce raiding at sea.[67] What was unacceptable was the reckless endangerment, or worse, the deliberate killing, of maritime civilians.

From the declaration of a blockade zone around the British Isles in February 1915 to the sinking of the *Lusitania* in May, U-boat warfare was the definitive German atrocity in British eyes.

The core of the dispute over right and wrong methods of war at sea was a culture clash. As the world's leading maritime nation, utterly dependent on imports and with large numbers of her subjects on ships, Britain had very strict views about what was and was not permissible in humanitarian naval warfare, and a massive amount of experience of war at sea. Germany was, by contrast, a complete newcomer: it had never before engaged in significant naval warfare.

The British view was that the *guerre de course* (commerce raiding) was legitimate, provided the safety of maritime non-combatants was privileged. This meant that raiders could stop ships, search for contraband and destroy ships carrying contraband. They could do this if and only if they did so with due regard for the safety of non-combatant passengers. Ideally this meant taking the passengers on board the raiding ship or setting them ashore. At the very least it meant warning them and allowing them to take to boats with a good chance of making landfall. The mounting of guns by merchant ships or the carrying of 'contraband' munitions did not in any way alter these humanitarian responsibilities, nor did the use of time-honoured ruses such as the flying of the flags of neutral powers.

The Germans, on the other hand, were applying analogies from land warfare to the war at sea. Thus, armed merchant ships were *Franc-Tireurs* and, as such, liable to destruction on sight. By extension, if some merchant ships were armed, German U-boats were entitled to assume that any merchant ship was armed and act accordingly. Ships carrying munitions could be treated the same way as military munitions stores, and destroyed regardless of the risk to civilians; the flying of false flags was analogous to the wearing of false uniforms, another offence punishable by death. Such views were utterly alien and barbaric to the British.[68]

Beyond this specific clash was a second-order clash of perceptions. To understand this it is important to explore the concept of *Kultur*, both what the Germans meant by it and what the British in 1914–1915 claimed the Germans meant by it. Initially in Germany the concepts of *Kultur* and *Zivilization* (civilisation) were not in binary opposition. Each referred to refinement and self-cultivation. But during the eighteenth century a usage of *Kultur* developed which was opposed to the idea of *Zivilization*. The former was seen as a specifically German phenomenon: the inward, honest self-cultivation of the German *Burger*, rooted in Protestant piety. This was opposed to the latter, a product of the 'artificial' court society of the aristocracy: alien, Latinised, immoral and French. The relationship remained an ambiguous one, with a tendency to clarify in times of crisis. In 1914, faced with a war against France and Britain, the concept of *Kultur* as a moral German opposition to hypocritical 'civilisation' underwent a huge revival amongst German intellectuals and became a method of self-justification by military and political elites. This proved a gift for British propagandists.

Prior to 1914 the British middle classes had often genuflected, sometimes uneasily, to the concept of 'German Culture'. Even anti-German sentiment could make an exception for the spirit of Beethoven and Bach, Goethe and Schiller. The former cases were probably more important; in an age where the middle classes were musically literate, the idea of the Germans as a 'musical' people was attractive.[69]

But once Germany began openly criticising the concept of 'civilisation' and, in British eyes, justifying destruction and atrocities in the name of *Kultur*, the very term took on a sinister aspect. When the Kaiser gave an interview to the American press attempting hamfistedly to explain the distinction, the *Daily Mail* responded as follows:

There is, it appears, some vital but elusive difference between Kultur and Civilization. Thus according to the Kaiser, anyone who enters an English drawing room can see at once that we are a highly civilized nation ...

But Kultur, in the true, the Teutonic sense, is denied us. It is some indwelling spirit, some attitude towards life, some set of instincts founded in 'the deepest conscientiousness and the highest morality' that altogether escapes us. In fact only the Germans have it. So far as we in Great Britain are concerned they can keep it.[70]

The collision course was now clearly marked out. For the British, civilisation meant the rule of law and humanitarian custom, which were essentially universal and non-negotiable. There were things that one simply did not do. For the Germans, in an early example of cultural relativism, these British pretensions to universality were simply the self-justifying ideology of a dominant power. That the British could claim that their blockade activities were legal, but that the German blockade was not, was simply hypocrisy as far as German commentators were concerned. Germany was being more honest: if Cathedrals were being used as observation posts to direct enemy shells, then they should become targets; if the bombardment of civilians or the use of poison gas speeded military victory and saved the lives of German soldiers, then wasn't it the duty of the German military to take these actions?

There is perhaps a whiff of stereotypical Luddism in the British attitude, at least initially. An anti-machine and anti-innovation conservatism is apparent. Later in the war the British became extremely proud of their technology, tanks in particular, but in 1914–1915, while the Germans had the technological upper hand, machine warfare was suspect. The Germans celebrated their innovative military technology: poison gas, Zeppelins,[71] flame-throwers and U-boats. The use of these same weapons was condemned as illegitimate by the British press. On 13 October 1914, the *Daily Mail* editorialised:

The German air men are renewing their inhuman pastime of dropping bombs upon Paris ... Bomb attacks are justifiable when some military end is gained, for example, the destruction of military stores, military workshops, oil tanks or magazines ... To kill non-combatants without motive and purpose is not war but murder. The pilots of the Taubes take women and children's lives out of sheer wantonness.

After the first air raid on Britain, on 20 January 1915 the *Daily Mail* editorial was entitled 'The Zeppelins at last':

The Zeppelins have made their first appearance in the country and taken their first toll of British blood ... To the victims of this cruel raid the sympathy of the nation, indeed the world will go forth. They have been slain for no military purpose. Yarmouth is not a fortified town, and if it were notice should have been given under the Hague Convention [so much for not quoting the rule book after Scarborough] which Germany has signed, to the civilian population before any bombardment. The Germans have acted at Yarmouth as they acted at Hartlepool and Scarborough and as their troops have acted in countless places in Belgium and France.
    It grows clearer with each month of the war that the immunity which non-combatants away from the actual scene of the fighting formerly enjoyed has passed away.

Asphyxiating gas in particular roused tremendous British hostility. On the day after the German Army first used chlorine at Ypres, G. Valentine Williams unleashed his own version of a poisonous vapour in the *Daily Mail* under the title 'The Mind of the Hun':

His methods of warfare do not bear comparison with those of even a savage but high-minded people such as the Zulus ... His savagery, however is not of the assegai and shield order. It is the cold blooded employment of every device of modern science, asphyxiating bombs, incendiary discs and the like, irrespective of the laws of civilized warfare ... The bewildering blend of primitive barbarity, low cunning and highly trained intellect which he comprises in the word 'Kultur'.[72]

One is left wondering whether it was the primitive barbarity or the highly trained intellect which was supposed to be most offensive to the *Daily Mail* readership. In fairness, the bewilderment could be genuine: the unspoken assumption of the age was generally that technological progress *ought* to promote better behaviour.

For the German High Command, poison gas was simply a method to expedite victory, arguably a humane action if it shortened the war – precisely the argument used later to justify Hiroshima. Technical illegality and immediate suffering were beside the point. For the British in 1914, they were the point.

These clashes of perception led directly to the greatest single atrocity of the war in British eyes: the sinking of the *Lusitania*. The story is too well known to require detailed repetition. It is worth, nevertheless, pointing to a few aspects that have been rather overshadowed in the neverending arguments about the ship.[73] The first is that however important the *Lusitania* was in shaping American attitudes, the vast majority of those who died on the ship were British. The second is that the *Lusitania* was a real case of 'babykilling'. Ninety-four of the victims were children; thirty-five of the thirty-nine 'babies' on board were drowned. Even today the photograph (genuine?) apparently from the Queenstown morgue published in the *Daily Mail* still has the power to shock.

The third point is that however much British propaganda exploited the case, the reaction in Germany was genuinely one of celebration, shocking to the British and Americans alike. This is a point that has been minimised by over-concentration on the British replication of the infamous 'Lusitania Medal'. This was a copy of a genuine, although unofficial, German medal produced by an entrepreneur, Goetz, on his own initiative. The British Government authorised a massive reproduction, far exceeding the original German one, and the medal was widely sold in aid of war charities in the United Kingdom and circulated in the United States. This was not strictly speaking, black propaganda. The British medals were clearly marked as copies and generally sold as such. The impression was given that the German original was somehow 'official', which it wasn't, yet this was less misleading than is sometimes assumed. The medal faithfully reflected the official German propaganda line on the *Lusitania*: the German public did celebrate the sinking, and the crew of the U-boat that sank the ship were decorated for it. The propaganda of the medal, like so much British propaganda, was grey rather than black, misleading but not fundamentally untruthful in its message.

The final point is that the numerous explanations, one might say excuses, that have been given for the German action, were dismissed in Britain at the time as irrelevant beside the cold-blooded murder of 1,200 non-combatants. That the *Lusitania* was carrying munitions, including in all probability an illicit undeclared component, was absolutely beside the point. The commander of the U-boat concerned did not and could not have known this. The *Lusitania* was not sunk regretfully *despite* the fact there were civilians on board. It was sunk *because* there were civilians on board as part of a sustained and consistent policy of naval terrorism.[74]

The line of Louvain – Scarborough – Zeppelins – poison gas – Lusitania was now drawn. *Kultur* stood condemned, but it was beginning to look like insufficient explanation. At the very start of 1915 the *Daily Mail* had reprinted a Will Dyson cartoon on its back page of two Pickelhaube-wearing apes in an aeroplane dropping bombs on civilians.[75] The *Daily Mail* did not carry many cartoons, but this image of technologically advanced but under-evolved 'sub-humans' opened the possibility of a worse explanation than a cultural one: that the Germans as a people were intrinsically flawed, probably depraved and possibly evil. This ape image attained classic form in *The Passing Show* in the week after the *Lusitania* sinking, with a cartoon showing Germans worshipping a graven image of a fanged ape carrying away a child.[76]

The net result of a year's escalation towards total war was a growing belief in the 'racial' depravity of the German people, a rhetoric of dehumanisation. An article in the *Daily Mail* on 7 July 1915 by an American journalist, Frederick William Wile, was entitled 'The German Murder Instinct'. Starting with an anecdote about a Chicago butcher, August Becker, who was hanged for murdering his wife and boiling her remains in a sausage machine, Wile then detailed three more particularly gruesome murder cases from Germany. These were described as, 'absolutely typical and quite common place stories of German crime'. Therefore, 'Louvain, asphyxiating gas, and the *Lusitania* are logical expressions of the brutality and callousness of modern German nature.' He then cites statistics for rape, illegitimacy (!) and murder in Germany and England, much to England's advantage and then repeats that 'Louvain, poison gas and the *Lusitania* are no longer mysteries.'[77] This view was reflected throughout the 'yellow' press. In *The Passing Show*, William Le Queux went as far as to suggest that blaming 'Prussian Militarism' was the action of 'Pro-German apologists'. The 'most shameful and brutal deeds of the German Army ... are cordially approved by the mass of that degenerate nation'.[78] It is possible to take the view that the escalating racism of the *Daily Mail* was a response to pressure from weekly journals further to the right. Northcliffe had come under pressure in May for 'unpatriotic' criticism of Kitchener. In the end it is doubtful that it was such an instrumental decision. Press and public ratcheted up the hatred together. The most poisonously racist weekly, *John Bull*, saw its circulation climb to 300,000 in early 1915, proving that there was a good audience for exterminatory rhetoric.

The implication and conclusion were clear: no more distinctions between good and bad Germans in the way that the earliest newspaper reports had suggested, no more restraint and fair play. The correct response was retaliation – poison gas to be met by poison gas and 'retaliatory' bombing of German cities. In short, kill them all and let God sort them out.[79]

Story-telling: atrocities and other wartime tales

In the Imperial War Museum it is possible to read atrocity stories in the making. Letters from the unmarried MacGuire sisters, Ada and Rho, living in Cheshire, to their married sister Eva in America, demonstrate the inventiveness of rumour. They were respectable people but with an apparent taste for lurid gossip.

On 6 October 1914, Ada wrote:

Mother has just had your letter. Yes, the German atrocities are quite true, but it is not true that Belgians have committed any cruelties ... there is a soldier now lying in our Fazakerly (?) military hospital who has had legs, arms, ears and nose cut off and his eyes are out. His father called to see him. They begged him not to see him, but he would and the shock has turned his brain. I do not vouch for this, but have heard it from two different sources. A gentleman in a train was talking to a friend of his. A.T. was in the same carriage. He said a couple he knows well wished to take a Belgian child as they had no children. To their horror the child sent to them had no hands. They had been cut off![80]

A week later Ada returned to the theme:

If they do come here they will have no mercy. There are children in Waterloo and Birkenhead who have no hands.

Mr Malvern says a gentleman he knows offered to adopt two little Belgian girls, but said he would like them to be of decent parentage. The authorities wrote and told him that there were two little girls, who judging by the fine quality of their underwear were of a refined upbringing. Their parents were dead & their nurse had been found bayoneted at their side, but both children had had their arms chopped off above the elbows. Now that is a fact. Poor wee mites, this gentleman had nevertheless offered to adopt them.

That is, I suppose, only one of many cases & some of the things are too dreadful to mention. Laura says that if the Germans come here she will commit suicide. However, I hope they will soon be smashed up.[81]

The first point to note is that in recounting these lurid atrocities there is no reference to the press. The 'evidence' is entirely oral. These stories are of a variety readily noted on a thousand university campuses and ten thousand pubs. They are urban myths.

Note that in each case they follow the classic model, the witness is a 'friend of a friend'. The evidence is precisely at two removes, near enough to be credible, far enough away to be unverifiable. The detail is exquisite and archetypal: the father who foolishly ignores the well-meaning medical staff; the respectable little girls with good-quality underwear. The process of oral elaboration is clearly at work: note the bayoneted nurse, necessary to establish the children's social status and allowing the import of another atrocity to compound the horror. The story in the first letter of the couple wishing to adopt a little Belgian child has evolved in the space of a week, gaining detail and then being retransmitted as a different story from a different source.

Timing is significant. These stories are a month after the first big press reporting of atrocities against Belgian civilians. First come the reports, necessarily vague, of actual atrocities. Then the inference that there were things too horrible to report. The public itself rushed to fill in the gaps.

Andrew Clark, the Rector of Great Leighs, was an energetic collector of rumours. In his diary of 29 October 1914 he too notes that he had been told by F. B. Rogers, a school music master, 'that there really *is* in the Convent at Bocking a little girl with her hands hacked off'.[82] The casual familiarity demonstrates that he had heard the rumour much the same time as the MacGuires. Clark noted down rumours of all sorts, in a Herodotean miscellany, neither believing nor disbelieving. But he did give considerable weight to recounting the tales of soldiers. On 12 October he recounted a soldier's account of the fighting in Belgium, in which he expressed severe doubts about the press representations and went as far as to state that the German soldiers had been acting in self-defence when 'Belgian girls aged fifteen or sixteen, revolver in hand, rushed into the streets to shoot Germans'. This image, actually favourable to the Germans, is of course every bit as much an implausible fantasy as the cut-off hands. But a later soldier's account fits the usual atrocity image much better. Travelling to Oxford on 20 November 1914, Clark met a 'wounded Army Service Corps' man:

He said that all that had been in the papers about German brutality was far short of the truth. In a Chateau the British troops found a large party of Germans who had murdered the inhabitants and set about themselves to drink everything in the cellar. While they were still drunk the British troops came up, and took no prisoners … In another village, the parents told of their two daughters, one sixteen the other eight – who had had both breasts hacked off and bled to death.[83]

Testimony like this turns conventional understandings of propaganda on its head. The press is criticised by a soldier for not giving enough detail of German atrocities. The active atrocity-monger here is the man in khaki.[84] He was almost certainly lying; he might not even have been at the front at all. He may well be playing to an audience of gullible civilians (as Sassoon did poetically). But this behaviour undermines our usual image of saintly suffering soldiers duped by the cynics of Fleet Street. The most infamous of all atrocity stories that appeared in the press had a similar origin. A 'Salisbury officer, just returned from the front' claimed to have discovered a Belgian baby impaled on a bayonet. This story, first printed in the Liberal-aligned *Daily Chronicle*, was picked up and expanded upon in the *Evening News* under the sub-headline, 'Baby on Bayonet'.[85] It is highly unlikely that the *Daily Chronicle* had deliberately invented such a story: they had been fooled by a lying soldier.

Soldiers spread rumours, but civilians were at least as bad. An advice booklet of 1914 has as one of its main suggestions to civilians, 'Don't pass on any idle rumours.' This must be one of the most ignored injunctions ever published.[86] Wartime Britain was a world of rumour. Atrocity stories were part of that world, but only one part. The most famous wartime rumour was 'Russians with snow on their boots'. In an anonymous published satirical 'diary' of 'Samuel Pepys Junr.', the entry for 15 September 1914 reads:

This morning 'tis given out by authority of the Press Office that no Russian soldiers have landed in France having passed through England. Which is I think, more strange than anything I ever yet heard tell of, seeing none of my acquaintance but hath a friend who hath beheld the Russians with his own eyes, either travelling in trains or marching upon the road, or encamped upon our commons and this in all counties from Land's End to John O'Groats.[87]

A poem by Marshall Steele likewise satirised the phenomenon:

> I have uncles, nephews, nieces, cousins, children (some are grand!)
> And each of them to me says
> They have seen the Russians land
> Or, since the truth cannot be hid
> Know well somebody who did.[88]

Significantly satirical as these comments are, they do not exaggerate, for by mid-September 1914 everyone knew someone, who knew someone, who had seen Russians. The German spy, Karl Lody, sent a report on Russian troops in Scotland to his superiors, citing three 'independent' sources.[89]

One of the best descriptions of the rumour, the logic behind it and the spirit of its transmission can be found in a diary entry of Winifred Towers on 29 August 1914:

We first heard the 'Great Rumour'. Between 40,000 & 22,000 Russians (accounts varied) were reported to have embarked at Archangel, to have landed at various places on the coast of Scotland, to have been brought by train through England & were now about to be poured into France in the rear of the German armies advancing on Paris & cut their lines of communications ... Everybody had a friend whose aunt's butler had seen them. They were reported from every part of the country; many of the stories were vague & far fetched & some were very amusing, as the one of the old lady who was sure that Russians had gone through Willesden, because she had heard them stamping the snow off their boots on the platform, but many were really authenticated & first hand, some even semi-official. It was reported that Southampton common crawled with Cossacks ... Of course, there were foolish sceptical people who said they could not possibly embark a large force in Archangel as there was only a single railway line ... that the supposed Russians were Highland regiments talking Gaelic, that the whole yarn was of German origin & set afoot to create a feeling of false security & stop the rush meant [to the colours] & so on, but these altogether ridiculous ideas were quickly suppressed. Everyone believed in the Russians & most people continued to do so, in spite of the very decided denial of the story issued by the Press Bureau.

The next day's entry is also revealing: 'The situation looked rather black & we all had a bad attack of the glooms, though the thought of the Russians did much to cheer us up.'[90]

This description begins to delineate the features of wartime rumour.[91] First, a sense of the absence or unreliability of 'official information'. The wartime press was quite heavily censored over issues that might have strategic significance, and this censorship was well known, even perhaps exaggerated. The press itself was complaining against censorship and at the very moment of incubation of the Russian story, *The Times* challenged military censorship by publishing the 'Mons Despatch', which had a massive public impact.[92] Resulting from this was an eclectic attempt to make sense of different gobbets of fact by tying them into an explanatory narrative. More and more 'supporting' detail accrues to the rumour. Then there is the process and motivation for transmission. What is striking about Towers is that she demonstrates considerable ironic detachment and justified scepticism, but told the story *anyway*. She did so because she found the rumour irresistible and basically cheering at a grim moment. Finally, and particularly striking in the case of the 'Great Rumour', was that even as it was being told, there was a consciousness that it *was* a rumour and even speculation as to how it started.[93]

An entire world of rumours. Andrew Clark recorded dozens in the course of the war. On 21 August 1914, the rumour that five foreigners had tried to poison the reservoir at Chingford is recorded. He mentions 'the Russians' on 30 August, and again on 3 September; on 26 September it is a rumour of German spies, and again on 20 October, 24 October, 26 October, 29 October, 30 October and 9 November. So it goes on.

In the course of 1915 there are many rumours around the village that a certain Seabrook of Waltham had been arrested as a spy and shot. On 24 October 1915, Clark notes that 'The Seabrook story is a fiction – Seabrook left because he has let – or sold his house.' The second-best rumour surfaces on 15 January 1916: 'A report is current that one of the Kaiser's sons is a prisoner in the Tower.' That took some beating, but a letter from his daughter topped it on 4 June 1917: 'We have now court-martialled and shot Sir John Jellicoe for losing the battle of Jutland and Lady Jellicoe was shot at daybreak on Thursday!'

On 28 June 1915, Clark noted, 'It is characteristic of the village mind that it is too feeble to accept simple fact, it has to add legendary details.' But examination of other diaries and accounts show that villages were no more prone to this than the urban environment. Michael Macdonagh's subsequently edited diary of life in London during the Great War shows just as much inventive rumour-mongering. There is good reason to think of atrocity stories primarily as a sub-category of rumour, along with spy stories, the 'Russians' and the 'Angels of Mons'. The attempt to consider atrocity propaganda as a 'technique', where stories are invented by identifiable agents with clear motives and then disseminated through the media, is based on a fundamental misunderstanding.[94] Rather than being imposed from above on a gullible public, most atrocity stories bubbled up into the media from this netherworld of rumour. A careful reading even of cases cited by Ponsonby actually suggests this interpretation: frequently the story appears to start not with journalism or editorial, but with a *letter* to the press.[95]

Atrocities, propaganda and the war

A fortnight ago I wrote a few lines in the *Church Family Newspaper* deprecating a too ready acceptance of atrocities ...

The paragraph which was written <u>before</u> the Belgian Official report and before the destruction of Louvain appeared <u>after</u> these events ...

Before the war began I was deeply anxious for peace ... the ghastly revelation of German aims and ambitions, the gross and vile barbarity of her methods of warfare have made me feel, as emphatically as any Englishman can possibly feel that we must make any and every sacrifice to stamp out a military tyranny which menaces the liberty of Europe and is a disgrace to civilization and to Christianity. (A. C. Benson, letter to the *Daily Mail*, 11 September 1914)

In a clever and nuanced discussion of the *Report of the Committee on Alleged German Outrages* (the Bryce Report), Trevor Wilson empathetically captures a Liberal's dilemma in 1915 regarding atrocity stories:

Bryce did not have the choice between telling the truth or telling a falsehood. If he proved so scrupulous in his investigations that he might deem the tales of sadistic crimes unproven, he would be helping to propagate a larger untruth: that the whole notion of deliberate and calculated atrocity committed on Belgium was unfounded.[96]

In a world of absolute standards, both Bryce's reasoning and Wilson's explanation can be dismissed as sophistry.[97] If we lived in a world in which no one ever committed atrocities, we should probably do so. In the meantime, was it genuinely morally superior to claim, as Ponsonby did, 'the injection of the poison of hatred into men's mind by means of falsehood is a greater evil in wartime than the actual loss of life. The defilement of the human soul is worse than the destruction of the human body'? Worse? Perhaps he should have told that to the citizens of Dinant and the survivors of the *Lusitania*.[98]

An agonised Liberal judge such as Bryce, favourably disposed to the German people, is perhaps an easier object of empathy than a ruthless Germanophobe press baron such as Northcliffe. But in many respects the *Daily Mail* faced precisely the same dilemma with atrocity stories: it printed them because it believed in the fundamental truth of the picture. In many respects the behaviour of the journalists, editors and proprietor of that paper is easier to understand than the Liberal reaction. Much of the detail Bryce presented in his report he knew in his heart was unreliable and probably untrue. By contrast most of what the *Daily Mail* presented was verifiably true and it seems a reasonable guess that most of what was false was to a large extent *believed* by a proprietor and staff who had or who developed a very low opinion of the German people. Finally, it should be remembered, newspapers print what people are inclined to read.

The greatest atrocity of all was the war. Most British people, by as early as the middle of September 1914, had no doubt in their minds that Germany bore responsibility for the war. Furthermore they had no doubts that there was something tangibly wrong with the way that Germany was conducting the war. One senses behind the atrocity stories an attempt to add detail to metaphors. For example the 'popular' story of the Canadian sergeant 'crucified' at Ypres in 1915 can surely not be understood without consideration of the undoubted fact that the Canadian division was attacked with poison gas in that battle. One also wonders whether the proximity of that event to Easter in 1915 meant that the image of crucifixion was 'in the air'. Stories of the victimisation of Belgian children and the rape of Belgian women do not seem unlikely when the language of 'Poor little Belgium' and the 'Violation' of Belgian neutrality was being used every day. It is a straightforward use of semiotics to spot how easy it is to leap from 'Poor mutilated little Belgium' to 'Poor mutilated little Belgians', or from the 'Rape of Belgium' as a metaphor to the rape of actual Belgian women.

In various ways the press did provide a framework in which atrocity stories flourished. By hinting at unspeakable horrors, the press more or less guaranteed that the horrors would be spoken. In creating an explanatory framework for atrocities, they made it likely that any atrocity would seem plausible.

But the press did not initiate the process of dehumanising the enemy; the German military and naval commanders did. In the end it was real atrocities, or military acts that would be perceived as atrocities, that stoked up popular fury. It was not the supposed mutilation of Belgian babies, but the all-too-real drowning of British ones, that brought the mobs on the street in May 1915.[99]

The idea that the function of propaganda in the war was to artificially stoke up hatred in a neutral populace is to fundamentally misunderstand the nature of the war.[100] When a positive story about an 'A1 German' appeared in the *Evening News* in October 1914, describing how a dying German soldier had refused water and insisted that it be given to a wounded British soldier instead, Andrew Clark wrote a marginal note dismissing it as 'a minor piece of fiction. One of the pests of wartime.'[101]

Being beastly to the Hun was good business; fair-mindedness might be ruinous. The public were more vehement haters than most of the press, and the press was far more inclined to hatred than official agencies. The process was bottom-up more than top-down. In September 1914, Horatio Bottomley was outraged at the confiscation of postcards which he had printed. These were seized by the police for libelling the Kaiser. That an arm of Government a month into the war was acting against the demonisation of an enemy head of state seems as extraordinary now as it did then.[102]

The real focus of Government propaganda efforts were 'positive': the repeated public assurances that Britain was not responsible for the war was in fact the single biggest propaganda message. But increasingly propaganda turned to two associated, but not easily reconciled, objectives: one was reassuring the public that victory was inevitable, the other was moral exhortation for greater participation and greater sacrifice. The iniquity of the enemy could largely be taken for granted; the question now was how that enemy should be defeated.

3 From spectatorship to participation; From volunteering to compulsion 1914–1916

> Your country knows that it is no light sacrifice that she demands of you ...
> If <u>you</u> do not go willingly to-day, you and your children and your children's children may have to go unwillingly to wars even more terrible than this one.   Recruiting advertisement, *Daily Express*, 10 February 1915

Spectators

A cartoon in *The Passing Show* in June 1915 shows a young man about town, monocled and smoking a cigarette through an exaggerated holder, standing in front of a shop window. The window carries a poster of soldiers going into battle and, underneath, the slogan 'Don't stand looking at this, Come and Help.' The caption, referring to the young man, is: 'Who's looking?'[1]

It was a complicated joke. The poster exhorts the move from spectatorship to participation, yet the 'knut' is not even engaged as a spectator. The line between spectatorship and participation could be blurred. In May 1915, the weekly issued a heavily ironic 'Six don'ts for patriotic civilians'. Advice included: 'be phlegmatic ... The Press Bureau will tell you when to get excited: till then forget there is a war on'; when troops go by, 'don't take your hat off ... it is liable to distract attention from shop windows'; civilians shouldn't cheer: 'Cheering is only permissable at horse races, football matches, strike meetings and in the trenches'; civilians shouldn't go out 'without a plentiful supply of White Feathers'; they should 'cultivate an upright and military bearing', so that even if they were not in the volunteer reserve, people would think they were. Above all, 'Don't be afraid of underestimating the enemy. *You* are not fighting him.' As a parody of the regular homilies in the press, it is spot on, and every bit as contradictory as the advice regularly issued. Civilians were regularly exhorted to be engaged and detached, serious and light-hearted, humble and proud.[2]

So far in this description of the British at war we have stressed the reactive rather than the proactive aspects. 'War enthusiasm', so far as it existed, was a reaction to war. Atrocity stories were a reaction both to the war and to German atrocities. But the move from spectatorship to participation was the story not only of Britain's entry into a continental war, but the narrative of the experience of the people.

The most famous poster image produced for the Parliamentary Recruiting Committee is the stern, moustachioed visage of Lord Kitchener over the message 'Your King and Country Needs You.' The most revealing poster is quite different. A poster image shows a sailor at a gun and a soldier on guard. Below them is a boy scout handing a parcel to the soldier, below this is a nurse with bandages and a female munition worker and in the foreground is a muscular smith working at an anvil. To one side is a middle-class 'loafer', hands in pocket. The bold caption is: 'Are <u>You</u> In This?'

The Kitchener image is remembered even though it was atypical. It suited later generations to believe that volunteering was based on an appeal to unthinking deference and outmoded traditional values. It was precisely this image which was rejected in the famous Oxford Union resolution of 1934 when the house voted against fighting for 'King and Country'. The image of the other poster, a vision of active citizenship based on a web of reciprocal obligation and duty, is disturbingly modern. Significantly it was designed by Robert Baden-Powell and expresses the ethos of voluntary participation central to the scouting movement.

Fear of mass passivity, and of an unwillingness to get involved, was every bit as much a rhetoric of 1914 as it would be in western democracies at the end of the century. The same villains were blamed: mass consumer culture, a cynical media and the bread and circuses of popular spectator sports. The argument about the latter would become a focal point of concern in 1914 and provides an insight into how the pressure to volunteer mounted.

In November 1914, the commanding officer of a battalion of Territorials (Lancashire Fusiliers) being raised in Bury wrote to the local newspaper complaining that his battalion was short of 500 men: 'Are we to do it all? … while you read the papers at home and go to picture palaces and football matches. Play the game and come and help us.'[3]

Defenders of professional sport rallied with comments such as the *Evening News* subheading 'Khaki in the Crowd', which noted that the majority of the audience at a Millwall versus Plymouth Argyle game were in uniform. Michael Macdonagh followed the controversy closely: attending a Chelsea versus Arsenal match in December he noted 'as big an attendance as I had ever seen', even though the *Globe* newspaper was attacking football. Moral pressure was being exerted on the crowd: in 'the good old days', the grounds had been surrounded by Sandwich men carrying placards with evangelical messages 'concerned with our eternal welfare', but now the posters 'ask the crowd such questions as "Are You forgetting there is a war on?"' In Macdonagh's opinion these attracted just as little notice as their pre-war equivalents.[4] A Liverpool–Everton match in January 1915 saw 'only' 206 men attesting in response to 16,450 attestation cards distributed on the instructions of Lord Derby. This was reported in highly negative terms although in fact it was a very good rate of return by this stage.

Perhaps more productive than an assault on the loyalties of football fans in the name of abstract patriotism was the attempt to harness that loyalty to the recruiting effort. Millwall fans were encouraged to 'let the enemy hear the Lions Roar' and to be in at 'THE FINAL'. Chelsea fans were asked to join the Middlesex Regiment and 'follow the lead of their favourite players'. At Elland Road, 200 Leeds fans were enlisted at half-time.[5] The claim that 100,000 men were recruited 'through' their allegiance to football clubs by the end of 1914 is clearly absurd, but the Army probably did include many more men who were at least casual followers of the game.[6]

Class contempt was never far from the surface in the attack on the 'working-class' game. In fact professional footballers, frequently singled out as shirkers, had a respectably high volunteering rate: 2,000 out of 5,000.[7] Amongst them was the extraordinary Walter Tull, the first pro-fessional black outfield player in the game, who enlisted in the sports-men's battalion of the Middlesex Regiment, and was commissioned as an officer in 1916. He was killed in action in 1918.[8]

It is likely that the erosion of audience and the deteriorating standard of performance would have led the Football Association (FA) and League to consider suspending activities, even if it hadn't been for the barrage of hostile middle-class comment. In some respects football simply moved to France for the duration, where it was a central passion of the Army.[9]

It is easy to take this assault on Association Football out of context. It was in fact part of a wider assault on inappropriately passive behaviour in wartime. Henry Cust, Chair of the Central Committee of Patriotic Associations, attacked horse racing, claiming that it would be monstrous for the crowds to cheer and lunch at Epsom whilst tens of thousands were suffering and dying in France. Similarly Henry Knolly hoped that, in 1915, 'the upper classes will forbear from assembling in their tens of thousands at ... Ascot peacocking in their plumes.' In Chester, the recruiting officer commented bitterly on the young men going to the races indifferent to the fate of the men at the front.[10]

Theatres faced similar problems. To a far greater extent than football grounds, the theatres were arenas of recruiting. Music hall and theatre were pervasive elements in the life of all classes, and much less gender-segregated than sports stadiums. The popularity of the song 'It's a Long Way to

Tipperary' rested, to a large extent, on the reference to London's theatre district: 'Goodbye Piccadilly, farewell Leicester Square.' Patriotic songs had long been a staple of the halls, the traditional repertoire was dusted off and new songs were added, including 'Your King and Country Want You' by Paul Rubens, with the now infamous line, 'We don't want to lose you, but we think you ought to go.' Individual actors worked up jingoistic monologues often incorporating the most patriotic speeches from Shakespeare. Many actors were not content with encouraging others to enlist; 800 of them had joined the colours by December 1914, reflecting in part a pre-existing tradition of voluntary part-time soldiering amongst actors. But for a young actor of military age who did not enlist, things soon turned ugly. Very few things seemed worse than playing a soldier rather than playing the soldier. Godfrey Tearle, playing the lead in *The Flag-Lieutenant*, was taunted by a woman in the audience holding up a white feather. An actor who had enlisted was particularly harsh on his former colleagues: 'Has father noticed how many people are still playing instead of fighting.' To anticipate slightly, when conscription was introduced, the persecution of actors became intense. A magistrate at the North London Police Court even threatened to invoke the vagrancy act, not used against actors since 1824, to punish an Irish actor who had failed to report to the military authorities. This magistrate lamented from the bench the passing of sterner Puritan days when those who fooled about the country with parties of players would be placed in the stocks as vagabonds. The ambiguous position of male actors was nicely illustrated by a Birmingham theatre's advertisement for 'fifty able bodied men for a long engagement at good pay', whilst pointing out that every member of the company had already served, was ineligible or had attested.[11]

The transition to war had become a problem of both etiquette and morality. On the one hand there was the call for 'Business as Usual'. The phrase was to become much abused, but it had started as a patriotic requirement. The Chancellor had wanted to steady nerves in order to avoid disruption of the domestic economy. Normal business of course included normal leisure: seaside resorts pleaded with their customers in August 1914 not to give up their holidays and ruin the businesses dependent upon them; theatres likewise claimed that the wealthy had a patriotic duty to attend, and so on. At the same time the public were being told not to behave as normal, but to volunteer their services.

Volunteers

In 1914 and 1915, Britain raised the second-largest volunteer army in history.[12] This fact has been utilised to generalise about the pervasiveness

3. Physical drill for volunteers. IWM (Q 53596).

of 'patriotism' and even 'imperialist' sentiment in Britain before the First
World War. Such an interpretation cannot be dismissed. In the final
analysis the willingness of so many men to serve was underpinned by
these sentiments, which were as natural as breathing to most of the
population. But it would be a mistake to think that this is the sole explanation required. These sentiments were generally shared both by those who
did volunteer and those who didn't. Other conditions were required to
move from patriotic cheering on the sidelines to actually joining up.

Some men entered the Army in 1914 for the most straightforward and
traditional of reasons: they were either bribed or they were forced to. The
spirit of the devious recruiting sergeant and the press gang were not
entirely dead. The concept of 'volunteer' was stretched to the limit by
the action of the Bristol Poor Law Guardians, who simply stopped paying
relief to all 'able-bodied' paupers in August 1914. With no real alternative,
it is not surprising that 90% of them joined the Army, a considerable
saving for the patriotic rate-payers. Likewise there were landowners such
as Lord Wemyss who threatened to sack and render homeless
able-bodied labourers on his estates who didn't enlist. But, even in
1914, actions such as these were generally felt to be reprehensible.

Bribery was much more patriotic. A very large number of businesses
across the country promised to continue paying men wages, or a

proportion of these, whilst on military service, in addition to their military pay. In at least some cases this would have been a real financial incentive, although in most it was more about removing the financial barrier. In a lesser number of cases employers paid a substantial 'bounty' to those who volunteered. Lord Burnham at Beaconsfield offered £10 to estate workers – a substantial sum – while in Gloucestershire, the Stroud Brewery Company gave volunteers a dinner and paid them £4.

Whilst compulsion and bribery played a role, as did economic distress in the first month of the war, the vast majority of volunteers cannot be explained in these terms. Fear of defeat and invasion, as suggested in the first chapter, was a vital spur to recruitment at the peak of enlistment between 25 August and 5 September 1914. German 'outrages' in December 1914 and May 1915 briefly revived this sentiment. Nor can the quest for excitement be ruled out. Clerks in particular, stuck in dull jobs with poor promotion prospects, seem to have been particularly drawn to the Army in 1914. From September 1915 the formation of 'pals' battalions tapped into existing sources of civic pride and sociability for recruiting purposes. Finally there was a barrage of propaganda from the Parliamentary recruiting committee, some of it quite sophisticated.

Perhaps most important was the continual local activity. Most localities held a series of large recruiting meetings through 1914 and 1915. Whilst the results were sometimes disappointing, they created an atmosphere in which volunteering was seen as the appropriate act. There is an aspect of recruiting meetings which is very reminiscent of a religious revival: platforms were set up from which a speaker appealed to the conscience of the listener, laying out in great detail the terrible consequences, literally 'hellish', of German victory. Men were then asked to 'attest'; those who did so would be applauded by the crowd. Those who came forward would then encourage others to do so.[13]

Often the resemblance was far more than accidental. Well-known local preachers would appear on the platfoms, local 'temperance' and 'chapel' bands would show up. Another useful analogy is the political platform meeting. Again this was quite conscious: most recruiting meetings made play of the political unity of the locality, with Conservative, Liberal and Labour representatives making speeches in turn. The transcendance of the frequently poisonous political atmosphere of the summer of 1914 was deeply impressive. The British had no word genuinely equivalent to Union Sacre or Burgfrieden, but 'party truce' was, in this context, not quite as bland as it now sounds. Both the political platform and the revival meeting were evoked by the appearance of Labour MP Will Crooks at many recruiting rallies. In Hyde he used both rhetorics and included the phrase: 'God never gave to man or woman an opportunity, but he meant it as an obligation.'[14]

Recruiting meetings embodied spectatorship and participation in an explicit form, issuing an invitation to individuals to step across the line from one to the other. Horatio Bottomley, by common consent the most effective 'recruiter' and one who was making a good living out of it, wrote an article on the 'Art of Recruiting'. He believed that in every human being there was 'latent patriotism'. But active patriots had to be made. The first trick was to get the 'man in the street' off the street and into the hall. He had to be convinced that the meeting was relevant to him. Once he was brought in, 'You must not lecture your man.' What was wanted was 'a plain homely talk'. The ordinary Briton was 'sorry for Belgium ... but he is not prepared to risk his life to avenge their violation'. He had to be made to understand that the threat was to his own home: 'the Kaiser means to invade our shores'. The man in the street should not be treated as a fool. This was the pragmatic argument, but the moral argument acted as the peroration: in the war, 'the peace and civilization of the world' rest upon the 'only man who really matters', the man who could 'shoulder a gun'. In this moment of trial, it should be explained, 'it is his soul which is at stake'.[15]

Reuben Farrow would have agreed. At a meeting early in the war he had denounced the warmongers who had caused it, but indicated his intention to volunteer. After the meeting Councillor Will Raynes approached him and asked, 'Do you profess to be a Christian?' Farrow assented and Raynes asked him, 'Do you think Jesus Christ would handle weapons and engage in the whole scale slaughter of human beings?' Farrow immediately took the decision to oppose the war.[16] This was to remain a minority decision, for both obvious and subtle reasons.

Recruiting meetings were designed to force the conscientious decision in the individual, but it was a decision taken in public. So meetings still required the spectators as well as the volunteers: the cheering crowd was a vital part of the dynamic. Should this dynamic be judged irrational?

That crowd behaviour can briefly overrule an individual's better judgement seems obvious; that some were carried away in the heat of the moment is undeniable. But it is equally likely that many who attended these meetings found them to be a moment of crystallisation of a decision that they had been considering for some time beforehand. Some volunteers may in fact have been manipulating the meetings rather than vice versa, milking the maximum public glory out of a decision to volunteer which had already been taken.

In an impressive effort to rescue the act of volunteering for rational choice theory, Avner Offer suggests a bounded rationality. The potential rewards of volunteering – excitement and social approval – were perceived as outweighing the risks of being killed and maimed, with the latter being seriously underestimated. Once again this goes some way towards explaining the phenomenon, but may not be entirely satisfactory. The possibility of 'conscientious enlistment' cannot be overlooked. There were men who appear to have enlisted because they thought it was the right thing to do, rather than the pleasant or profitable thing.[17] Not that this entirely undermines Offer's point. The classic anthropological distinction between social actions motivated by considerations of honour against shame, in other words external features, compared to those motivated by conscience to avoid guilt, in other words internalised concepts, is overly crude if applied to 1914–1915. One could viably argue that 'conscience' was still a matter of social conditioning, and that the appeal to conscience was simply one to social acceptability at one remove. This is both hard to deny and ultimately hard to prove.

Contemporaries indulged in a good deal of double-think on the issue of the voluntary act of enlistment. There was a widespread belief that volunteering ought to be a free act, not one motivated by social pressure; but at the same time there clearly was a great deal of social pressure. Some women handed out white feathers to ununiformed men, at the same time the practice was widely disliked, which is one of the reasons why it was remembered. Defining the practice, Andrew Clark wrote: 'To show the "white feather" is the longstanding proverbial expression for to be deficient in courage.' He went on to comment: 'At the beginning of the war hysterical feminists made themselves objectionable by sending white feathers to young men who had not enlisted.'[18] In the last months of the voluntary recruiting campaign there were people who felt that social pressure was becoming immoral and counter-productive, and that it was inimical to the genuine volunteer spirit. Some believed that straightforward compulsion would be both more honest and more just. As early as January 1915, Clark comments to this effect in response to some of the advertisements appearing in the press.[19] Harry Cartmell states that, by mid-1915, 'the average recruiting speech became a mixture of abuse, cajolery and threats', and that 'men secured by pressure of this kind could hardly be described as volunteers'. Worse still, 'the whole business had become manifestly unfair ... men were induced to join whose business and family obligations ought to have secured for them a respite, while insensitive people with no such responsibilities smiled and sat tight'.[20] Cartmell experienced 'a feeling akin to humiliation' when seeing poster appeals for the 'co-operation of the "best girls" of the men who were wanted for the army'. But the 'depth of banality' was reached in 'the final production', a great sheet 10 feet long, which announced that the last day for voluntary enlistment was 2 March 1916 and appealed to young men with the slogan, 'Won't you march too?' Cartmell finally rebelled: 'This *jeu d'esprit* as "Punch" called it, was withheld from the public of Preston.'[21]

There is a powerful tradition of thinking about volunteering as an abstract merging of individuality with the 'Nation's Cause'. In reality, it was naturally a good deal more complex. In many cases, far from overcoming the divisions and barriers of civil life, the processes of volunteering reinforced them. Some 'pals' battalions were actually less about who you served with, but much more obviously about who you didn't serve with. Middle-class fears of the possibility of serving alongside coarse working-class soldiery go a long way to explaining the early foundation of 'public schools' and 'stockbroker' battalions. This impulse continued through 1914–1915. In December the advertisement in *The Scotsman* for recruits for the 2nd Sportsmen's Battalion offers a unit of 'university men, public school boys and sports men'.[22] The ideal might be to become an officer or to serve in an acknowledged elite pre-war volunteer formation, such as the Honourable Artillery Company or The Artists' Rifles; but demand for entry in such units was outstripping supply. Whilst an idealistic middle-class socialist such as R. H. Tawney might choose to merge his fate with the common people by joining an ordinary working-class battalion as a private soldier, it seems fair to point out that Tawney was exceptional, even perhaps amongst middle-class socialists. There were other 'gentleman rankers': Stephen Graham, Henry Williamson and Frederick Manning come easily to mind, but in each of these cases there was a deliberate element of 'slumming' and perhaps a clear literary agenda – an ambition to describe the common soldier's war. Those with no such objectives were drawn instead to units with a clear class identity. The best studied of these is the London Rifle Brigade (LRB). Prior to the war the LRB had charged a joining fee of 21 shillings, which was more than a week's wages for a labourer. It might seem strange to a modern reader, but the joining fee was continued up to 1916. This was a payment for social exclusivity. Prior to the war one potential recruit had been told in no uncertain terms, 'the battalion for the bobtails is the Tower Hamlets'. In June 1915, *The Despatch* described the battalion as one where 'Clerks, solicitors, barristers and businessmen fight side by side.' The wartime LRB was willing to broaden its geographical base, but reluctant to shed social exclusivity. Letters were sent to the provincial press, such as one in *The Sheffield Independent* inviting clerical and professional workers to apply, pointing out that the military life would be 'far pleasanter if carried out with others whose civil occupation is the same'. The fee was discontinued, significantly, when the LRB was forced to accept substantial drafts from 'lower class' regiments after catastrophic casualties.[23]

At the other end of the spectrum from the LRB was the 'Fellowship' company of the Cheshires, a 'pals' unit organised by J. Hunter Watts of the Manchester Clarion Club and the British Socialist Party, which was advertised in *Clarion* in July 1915. This offered men the chance 'to fight side by side with SOCIALIST COMRADES'. Whilst this might sound like the ultimate ironic collapse of socialist idealism, it was actually of a piece with the pre-war stance of the editor of the *Clarion*, Robert Blatchford, who had been a firm advocate of compulsory 'democratic' military service.[24]

A poignant example of class perceptions carried into military service can be found in the case of the grammarian Henry Fowler. Initially he had come out of retirement to assist in the recruiting campaign, but became troubled at asking others to run risks that he would be spared. He lied about his age, which was well above the maximum for enlistment, and joined the sportsmen's battalion. On arrival in France his real age was revealed and he was sent to work at a base camp. In February 1916 he wrote to his commanding officer protesting bitterly that he was being made to perform 'menial' duties such as dishwashing, coal-heaving and porterage, and that the conversion of those who had enlisted for active service into 'menials or servants' was an incredibly 'ungenerous' policy. Fowler did manage to return to the trenches, but he passed out on parade and was discharged on medical grounds. It says a great deal about the relationship between class and patriotism, and about the limits on 'unconditional' service, that a man might be willing to die for his country, but not to wash dishes for it.[25]

Class was not the only prejudice expressed in recruiting. It may be apocryphal that men of Irish Catholic descent and Nationalist sympathies were particularly attracted to the symbolically appropriate 'Green Howards', which was a Yorkshire Regiment with no particular Nationalist heritage; but it is certainly true that one of the motivations of Irish Nationalist politicians on Tyneside in forming the Tyneside Irish was a desire to prevent good Catholic boys from being corrupted in a predominantly Protestant and possibly 'Orange'-tinged army. Similar ideas from a nonconformist Welsh perspective were apparent in the raising of the 38th New Army Division. A great deal of effort was made to convince the Welsh public that the religious identity of Welshmen would be protected. Lloyd George bearded Kitchener on the provision of adequate numbers of nonconformist chaplains.

A battalion which combined both 'ethnic' and class exclusivity, formed in a city defined by such considerations, was the Liverpool Scots.[26] It serves as a case study of the extent to which the structures of peacetime sociability, with all their snobberies and solidarities, were transmitted into enlistment. Pre-war members such as Lieutenant Anderson were members of the Territorial battalion as part of a package which included the Birkenhead Dramatic Society, the Oxton Cricket Club, the Birkenhead Park Rugby Football Club, the Methodist Church and the Liverpool

Conservative Club. These associations, along with areas of residence and business ties, were shared with many other members of the battalion. The pre-war rules excluded manual labourers, demanded Scottish 'ancestry' and charged a 10 shilling entrance fee. Even before the outbreak of war a few manual workers were accepted and the 'ethnic' consideration was allowed to broaden the scope by comparison with the Liverpool Rifles, which were more homogeneous in class terms.

Wartime broadened the recruiting structure. The occupational distribution of recruits shows the presence of men who would have been unlikely to be accepted in the pre-war battalion, even to the extent of including 23 labourers. In all, 148 known occupations are listed for the 614 recruits, with 124 listed as unknown. But the balance is still overwhelmingly middle class. Fully 120 of the recruits are listed as clerks; no other single occupation approaches even a quarter of this figure. Other occupations with more than 10 men listed are: butcher, musician, shopkeeper, shopman, painter, labourer and steward. The overwhelming majority of recruits were from white-collar or skilled working-class backgrounds. Wartime casualties slowly diluted this class identity, although the regional identity lasted longer. Yet even within the battalion, the old standards were upheld in one respect: the Liverpool Scottish ended the war as it had begun, officered almost entirely by a narrow circle drawn from Liverpool's social elite.

The last military formation raised with a distinctively sectional ethos, the Jewish Brigade of the Royal Fusiliers, created in 1917, had an explicitly Zionist agenda. But it was also an attempt to overcome widespread doubts in the Jewish community about the capacity of the Army to allow practising Jews to retain their identity. This was the last British formation raised in the war which could be characterised as at least partially a volunteer unit, although in a very qualified sense.[27] But the idea was not universally popular. In an impassioned memorandum, the Secretary of State for India, Edwin Montagu, the only Jewish member of the Cabinet, condemned the idea for its implication that English Jews were not simply English. In doing so he showed a different concern about social exclusivity. For Montagu class and culture trumped what he saw as a spurious 'ethnicity' and religion:

I am waiting to learn that my brother, who has been wounded in the Naval Division, or my nephew, who is in the Grenadier Guards, will be forced by public opinion or army orders to become an officer in a regiment which will mainly be composed of people who will not understand the only language which he speaks – English.[28]

Burke's aphorism of men preferring to associate in small platoons was to find a literal embodiment in the British volunteer army. There were limits to this: the proposal to form a 'vegetarians' battalion of Kitchener's Army was, if not a joke, at least treated as one. If this army was a mirror of the nation, then it was a mirror in the very particular sense of the fragmented and localised structure of social life, based on 10,000 scout troops, trade-union branches, chapels, football clubs, schools, masonic lodges; on rural estates, offices and workshops. The record of Hyde's recruits show volunteers coming from the swimming club, rugby club, football club, hockey club, the Young Unionists, all of the chapels and churches, the Boiler Makers' Union and the Labour club, the Sunday schools, Good Templars, Oddfellows, Kingston Mills Band and PSA, as well as the more obvious Territorial Association and rifle clubs.

This army was not a cross section of Britain. It included more clerks than miners and railwaymen combined.[29] Contrary to the conservative mythology of 'deep England', the rural population was generally unmoved by an impulse to volunteer: the archetypal urban activity of omnibus transport had double the volunteering rate of agricultural workers.

Once in uniform, men became 'patriots' whatever the initial impulse for volunteering had been, but it should always be borne in mind that the process was itself a great deal more complex than that.

Scots wha' ha'e with Wallace bled

Scotland laments the glorious, England mourns the dead.
Lawrence Weaver describing the intentions of the Scottish
National War memorial in 1923[30]

All generalisations break down somewhere and in a multi-national state it is unsurprising that they tend to break down on national lines. During the war the failure of the Southern Irish to volunteer proportionately excited a degree of hostile comment. In fact Ireland, predominantly rural, was not particularly out of line initially with rural England and Wales. In retrospect the more interesting question is why there was a disproportionately high number of volunteers from Scotland.

Recruitment up to 4 November 1914 per 10,000 population

Southern Scotland	237
Midlands	196
Lancashire	178
London and Home Counties	170
Yorkshire and North East	150
Ireland (North and South)	127
West of England	88
Eastern England	80

Parliamentary Recruiting Committee report, cited in P. Simkins, *Kitchener's Army* (Manchester, 1980), p. 112

This is an awkward subject. At the time, resentment of Scottish patriotic arrogance was fairly widespread amongst the volunteers in English line regiments, and that competitive spirit is far from extinct. Overall the table above is perhaps best explained in terms of an urbanisation index. Just as in England, there were specific economic incentives at work. The high proportion of Scots enlisting from the building trade, moribund in August 1914, played a role. The discrepancy in enlistment between the two main Scottish coalfields is also explicable in economic terms. The west coast mines were kept busy by orders for the steel industry; the eastern mines were heavily disrupted by the loss of continental markets. As a result, in East Lothian, 36.5% of miners had enlisted by August 1915; in Ayrshire only 20%. This compares with 22.9% of English miners and 22.5% of Welsh. But even the strongest economic motivations did not operate in isolation. Quarrymen in North Wales found their employment massively disrupted by the war, to the extent that only 700 out of a pre-war workforce in Gwynedd of 8,400 were in full-time employment in January 1915. Despite this only 1,200 (14.3%) had joined the Army. By contrast every Scottish occupation saw above average enlistment rates.[31] Similarly the civic considerations behind battalions such as the Glasgow Tramways are not dissimilar to cases in Birmingham, Manchester and Liverpool. Scotland had its own 'class' battalions, and the Edinburgh Territorials of the Royal Scots had as strong a caste identity as the London Territorials. Leith dockers naturally joined the 7th Battalion, whilst the 4th had post office and civil service companies. The 5th Battalion recruited heavily from the fee-paying schoolboys of George Herriot's School, whilst their traditional rivals on the rugby field, George Watson's, made up a high proportion of the 9th Battalion.[32]

But this doesn't tell the whole story. It seems rural Scotland also had a much higher rate of volunteering than comparable areas in other parts of the United Kingdom: 93 per 10,000 population.[33] For example, in the course of the war, the remote Highland parish of Gairloch sent 507 men into the armed forces from a total population of only 3,317 (15.2%).[34] This was by no means exceptional: Turriff town and parish had 170 men already serving by the end of 1914, which compares with 295 men of military age not in uniform in May 1915.[35] At the end of September 1914, it was claimed of the Outer Hebrides that nearly all of the men were away on military or naval service, and only women were left to work the crofts.[36] Almost two-thirds of the fishermen of Scotland volunteered for dangerous service with the Royal Naval Reserve, one of the highest rates of occupational mobilisation in the country. This might be usefully contrasted with North Wales, where one recruiting meeting at the Pwllheli hiring fair produced no recruits at all and where the 30,000 recruiting leaflets which were distributed at hiring fairs in May 1915 produced a total of 23 volunteers.[37]

The high national rate of volunteering in Scotland is undoubtedly significant. Neither the age structure nor the health of the population would predict this overall result – if anything they would provide a slight bias against Scotland. Nor is it clear that better local organisation was in itself the reason, although 'clan' mobilisation and well-organised regimental structures probably played a role in the Highlands and Islands. One is forced to consider a cultural explanation.

In important cultural respects Scotland was definitely a different country from England in 1914, although there was obviously a fair amount of overlap, particularly in urban life. Some of the features of the English picture simply do not apply. In particular, it is difficult to convincingly argue that more Scots volunteered because of a greater fear of invasion. Quite the contrary: even William Le Queux at his most inventive couldn't come up with a plausible German invasion which would march via Edinburgh and Glasgow (although, if there had been more potential *Daily Mail* readers in those cities, he might have tried harder). The religious picture in Scotland was different and distinctive as well, and it is possible to argue that it was one more compatible with military service. In particular, the concept of 'covenanting', intrinsic to Presbyterian culture,[38] carried a distinctive charge when it came to military service. Because of events in Ireland in 1912–1914, the concept was still very much a live one, and its importance may well have stretched beyond Ulster to Southern Scotland as a motivation for enlistment. It is revealing that 90% of the military-age sons of Church of Scotland ministers volunteered, probably the highest ratio of volunteering of any group on record in Britain.[39]

The simplest answer may still be the best: that Scottish culture was more patriotic, perhaps even more militaristic than English. A few possible indicators could be suggested. One is speculative and retrospective, but nevertheless intriguing. At the height of the literature of disillusionment in the late 1920s and early 1930s, when some middle-class volunteers – English, Welsh and even in one case an Ulsterman – were writing anti-war novels and memoirs, the Scottish middle-class veterans were deafening in their silence.[40] One in six British soldiers of the war were Scottish, but apparently not a Graves, Sassoon, Aldington, Williamson or even a Crozier amongst them. In the event, the great Scottish war memoir of the 1930s remained unpublished, and for good reason. John Reith's *Wearing Spurs* was written in 1937 from his original diaries. His friends persuaded him to suppress it because it would have given ammunition to his enemies as Director General of the BBC. It certainly would have; at the high point of British pacifism, the publication of what might be subtitled the 'story of a war-lover' would have made Reith's job impossible. It finally appeared in 1966.[41]

An argument by absence, long after the event, is of limited use; although it is worth noting as a counterpoint the unusually high proportion of Scottish cases amongst published British 'Rolls of Honour'. But it might be taken in conjunction with a very real presence. The patriotic bestseller (in prose) of 1915–1916 was *The First Hundred Thousand* by a Scot, 'Ian Hay' (Ian Hay Beith). The tone of this book, with Army life and the war as a glorious and amusing adventure, is not undermined by the final scenes of battle at Loos in autumn 1915. In reality, Loos was literally a bloody disaster, but the book presents it as glory; the deaths only serve to reinforce the patriotic message. This was not written by some detached civilian: Beith went through the battle and was sufficiently uncowed to rush out a sequel, *The Second Hundred Thousand* in time for an even bigger bloodbath on the Somme.[42] Generally taken as expressing the ethos of the Kitchener Armies in general, it is worth wondering whether there might be something specifically and self-consciously Scottish about these books.

Although popular militarism may have existed as a stronger potential cultural resource in Scotland, this should not be taken as a simplistic stereotyping. Scottish reactions were as complex and nuanced as those in any other part of the British Isles. Indeed, it could reasonably be objected that there was also a strong anti-militarist strain observable amongst Scots. Scots were very slightly under-represented in the pre-war army, although post-war they would be over-represented.[43] Keir Hardie was one of the few democratic socialist leaders in Europe to hold firmly to the anti-war resolutions of the Second International, and James Ramsay MacDonald quickly became Britain's most reviled 'pacifist'. They exemplified a distaste for war and distrust of the military which certainly existed in Scotland. Although the widespread anti-militarism which proliferated in English and Welsh nonconformist circles had no real Scottish equivalent, Scotland had its own vigorous Liberal and Radical traditions. Political Liberalism still dominated Scotland in 1914, even as it was challenged in England. Among these Liberals the spirit of Midlothian lived on, and the Gladstonian appeal of 'Peace, Retrenchment and Reform' still had a resonance in Scotland. Even at the height of the war, militant anti-war speakers could probably get a fairer hearing in Glasgow, with less chance of becoming victims of violence, than anywhere in England. Bruce Glasier, an ILP activist, reported in 1916 that Scottish anti-war feeling was 'more energetic and aggressive than in the English branches'.[44]

Pre-war working-class scepticism about matters military was widespread in urban Scotland, just as it was in other parts of the United Kingdom. John Reith mentions that his Territorial Army unit was mocked in the rougher areas of Glasgow prior to the outbreak of war. But after the outbreak of war, in the same districts, the tone changed to respect: 'we were soldiers, our status and potentialities realised'.[45]

The status and potentialities of soldiers is an indicative phrase. Although in certain respects it had been latent before 1914, the sheer glamour of the Scottish military tradition does seem to have played an important part in mobilisation. Even south of the border the peculiar appeal of kilted regiments was noted; the Liverpool, Tyneside and London Scottish had little difficulty in finding volunteers, Scot and 'Saxon' alike. It is also significant that, uniquely in the United Kingdom, Scotland appeared able to identify with equal force with Territorial, New Army and Regular Regiments. Scotland raised thirty 'new army' battalions, second only to Lancashire, whilst at the same time filling the ranks of no fewer than four Territorial Army divisions. A further dimension is suggested by the fact that Scotland had two competing warrior traditions: Lowland and Highland, 'Scots' and 'Gaelic'. Competitive emulation was a powerful spur: neither tradition wished to be overshadowed by the other, and both were determined to outshine the mere Sassenachs.

Scottish patriotism, imbued deeply with an imagined warrior past, was distinctly pervasive and peculiar. That Robert Burns, humane, internationalist, Enlightenment poet that he was, could pen the most stirring and bloodthirsty call to battle in the British Isles, was typical. The appeal to a race that had bled with Wallace and fought for the Bruce was amongst the subconscious conditionings of a nation in 1914. Many, perhaps most, Scots knew chunks of Burns by heart. At other times and in other places, 'A man's a man for a' that', might be more relevant, but in the autumn of 1914 it isn't hard to guess what came to mind. Whilst 'Men of Harlech' doubtless rang out at a few Welsh recruiting meetings, it is still doubtful that any other part of the Islands had so internalised a warrior self-definition.[46] In 1897, 6,000 Scottish 'total abstainers' had marched to the field of Bannockburn to battle against drink.[47] It would be difficult to point to anything analagous in other parts of Great Britain. The militarised rhetoric of the English Salvation Army was not so specifically rooted in *actual* military history. Of course, the English had also glamorised elements in the martial past: there was a tradition of 'Soldier Heroes'. But, traditionally, popular patriotism had been more focused on the Royal Navy and its exploits. This was less useful for persuading men to don khaki.

The Carnegie history of the war in rural Scotland takes on an uncharacteristically poetic note in describing the mobilisation of Highland reservists. As the train delivering them to their Regiments stopped at stations throughout Caithness and Sutherlandshire, 'houses were lit up and people stood at the doors waving torches and chanting a high-pitched battle song. Except for the railway, nothing had changed. It was thus through all the ages the clans had mustered.' The descriptive language is as indicative as the actions.[48] In the foreword to a local history and roll of honour, the extensive recollections of local veterans are justified in the following terms: 'What should we not give for a detailed record of the Scots whom we merely sing in slump as having bled with Wallace, the Scots, say, whom Bruce led at Bannockburn.'[49]

Confirmation of this peculiarity of the Scots comes from an unlikely quarter. David Kirkwood, a leading ILP man in Glasgow, would find himself deported to Edinburgh on the orders of Lloyd George after leading strikes in the munitions works. In his memoirs, apparently half-embarrassed, he wrote:

I hated war. I believed that the peoples of the world hated war ... Yet I was working in an arsenal, making guns and shells for one purpose – to kill men in order to keep them from killing men. What a confusion! What was I to do? ... I resolved that my skill as an engineer must be devoted to my country. I was too proud of the battles of the past to stand aside and see Scotland conquered.[50]

An English trade unionist might have expressed similar sentiments, but the last sentence is striking: Kirkwood hated war whilst being specifically proud of Scottish battles in the past. He was not unique; of the three Labour councillors in Edinburgh, whose responses to the war are known, one became strongly pro-war, and the other two quickly volunteered, despite all three being ILP men. In Glasgow only two out of nineteen ILP councillors expressed opposition to the war. The vice-president of the Scottish Trade Union Congress volunteered for military service and was killed in action. Even in 1916, no Scottish Labour MPs voted against conscription.[51]

The English had much more difficulty keeping an entirely straight face about military tradition: the accent of 'Fred Karno's Army'[52] ('we cannot fight, we cannot shoot, what f***ing use are we'), is distinctively English, and so is the tune.[53] For Scots it sometimes appeared that spectatorship was simply not an option. The language of martial history, whether expressed in Gaelic, Scots or English, forced involvement:

> Bi'bh deas gu leum an airdhe
> Le ceum gaisgeil, neo sgathach, dana
> Bi'bh null that comhnard na stri
> (Be ready to leap up, with firm step, bold, fearless, crossing the plain of
>   strife)   John Munro, Isle of Lewis, killed in action, April 1918

Scotland! Scotland! little we're due ye,
Poor employ and skim milk board
But youth's a cream that maun be paid for,
We got it reamin, so here's the sword! ...

Fars the cry from Leven Water
Where your fore-folks went to war
They would swap wi' us tomorrow,
Even in the Flaunders glaur!   Neil Munro, born Argyll, Glasgow journalist

Nae ours to blame, but when it came
We couldna pass the challenge by
For credit o' our honest name
There could be one reply ...
We'll show them a', whate'er befa'
Auld Scotland counts for something still
                    Charles Murray, born Aberdeenshire, served in South African army

Even one of the most cynical and bitter condemnations of the war in the Scottish poetry,[54] Ewart Mackintosh's poem, 'Recruiting', a savage 'Sassoonesque' condemnation of all the iniquities of women, profiteers, journalists and civilians in general, and which was written surprisingly early, ends with a straightforward recruiting appeal, unthinkable in Siegfried Sassoon:[55]

Lads you're wanted, come and learn
To live and die with honest men.

You shall learn what men can do
If you will but pay the price
Learn the gaiety and strength
In the gallant sacrifice.

Take your risk of life and death
Underneath the open sky
Live clean or go out quick
Lads you're wanted, come and die.

Mackintosh was killed at Cambrai in 1917.

On not volunteering

British men, do you want your women violated?
Your children mutilated
Yourselves shot down?
The Germans have done these things to men, women and children in
    Belgium,

They will do the same to you and yours if they come here
Every British Soldier is the bodyguard of every woman and child.
Imperial Maritime League poster, early January 1915[56]

Send out my brother, my sister or my mother, but for God's sake don't send me.
Lyric from anonymous soldiers' song of 1914, parodying a recruiting song[57]

If Scotland had the best record for volunteering, Leicestershire had one of the worst. The civic history of Leicester is unusually frank about this. There certainly were large recruiting meetings in Leicester: at one meeting in 1914 there were 15,000 people 'surging in the market place, the National Anthem and patriotic songs, but recruiting was slow'. That is an understatement – it was practically nonexistent. A great meeting at De Montfort Hall yielded nine pledges to enlist, but only four of these men actually showed up and two of those were rejected as unfit. By 30 March 1915, Leicester's record was a serious civic embarrassment. A recruiting speech pointed out that in Newcastle 18.5% of those eligible had joined the colours, the same in Nottingham, 10.5% in Swansea, 7.6% in Wakefield, 7.1% in Hull, 6.7% in Sheffield and Leeds, 5.2% at Derby, 4.1% at Bradford, 4% at Oldham and only 2.6% in Leicester. Leicester was already suffering further acute embarrassment because the ILP leader, Ramsay MacDonald, was one of the local MPs. He was being lambasted in the press as a traitor and pro-German. It is tempting to connect the two and suggest that there was a sustained anti-war sentiment in the city and county. But this would be difficult to sustain. MacDonald actually spoke in favour of volunteering on several occasions and addressed a recruiting meeting in 1914. Two other possible explanations rest in the structure of the county regiments and in the early boom conditions of the bootmaking trade from September 1914. Both undoubtedly influenced these figures, but are unlikely to be the whole explanation. Perhaps Leicestershire's remoteness from the coasts may have diminished invasion fears and reduced the sense of urgency. But the most likely explanation was a widespread failure of local leadership. The local recruiting committee met twenty-five times, but thirteen members of the committee failed to attend a single meeting, and twenty-two had only been to one as opposed to thirteen who had been to two or more. In a desperate attempt to whip up some patriotic fervour, the committee sent 438 letters to clergy requesting that a patriotic sermon be preached. One hundred and forty-four Anglican priests and thirty-six Free Church ministers agreed to do so, but eighteen Anglicans and twenty Free Church men declined and the rest didn't bother to reply. This may suggest that in the heartlands of 'old dissent' a certain ambivalence about the war had not been overcome in 1915. This was ambivalence rather than active hostility: the Free Churches of Leicester were very active in war charities. Whatever the reasons, the net result was that most of those eligible did not join up. The civic history notes that there were 60,000 men of military age in Leicestershire and Rutland who were not with the colours in summer 1915. The main reason according to the author was a widespread passivity – an understanding amongst men that they would go when they were called.[58]

By way of contrast, the civic history of Hyde in Cheshire, published in 1916, has a whole section dedicated to what it describes as fighting families. The Smiths of Castle Street had four sons serving out of eight: two of them had been killed by July 1915. The Long family of Cheapside had six sons who had served – by 1916 two were dead, two were wounded and one was a prisoner. The Oldham family of Dunkirk cottage and the Ellisons of Frank Street each had five sons in uniform; the Williamsons three sons and their father.[59] It is easy to miss the point about such cases. They were publicised precisely because they were not typical. For every family with multiple volunteers there was another with none, and it was these who were being shamed by such publications.

It needs to be remembered that the vast majority of the men of military age in Britain during the First World War chose not to volunteer for the armed forces. Communities where the majority volunteered, such as the public schools and the universities, were the exception rather than the rule. Such cases were not exclusively among the social elites. In Swindon the local authority teachers had an impressive volunteering record, sufficiently so to be recorded in the civic history.

Enlistment of Swindon school teachers

Males: January 1916	Elementary	Secondary
Serving	31	6
Attested	10	16
Unfit	16	2
Unattested	0	1
Over age	32	4

Bavin, *Swindon*, p. 63

A substantial minority of all male teachers of military age in Swindon were with the colours before the introduction of conscription and, among elementary school teachers, those most easily substituted by women, this rose to a clear majority. Furthermore, all but one of the men eligible under the Derby scheme had indicated a willingness to go when called.

Whilst within many communities similar cases could be cited, the aggregate figures for most areas tell a different story.

A fairly typical urban area, such as Todmorden in Lancashire, which had somewhere between 5,000 and 6,000 men of military age (based on 1911 census), found in the registration survey that at the end of voluntary recruiting there were 700 'starred' workers exempt from military service, 273 judged unfit, 515 single and 878 married men who had attested to serve under the Derby scheme if called, and 509 of the eligible single men and 862 married men had refused the 'invitation' to serve altogether. Therefore about 3,750 men in the town were not serving at the end of fully voluntary recruitment, allowing a degree of evasion. If the eligible population was 5,500 this would imply about 1,750 volunteers. The final voluntary enlistment rate of about 30% is quite in line with the regional average.[60]

Even in a town with an exceptionally high enlistment rate, such as Turriff, a slight majority of the men of military age chose not to join up. I use the term 'chose' deliberately. We tend to think of volunteering as a choice, and not volunteering as perfectly normal, or perhaps as the obviously rational action. Of those who chose not to volunteer, nearly 3 million would later be compelled to serve. Many others were able to avoid military service entirely. But in 1914–1915 in particular it seems fair to say that at some point a fit man of military age would need to be able to rationalise to himself and to others why he was not in uniform.

Those who did not volunteer in 1914–1915 were failing to enlist at a time when volunteering was weighted with massive 'social approbation' and, as a corollary, not volunteering was met with social disapprobation. Andrew Clark notes the term 'shirker' in use by 29 August 1914, and the term 'slacker' by 5 September. Non-volunteers often found these damning labels applied to them and not volunteering was, therefore, in important respects, a real choice.[61]

Not everyone had this choice; many men were unfit for military service, even though this was not apparent at first glance. The actor Frank Pettingell was one of them and he wrote and published a monologue entitled 'We cannot all be soldiers.' In it he speaks of the young and healthy who join the khaki ranks receiving a glance of praise and pride from the people they met. Men who were clearly above military age could likewise be as ostentatiously patriotic as they liked, but:

> Now in the shops and in the streets and everywhere you'll see
> A lot of men who look as fit as anyone can be
> And you'll say with bitter feeling, 'Why don't that fellow 'list …
> And you'll dub him as a coward and you'll treat him with disdain.

He ends with the appeal:

> Just think a little better, just be a little kind,
> And don't class as a shirker every man who's left behind.[62]

If those who could not join up felt these pressures, it is not difficult to imagine the pressure on those who could.

Avoiding military service is usually considered in the literature in terms of conscientious objection. Uniquely amongst the warring nations of 1916, the British, on introducing conscription, allowed the possibility of a moral objection to killing to exempt a man from combatant service. Yet it is overwhelmingly likely that very few of either those who didn't volunteer, whether later conscripted or not, had had overwhelming moral compunction on this particular issue. The vast majority of the non-volunteers did not hold back either because of moral objection to the act of killing or because of ideological objection to the war. Broadly ideological qualms may have played a secondary role in some cases, for example a lack of desire to die for England may have held back recruiting in Nationalist rural Ireland or in parts of Wales. But rural indifference was probably the main reason in 1914–1915, and was equally observable in many parts of England. Some 'badged' men in industry may have had socialist objections to war which were never tested. But it is difficult to argue that anti-war sentiment was generally the reason that men held back any more than that irrational enthusiasm for war explains why so many volunteered.

The most obvious reason for not volunteering was a disinclination to be killed or maimed. This was obviously the motivation that dared not speak its name. In the climate of the First World War a straightforward admission to cowardice was unlikely to be met sympathetically. In all probability those who were scared, a legitimate enough reaction one might think, would be unlikely to admit it even to themselves. But it would probably be a mistake to think that every reason and rationalisation for not rushing to the colours was simply a cover for fear. When conscription was introduced, resistance to joining up doesn't appear to have been any stronger among men who were medically adjudged to be 'A1', and therefore fit for frontline service, than it was among men graded B and C who would therefore be drafted for non-combatant roles.

Of course, what could be seen as an equally morally dubious rational motive could play a part: the possibility of economic advantage. By October 1914 the large numbers of volunteers were causing a labour shortage. For the working class in particular, it heralded the beginning of genuine full employment, potentially enhanced wages and enhanced bargaining power. At the least derogatory, this could be seen as a moment when men who had been living on the margins could for the first time provide some comfort and security for their families; at the most derogatory as a golden opportunity, ruthlessly exploited, to make some real money. The latter interpretation naturally dominated the increasingly shrill complaints of the middle classes. But, once again, few would be likely to admit that they were staying out of the Army to make money. In fact it is easy to make too much of this: the co-relation between high wartime wages and low enlistment was present but at the same time fairly weak. Some trades where wages had risen by 1916, such as dockers, did show low enlistment rates, whilst compositors, whose wage rates rose very little, did prove apt to volunteer. But railwaymen had a lower enlistment rate than coalminers whose wages had risen more.[63]

The rationales that actually were used tended to be on the following lines: 'They don't really need me'; 'I'm not suited to the army'; 'I'm more useful at home' or; 'I have other and greater responsibilities'. These would come to be supplemented, ironically, with the argument, 'I'll go when all the shirkers have been rounded up.'

The fourth of these arguments was probably the most frequent. Ada MacGuire wrote in October 1915:

recruits are not coming in quick enough because we have now got to the men who have dependants & who would have to sacrifice them for their country. The pay they get won't pay their rent & rates, so what are they to do. The Government won't pay the rent for them. The working classes are no worse off, it is with the middle classes that the difficulty lies. A man has to face the fact that if he is killed, his wife or his mother as the case may be, will have to turn to and work for a living. However something will have to be done.[64]

This fear of army service leading to 'loss of caste' for the families of the middle class was real enough. In his diaries of 1915 and 1916, Harold Cousins, a middle-aged and married Oxford graduate, living in St Albans and working for the 'Alberta Land Company' in London, found himself confronting his own civilian status. He did join the local volunteer corps quite early in the war, but, near the upper band of military age, he felt little obligation to enlist in the Army proper. His wife was 'delicate' and he seems to have genuinely seen his first duty as being close to her.

Cousins on occasion could be a rather unselfconscious spectator. He attended a recruiting meeting on 2 October 1915, where 'everyone I spoke to thought it was rather a farce ... conscription must come & it will not be unwelcome'. There is no sense in this case, or in his other descriptions of such meetings, that he felt the appeal might apply to him personally. Although he was of military age, Cousins was convinced that his own reasons for not joining the army were overwhelming. When canvassed for the Derby scheme, the 'chief difficulty was to find room for a recital of my circumstances on his card, rendering it impossible for me to do more than I am doing at the moment … These reasons include physical, financial and business considerations.' But on occasion a strange self-awareness sets in. After criticising 'slackers' in Wales, he states, 'Perhaps, I am a slacker myself, however much I might be otherwise in other circumstances.'[65] Cousins refused to attest and, when attested married men were called up, he had no sympathy: 'it seems to me that married men, who like myself, have heavy obligations which render their enlistment almost impracticable, should not have attested. They were praised for doing so and now they are asked to fulfill their engagement, they ask to be let off.' After the introduction of conscription on 26 April 1916, he commented at length on the detail of these obligations: 'The assistance to be rendered to married recruits to relieve them of mortgage & rent payments is not to exceed £104 per annum. This would not be enough for me as there would still be another £30 or so per annum to be found before there would be anything for Marjorie and John to live on.' On 2 May, he claims: 'If I were free I would go like a shot.'

On 11 May 1916, he was confident that he would be exempted for 'business and domestic reasons': his company was claiming exemption on his behalf. On 11 July 1916, Cousins received his call-up papers. He wrote to the recruiting officer pointing out that his exemption application was pending, but, in the meantime, 'Poor Marjorie got quite a turn when the papers arrived as if I had been ordered straight to the trenches … I must say that I should think it rather jolly and exciting to join up if I were free.' The comment might sound like civilian ignorance, although it is clear from his diaries that in fact Cousins was very well informed about the real conditions on the Western Front. He was medically examined on 21 July and granted three months' exemption on 9 August, 'with leave to appeal'.[66]

Cousins' employment exemption lasted until 2 February 1917. Then came a 'day of great commotion'. The Alberta Land Company faced liquidation. His reaction crystallised his thinking for a year:

If this is decided I am done, for my salary would cease, my reason for exemption from Military Service would disappear, for having no means of subsistence I should be better off in the Army than out of it, no one being willing now to engage anyone of military age. So far as I myself am concerned this would be alright, but it would be all wrong for Marjorie and John.[67]

There was a brief respite. Initially the company did not file for bankruptcy and Cousins willingly took a salary cut: 'the sense of relief is very great'. But the relief was short-lived. His job was lost and so was

his exemption – on 14 February 1917 his exemption claim was dis-
allowed: 'So here begins a new era. I cannot think connectedly & must
get back to Marjorie. Poor Girl. I suppose it means another upheaval
for her just as she was getting stronger.' The next day he writes:

> they can do what they like to me ... I am much worried over financial matters and
> must try to get something from the Alberta Company ... I believe Marjorie will get
> 25/ a week for herself and John & I shall try to get £2 a week from the Civil
> Liabilities Committee. But this alone won't be enough to meet all our fixed
> obligations. Everything feels very blank, but I suppose one will soon settle down.[68]

In the end, Cousins accepted the fact of military service with a degree of
stoicism for himself, but with real distress regarding his family. His diary
comments are too consistent with his ultimate reaction to be easily dismissed as the self-justification of a coward. I doubt that the diary was ever
written for a wide audience; I suspect it was written for Cousins himself
and to a certain extent for his son. His intended answer to the question
'What did you do in the Great war, Daddy?', was, clearly, 'I tried to look
after you and your mother.' Whilst this might lack the grandeur of Bob
Smillie's supposed response, 'I tried to stop the bloody thing', it had its
own quiet respectability.[69]

Cousins was not alone in putting family first. Throughout 1915 there
was a running public debate on whether or not married men ought to
volunteer. In 1914, *John Bull* had come down firmly in favour of their
doing so, but in 1915 the position shifted: 'The men who have women and
children dependent on them, who have established homes, who have
taken upon themselves the full burden of citizenship, may, in the last
resort be compelled to defend their country', but, 'that time, I submit,
has most emphatically not come, so long as men without responsibilities
or family ties are at liberty to waste their time at football matches and
picture palaces'.[70] This amounted to a public sanction for hanging back.
The age structure of recruitment and of casualties, and the surprisingly
small number of war widows and orphans relative to deaths in the war,
indicates that married men were much more reluctant to volunteer. So
does the storm of protest over the decision to take attested married men
in 1916 under the Derby scheme provisions in advance of the call-up of
unattested single men. Admittedly there was a strong counterblast from
both the single and married who had not attested, accusing the attested
married of gross hypocrisy in claiming willingness to serve, and therefore
benefiting from public approval, but then being unwilling to deliver on
their promise.

But single men could also claim higher family responsibilities. A
young gardener in Essex, conscripted in 1916, had declined to volunteer

according to the Rector of Stoney Massey because 'He felt he owed a greater duty to his mother at home than to King George, for his mother had done much for him, whereas the King, so far as he knew, had not rendered him any service!'[71] Undoubtedly intended as an example of innocent or wise rusticity, it remains a rather good example of the countervailing pressures that kept men out of uniform.

A letter in *The Scotsman* at the height of voluntary recruitment had rhetorically asked about a case where one of two brothers had enlisted whilst the other had remained at home to care for his mother and sisters: 'Is the former a hero and the latter a coward. The dilemma is of course absurd.'[72] Much of the rhetoric of volunteering was centred on concepts of the protective duties of men towards 'helpless' women, but this meant that men could also honourably claim a higher duty to their immediate families. Two concepts of masculine duties came into conflict.

Even after compulsion was introduced, there would be those who would accept such a view as honourable enough.

The voluntary ethic

The civic history of Hornchurch states, of the early war years, 'Never was there such a time for individual effort … everybody served.'[73] Extracts from the diaries of the Lord Mayor of Leeds published in the city's civic history, the wartime letters of Neville Chamberlain, Lord Mayor of Birmingham, the post-war reminiscences of Harry Cartmell, Mayor of Preston, demonstrate the pervasiveness of the voluntary ethic. They show the tremendous call on the time and effort of these civic luminaries, and the enormous number of voluntary organisations with which they interacted. E. G. Brathchell, a local Justice of the Peace in Essex who was 46 years old at the outbreak of the war, held no fewer than 31 voluntary appointments during the course of the war.[74]

This ethic of doing one's bit extended into all spheres of life, some fairly unlikely. Isabel Hutton noticed that her mentally ill patients began knitting for the Red Cross, as well as singing war songs and keenly following the war news. It is worth remembering that this is not a reversible syllogism: just because the mad threw themselves into the war effort doesn't imply that everyone who did so was mad, dissenting views of 'war hysteria' nothwithstanding.[75] Nevertheless the new expectations could give rise to considerable pressures.

It was a deeply improbable combination of such pressures, specifically the rhetoric of Free Church teetotallers and the example of the Tsar, which persuaded King George V in 1915 to voluntarily abstain from alcohol for the duration of the war. With a few lapses 'for medicinal' purposes, he carried out the pledge. The failure of 'Squiffy' Asquith to follow suit was not viewed favourably in many circles. A three-sided struggle between compulsory prohibition, voluntary abstention and the liberty to drink in moderation (no one actually advocated excess), had been going on for years before the war. Mobilisation had created new anxieties and changed the framework of the drink question. Gender and class perceptions played a role: there was a widespread fear that working-class women were taking advantage of separation allowances to indulge in public drunkenness. The Archbishop of Canterbury had written to Lord Kitchener as early as October 1914 that 'although it sounds horrid', his information was that there was something in this.[76] One result was the Caxton Hall public meeting on 12 November 1914 calling for total abstinence for the duration, which was chaired by Davidson himself and addressed by an improbable combination of Arthur Henderson, Cardinal Bourne, the Lord Mayor of London, Lord Roberts and Lady Jellicoe. Davidson's correspondence with both Anglicans and Dissenters show a groundswell of religious opinion in favour of harsh measures, although Davidson himself was open to argument against prohibition, tactfully making the case to the Bishop of Willesden that a small whisky and soda at luncheon might not be the end of the world.[77]

In the spring of 1915, Asquith asked Davidson to survey his clergy on the drink question in the localities, with a view to informing legislation. Lloyd George was playing to the nonconformist gallery on the issue and Asquith was under pressure to respond. But the gradualist legislative approach was to some extent pre-empted by Lloyd George upping the stakes on 1 April with a telegram asking the Archbishop to co-ordinate a voluntary pledge by all religious leaders to set an example of abstinence in response to the King's Pledge:

The King is now anxious that the public should follow his example and more especially the leaders of public opinion in every branch of life should give the same pledge. There is no doubt that members of the Cabinet, judges, the heads of professions, the great employers of labour and Trade Unions will follow. If this is enforced by a special appeal of the Archbishop ... the Chancellor believes that legislation would have very little left to do and it would only be required to co-erce a minority who are hopeless slaves to drink.[78]

Davidson did as requested and delivered a Sunday sermon appealing for abstinence. R. J. Campbell, a prominent Unitarian minister, wrote to congratulate him and urge organisation of a 'King's pledge'. He stated that he 'would sooner see a moral movement of this kind begun than any amount of prohibitive legislation, the good effect would be enormous ... You can rest assured that the free Church organisations would readily follow your Grace's

4. A voluntary canteen for soldiers. IWM (Q 54274).

lead.'[79] After Davidson published an open letter to *The Times* in conjunction with the Archbishop of York, Cardinal Bourne and the Free Church leaders, the momentum grew. The letter called on the public to follow the King's 'unprecedented lead'. It urged the 'duty and privilege' of 'bearing voluntary part in the Nation's self-discipline and self-sacrifice by abstaining'. This voluntary act was 'due to our brave men, to the nation at large and to God'.[80] This appeal implied the formation of a national voluntary effort in favour of abstention. Frank Briant, a nonconformist in Lambeth, wrote to his 'neighbour' that he felt a national temperance movement led by the King would be far more effective than the dozens of existing groups.[81] By this time Davidson and indeed George V were becoming nervous at what they had unleashed at the request of Lloyd George. In a letter to the Bishop of Croydon he suggested that it was time to apply the brakes.

To tell the truth the King is placed at present in an extremely difficult position, by those who believe what he has done as being a movement in favour of abstinence generally rather than an action taken in connection with a war emergency. The King is, I believe, inundated with letters on the subject and appeals, that he should let himself, so to speak, become exploited as the leader in a temperance movement generally … Very real harm is being done, and I even have heard it said that if this pressure continues the King may find it necessary to say something modifying what he has already said. That would be disastrous.[82]

In the end voluntary abstinence was not enough: the hard core of incorrigible imbibers proved larger and more determined than the optimistic temperance advocates hoped. But the King's Pledge illustrates how the war called forth intensified efforts on the part of existing bodies and expanded their scope. In many ways temperance was the archetypal voluntary cause of the Victorian age, both as individual act and as pressure group for social reform. The early years of the war gave renewed impetus to such sentiments and called forth a host of new initiatives.

The scale and scope of voluntary action of all varieties was breathtaking. In just one attempt to co-ordinate it, an 'Active Service League' initiated by the sister of Viscount French, mobilised 53,000 subscribers, and 2,000 volunteers were classified and passed on to organisations that could make use of them. In Leeds alone there were 10,000 women involved in volunteer activity by the spring of 1915.[83]

By 1917 Violet Markham, by this time officially employed by the National Service Department, was actually complaining that there were simply too many volunteers: 'It is most perplexing to know how to fit in all these amateurs.'[84]

Lady Limerick began a free buffet at London Bridge Station, 'where the travelling soldier can get a free meal at any hour between 8am. and 10pm'. On average 1,200 men were served each day with cocoa, sandwiches, cake and cigarettes as well as writing paper for those going to the front. Thirty to forty volunteers manned the buffet each day. Of course it had another agenda – to keep soldiers 'away from the public house' – but the idea spread rapidly, even to the extent that it was British middle-class ladies who began providing this service for the French Army.[85] All over the country 'Sister Susie' was knitting socks for soldiers. In Turriff the 'Parish War Work Party' sent 2,012 garments between October 1915 and October 1916, 3,247 the next year and 3,684 the year after – highly impressive for a very small community.[86] This kind of voluntary and charitable activity was ubiquitous. Over 400 charities were registered in Scotland before 1917. They included the Forres Town Vegetable Committee for the British fleet, the Tayport War Dressings Fund Bottle Collection, the Fearnought Glove Fund, the Leith Ladies branch of the National Egg Collection, the Greenock Telegraph wounded in Malta Fund and the Footballs for Soldiers Fund. The second edition of the Liverpool social worker's handbook, published in 1916, listed new associations founded for war work. There were the local branches of the large national organisations: Prince of Wales Fund, The Royal Patriotic Fund, The Soldiers and Sailors Help Society, Women's War Service Bureau, Lord Roberts Workshops for Disabled Soldiers and Sailors, British Red Cross and the War Economy branch of the Women's Industrial Councils, the NUWSS Women's Patrols. There were also the local initiatives: Town Hall Committee for Widows and Dependents, the Liverpool Reception Committee for Belgian Refugees, Liverpool War Dressings Association. There were class-specific organisations: the Professional Classes Relief Council, and Officers Family Fund. To co-ordinate the activities and assign volunteers there were the Civil Service League, Town Hall Association and the Liverpool Joint War Committee. This was in addition to an increased call on the services of existing organisations.[87]

Local initiatives were a testing ground for effective voluntary action. Bristol took particular pride in the 'Inquiry Bureau' which became a model for the nation. Shortly after the 2nd Southern General hospital began receiving wounded, the Officer commanding found himself inundated with inquiries regarding the patients, and appealed for voluntary assistance. 'A little band of workers' offered their services, mostly local businessmen. Their numbers increased rapidly, 'including several ladies', until they numbered in the hundreds. The Inquiry Bureau organised lodgings for the families of wounded soldiers close to the hospitals, which were 'clean and respectable'. They provided assistance 'after careful inquiries' to the 'deserving', paying railway fares and board and lodging. The work of the bureau expanded into organising entertainment for convalescent troops: 400 local artists provided 4,500 entertainments, and 500 visiting artists provided 5,000. Some 32,450 men were entertained at the Zoological Gardens, 50,000 at the Museum and Art Gallery and 20,000 at the Prince's Theatre which reserved 50 to 100 seats at each matinee for the wounded. On a single occasion 2,270 men including 400 'crutch' cases were entertained at the Bristol Hippodrome, a national record. The Inquiry Bureau activities expanded out to cover the whole of the South West and South Wales.[88]

The gendered aspects of the volunteer ethos should by now be apparent. The male volunteer was appealed to in terms of protecting women and children. Women were appealed to in order to show solidarity with their menfolk, but also to avoid being seen as 'useless'. From the outset the newsletter of the National Union of Women's Suffrage Societies had considered the war an opportunity to 'show ourselves to be worthy of citizenship, whether the claim is acknowledged or not'.[89] Notoriously, the leadership of the Women's Social and Political Union, the suffragettes, threw themselves into the war effort. Sylvia Pankhurst broke ranks and maintained an oppositional stance, but her mother and sisters were militant supporters of the war effort.

Explaining that decision has not always been easy for historians. Some see it principally as opportunism, others as a logical outcome of pre-war militancy and the willingness to embrace violence. One intriguing

suggestion has been made by Jacqueline de Vries that points to the con-
sistencies in the rhetorical positions of Emmeline and Christabel with
their pre-war stance. At a war service meeting, Mrs Pankhurst claimed,
'Prussianisation is masculinity carried to the point of enormity and
obscenity even.' Christabel stated, 'if German victory would be an appalling calamity for men, for women it would be infinitely worse. To defeat
the Germans is the Woman question of the present time.' Both women
identified 'Prussianism' specifically with the violation of women by men.
The symbolism of atrocities against non-combatants and neutrals paral-
leled state violence against suffragettes prior to 1914.[90]

Such rhetoric must have seemed perfectly natural in 1914–1915.
Furthermore it parallels similar thinking on the part of Liberals,
Christians and socialists. The events of 1914 had transferred an internal
struggle into one against an external enemy perceived as antithetical to
core values. In retrospect it seems grossly exaggerated, but it had an
internal coherence at the time.

By 1915 leading feminists had come to the conclusion that it was vital to
stake a larger claim for women to active citizenship. The Women's Right
to Serve march was an apparently spontaneous attempt to force the
government to make more and better use of women in the war effort.
Decked out with the purple and green colours of the suffragettes, it made
an enormous impression directly on those in central London and indi-
rectly on those who read the press coverage.

The march was in reality deeply disingenuous. Superficially it appeared
to be a spontaneous demand to force the government into incorporating
women into the war effort. In fact it was the product of collusion between
Lloyd George and the Pankhursts. The Minister of Munitions was pres-
surising male trade unionists to accept 'dilution' in the form of female
labour. Women demanding the 'right' to serve was a very useful lever
towards this end. In a broader sense it marks an important phase in the
increasing governmental attempt to channel and organise the volunteer
ethos. As with the issue of drink, an apparently voluntary action was in fact
prompted. Voluntary actions were also increasingly supplemented with
legislative or executive measures. Tightening regulation of the drink trade
began early in the war. By the middle of the war a whole panoply of
regulation was in force: the strength of beer was reduced, licensing
hours limited, 'treating' was forbidden and actual prohibition enforced
in some military and munition districts. In the case of women's war
service the British Government during the First World War never abandoned the voluntary framework, but the demand to serve was helpful in
the movement towards compelling men. By the end of 1915 a hybrid of
voluntary action and compulsion was emerging.

Compulsion

In the first full-scale study of the conscript majority of the British Army in the First World War, Ilana Bet-El claims that conscription, unlike volunteering, was a bureaucratic process in which the individual was passive and events progressed automatically 'without his consent and without his knowledge'.[91] Doubtless true of most times and most places with compulsory military service, this was emphatically not the case in Britain from 1916 to 1918. The reason was the real possibility of appeal against conscription. Built into the Derby scheme and its successor, the Military Service Act, was a safeguard procedure. It was intended to protect the rights of genuine conscientious objectors, but also, and more importantly, to avoid doing needless damage to the economic fabric of localities, to protect families from unnecessary hardship and to allow the process of conscription to be fair and be seen to be fair.

Except in regard to conscientious objectors, the Military Service Tribunals have largely disappeared from the history of the First World War.[92] This is doubtless due to the fact that the vast majority of tribunal records were deliberately destroyed in the 1920s. Yet they were a key, in some respects *the* key, institution of 1916–1918. Conscientious objectors made up a tiny part of their total activity. For example, at the Banbury Local Tribunal, the first session saw approximately 40% of appeals on domestic grounds, 40% on employment grounds, about 10% on both domestic and employment and less than 10% on conscientious grounds. Arthur Gleason in 1917 would claim that only 2% of appeals were made on conscientious grounds. Even this might be an overestimate. In Huddersfield, which was described as 'a hot bed of pacifism' and which had a well-organised support network for conscientious objection, less than 1% of appeals to the tribunal were made on conscientious grounds.[93]

The scale of tribunal activity was immense. The Birmingham Local Tribunal, which had to divide into two parallel 'courts' sat 1,765 times from 1916 to 1918, and gave 90,721 decisions. Ultimately 34,760 men were sent into the army. The Croydon Local Tribunal sat 258 times and heard 10,425 cases in the same period. It is not absolutely clear how cases relate to individuals, although we know that the Bristol Tribunal heard 41,000 cases relating to 22,000 men, of whom 17,000 were ultimately refused exemption. In Leeds the Tribunal sat 435 times and there were 55,101 hearings involving 27,000 individuals. Of these, 13,897 cases were dismissed outright and 41,204 claims were either withdrawn, or exemption, usually temporary, was granted. Together these four Tribunal districts dealt with roughly 100,000 individuals claiming exemption.

There were some 1,800 local Tribunals in the country. Admittedly Croydon, Bristol, Birmingham and Leeds would be among the biggest, but it is quite clear that the usual response to conscription was not passive acceptance, but an appeal. This was certainly the contemporary impression. If the figures above are projected, it must have been a rare individual who did not make a claim for at least temporary exemption.

The Huddersfield Military Tribunal heard 12,543 initial appeals in 1916 alone. The employed male population in the 1911 census had been 35,662.[94] Given that the majority of the working-age population was either 'badged' in reserved occupation, outside the parameters of conscription due to age or health or had volunteered before 1916, these figures strongly suggest that appeal was the automatic response to being called up in Huddersfield.

Macdonagh in February 1916 described the Tribunals in general as 'clogged with work' and that the City Tribunal sitting at Guildhall had to deal with 20,000 claims for exemption. One of these, Harold Cousins, noted in his diary on 11 May 1916, that it was unlikely that the Tribunals would be able to get through the immense number of appeals by attested men in that month. It should be remembered that these appeals were conducted after medical examination, which had already rejected a proportion of those conscripted. Success rates were wildly variable, but generally ranged between 20% and 50%, usually for a temporary exemption.[95] In some cases the rate of success was probably much higher. The Huddersfield Tribunal gave few total exemptions, but at the same time only 24.5% of applicants were refused outright.[96]

The odds of gaining at least a temporary exemption suggest that appeals were not purely formal; indeed the very numbers appealing clearly indicates that an appeal was felt to be worth trying. The audacity of some appeals almost defies belief, for example, the man who appealed in Leeds for three months' delay in order to complete a course of hair-restoration treatment; but such examples, which attracted much contemporary attention, were untypical.[97]

One young man who appealed was Frank Lockwood. Lockwood was a young and single lithographic artist working in the Colne Valley. Privately, he was clearly horrified by the war and its consequences. He did not attest under the Derby scheme and as a result was called up in early 1916. His experience with the local Tribunal at Linthwaite was an unhappy one: they spent only a few seconds in dismissing his case. With the aid of legal representation he challenged the decision at the East Central Appeal Tribunal. On 3 April 1916 he turned up at the Huddersfield Police Court and secured exemption until the end of his apprenticeship. The Linthwaite Tribunal had turned him down on the grounds that his trade was not of national importance, but Lockwood had appealed on educational grounds. The appeal tribunal accepted his argument that the relevant clause was 'if a man is being trained or educated for any work ... it is expedient that he should continue to be so trained'.[98] As a result it was nearly a year before Lockwood found himself in uniform.

The value of even a temporary exemption was immense. It allowed men time to get their affairs in order, and also significantly reduced the chance of being killed. It turned out that Lockwood did not serve in a fighting arm, but he was spared a year of uniformed discomfort.

This system was anything but a model of bureaucratic anonymity. It was rooted in the localities and conducted in the full glare of publicity. One of the paradoxes of conscription in Britain is that the system could only be made to work by a massive volunteer effort. The canvass for National Service registration was entirely voluntary. In Leeds this involved 200,000 separate visits by thousands of volunteers. Who these canvassers were varied from area to area and sometimes within areas. The listing and photographs from Hyde in Cheshire shows them to be predominantly middle-aged men: seventy-one of the canvassers named were male and nine were female. Most of the sub-districts had no female canvassers.[99] After the canvass was completed, the next stage was to constitute the Tribunals.

Neville Chamberlain, active in every voluntary activity, both locally and nationally, noted in a letter in January 1916 that the Tribunal was his 'most tiring work', sitting for seven hours on three days of the week. Charles Repington sat on the Hampstead Tribunal. At the first sitting it took two and a half hours to hear ten cases. In May he abandoned plans to travel to Yorkshire 'owing to the pressure of tribunal work', and in August after a 'long sitting' he did not get home until 9 p.m. In his view 'the Hampstead Tribunal have worked like Niggers'.[100]

The total numbers who served on tribunals must have been substantial: 20,000 minimum and, allowing for turnover, a figure of 40,000 is much more likely. Many Tribunals were sitting twice or more per week from early 1916 onwards. The men who served, for they were overwhelmingly men although some women did sit on Appeal Tribunals, have been aptly described as the type of people who would be approached to verify a passport application – in other words the locally prominent. Thus in Hyde, the Tribunal included the Mayor, a Justice of the Peace, a councillor, a solicitor, the chairman of the board of the local cotton mill and a businessman. It should be noted, however, that Tribunals at both the local and appeal levels were actively encouraged to appoint representatives of labour, usually trade-union officials – the secretary of the local Carders Association in the case of Hyde.[101] The Tribunals were often supplemented by an advisory committee which ruled on exemptions prior to hearings. Repington in Hampstead wrote of the 'advisory committee' that it consisted of a barrister, one 'labour man' and five tradesmen of the 'better class'. The trade unionist was the 'hardest man of all on the poorer classes'.[102]

Some sense of the complex process of recruiting a tribunal can be found in the files of the Bedfordshire Appeals Tribunal. The process was initiated by a memorandum from the local government board written by Walter Long. It called on the chairmen of county councils to choose persons of 'judicial and unprejudiced mind', a phrase underlined in the Bedfordshire copy, who would 'command the confidence of the community'. A fair proportion were to be direct representatives of labour. The Tribunals were not to include those eligible for military service or those who already sat on Local Tribunals, unless they were willing to resign that post, and 'women may be placed on the tribunal with advantage'.

Informal soundings were then made across the county. A Luton businessman, Thomas Keen, was recruited and, in turn, asked to suggest names to represent labour in the town. He suggested several names from the local Amalgamated Society of Engineers, but noted that they would be reluctant to serve unless mandated by a union vote. The President of the Local Trades Council agreed to serve and his employer granted him one day a week to participate. The Council Clerk, meanwhile, was looking for a suitable representative for agricultural labour. This proved difficult because such men were nervous about the expenses involved in travelling to serve on a Tribunal.

Furthermore there were legitimate doubts about appointing someone who would be thought susceptible to landowner influence. It was concluded that what was ideally wanted was 'a man who all his life had been a wage earner but was now independent of everyone'. Finding a representative of urban labour in Bedford proved equally difficult. The name of a Mr Seamark was forwarded, 'an advanced Trade Unionist and Socialist leader – the type of man who ought to be on an Appeal tribunal'. Barbara Prothero was approached to sit as a woman on the Tribunal. She agreed provisionally: 'I should like to do all that I can in the present crisis.' The Tribunal was finally able to sit on 22 March 1916. It was soon swamped with work and indeed in the first three months several members resigned, including Mr Marks, the clerk who had kept the correspondence file.[103]

The Bedfordshire Appeal Tribunal was not directly elected; it was compiled through an extended version of the old-boy network. At the same time there was a scrupulous effort to correspond with the spirit of the original memorandum. When advanced left-wing views were being put forward as a recommendation for Appeal Tribunal service, it is hard to dismiss the Tribunals as failing to secure balance. One weakness was the interpretation of labour representation. Not unnaturally the Tribunal recruiters looked to the ranks of organised labour. But this meant that workers without the protection of a trade union could be seen as peculiarly vulnerable.

The consensus judgement of Tribunals as 'muddled, inconsistent, prejudiced and unjust' springs mainly from their treatment of conscientious objectors and socialist dissenters in particular.[104] There is some truth in this charge, regarding the tiny minority of conscientious objectors, although even there the tribunals could be much more generous than is often realised; but it is much harder to be certain about the Tribunals dealings with the other 98% of appeals.

The best description of a Tribunal in operation, as seen from the bench, is by Harry Cartmell in Preston. Some of the cases before the Preston Tribunal seemed to be drawn from the bumper book of Lancashire stereotypes. In all seriousness, boot repairers presented themselves as clog makers and as such indispensable to local industry. An advocate argued the case for exemption of a tripe dresser on the grounds that tripe, trotters and cowheels were essential food. The Mayor dryly responded that these were very delectable, but 'not perhaps essential'. Subsequently, in Cartmell's own words, 'from tripe to black pudding is an easy transit'. A black pudding maker explained that his wares were very popular amongst the troops. Attempts to automate the process had failed and the job was unsuitable for women. Giving a lurid description of the processes involved, he had no difficulty in convincing the Tribunal that his was not a profession open to dilution. Cartmell claimed that their only hesitation before exempting him was because 'a man accustomed to this sanguinary business might find better scope for his skill in the army'.[105]

The panel found themselves undergoing a rapid and thorough education in the ordinary working lives of Preston men. Impromptu demonstrations of skills were staged before the Tribunal, products were displayed and even on some occasions field trips were carried out to workplaces.

Not everyone appealed in good faith. If the testimony of the many businessmen's sons who appealed on the basis that their father was too old to work at 50 was to be believed, Cartmell suggested that 'senile decay sets in at a very early age in Preston'. Conversely many men in their early twenties were presented as surprisingly indispensable to their businesses, despite the fact that they were only receiving the salary of ordinary assistants. But the social investigation aspect of the Tribunal revealed many cases of quiet virtue, which Cartmell recorded with approval. There was a young man who revealed reluctantly under questioning that, since his mother had died and his father was confined to bed by illness, he was the household's sole wage-earner, but he also cared for his younger siblings and did all the domestic tasks. He was exempted temporarily. Even more striking to the Tribunal was a widower who ran his business whilst bringing up five children 'without female assistance', and who displayed no awareness that he was doing anything remarkable. The Tribunal exempted him unconditionally with praise for his devotion to duty. Referring to unmarried young men who had apparently made the decision to put their own interests second to caring for aged parents, Cartmell remarked, 'we met many heroes of that kind'. Indeed Cartmell believed that young single men had been revealed to be admirable in their familial responsibility, more so than many of the married men.[106] Most of those who appealed in Preston had legal representation. On the whole the local solicitors were conscientious in making a legitimate case for their clients, although in the case of a travelling fairground worker, the solicitor was largely pushed aside by the man's mother who conducted the appeal to the amusement and exasperation of bench and brief alike.

The few remaining solicitors' briefs for Tribunal hearings give a good feel for the process. The firm of Brundrett, Whitmore and Randall preserved a number of files on appeals which went before the City of London Tribunal. An umbrella and walking-stick manufacturer appealed on behalf of two of his employees. One was his accountant and traveller, who was also his brother-in-law. His assistance was needed because the employer claimed defective eyesight. The other appeal was for a skilled worker. The firm had already lost ten out of fourteen men to the colours. There was no chance of substitution: 'even if I could obtain women sufficiently skilled, I could not employ them because the buildings could not be altered to comply with LCC regulations.' The employer needed these men to keep his business going, the profits of which kept himself, his wife and three children. The solicitors charged the not inconsiderable sum of £3 3/- for their advice.

Walking sticks and umbrellas were clearly not an essential industry, but a claim by a family of ironmonger business to maintain the son of military age, centred on their production of 'trench barrows'. The firm had been reduced from twelve to five men, and the unmarried 35-year-old man concerned was 'the only one left who knows anything of the business'.

The most detailed claim was from a small businessman on his own behalf. Both as a snapshot of society in January 1917 and as an example of the hundreds of thousands of detailed appeals being lodged, it requires quoting at length and has been included as an appendix. The appeal was supported by several other documents verifying details of the claim, which was both domestic- and business-related. It illustrates the way that the conscription net was scooping up the owners of small businesses, and illustrates one of the mechanisms they used to cope with this. Amongst the letters included is one from another businessman, who requests that he take over the business in order to keep it going, so that his family will receive support.[107]

Cartmell points out that the Tribunal sat solely to hear appeals against conscription; that it had no power to initiate the process. This was not well understood. The Tribunal received letters denouncing 'shirkers' and demanding that they be called up. The most extraordinary of these came from discontented wives. One woman wrote of her husband, 'I cannot understand him getting off every time ... Come for him now, it will make a better man of him ... he might be the missing link.' Another wrote that her husband 'was impossible to live with through his drunkenness and temper ... I have lost relatives in this War whilst he hides there to live a life of laziness.' In the latter case Cartmell wrote that the lady wanted a separation and felt that the Tribunal would be just as effective as the magistrates, with the added advantage of a regularly paid allowance.[108] In conclusion, Cartmell wrote, 'we were appointed to give effect to a pledge that the circumstances of men should be fully and carefully considered before they were called up to the Army. That pledge was carried out in Preston.'[109]

Chamberlain appears to have been less sympathetic than Cartmell, but also saw humour in the situation:

One man begged to be postponed as unless he were there he did not know what would become of his troop of boy scouts! Another said he made Jews Harps for the export trade. I asked where he sent them to. 'To South Africa mostly, sir.' 'Well' said I gravely, there are a great many jews there,' & the Committee all looked very solemn.[110]

Joking about cases, given the grave nature of Tribunal activity, was to say the least, in bad taste. Frank Lockwood was furious about his Appeal Tribunal hearing even though he was successful. He had been collecting examples of bizarre and perverse Tribunal decisions in the form of press clippings.[111] Immediately after his own first unsuccessful appeal he had clipped an example from Market Bosworth where the men employed by the Atherstone Hunt were exempted on the grounds of their importance in maintaining the stock of horses, and commented, 'could farce go any further?' This did not stop him being hurt when he found himself pilloried in the local press as just such an example. At his successful appeal, it was claimed in the press that his solicitor had argued for exemption on the grounds that as an apprentice mapmaker he would be needed to 'alter the map of the world'. Lockwood was furious to read this, he was a lithographic artist and mapmaking was just a sideline, and it had not been his solicitor who had made the comment but a member of the Tribunal. In his diary Lockwood vents his anger at such comments at both his Tribunal hearings. The joke continued to rankle: he copied a quotation from the popular weekly, *The Passing Show*, which had coined a new definition: 'TRIBUNAL – Formerly a court of justice. Now a collection of local celebrities who send other men's sons into the army.' To which Lockwood added his own bitter coda: 'and make jokes about it'. Lockwood also cited a case of a woman whose seventh son and sole support was conscripted.[112]

But were the Tribunals unfair? Lockwood might have paused to reflect that even if his pride had been offended he had been dealt with generously. The Appeal Tribunal in Huddersfield had in fact used a very loose construction of the law to allow him to finish his apprenticeship and, joking apart, he had been extremely lucky. Repington had initially been suspicious of his colleagues, but quickly concluded that they were 'careful, sympathetic and thorough', and that their decisions were very just. Repington had a *parti pris*, but the image of the Tribunals as tyrannical owes more to the martyrology of conscientious objectors than to social reality. The real problem was less tyranny than apparent whimsicality and the defence of local interests. A memorandum from Auckland Geddes to the War Cabinet in July 1917 complained that 'the present exemption system is based almost entirely on individual or local considerations'. The result was that one Tribunal in a seaside town would exempt all of its bathing box keepers and boatmen on the grounds of the vital interest of 'the national health', whilst another up the coast would indiscriminately call up fishermen. Geddes was worried about the impression given: 'confusion breeds inequality of treatment; inequality of treatment, a sense of injustice; a sense of injustice, hatred; hatred of government revolt and revolution'. Whilst this was overstating a bit, there can be little doubt that compulsion, introduced in the name of fairness, had thrown up its own contradictions.[113]

Duty and sacrifices

The firmest rejection of wartime values could be found in the close-knit circle of 'Bloomsbury'. For many of these Liberal intellectuals and artists, mostly from Cambridge backgrounds, the war was simply a disaster and antithetical to civilisation. Real freedom was the freedom to cultivate the self, to pursue, as an individual, beauty, truth and happiness and to be bonded with others in honesty. In traditional philosophical terms they remained committed to otium and resisted the wartime lure of negotium, civic commitment. There was a snobbishness and complacency intrinsic to this which cannot be overlooked. The comment sometimes attributed to Lytton Strachey, 'I am the civilisation they are fighting for', still has a distasteful ring to it. Yet for all the flaws and accusations of selfishness that could be applied to this stance, it is difficult not to feel that there was a certain real courage in this position. It has to be acknowledged that some of the circle paid a heavy personal price in defence of libertarian values. Bertrand Russell, in particular, could have taken a much easier path than his principled objection to conscription, as the example of his fellow Bloomsbury intellectual John Maynard Keynes demonstrates. Keynes, despite his many misgivings and, indeed, cynicism about the war, dutifully advised on the running of the war economy. Russell, by contrast, suffered the rejection of his colleagues and the threat of imprisonment. In the long term these things helped establish him as the country's leading public intellectual, but this doesn't seem to have been a long-term calculation for him at the time. His bravery should not be questioned.

The fear that the rhetoric of sacrifice was being used to push through infringements of liberty was not confined to Bloomsbury liberals. A 1915 pamphlet, published by the ad hoc 'League of the Man in the Street' (of which the President was W. J. Ramsey, also Vice Chairman of the Metropolitan Radical Federation), attacked the assault on the drinking habits of the working man: 'The average citizen, ready, eager, indeed to make any sacrifice to help his country … has patiently submitted to irritating, unnecessary and useless restrictions which in normal times he would stubbornly have resisted.' But the impositions of 'a noisy *Clique of Teetotalers*', had gone too far, and the league had been formed to defend the 'social relaxation' and 'habitual beverage' of the poorer classes from the assaults of 'cranks and faddists', in their 'insidious attempts to interfere with the rights and liberties of the man in the street'. Instead of the Government 'wasting [its] time in hopeless attempts to make people sober by restrictive legislation', it should save the people from '*exploitation by shipping rings and food speculators*'. The pamphlet even suggested that men would cease to volunteer if they believed their absence would allow the Government of the country to be usurped by 'pump puritans', and that they would not fight the tyranny of German militarism to 'forward the *oppressive tyranny of the killjoy*'.[114] The League was to be open to all 'persons of British nationality'.

John Bull welcomed this defence of the popular freedom to drink. Suspicious of nonconformist agendas it suggested that the whole issue was being promoted to cover for incompetence in high places, 'a mere device to shield ministers … a damnable libel on the working class'. Cartoons were published mocking Lloyd George as a phony St George slaying the dragon, drink. Furthermore it suggested that the advocates of voluntary abstinence actually wanted it to fail so that they could force through prohibition.

In a cartoon 'The Drink Problem solved', *John Bull* recommended:

> Give liberty to sober men
> Who with restraint will use it
> But take away the right to drink
> From loafers who abuse it.

Typically *John Bull* had come up with a 'common-sense' answer which was in fact completely vacuous.[115] Such populist sentiments are hard to categorise in traditional terms as either left or right wing. The defence of popular liberties was what the war was supposed to be about, but liberty was prone to be abused and those who were voluntarily taking the 'moral' path demanded coercion. Libertarian resistance to compulsion in all its forms never died away in Britain during the war. The Labour movement fought tooth and nail against the 'conscription of labour' with a great measure of success. But compulsion and interference gained ground as the war progressed and people lost faith in the ability of purely voluntary measures. The same Labour figures who resisted conscription, military and industrial, were at the forefront of the demand for draconian measures against profiteers, whether in the form of confiscation of wealth, national control of the food supply or the complete removal of property rights in housing. Even within the movement there was growing suspicion that trade unions fighting hardest against 'comb-outs', particularly the engineers, were quite willing to use the cry of liberty whilst fighting the war unto the last unskilled labourer. This loss of faith in good will and voluntary measures was based on an ever-increasing fear that there were many who, for selfish reasons, remained uncommitted, leaving those who took voluntary action shouldering an unfair burden. *The Passing Show* encapsulated the developing mood with a satirical cover cartoon of Asquith dressed as Nelson issuing a 'revised' signal: 'England will be ever so much obliged if every man, will, within reason of course, do a little bit of something or other.' The inadequacy of such sentiments played a large role in discrediting the voluntary ethic of Liberalism.[116]

Eva Isaacs, a young mother who had stoically endured her difficult separation from her husband with a maturity well beyond her youth, was highly critical of the proposed voluntary National Service scheme in a letter to her husband. It was a 'great nuisance'. She resented the idea that conscientious people such as herself were being pressured to encourage their servants to enrol whilst other more selfish people were able to ignore the national need. She stated that she wished the scheme was compulsory and 'entirely out of ones hands'[117] even though she understandably dreaded the additional burden of housework that would fall upon her with the loss of her housekeeper Mrs Flynn, who had been a rock of support to her through a very difficult time. Isaacs was prepared to make serious sacrifices as long as she felt that others in the same situation would do likewise.[118]

Isaacs is fairly consistent on this point in her letters when it comes to sacrificing her own comforts as well. She voluntarily reduces her consumption of bread, meat and sugar when requested, the latter a real hardship for her. She complains about, but accepts, reduced consumption of petrol and coal.

The thing that angers her by 1917 is that voluntary measures are allowing some to 'free ride' upon those who take voluntary action. In almost every sphere she actively welcomes the imposition of regulations and compulsion. This is crucial: state interference and intervention were not forced upon an unwilling populace – they were based upon a popular demand for such interference. Individuals and groups had different ideas about who should suffer most from it. Labour sometimes demanded 'the conscription of riches'; the middle class were more drawn to industrial conscription of the workers. But almost everyone came to feel that the state should compel support for the war effort in the name of 'equity'. If someone as pampered as the daughter of a plutocratic Cabinet minister could be swept along by the rhetoric of equality of sacrifice, it is unsurprising that those with far less to lose found it attractive. The working-out of an economy of sacrifice was at the heart of the war.

4   Economies of sacrifice

The value of blood

On All Saints' Day 1914, the vicar of Bradford preached a sermon entitled 'Precious Blood'. His opening line betrayed a Yorkshire inflection that gives an immediacy to the published version: 'Blood! An awful word is that. A solemn word.' He continued: 'A word that takes you straight to the sublime sacrifice of the Incarnate God. A word which reeks in our newspapers these days.' On All Saints' Day, when, 'we commemorate those who have given themselves, whether in life or in death for the Imperial cause of Christ', then, 'it is obviously fitting that we should think of those who during the last weeks – weeks which seem like years', had given themselves for love of the country. The German Army had been thwarted, great things had been achieved: 'To the noble army of Liberators we pay homage. But the moment we do so we are up against the stupendous fact ... the power which achieved it was one and one only – Sacrifice.'[1]

This was a particularly Anglican version of the universal language of wartime. The relationship between Christian rhetoric and wartime values was an intimate one. This was not accidental, and will be expanded upon later. For the moment it is the issue of this national language and local inflection which needs to be explored. If blood was the currency, how did the books balance?

Sometimes the idea of wartime sacrifice as an economy became explicit. Writing in early 1917, Eva Isaacs tells her husband of a dinner party where one of the guests was Cecil Langton, an officer blinded in the war:

Poor chap, it makes one's heart ache to see him. I feel as if I was his *debtor* for life, for after all it was for me and all of us at home that he lost his sight. I feel much the same to all the wounded I see or for that matter anyone in khaki, they seem to have a tremendous hold on one, nothing one can do is enough & one can never *repay* them for all they have lost or all they have risked.[2] (My italics)

From the opposite end of the social pyramid, we can see a similar idea being expressed. Alfred Reeve, an autodidact Newcastle labourer with a taste for the poetry of Robert Lowell, produced a poem entitled 'The Separation Allowance':

> The money is paid out, there is no eagerness.
> Money for Mons!
> Money for Neuve Chapelle, Loos, The Somme!
> The banks of the universe could not meet the debt –
> All the world's a creditor.
>
> The soldier's wife enters a little city church
> And the door folds her from the clang'rous city street
> I peer through the dim light from sacred windows
> As she kneels and prays
> Hoping with her that he will come back
>
> The world's a creditor
> But if he does not return,
> Heaven will repay the debt.[3]

Similar imagery can be found in other poetry. Moira Armstrong wrote war poems entitled 'The Debt', 'We Are Paying in Blood! We Pay in Blood!' and 'Are We Worthy of the Sacrifice?'

> Filled with overwhelming love and wonder
> Of the vast sacrifice of matchless price
> And some of us, who watch them, sadly feel
> How all unworthy are we of the lives laid down
> Humbly we pray that we may take our share
> Nor leave to them alone the honour or the cost.[4]

This economy received official backing in the form of a heart-shaped medal issued by the women's branch of the new National Service department in 1916. Costing one shilling, 'The pendant of service and sacrifice' was limited to those who could prove that they had relatives serving and was emblazoned at the top with the word 'sacrifice'.[5]

This idea that there was an economy of sacrifice led naturally to the idea that this should be a balanced and equitable economy. The self-evident problem was the practical arbitrariness of the expenditure of the central currency in that economy: blood. In theory this was a universal tax upon the population; in practice it was potentially divisive in terms of region, class and occupation.

'Cook's son, Duke's son, son of a belted Earl'[6]

Death in Croydon

After the war, the London suburb of Croydon produced a long and detailed roll of honour. Compiled by inquiries of families, firms and

associations and using press reports, it is doubtful whether it was absolutely definitive, but it does provide an unusual amount of detail about the
impact of wartime death on a locality. Particularly useful is the fact that 997
of Croydon's 2,504 war dead are listed with clearly identifiable occupations prior to enlistment. Thirty-eight of the dead were professionals,
twenty-one of them were in higher education, eighteen were teachers
and three librarians; combined this represents 3.1% of the total and 8%
of the identifiable occupations. Two hundred and six were in clerical
occupations, 8.2% of the total and 20.7% of the identifiable. Commerce
excluding food trades accounted for eighty-five dead: 3.4% and 8.5%
respectively. The food and drink trades saw sixty deaths: 2.4% and 6%.
The media and communications including printing, journalism, cinema-
tography/photography and telephone/telegraph saw forty-three deaths:
1.7% and 4.3%.

Broadly, the professionals, clerical, commerce and related areas made
up around 17% of the total and about 45% of the identifiable casualties.
Utilities, police, post office and other uniformed workers suffered fifty
dead; transport including the merchant navy sixty-seven dead; skilled
building trades forty-nine dead; the metal trades including apprentices
twenty-five dead; and the 'unskilled' seventy dead, including forty-six
listed as labourers. In total this broad swathe of the working class made
up 10.5% of all deaths and 26% of known deaths. One hundred and
forty-eight deaths fall into a category of 'miscellaneous', a staggeringly
diverse range of occupations including fourteen 'farmers' who were
clearly emigrant, eight domestic servants, mostly chauffeurs, and nineteen
gardeners. 'Miscellaneous' also includes hairdressers, jewellery makers,
cement workers, golf caddies, a billiard cue maker, tailors, bootmakers,
ironmongers, drapers, an apprentice organ builder, an actor, a stage
manager, a cellist, drivers, a park boatman, an undertaker's assistant, a
professional goalkeeper, a 'society entertainer', hosiers, hospital workers,
waiters, a docker, sign painters, a lithographic artist, a car body builder,
cleaners, glass stainers, laundrymen, a chef, a pastry cook and an auction-
eer. They make up 6% of the total and nearly 15% of the known
occupations.

The balance of the dead is 122. They are all men apart from one
woman, already serving with the armed forces in 1914. This roll is not
systematic or definitive. It lists people with Croydon connections, including large numbers with family in the borough who had themselves moved
away. It also lists civilian casualties, including a Belgian refugee who died
of a heart attack during an air raid. It includes men who died of
war-related illness after their return to civilian life, and men who died
serving in volunteer units at home, including those who died up to a year

after the Armistice. Nevertheless it is clear that the roll includes the overwhelming majority of the borough's military casualties and is also, principally, a list of men, resident in the borough on 1 August 1914, who died on military service. All of these figures are minimal. Many of the entries are sketchy and unhelpful.

It is certainly probable that this occupational sample is heavily biased. The occupations of professionals are far more likely to be listed than those of the unskilled working class. Still the prominence of the middle class broadly defined is striking. Those explicitly described as clerks almost equal the known workers from transport, building, metal trades and unskilled labourers combined. Certainly there is distortion, but it cannot be assumed that all professional and clerical workers are listed by occupation. In many cases, prior Territorial or volunteer service is mentioned, rather than occupation. Many of these men appear to be clearly middle class. Counterbalancing this, regular Army reservists were likely to come from lower down the social scale; many of these are also listed only by prior service. So whilst the figure for the commercial and professional middle classes must fit somewhere between a high of 37.5% of all deaths in Croydon and a low of 14.7%, it would be difficult to calculate precisely where it fits. What about those with no occupation listed? A proportion of them are clearly emigrants. A further proportion are probably men already serving in 1914 but not specified as such. There are many listed who look very likely, but it is not unambiguous enough to be sure. Another group must be those enlisted directly from school during the war, and those who had left school but had not settled to an identifiable 'trade' before enlistment. Many other names are listed by employer rather than by job. It is impossible to tell whether someone simply listed as employed by the *Croydon Advertiser* is a journalist, a printer, a clerk, an office boy, a van driver or a sweeper. It is safer not to guess.[7]

Occupational losses are a story of broad patterns and local variants. Nationally, 186,745 railwaymen enlisted and 18,597 were killed – 10.16% of the total. This figure conceals variations. For reasons that are ultimately obscure, the losses of the Great Western Railway were fewer than 2,000 from 25,479 enlisted or about 7.5%. The British American Tobacco Factory at Ashton Gate in Bristol saw 1,255 men enlist and 129 killed, a casualty rate of 10.5%, roughly consistent with the losses of Imperial Tobacco in the same city. J. S. Fry, chocolate manufacturers in the same city, saw 1,050 men enlist and 127 killed, a death rate of 12.1%. But it would clearly be mistaken to confidently state that chocolate makers suffered proportionately more losses than cigarette makers.[8] In any of the smaller samples differential age structures and straightforward random statistical variation skew the picture. The point of greatest danger

was not necessarily where one might think. Shockingly, a Grimsby traw-
lerman who volunteered for the army in 1914 might actually have
improved his life expectancy despite the slaughter of the town's pals
battalion on the first day of the Somme: 5,875 trawlermen were fishing
or minesweeping during the war and of these 1,072 were lost – a death rate
of 18.2%.[9]

Amongst the members of the Accrington Pals who died on the first day
of the Somme there were fifty different occupations listed, reflecting not
only the predominant occupations of the Lancashire towns from which it
was drawn – engineers, coal-miners and textile workers – but also large
numbers of shop workers and clerks, as well as the professional men
amongst the battalion officers.[10]

After all qualifications, two conclusions, which correspond with the
subjective observations of most shrewd observers, can still be proposed.
The first is that 'white collar' workers bore a disproportionate part of the
human cost of the war. It is true that one fairly complete occupational
sample, the London County Council (LCC) Roll of Honour, shows only a
slight bias in this direction:

	Manual Occupations (approx.)	Non-Manual (approx.)
Enlistments	6084	4080
Deaths	614	451
Enlistments	59.8%	40.2%
Deaths	57.7%	42.3%
Deaths/enlistments	10.5%	11.05%

J. L. Robert and J. M. Winter, *Capital Cities at War: London, Paris, Berlin*,
Volume 1, Cambridge, 1997

But this should be treated with caution. The LCC had an unusually large
number of Army reservists in manual occupations in 1914. Furthermore
this only provides one half of the equation – deaths as a percentage of
enlistment. It does not indicate the *percentage of enlistment.*

The second conclusion, which follows from this, is that, despite the
voluntary system and the chaos in manpower planning, the workers
most obviously valuable to the war effort were generally spared.
Although the British manpower budgets didn't operate with the type
of cold-blooded efficiency associated (perhaps wrongly) with the
pre-war conscriptionist powers, the overall result, judged from a rational
military point of view, was not unfavourable. The trade-off for such
inefficiency as there was, in terms of a degree of consent towards the
processes of enlistment, may even have been favourable for both military

and civilian morale. But it would be a mistake to become too enamoured of this view. By 1917 some very real tensions were apparent, based on an unequal blood tax.

Norfolk farmers and others

There is another helpful snapshot of a particular moment in the war in one locality. It is both helpful in establishing figures and in establishing a mood; but for the same reasons it has to be approached with some caution. Walter Rye had taken it upon himself to compile a Roll of Honour for the county of Norfolk. In doing so he became conscious of a disparity. In August 1917 he published a polemical pamphlet comparing the sacrifices of tenant farmers with other occupational groups, a set of statistics that he believed 'might be of some historic value'.[11] Using the local directory for 1912 and making inquiries of individuals and recruiting agencies, he established that in North and East Norfolk there were 1,725 tenant farmers, including their sons. From this number he could firmly establish that 245 were serving or had served in the armed forces. He added twenty-five, 'for men whose names have escaped me, though I think the figure excessive', and concluded that 15% of farmers and their sons had answered the call. He proceeded to compare this figure with lawyers and clergy. Of the lawyers, comparably assessed, of whom there were 211 at the last census, 91 were serving (42%). Of the clergy, 685 at the last census, 231 men were serving (33%). Rye was not perfectly clear on the comparability of his baseline and it is just possible that it is all nonsense. It is impossible to check his figures in detail today. But it wouldn't have been too difficult to do so at the time and Rye was already engaged in a polemic on the subject. An obvious mistake would have discredited him utterly.

So with this qualification noted, this further conclusion on the scale of losses can be presented. As of mid-1917, twenty-three tenant farmers and their sons had been killed, fifteen lawyers and sons, twelve clergy and sons. Comparing these figures with the total population, the 'blood tax' by mid-1917 on each group was:

Tenant farmers	1.3 %
Lawyers	7.1 %
Clergy	1.7 %

Rye doesn't make this calculation, perhaps because it shows that the clergy were not really so different from farmers in this respect. But the comparatively high figure for Norfolk lawyers is very clear. Having made this statistical case, Rye condemns the farmers as a class, betraying his bias and purpose:

As I anticipated, they prove the educated and thinking classes felt the supreme necessity of giving their personal service far more than the farmers, whose slower minds and greater personal interests led them to stay at home and manage what has proved to be a most remunerative business.[12]

Rye's conclusions corresponded perfectly with a growing popular prejudice that tenant farmers were both shirking and profiteering and, worse still, were using their influence on military service Tribunals in the country to exempt each other's families from service. He further suggested a specific accusation:

The worst part of the whole thing is to be compelled to come to the conclusion that there were large parts of East and North Norfolk where bad local influences were brought to bear to stop recruiting, and where, in fact, it was actively discouraged. That the districts that show the worst on the map coincide with spots under certain dominations of religious and political influences *may* be accidental.

It seems unlikely that he would be referring to the Labour Party in the context of tenant farmers; the implication is that this is a jibe at non-conformists and the Liberals. Rubbing salt into the wound, he continued, 'These remarks, of course do not relate to the actual working-man, whether farm labourers or mechanics – they have mustered up a number which we are told makes Norfolk the best recruiting ground in England.' Likewise, Rye praises the contribution of the aristocracy in the districts.

It is not surprising in light of this that one Norfolk farmer, J. H. Bugden, had accused Rye in the *Eastern Daily Press* of 'inciting class hatred'. Bugden and another critic, Mr Davis Brown, presented Rye with a serious problem, which he addressed in a footnote:

Since the correspondence, I have been told that both of these gentlemen have lost a son in the war. No doubt they were naturally hurt at my remarks, which of course referred to a class and not to individuals, and I should not have written as I did had I known this fact.

Whether Brown and Bugden were therefore to be exempt from having 'slower minds' and implicit profiteering is less clear. This specific prejudice against tenant farmers was not unique to Rye. Was it true and did it have a more general applicability? There is good reason to believe that it was and did. Some of the stories circulating may simply have been malicious, although not implausible: one farmer was accused of having got two sons 'starred' as shepherds even though the farm had no sheep. But the record of the *Local Tribunal* in South Caernarvonshire, which had granted exemptions to all but 180 of 1,500 applicants by June 1916, suggests an extraordinary degree of self-interested rural collusion in evading military service. Some of the farmers whose families had responded personally to the call for men were, unsurprisingly, the most bitter about their neighbours. A Cambridgeshire farmer wrote to E. S. Montagu at the beginning of 1916 that a fellow farmer had delivered one of his workers to the Tribunal whilst getting his own son exempted, and that there were ten men working on tasks of no military importance in nearby villages who had been granted exemption. This farmer had had two sons at the front, and one who was sent home for enlistment under age. His view was 'as this is a people's War, all should take their share'. He was sufficiently angry to sever his connection with the Liberal party.

A comparison of the census figures for England and Wales of 1911 and 1921 show a fairly sharp drop (-18%) in the number of farmers' sons and male relatives employed. But it shows an equally sharp rise (+17%) in the number listed as farmers and graziers themselves, and in absolute numbers the former fell by 17,000 whilst the latter *rose* by 36,000. For comparison, there was a fairly large decline in the number of male agricultural labourers, from 622,279 to 549,329 (-12%). Whilst these figures cannot prove a loss differential between the two groups, because they cannot distinguish changes in category or migration, they are not incompatible with the subjective evidence. The most striking decline in the countryside is in the number of gamekeepers listed between the two censuses, which fell from 17,148 to 9,367. This may well reflect high casualties both within this group and amongst their employers.[13]

So was there a serious inequality in losses in the countryside? The Roll of Honour for Tetbury in Gloucestershire suggests a serious discrepancy in the social class of rural casualties. Although occupations are not given, only two of the sixty-eight dead listed were officers. One of these was a pre-war regular.

This evidence raises a final question. Most samples from urban England point to a death rate very slightly below the overall death rate for enlisted men in the British Army. Even Leeds, which had a high ratio of volunteers amongst its enlistments and as a result saw casualties above the urban norm, suffered 11.68% deaths, very slightly below the national average. Was the English countryside making up the balance? There were undoubtedly villages and estates that suffered heavily, for example the memorial for Sandon, Gayton and Marston in Staffordshire shows eighty men enlisted and twenty who died, a figure of 25%. Most rural areas indicate losses above average: the Roll of Honour for Hatfield in Hertfordshire shows 16.2% of the enlisted died in or immediately after the war. The figures for Windermere parish indicate a loss rate of 14.9%.[14] Yet it might not be so simple.

The Tetbury figures demonstrate some definitional problems. Supposedly 560 men enlisted from Tetbury. The analysis by the local historian John Davies points out that this is an implausibly high figure suggesting the enlistment of almost every man of military age in the village. The figure must refer to the district, since the population in 1916 seems to have been circa 5,400. So about 20 to 21% of the total male population served and, of those who did, 12% were killed, a death toll of 1.2% of the total population. But the memorial is for the village rather than 'Greater Tetbury'. As this is less than half the total population, this would imply a substantially higher death toll than the national average – almost double. However, this is also unlikely to be the case for a series of technical reasons. For example it seems likely when examining some of the cases that men being claimed had in fact emigrated well before the war and therefore were absent from the census figure. What we can say with some confidence is that the percentage death toll for Tetbury was higher than the urban average, possibly substantially higher. The figures for Attleborough in Norfolk seem to confirm this. It is claimed that from a total population of 2,500, 550 men served and (depending on definition) 100 or 108 died. As with Tetbury these figures might have to be treated cautiously, but even the conservative estimate suggests a loss rate amongst the enlisted of 18.1%.[15]

But the disproportion between the populations of urban and rural England was such that the male population of rural England would need to be almost wiped out to counterbalance even the slight under-representation of English towns. This clearly did not happen. Given that agriculture *overall* had low rates of enlistment, it may be the case that losses among those enlisted were high, but still not high enough to make up the balance.[16]

County towns and commuter suburbs in England are a more likely source of the 'missing casualties'. Colchester claimed to have lost 1,248 men from a total population of 43,377. At 2.8% of total population this was an exceptionally high figure, even when allowance is made for it being a 'garrison town'. But dozens of such cases would not counterbalance the shortfall of the conurbations.[17]

The ultimate answer as to where the balance came from is that it was probably Scotland. Not only did Scotland have a higher volunteering rate per capita, it clearly had a higher death rate amongst those enlisted, probably as a result of the former. Turriff and district had 2,670 men enlisted in the armed forces of whom 597 died, a death rate of almost 22%; within the district the villages of Crudie and Upper Brae 94 men had enlisted of whom 26 died – almost 28%. Similarly Selkirk had an enlistment of 1,296 and listed 292 deaths, a death rate of 22.5%. Given the previous comments one therefore might expect that retail workers in

Scotland could be expected to have an extremely high loss rate. Yet strangely the Roll of Honour for John Menzies, at that time an almost exclusively Scottish firm, shows a loss rate of 17.1%, far above the British average, but possibly below the Scottish one.[18]

But the John Menzies figure may be a useful control because it lists men who were actually in Scotland in 1914. As with rural England, many of the Scots listed were pre-war emigrants, and there was an even higher proportion in Scottish rural communities. The slipperiness of definitions of what a given community's losses actually were should always be borne in mind. The young male population of the British Isles (and indeed of the British Empire) was highly mobile. With the significant exception of Ireland, men were most likely to be commemorated where their parents lived. Given rural out-migration this produced a natural bias to overstate rural losses and understate urban ones.

Despite this qualification it is clear that disproportionately early volunteering led inevitably to a disproportionately high casualty rate. It is important to be precise about this. Scotland had a higher casualty rate *amongst* the enlisted, but it must be remembered that it *also* had a lower final percentage of men *enlisted* than England. By 1916 the wartime boom in steel, shipbuilding and coal mining had placed a higher than average segment of the male population in reserved occupations. Nor was rural Scotland universally in uniform.

Even in Scotland the problem of tenant farmers specifically evading the call to serve was clearly not unknown. Whether it was serious is difficult to tell: in the Aberdeenshire rural community of Alvah, the service roll shows that thirty-four of those who served were agricultural labourers, ten were white-collar and professional, two were regular Army, two had been schoolboys, fourteen were crofters' or farmers' sons and thirty-three were drawn from retail and manual trades. But in all the categories other than agricultural labourers, a large proportion of those listed were out-migrants. This was particularly true of the farmers, most of whom had left for the Dominions prior to the war.

The perceived 'shirking' of farmers everywhere aroused a certain amount of popular anger and contempt. In Scotland, understandably enough, there is an indication of real bitterness at those who claimed exemption on flimsy grounds. Charles Murray's poem, 'Dockens before His Peers (Exemption Tribunal)', is a vernacular polemic far more vicious than Rye's statistics. 'Dockens', a corrupt and corrupting farmer argues for the exemption of his sons. Urban dwellers are more dispensable:

> There's men aneuch in sooters' shops and chiels in masons yards,
> An coonter-loupers, skleters, vrichts and quarrymen and cyaurds
> To fill a reg'ment in a week, without gyaun vera far.

His eldest son is indispensable:

> There's Francie syne, oor auldest loon, we pat him on for grieve
> An' fegs we should be at a soss, gin he should up an' leave.

But when the Tribunal point to the younger son:

> Fat? Gar him 'list! Oor laddie 'list? 'Twould kill his mother that,
> To think o' Johnnie in a trench awa' in fat ye ca't
> We'd raither lat ye clean the toon o' ony ither twa;
> Ay, tak' the wife, the dother, deem, the baillie wi the mant,
> Tak Francie an' the mairret men, but John we cann want.

By evasion and intransigence the tribunal is worn down. At the end, Dockens calls in old favours:

> Aul' Larickleys, I saw you throu', an this a' my thank;
> An Gutteryloan, that time ye broke, to Dockenhill ye cam' –
> 'Total exemption' Thank ye sirs. Fat say ye till a dram.

There was a widespread urban suspicion that rural Tribunals everywhere were engaged in mutual back-scratching and corrupt deals over a glass of something. But it is obvious that few people were shirkers in their own minds. The standard rural defence was that farming was work of self-evident national importance. The Government desperately wanted to increase food production, an objective that became more and more important as the war progressed. Whatever urban dwellers might think, farmers presented themselves as patriots. Because domestic food supply was so vitally important as the blockade tightened, they *ultimately* avoided popular anger to a surprising degree.

It is difficult to avoid the conclusion that they were helped enormously by the existence of conscientious objectors. Public anger against 'conchies' diverted attention from a problem which, in absolute terms, was a far greater one. Furthermore it was not in the interest of the Government to publicise the issue. It had obvious pragmatic reasons for sheltering farming, and by 1916 the composition of Government had been heavily shifted towards rural interests which had no desire to stir up tension between town and countryside. Murray's poem aside, the Dockens family largely got away with it.

The importance of timing

Differentials in the human toll between occupational groups and classes were compounded by differences in the underlying chronologies of the death toll. Aggregating the British death toll and projecting the impact of casualties on morale from an overall figure misses the essential localism that lay behind casualty lists.

It is important to examine how death impacted on particular groups and localities, but at the same time small samples are vulnerable to the vagaries of statistical variation.[19] To minimise this problem, ideally one needs samples that are reasonably large and complete. Even so a careful attention to biases is required.

In extreme cases local patterns of military service in itself could be wildly divergent, with an important impact on local death tolls. A comparison between Leicestershire and Shetland illustrates this: in Leicestershire, 76.5% of the other ranks' war dead came from men serving with regiments affiliated with the county, whilst only 2% died serving in the Royal Navy;[20] by contrast, 20% of the Shetland war deaths occurred whilst serving in Dominion forces, 29% serving in the Royal Navy or RN Reserve, 17% serving in the Merchant Navy and 34% serving in the British Army, mostly, but not exclusively, Highland regiments.[21] In terms of casualties, Ultima Thule was far less insular than the Heart of England. This had implications in terms of chronology. Leicestershire's casualty lists would increase drastically when local regiments were in battle, Shetland's would be spread far more evenly. This isn't a straightforward comparison of England and Scotland; Shetland was probably peculiar even in Scotland. The 1915 death toll for Arbroath, which is conveniently roughly 100, shows that just over 50% died serving in the Black Watch, another 15% in other Highland Regiments and a further 16% in other Scottish regiments. Losses to a single regiment could seriously affect the chronology of a death toll, particularly in the first two years of the war.[22] An analysis of the London County Council Roll of Honour shows an extraordinarily high death toll of 'white collar' workers in the month of May 1915, a proportion which was far above the national average. The specific reason was the massacre of certain regiments of London Territorials in a futile offensive at Aubers Ridge, which came on top of heavy casualties at Gallipoli and Ypres. The 23rd Battalion of the London Regiment suffered 237 killed, roughly a quarter of its strength, on the 26 May 1915.[23] It is certainly tempting to point to this as a contributory element in several events in the metropolis, such as the widespread anti-German rioting of that month and the fierce public controversy surrounding the 'shell scandal' promoted by the Northcliffe press.

The very specific resonance of the 'blood sacrifice' of the 36th Ulster Division on 1 July 1916 at Thiepval on the Somme had a profound impact on popular attitudes in Protestant Ulster. Likewise the 'Lancashire Landing' at Gallipoli became a focal point in the memory of Bury in Lancashire.

It is therefore important to try to reconstruct the differential impact of losses not only by social strata, but also by examining when they occurred. At the top of the social pyramid, a society columnist in *The Tatler* claimed that by the end of August 1914 'everyone' knew a family in mourning. This may sound hyperbolic, but by the end of 1914 at least three peers and fifty-two sons of peers had been killed in action. This can be compared with losses in the whole of 1917–1918 of six and sixty-five respectively. The aristocracy really did lead the nation into battle and suffered early as a consequence.

To a slightly lesser degree, this can be generalised to a broader section of the British elite. Alumni of Eton College, the most prestigious school in the country, suffered 1,031 combat deaths in the war (and a total of 1,157 deaths). Of these 192 (18.6% of all combat deaths) were suffered before the end of 1914. Roughly half of Eton's total losses had been suffered by February 1916. Given that almost 20.5% of ex-Etonians who served in the war died as a result, it is fair to conclude that losses amongst old Etonians were shockingly high at a very early stage. *The Tatler was* being a little hyperbolic: only about thirteen Etonians had actually died by the end of August 1914, but by the end of the year the statement must have been broadly speaking true.

As always, a degree of caution is useful. An examination of Lancing, a major public school, but somewhat less prestigious than Eton, shows that 820 ex-pupils served in the war, of whom 163 died (19.9%), well above the national average. In this case, the death toll for 1914 was not particularly heavy. There was one death in August and one in September and a further five by the end of the year. A total of seven deaths suggests that at this early stage the losses for alumni of this school were actually well below the national average. This suggests that Lancing was under-represented in the pre-war army. Subsequently the losses began to catch up: thrity-six ex-pupils died in 1915 and a further forty-four in 1916. Despite this, the median date of death was December 1916, at the end of the battle of the Somme. This was a bit later than the national average. Because the *overall* death rate of these alumni was high, it is fair to note that Lancing's ex-pupils *had* suffered disproportionately by the summer of 1916, but a bias towards early losses is far less apparent than in the case of Eton.

The social implications of disproportionate and early losses in 'the best circles' were profound. Cynthia Asquith's wartime diaries show a tightening net of personal bereavement. Not all losses were equal. Initially she is aware of losses in her social circle, but it is the death of her friend 'beloved' Billy Grenfell, a year into the war, which was 'the first that has been much more than vicarious to me'. In October 1915, her brother Yvo Charteris was killed: 'sheer finality and silence – a complete precipice – *nothing* one could do'. She noted ' the extraordinary difference between people – even Billy whom one thought one was so fond of – and one's own little brother'. In July 1916 a second brother, initially reported missing, was confirmed killed and, in September, she responded with a resigned numbness to the death of her brother-in-law, Raymond Asquith: 'Now I feel I have relinquished all hope and expect no one to survive.'[24]

Arthur Gleason, an American with little sympathy for the idle rich, paid a back-handed compliment to the young men of the upper classes, by claiming that 'for the first time in their lives they have found something active to do through noble sacrifice'.[25] There is a good deal of evidence that this is true. The hedonistic youth of the Edwardian summer do appear to have undergone an awakening to the price of privilege, expressed in age-old terms of *noblesse oblige*. It is readily observable in the letters of Eva Isaacs to her husband, doubly poignant and perhaps more forceful in that their respective families, Mond and Isaacs, were Jewish in background and were dismissed by many as *arriviste*, as well as being the targets of some unpleasant anti-semitic slurs from the 'patriotic right'.[26]

Eva found separation agonising, but repeatedly expresses the moral imperative of service. On 12 August 1914 after Rufus enlisted she stated, 'you are doing the only thing that is right'. In November 1916 she admitted that seeing young officers from the War Office made her wish that he would take a home posting but, then, 'I am glad that my man is in France, for I know it is right.' In December she mentioned her pride in being able to tell people her husband was on the Somme. She concedes that Whitehall remained 'tempting', but 'the duty we submit to is as you say greater & more powerful than ourselves'. It would 'compel us by force if we did not follow it voluntarily, but it compels our minds & souls to acknowledge its right & so find honour in following it ... it is like a purifying fire that cleanses us by supreme sacrifice'. In January, when Rufus returned to the front from a short leave, 'I would not keep you ... I know you could not be content to be at home ... if others can stick it so can we.' At the end of the month, 'when one meets men who have been wounded & are going out again, one is glad that one can say that ones very own man is out there too.' She admits that she was very glad that he was temporarily out of the danger zone, but she was also 'very proud that you have been there'.

These sentiments might seem utterly conventional, nevertheless they were quite clearly heartfelt: few other writers repeat them with such insistence and consistency. They were not based on any illusions about the nature of the war. Eva is openly contemptuous of the 'eyewash' of the press. It is quite clear that her husband's frank descriptions of the front line whilst he was on leave had horrified her. These impressions would soon be reinforced by graphic descriptions from her brother who went out to France in 1917. In the latter case she wrote to her brother agreeing that the grim details of a bombardment he had experienced were best withheld from their parents. The best evidence of her realism about the trenches is that when Rufus was appointed to a job at brigade staff, she was genuinely relieved. She squared this with her sense of their social obligations on the grounds that he had already done his share. Even *noblesse oblige* had limits.

Did the courage and disproportionate early losses of the elite serve as a cement for the existing order? Some hoped that it might. Arthur Gleason reports a conversation with a 'distinguished English writer', who asked him: 'Do you think working men will ever feel bitterly again, now that they have seen their officers leading them and dying for them?' It wasn't a totally unreasonable question, and it is worth pointing out that in the brief flurry of 'soldiers' soviets' in 1917 one of the demands of the ordinary soldiers was that more respect should be paid to the junior officers of the infantry. In 1915, *John Bull* had repeatedly returned to the theme. Conflict between the 'masses and the classes' had ended in the trenches as soldiers learned to respect their officers. A cartoon in September showed a workman and noble in khaki shaking hands: 'Now we understand one another.'[27]

Although class barriers were in no respect dissolved in the trenches, public-school officers and working-class soldiers do seem to have developed a remarkable degree of mutual respect. But Gleason's response was still apt: 'It did not occur to her to inquire how gallantry in an infantry officer would prove a substitute for a living wage.'[28] The hedonistic behaviour of some of these junior officers whilst on leave exacerbated the problem. Diana Manners and Duff Cooper, who later married, were very much involved in the fast set of the well-connected, and both make extensive reference in their memoirs to the atmosphere at the time, using their original diaries. For Manners the mid-war period was a 'dance of death', a wild attempt by doomed gilded youth to experience a final period of pleasure.

The literal decimation of social elites of military age by the end of 1916 led Lord Lansdowne, the most 'ultra' of Tories, to a pessimistic conclusion which was the polar opposite of Gleason's anonymous writer. The war had to be stopped before the elite were exterminated and the country slid into revolution. Lansdowne's view was untypical; generally these losses strengthened rather than weakened resolve, but amongst social elites it is possible to see the experience of bereavement as generalised to the point of trauma, a phenomenon of some importance in constructing the post-war idea of a 'lost generation'.

In small rural communities the impact of chance, statistical variation and local circumstances made for an uneven toll. The village of Bowerchalke in Wiltshire suffered sixteen deaths in the course of the war. Three of these were in June 1916, a generally unremarkable month; whilst none of them were in July, August or September of that year, three of the bloodiest months of the war. Great Leighs in Essex suffered eighteen deaths; precisely half of these occurred in just four months of the war, October 1914, May 1915, November 1917 and October 1918. For both of these villages the median date for deaths came in 1916, June for Bowerchalke, October for Great Leighs.

Casualties in rural Scotland appear to have been spread more evenly. The thirty war dead of King Edward's occur on nineteen separate months, with the median date July 1916, coincidentally the bloodiest month with four deaths. Nevertheless variation was equally possible in Scotland: of the thirty-seven known dates from Marnoch, the median is as late as May 1917, which is also the bloodiest month with five deaths. There is only one death in July 1916.

Industrial towns were even more vulnerable to particularly catastrophic losses associated with a single battle. The decimation of the pals battalions of the industrial north on the first day of the Somme is too well known to require lengthy repetition.

For London, 1 July 1916 was just a particularly bad day amongst many such, and the same was true for Glasgow; but for Bradford, Newcastle, Belfast and many other towns it was definitely the worst day of the war. The Leeds civic history devotes two pages to the impact of the battle on the city.[29]

On the 1 July 1916, 235 men of the 'Accrington Pals' battalion were killed, 17 more died of wounds sustained and a further 350 were wounded. To some extent the battalion was misnamed; the more prosaic official title, 11th East Lancashire Regiment was just as accurate, since only about half the battalion came from Accrington and district, and large numbers actually came from surrounding towns, particularly Chorley. Indeed, by 1 July the battalion had received a draft of 78 Yorkshiremen from Hull. Nevertheless about half of the battalion dead on 1 July were from Accrington.

During the course of the war as a whole 865 men from Accrington and district died.

So losses on the first day of the Somme represented about one in eight of Accrington's war dead. It is unsurprising that the town chose the sixth anniversary of the battle to dedicate the war memorial. The horror of

1 July 1916 has in recent years become a definitive image of the war, but, although no part of the nation was left entirely untouched, it was essentially a sectional tragedy. The high proportion of losses on 1 July was not universal: about one in forty of the nation's dead fell on that day.

Even towns that suffered as badly as Accrington on the Somme would experience other bad moments. The battalion was painfully rebuilt in 1917, but in 1918, the 'pals' would suffer 240 killed, missing and wounded at Arras at the end of April, and 370 killed, missing and wounded in clearing Ploegstreet Wood at the end of September. By the middle of 1918 the battalion had been rebuilt by drafts from all over the country, lessening the local impact of such battles, but even so Accrington and Chorley would suffer smaller scale 'black days'.

The Battle of the Somme, not just on 1 July but on subsequent days as well, could overshadow even large urban areas because of the nature of associational recruiting. On 8 July 1916 Neville Chamberlain wrote to his sister that he was 'rather depressed. Birmingham has been hit with a vengeance this time & both the City Batts and the Territorials have been terribly cut up.' Chamberlain was busy writing condolence letters: 'One of our Councillors is killed, two of our principal officers have lost their sons and among our own friends Harry Field's son, Harry is killed and Guy is missing & Arthur Dixon, Hallewell Rogers, Cary Gilson, Harry Marin and many others have had a son in the list who is dead ... That is the worst of local battalions, it does hit a district when they get cut up.' A week later he wrote to his other sister that 'two of our Territorial battalions have been wiped out'.[30]

The Battle of the Somme continued for five brutal months. Some communities which had been spared heavy losses on the first day would still suffer disproportionate casualties before it ended. A particularly clear example is the district of Ruthin, Denbighshire. During the course of the war ninety-nine men from the district died. Up until 1 July, Ruthin had suffered eighteen deaths. During the battle it was to suffer a further thirty-three, precisely one-third of the wartime death toll. The reason is obvious: the deployment of locally recruited units of the 38th Welsh Division in the battle from end of the first week of July.[31]

July 1916 was a bad month for most large communities, but it was not automatically the worst month throughout the country. Local variants were very strong. In Guildford, for which we possess a good record, July 1916 was the second-worst month of the war, but overall the Battle of the Somme was only the first of four bad periods and not the worst.

Guildford known dates of death (437 cases from August 1914 – July 1919)

	1914–1915	1915–1916	1916–1917	1917–1918	1918–1919
August	0	4	6	7	19
September	6	8	12	14	19
October	5	4	8	19	12
November	10	1	4	14	16
December	4	2	4	15	5
January	1	1	2	4	1
February	3	1	4	5	7
March	2	6	2	16	3
April	3	4	16	25	1
May	15	6	7	5	1
June	0	4	4	10	1
July	2	22	15	9	0
Year total	51	73	80	143	84

This table tells a striking story. The median date for fatalities from Guildford was August 1917. The worst single month was April 1918. Although not unscathed for the first three years of the war, the agony of casualties intensified rapidly from the opening of the battle of Passchendaele. More than half of Guildford's war losses were concentrated in four clearly identifiable periods, three of them after this point. Fifty-two deaths came during the Battle of the Somme; eighty-four during the battles of Passchendaele and Cambrai in 1917; fifty-six during the German Offensives of spring 1918; and sixty-six during the final Allied Offensives and the influenza epidemic. The post-Armistice death toll illustrates the continued significance of the latter.

Guildford's losses are substantially and significantly later than the national average. This seems true at every stage: Guildford had its first war death in September 1914.

It would be dangerous to generalise from Guildford to the south east of England. Very local features were at play, such as the precise operational record of the local regiments. For example, Todmorden in Lancashire shows a similarly 'late' profile of losses:

4 August to 3 August	1914–1915	1915–1916	1916–1917	1917–1918	1918–1919
Deaths	61	86	175	219	119

J. Lee, *Todmorden*, pp. 162–3

Like Guildford, Todmorden had a median date of August 1917 and, similarly, Todmorden suffered horrendously during Passchendaele, with seventy dead and forty missing, which was worse than the Somme. There were also seventy deaths between August 1918 and the Armistice.

Hornchurch in Essex provides a third 'late' profile. The information is fairly incomplete, but where the month of death is given in the record, the picture is conclusive:

Year	1914	1915	1916	1917	1918	1919
Deaths	3	8*	26	33	40	5

*This figure is too low – a number are listed simply as missing or dead at Gallipoli, but were excluded for strict comparability.
C. Perfect, *Hornchurch*, Roll of Honour

Once again, late 1917 appears to be the median. There is a risk of distortion towards better reporting of later casualties. A memorial in Willesden in North London has a distinctly peculiar profile:

Year	1914	1915	1916	1917	1918	1919
Deaths	2	3	12	4	20	10

C. Macintyre, *How to Read a War Memorial*, pp. 58–60

Whilst it is possible that Willesden suffered more than half of its war-related deaths after spring 1918, it seems very unlikely.

For Hatfield in Hertfordshire, the known dates of death are somewhat more evenly spread, but there is still a 'late' bias:

August–July	1914–1915	1915–1916	1916–1917	1917–1918	1918–1919
Deaths	12	24	38	45	18

In Hatfield the median date falls at the start of Passchendaele. In this case it doesn't seem likely that this is caused by biases in reporting. Taken in conjunction with other evidence, there is some reason to think that the perceived casualty burden of the war as a whole was intensifying, particularly in the Home Counties from the middle of 1917. To conclusively demonstrate this would require more evidence, but as a hypothesis it is not implausible. This would not be surprising. Heavy early casualties in the social elites and the expansion of the army meant that the recruitment of junior officers had to be broadened and junior officers were peculiarly vulnerable in combat. In broad statistical terms, Scotland aside, the population was being killed in order of social precedence. By the second half of the war these losses were reaching deep into the lower middle class.

One example of the high rate of officer casualties in the south east can be drawn from the Hove Roll of Honour. The ranks of those listed dead and missing presumed dead reveal that Hove lost 474 other ranks and 121 officers. Just over 20% of all Hove's losses died with a commission. This can be compared with the county of Leicestershire which suffered 443 officers dead and 8,905 other ranks, indicating that commissioned ranks made up less than 5% of Leicestershire's dead. In the case of Tetbury, mentioned above, officers were less than 3% of the total. Whilst Hove's officer casualties must have started amongst the social elite, they obviously cannot have been confined to it. Hove must actually have seen officer losses extending down into a much broader swathe of the middle classes.

Duff Cooper in a letter describes the social composition of his little group of officer cadets training in 1917. Four out of the six were ex-rankers. One is identified as a Nottingham shoemaker; the rest, apart from himself, appear to be lower middle class, from a wide range of regional backgrounds.[32] Whilst the replacements for the social elites were drawn from a wide sub-urban and middle-class pool, it was natural that the service economy of the south east would be disproportionately affected. The potential for resent-ment was very real. This will be explored subsequently.

Chronologies of loss mattered; the war did produce a steady back-ground of losses, even during the relatively quiet winter months, but social groups and geographical areas also suffered sudden moments of mass loss. The social elites were hit hard and early: Scotland suffered badly in 1915; London reeled briefly in May 1915 and then had a series of bad months throughout the war; the first day of the Somme saw devastation visited on many northern English industrial communities and the continuation of the battle saw other communities drawn in (including, of course, the Dominions). Finally there is some reason to suspect that the suburban south east saw a marked acceleration of losses in 1917–1918.

The social, cultural and political impact of these variations mattered.

Soldiers and civilians

Is there any man, woman or child who does not think of the men in the trenches? Most people are so impregnated by the war, that they live with it, they sleep with it and eat with it. It enters into every thought and action, it is never absent, either awake or asleep. (Frederick Robinson, diary entry for 19 March 1918[33])

Robinson was reacting angrily to yet another exhortation to think of the soldiers.

5. Post for the Army. IWM (Q 54267).

In an attempt to express the mood of Britain in 1917, Arthur Gleason, an American social commentator, interviewed various statesmen and writers. He concluded that none of them 'had quite revealed the central flame'. Instead he pointed to the case of a wage-earning girl in London who every day commuted past the Fishmonger's Hall which was serving as a military hospital, and who hand-delivered a letter which he quoted:

Dear Sir,
   I am taking the liberty to write to you to ask if it is true that often soldier's wounds could be the easier and the better healed were there plenty of skin available to graft onto a wound … I am prepared to give as much as would be practicable to take from me.
   This is no impulsive movement on my part. I am obliged to come to town each day to earn my own living and am therefore debarred from working for the soldiers as other girls of my own age are doing. I have two brothers fighting, and for their sakes, I feel I must do something. I am writing to your hospital because I know of nowhere else.[34]

Gleason was an Anglophile, although not an uncritical one. His book was written to influence American opinion in favour of Britain. This letter could be dismissed as propaganda or even invention. Despite these reservations, it is likely to be real. Gleason, where he can be checked, seems reliable and this letter is, in context and content, very plausible. It is worth pondering the centrality he gives this idea of sacrifice, as embodied not in the rhetoric of leaders, but in a very literal sense, by an ordinary female clerical worker.

The alienation of soldiers from civilians is such a literary stereotype of the war that the obvious point has been forgotten; the two were inevitably intimately linked in countless ways. The constant flow of letters to and from the armies and leave, increasingly regularised, although never frequent enough from the soldiers' point of view, maintained the links.

Soldiers could not fully express their experiences and emotions about front-line service – such alienation is common to all wars – but they tried to recount conditions far more than is sometimes realised, and were listened to by their friends and relatives, much more so than is usually acknowledged. Harold Cousins recounts in his diary in early 1916 a horrendous account of the battle of Loos which he heard first hand from a former office colleague home on leave: three months later the bodies were still unburied, causing 'a dreadful stench'.[35] This is one of several such cases. Similarly, Elizabeth Fernside in a letter to her son gives an account, heard from a relative, of Passchendaele as a dismal disaster. Robert Saunders was shocked by the condition of one of his sons home on leave in 1917 and clearly spoke to him at length about the front. Eva Isaacs evidently knew a great deal. Indeed it is difficult to find a contemporary civilian account that doesn't demonstrate a fairly high degree of knowledge about conditions at the front. No one was entirely convinced by the more romanticised and sanitised accounts that appeared in the media, and the media itself was far more honest about front-line conditions than legend suggests. That there was ultimately an existential gap should not be denied. A 1916 poem entitled 'Home Again' expresses it well:

> They give us sweets and picture books and cigarettes and things
> And speaks to us respectful-like as though we all was Kings ...
> And we talks a bit to please them when the ladies come to call,
> But the things that we have seen and done, they 'aven't seen at all ...
> The're things that don't bear thinking of and things you never tell;
> It's a waste of breath to talk to folk who haven't been in 'Ell.

This sentiment is the essence of many post-war memoirs and poems. It is therefore significant that this was written by a female civilian at the height of the war.[36]

The bonds between civilians and soldiers were not broken by war on either side. A poem published by Aimee Eagar in 1916, dedicated to the memory of her brother and two nephews and entitled 'Our Heroes', indicates a far greater sensitivity to the plight of the soldiers than the title would suggest:

6. Policewomen and soldiers on leave. IWM (Q 31090).

> It is not 'glory' in man's blood to deal,
> Man's blood outpoured upon the teeming earth.

It emphasises both the suffering of the soldiers and their families:

> Glory and Honour? Not to sit afar
> And look for news that may be news of death;
> Pride of battle? Not for those who wait
> With long drawn out suspense and baited breath.
>
> I am no traitor to my country, I,
> If in a ruined home I sit apart
> And watch my orphaned children, and awhile
> In silence listen with a broken heart.

Soldiers had families – something so blatantly obvious that it wouldn't need mentioning were it not for the fact that it is possible to read whole anthologies of First World War prose and verse without being provided with any suggestion of this fact. Such is the emphasis on the emotional bonds between the soldiers in the most famous literature of the war that the significant bonds with the home front have disappeared from view. Compared with the paeans to fallen comrades, expressions of domestic affection inevitably do not rise to great literary heights; but they are there for those who care to look, and mediocre poetry is usually more representative than the first-rate. Dyneley Hussey, a Lieutenant in the Lancashire Fusiliers wrote for 'Francesca in Her Cradle':

> Ah! How blest thou art Francesca,
> In this reign of murderous might
> To be infant and unwitting
> Of the world's tremendous blight.

Eric Wilkinson, a Lieutenant in the Leeds Rifles dedicated his little book of poems, 'with deep affection to the Dearest parents a man ever had', several of the poems address them directly. He wrote for each of them on their birthdays:

> Little mother, Little mother
> How I'd like to see you now.

For his father's birthday, whilst he waited to go into action on the Somme, he wrote the poem 'Dad o' Mine':

> Mid-summer Day, and the mad world a fighting ...
> Yet for one day, we'll let all slip behind us
> So that your birthday, Dad, still may remind us
> How strong, yet supple, the bonds are that bind us.

Such emotions were liable to take on a 'birthday card' quality when poetically expressed and this was no exception, but clichéd sentiments are not by definition any less true. Fathers and mothers, children, wives and sisters, were not aliens to most soldiers – they were precisely the people they were fighting for.

Civilians reciprocated with deep respect. Even those with little personal connection to the war were loath to treat the soldiers' conditions with anything but the highest consideration. Robert Roberts many years later remembered being disciplined by his mother for singing the song 'Oh What a Lovely War'. She told him in no uncertain terms that it was offensive to the men who were undergoing such terrible hardships. He pleaded in vain that it was a soldier's song and was meant ironically, but she felt strongly that such sentiments were entirely inappropriate to civilians. A pamphlet addressed to children advised them: 'avoid selfishness like poison ... our soldiers are doing as much for you. Remember them and follow their example.'[37]

The idea that civilians were indifferent to the suffering of the soldiers is manifestly absurd. The suffering of soldiers stood at the very centre of wartime values. Some apparently trivial but actually significant stories from 1916 make the point eloquently. There was an increasingly angry demand that private 'squares' in wealthy areas of London be opened for the use of wounded soldiers. Likewise there was a demand that wounded soldiers be given priority in first-class seating on commuter trains. Neither is perhaps very surprising until considered in light of the status consciousness of British society and the high regard given to property rights. In each case rights conferred by mere money were being told to make way for the higher claims of blood. This was not a revolutionary sentiment – levelling for its own sake was not generally a popular demand – but an acknowledgement that the hierarchy of values had changed significantly as a result of the war. No one stormed Buckingham Palace in 1917, but it was frequently used for garden parties for wounded soldiers. The paramount moral claims of soldiers and their families were widely acknowledged, but who were those claims made against?

Profiteers

The question of relative sacrifice in financial terms was addressed by a Government memorandum on soldiers' pay and benefits in September 1917. It cheerfully concluded that soldiers were doing reasonably well out of the war. Taking together the pay, benefits and separation allowance, it concluded that the recompense for a non-commissioned soldier with a wife and two children ranged from 47/6d minimum to 94/6d maximum and for a single man between 30/- and 73/6d. By implication, the best-paid common soldiers, NCOs and technical specialists, were doing better than skilled munitions workers, and the 'Poor Bloody Infantry' were being recompensed in line with the unskilled.

As with many attempts at quantification, the result depended on the assumptions. The reasoning would be familiar to cost accountants in higher education. A substantial component of the 'recompense' was benefit in kind. The soldiers were being provided with an estimated 20 shilling value in 'board and lodging'. It isn't difficult to imagine the reaction of men desperately searching for a 'better hole' in the muddy shell swept wasteland of Passchendaele if they had known that their improvised trenches and cold Machonochie stew had been valued by the Government bean counters at a pound a week.[38]

Inept as it clearly was, this was at least an attempt to tackle the problem of relative sacrifice. Blood was being shed, and the question had to be asked whether there were immoral monsters who were growing fat as a consequence. A letter in August 1917 from G. V. Wellesley, an ex-Etonian officer known as 'father', to *Chin-wag*, the newsletter of the Eton Manor Club in East London, attacked the perceived greed of workers:

What shall we say to the Amalgamated Society of Engineers who last week proposed to strike for higher wages? Has it ever occurred to them that their fellow country men in the trenches are hourly facing mud and misery, exhaustion, shells, gas, death – all for a paltry 10/ – and their keep, without the power or the wish to strike for higher wages? For these it is enough that they fight for their country. *Let that also be good enough for those who work at home.*

There is no need to wear a long face. *Keep yourselves and others cheerful and get on with your jobs.* (Original italics)

Whether the young working-class readers of the newsletter took this to heart is unknown.[39]

Supposedly greedy workers were one but by no means the only group accused of turning blood into money. In Chester 'that curse of every civilization began to thrive – the "War Profiteer". He drew his representatives from every social class. What did our city folk say? "All profits made during the war were the price of the blood of those who fought without hope of monetary reward."' The image of the profiteer was the image of the vampire.[40]

A significant amount of this vocabulary, which became pervasive in wartime, appears to have had its origins in pre-war socialist rhetoric. The *Daily Herald* was using two key words well before they were generalised. On 31 July 1914, it stated that a war would bring 'Gore for the worker and gold for the shirker.' The next day it published a cartoon with the caption: 'Even the war cloud has a silver lining for the profiteer.'[41] This rhetoric spread very quickly in the first months of the war, in part one suspects because local Labour men were making their voice heard at local meetings protesting rising prices. On 12 August the *Daily Herald* commented on the perception of double standards:

In Staffordshire a man has been fined … and another sent to prison for smashing windows of shops where the price of provisions was alleged to have been raised. From no part of the country do we hear of the prosecution of those who are trying to grow richer by squeezing the poor. They do not offend against class law – only the moral law.[42]

Yet the socialists were also aware that this was a stance that had spread rapidly beyond socialist circles.

In an ironic cartoon comment on 14 August 1914, the *Daily Herald* showed a fat 'John Bull' carrying a banner inscribed: 'To seek private profit at public expense is today a crime against the nation.' The moral was supposedly: 'All England is socialist today'; but the newspaper made it quite clear that this rhetoric should be treated as superficial.[43]

'John Bull', in the shape of Horatio Bottomley's weekly, *John Bull*, was soon waving exactly the banner that the *Daily Herald* claimed as its own. In early January 1915 it referred to the 'War Prices Swindle', claiming 'The noble British pirate is at his game again. One after another essential commodities have risen in price.' The blame was placed on 'shipping

rings'. A cartoon of 'The New Deity' showed a fat 'capitalist' being
beseeched by a ragged woman and her children. On his waistcoat was
the legend 'Wheat and shipping rings', and he clutched a fat bag marked
'war profits'. Editorially the paper commented on the 'brigands who are
robbing the widows and orphans of our soldiers and sailors ... our own kin
fatten off our own lean bodies ... they pray and philander whilst they
plunder the gallant men who are being maimed and killed.' Criticisms of
war profiteering were more than a little bizarre when voiced by Bottomley.
His body was anything but lean and he was a swindler of epic proportions,
indeed not averse to preying on widows and orphans while voicing pieties.
The resemblance between the 'New Deity' profiteer and the regular
portrayal of 'John Bull' himself leads the reader to suspect the cartoonist,
Frank Holland, might have been engaged in a private joke at Bottomley's
expense.[44]

This rhetoric sharpened in intensity and frequency in 1917. In January
the *Daily Herald* remarked: 'this is undoubtedly a lovely war for some
people, the official estimate of excess profits to April was £86,000,000'. In
April, A. G. Hales blamed the 'profit pirates' for jeopardising victory.
According to the paper, bread was dear, not because of shortage of supply,
but because of the dirty practices of cartels: a baker who had tried to sell
cheap in Abertillery was forced to make more profits when threatened
by a boycott from the mills at the behest of the local Master Bakers
Association. Potatoes were being kept off the market deliberately to
increase prices. An internal memorandum from Sainsbury's showed
them withholding tea and sugar until prices increased. The weekly published the 'Song of the Profiteer':

> Some people declaim on the blessings of peace, but not many tradesmen,
>   I'll warrant:
> The profiteer was immune to public censure:
> By some profiteering is reckoned a crime,
> Like murder though rather less gory,
> Such persons are rather too moral for words.
> They sheltered behind the fighting man,
> Kept safe by the lads who are fighting abroad ...
> And dying in thousands, I'm told,
> The profiteer gloats on the growth of his hoard.

The profiteer positively revelled in others' misfortune: 'here's to the war
that is making us rich, while it takes the last copper from others'.
Indicative of a leftward shift in the tone of *John Bull* in 1917, this representation climaxed with a cartoon by Frank Holland showing a worker
assailed by top hat wearing leeches labelled 'profiteers'. The profiteer was
now not only battening on the soldier, but also upon the working man.[45]

This shift was apparent earlier in *The Passing Show* which published a poem entitled, 'Socialists, Forward', suggesting that the nation should become 'Socialists, pro-tem'. From a publication which had usually tended to side with small business this was remarkable, but rising prices were forcing the issue: 'now in wartime when one hears, complaints of grasping profiteers'. The state should commandeer food supplies 'to squelch the domestic foes who bleed. Our people in their time of need.' In a 1917 cartoon, an exasperated customer is shown saying to a pork butcher, 'I said how much is a pound of chops, not what is the daily cost of the war.' Images of profiteers now regularly appeared on the cover, such as one of a pig in a top hat marked 'profiteer' surrounded by money bags.[46]

By 1917 profiteering had become a widespread term of abuse, a central concept in the discourse of the war. So ubiquitous was the discourse of profiteering that it is sometimes dangerously tempting to see it as only a discourse and forget that it described a social practice, one moreover which was in certain cases legally defined. In August 1917, the Ministry of Food began arguing for a harder line against profiteering shopkeepers. Messrs Little and Ballantyne were prosecuted at Carlisle at the request of the Ministry. Fourteen charges were laid and illegal profits of £216 were proven. But the firm was only fined £80: 'No clearer case of illegal trading in potatoes has been established and the fact that on conviction the magistrates merely deprived the offenders of one third of their illegal gains is discouraging.'[47] Prosecutions under the food orders gathered pace as the month progressed. Messrs Gunn & Co. of Liverpool were fined £180, and a Cardiff greengrocer £100, for selling potatoes for illegal profit. Seventeen defendants in Luton were fined for obtaining sugar by false declarations. In London a magistrate announced his intention of imprisoning repeat offenders.[48] In September, George Thompson, a farmer from Long Sutton in Lincolnshire, was charged with fifty-five infringements resulting in an illegal profit of £5,525. He was fined £5,500 and £250 costs, but the Ministry remained disappointed having pressed for imprisonment in addition to the fine.[49] Cases such as these indicate that tangible profiteering could be discovered. In a more general sense, there were some indications of excess retail profits. Comparing wholesale and retail prices in August, the Ministry pointed out that whilst the wholesale price of beef had fallen 10% in the month, the retail price had risen slightly and that there was no change in the wholesale prices of frozen mutton, tea or sugar to account for the rise in the retail prices of these items.[50] At the same time the memorandum clearly indicates that these were the exceptional items and that otherwise retail prices had risen, fallen or stayed the same in line with wholesale.

The final point is crucial. Whilst profiteers unquestionably existed, it was wartime inflation in itself which was creating the perception of profiteering. In this context the issue of prosecuting profiteers placed the Government in an impossible double bind. Failure to prosecute would lay the Government open to the charge of conniving with profiteering. But every well-publicised prosecution became evidence of the existence of profiteering and confirmation of the belief that it was profiteers who were causing the rise in prices.

Next to retailers, the second major target of profiteering accusations were manufacturing capitalists and mine owners. This was perfectly understandable because it became the rationale for industrial militancy. It is unsurprising that it was the South Wales Miners' Federation which presented a table of figures for their industry to demonstrate how mine owners' profits were outstripping wages.

% of turnover	Wages	Profits
April 1910 – June 1915 (average)	67.00	9.60
June 1915 – June 1916 (average)	61.79	16.35
July 1916	56.46	24.05

Gleason, *Inside the British Isles*, p. 322

The straightforward implication of this was that profits were achieved by holding down wages – a moral justification for strikes, which were not therefore against the nation, but against profiteers. Such figures were obviously self-interested, and coal owners vigorously denied or explained them. But the published profits of the Lewis Merthyr mining company showed a marked wartime increase, which certainly seems excessive. Profits in the four years up to 1914 had been a respectable £98,000; during wartime they averaged £200,000 annually. This was somewhat above inflation, but also undoubtedly an underestimate, because the company reserve rose £220,000 in 1917 alone with a further special reserve of £100,000, and in 1918 a profit of £418,807 was declared.[51]

Gleason cites published figures for parts of the textile industry. Fore Street Warehouse Company had made a profit of $140,000 in 1914 and $315,000 in 1916; even allowing for inflation this was more than respectable. Apparently even more blatant was the case of the Pawson and Leaf drapery house where 1913 profits had been £7,639 and 1915 profits were £35,853.[52]

The largest single survey of wartime profit-making was the investigation by the *Economist* of the declared profits of joint stock companies. The survey of just under a thousand companies (numbers obviously varied from year to year), indicated that the average profits initially declined, probably reflecting the initial onset of wartime depression, but that overall profits began to show a sharp rise as the economy moved into high wartime gear.

Financial year	1913–1914	1914–1915	1915–1916
Average profits	£76,000	£72,000	£93,000

S. Litman, *Carnegie Endowment: Prices and Price Control during the War* (Oxford, 1920), p. 71

As with retailers, the relationship between fact, rhetoric and official attitudes was complex. In this case, the Government walked a tight-rope. Accusations of capitalist profiteering were potentially dangerous, but they were also useful. If the condemnation was allowed to get too far out of hand it would be very dangerous in terms of labour unrest. But within limits it was an extremely useful weapon against manufacturers in order to keep the cost of the war under control. A public rhetoric of profiteering could be used as an excuse to fix prices and impose taxes.

This may explain the extraordinary tolerance afforded to such rhetoric.[53] In fact, the real kings of profit-making by 1917, were almost certainly neither retailers nor industrialists, but farmers. A survey of farm profits per acre, roughly half of it arable in 1917, shows the average gross profit per acre running at 445% the level of 1913–1914. While it is certainly true that, prior to the war, farming had been a rather unprofitable business, this baseline, 1913–1914, had actually been a better than average year.[54] To this should be added four further considerations. First, these were *average* profits per acre, so some farmers must have been doing considerably better. Second, farmers had a very favourable tax regime up to 1917 by comparison with other groups. Third, these are profits per acre, but some farmers were actively expanding the acreage farmed. Finally, these are legal profits. Unscrupulous farmers, such as the Lincolnshire man cited above, could make even greater profits. Whilst these profits were made, to some extent, by cutting down on certain expenses to the long-term detriment of viability, it is also worth remembering that the inflationary pressures in the countryside were probably not as great. Rural rents had been pegged, a point that caused an estate agent in Yorkshire to comment bitterly, 'you can see the profits oozing out of the farmers, but the unfortunate landlord doesn't get a look in'.[55] Tenant farmers as a group were having a very good war. In the circumstances the wails of the farming community about income tax changes in 1918 look deeply insensitive.[56]

Of course, as with the issue of military service, farmers could claim patriotic justification. Increasing domestic food production to substitute for imports was a major strategic priority and one which grew stronger

after the declaration of unrestricted submarine warfare by the Germans
in February 1917. The Government was constantly urging greater production. Nevertheless, some farmers' behaviour bordered on the outrageous. Opposition to price controls in 1918 led to farmers' 'strikes'. Harry
Cartmell recounts in some detail the blackmailing tactics of Lancashire
farmers:[57] one of his fellow mayors, not named, lost patience entirely and
set out into the countryside where, 'by threats and menaces', he secured
his town's food supply. Cartmell comments: 'this opened up a rather
terrifying vista, for it seemed that the gentle art of cattle lifting was to be
added to the accomplishments, already somewhat diversified, of war-time
mayors'.[58] As with the issue of exemption from military service, one might
have expected a more widespread public condemnation of rural 'profiteering'. The reasons why it was not more frequent were probably similar:
food supply was simply too vital to interfere with and, whatever the moral
issues, the farmers were spectacularly delivering the goods.

Thus, in 1917, whilst the condemnation of retailers was reaching fever
pitch, *The Passing Show* actually advocated a 'Bounty for Farmers' bill and
criticised its obstruction. *John Bull* proved more ambivalent and published quite a number of stories hostile to farmers' profiteering, but they
were never a major target.[59] Small shopkeepers and large capitalists were
easier targets, the former being the interface with the consumer, the latter
as 'the villains' in wage disputes.

Profiteers were supposed to be moral pariahs, outside human sympathy. Social reality was rarely that tidy. Nevinson, the most subversive and
astute of all British war artists, commented brilliantly upon this in his
portrait of a 'profiteer' entitled 'He Gained a Fortune, but Lost a Son.'

Somebody else's dustbin

We are all, I suppose, more prone to condemn extravagance in the field
of our own virtue.

H. G. Wells, open letter to Hedley Le Bas in support of War
Savings drive, 1916[60]

The demand for greater sacrifices was increasingly a demand made of
other people. The notoriously scruffy Wells commented in 1916 that he
was happy enough to give up buying smart clothes for the duration and to
urge others to do likewise, but he could not follow the example of Mrs
Sydney Webb, who was renouncing the cinema and alcoholic beverages
for the duration. He doesn't directly suggest that his puritanical Fabian
friend might not be making any real sacrifice either.

In April 1916 a poem by Alfred Berlyn in *The Passing Show*, 'Very like a
Wail', detailed a set of wartime tribulations:

7. Digging for victory. IWM (Q 54566).

> My landlord asked me for the rent,
> I made him this appeal
> On Sacrifice you're surely bent
> To serve the common weal.

The landlord turns a deaf ear, as do the tradesman, butcher, tailor and baker. Berlyn concludes:

> With patriotic calm I'd bear
> The doom of poverty
> But is there no one keen to share
> My sacrifice with me?[61]

The authenticity of other people's sacrifices was now a subject of widespread doubt.

Sir Charles Lucas felt it important to point out in 1917 that 'Sacrifice means giving something it costs us to give.' The viewpoint of Mark Twain who allegedly promised that in the event of an invasion he would be 'prepared to sacrifice most of his wife's relatives', was Lucas suspected, 'the attitude of many at this time. They are ready to give up what they would rather be without, and they call upon others to give up what they do not feel the want of themselves.'

Lucas used the by-now traditional touchstone: 'Think of those who have made the great sacrifice, joyfully and willingly ... Think of the fathers and mothers who have not with held their sons.' In respect for them 'we at home can give something, time, money, work. We can forego some pleasure, some luxury, even some food.'

For Lucas, the great evil of war was 'waste'. It was a scandal that 'even to-day pieces of bread are thrown about on the streets of London ... it is the poor, who cannot get other food, that need the bread.' Lucas claimed that those who were better off were doing something and he condemned those who were spreading dissention. He stated that his own West End Club had instituted meatless days and potatoless weeks, but he admitted in passing that the clubs in general, 'with some reason', were held to be 'homes of luxury and wastefulness'. This feeling that someone, somewhere, but of course never oneself, was failing to sacrifice adequately was becoming widespread by 1917. Occasionally these moral exhortations contained a self-evident hypocrisy: the popular novelist Marie Corelli published an open letter in 1916 calling for an end to the extravagances of the rich, but was herself exposed as a hoarder in 1918, being fined £50 and 20 guineas costs for possessing 183lbs of sugar.[62] Yet even those who were largely righteous slipped easily over the line into self-righteousness.

The short story 'War Economy' by J. E. Buckrose captures this tendency perfectly. East Yorkshire housewives are being addressed by a local female dignitary at a public meeting, 'When she closed by saying that women could pay for this war by what they saved from the dustbins of England, if they only would, we felt our spirits respond to hers. We all thought, immediately, of somebody else's dustbin.'[63] There is a slight distancing through fiction, but this has the ring of truth. A self-satisfied comment in the immediately post-war history of Hove showed that this mindset was still at work. A house-to-house survey of the parish of St Thomas had indicated that '90%' of the residences had already committed themselves to 'carry out the economies called for by His Majesty'. The history goes on to state: 'If every parish in the land had shown so good a spirit there would have been no need for rationing, but there were always the selfish or dull people to reckon with, and in this matter as in others, it was they who were responsible for the compulsion that followed.' The thought that very few households in St Thomas would have answered such a loaded question otherwise simply doesn't appear to have occurred to the author in his civic complacency. The only real surprise is that 10% of the people of Hove were willing to admit that they were ignoring the request.[64] In a typically trenchant cartoon in *The Passing Show*, 'A Tea Shop Criminal'

8. Allotment holders pledge allegiance. IWM (Q 54729).

is depicted surrounded by a disapproving crowd of waitresses and customers. The caption identifies him as 'The man who inadvertently let his lunch bill come to 1s 3½d.'[65]

It was a short step from seeing others as heedlessly wasteful, to seeing them as actively undermining the war effort through lack of patriotism. Typical of this was the 'Bottomleyite' philosophy of attacking both local and central Government as hotbeds of waste, corruption, inefficiency and nepotism. This was simply the pre-war radical populism of *John Bull* extended into wartime. Practically every page of the paper calls for a 'business' mentality to eliminate waste. It is peculiarly transitional, looking back to nineteenth-century radical attacks on 'old corruption' and at the same time anticipating the populist conservatism of the twentieth century. The rhetoric of targeting other groups as profiteers and shirkers was an ever-increasing feature of wartime.

The language of sacrifice was immensely malleable. It could be turned to the purposes of almost any political agenda. Class antagonism could be justified through accusations of inequity. Harold Begbie, whilst 'Business as usual' was still the official slogan, could poetically lambast the gentry as hypocrites on behalf of the little man. When 'Sir Joseph Jingo' arrives at the pearly gates, he declares:

> I never committed a traitor's sin, disloyal men I shunned
> Tho' up to the neck, I sent a check to the Prince of Wales Fund

> I offered my house as a hospital and made my clerks enlist.
> 'You haven't my peer', he said, 'in here' and brought down a British
> fist.

The heavenly bureaucracy is not impressed:

> Saint Peter raised his head from his book, 'Did you serve your country
> well?'
> Draw near old bear, there is something here, another tale would tell,
> For it looks, do you see, that you gave not thought to the toiling trades-
> man's till,
> Subscriptions yes, with your name in the press, but what of your grocer's
> bill?

Begbie, writing for the Liberal *Daily Chronicle*, sets middle and working
class together against the rich:

> O the poor man pays and the rich man owes, and there's war, fierce war,
> in the shop
> The daily till must balance the bill or the wheels of trade would stop;
> Pay up, pay up, owe nothing now, for the price of life is at stake,
> And children weep when food's not cheap, and the hearts of mothers
> break.

This is obvious special pleading to deflect the charge of 'profiteering' in
inflationary conditions from the small retailer and retain a shred of solidarity between customer and shopkeeper by blaming someone else.

Another and more successful example of the persistence and adaptation
of pre-war concerns to the new rhetorical environment is the Glasgow rent
strike of 1915. This has occasionally been assimilated into the history of
anti-war protest and certainly some of those involved emerged as anti-
war protesters later. Yet at the time the rhetoric of the strike was heavily
conditioned by a successful appropriation of the patriotic language of
sacrifice, with the stress placed on the actions of profiteering landlords
persecuting the families of soldiers.

This was a particularly blatant case of the war being used to further a
pre-war agenda. The dismal and exploitative rental market in the city had
been a scandal for years. Whilst there is no doubt that the impact of war
worsened things considerably, and it is likely to be true that the families
of soldiers were suffering with peculiar intensity, the targeting of landlords reflected a long-standing local issue. Furthermore it was one with a
particularly Scottish resonance: the radical tradition in Scotland had
always had a particular niche in its rogues' gallery for the heartless
'laird' mercilessly battening on his tenants. This loathing was brought
by migrants from the crofts to the slums and translated to the issue of

urban rents. During and after the rent strike 'old' radical literature condemning Scotland's curse of landlordism circulated freely in the cities.[66]

The major difference in 1915 was that the tenants now occupied the moral high ground to an even greater degree: they were not simply victims but patriots, and their oppressors were not simply villains but traitors. A handbill advertising the inaugural meeting of the Glasgow Women's Housing Association made this clear: 'While at the moment all sections of the community, especially women are being called upon to make sacrifices, the patriotic president of the Houseowners association, stated "this is the moment to raise rents".' Patrick Dolan, a leading agitator, described the landlords as 'no better than Huns'. Significantly the rent strike began amongst the respectable tenants of South Govan, primarily clerks and skilled workers. When it spread to the poorer Shettlestone district, the focal point was initially the McHugh family home, a household where the father had been wounded and which had sent two sons to the front. A crowd gathered to oppose their eviction and a Union Jack was nailed to the door. A photograph of a procession on 8 October 1915 shows women and children carrying banners bearing the slogans, 'we are fighting landlord Huns' and 'My Father is fighting in France, we are fighting Huns at home.'[67]

With this rhetoric the protesters won a crucial public-relations victory, which was quickly translated into a political one: the imposition of rent control. This measure, one of the most enduring legacies of the war and perhaps the most significant piece of social and economic legislation in the first half of the twentieth century, was forced through both to quell potential disorder and because traditional property rights were being forced to take second place in wartime.[68]

This Scottish identification of 'profiteers' in general as an enemy within reached its climax in 1918 when Tom Johnston, the editor of the labour journal *Forward* published a pamphlet entitled, *The Huns during Three Years of the Great War* in 1918. The title, which at first glance implied kinship to the stream of literature issuing from the 'radical right', camouflaged a 'patriotic' assault on the exploiters of the working class.

The term 'Hun' was appropriated for use against traditional capitalist enemies in the valleys of South Wales as well. In October 1915, Councillor Hubert Jenkins attacked the landlords of the Aber Valley as having the same 'greed for power' as the Prussian militarists: 'If these "Huns of Britain" wanted to start a revolution in this country, let them start by raising the rents.' Rent rackers were described by Edwin Lewis as 'rag a muffins, dirty scoundrels', preying on the poor wives of servicemen.[69]

'Other bugger's efforts'

I knew a man of industry
Who made big bombs for the RFC
Who pocketed lots of LSD[70]
And he (thank God) is an OBE.

I knew a woman of pedigree
Who asked some soldiers out to tea
And said 'Dear Me' and 'Yes, I see'
And she (thank God) is an OBE.

I knew a fellow of twenty-three
Who got a job with a fat MP,
Not caring much for the infantry,
And he (thank God) is an OBE.

I had a friend, a friend – and he,
Just held the line for you and me
And kept the Germans from the sea
And died without the OBE,
Thank God!
He died without the OBE.[71]

In the summer of 1917 Britain acquired two new Orders of Chivalry. The senior of them, the order of Companions of Honour, was exclusive. The other was an entirely new phenomenon, perhaps a contradiction in terms, an unlimited chivalric distinction: the Order of the British Empire. It was described as 'Democracy's Own Order' and was, among other things, the first order of Chivalry to admit women on equal terms with men. One might have thought that this recognition of the immense efforts being made by the civilian population would be a popular success. Not at all – it soon came in for fierce criticism. Popular nicknames included 'Order of the Bad Egg', 'Order of Bloody Everybody' and 'Other Beggar's (or Bugger's) Efforts'.[72]

The widespread impression arose that this 'honour' was being handed out wholesale to time-servers, shirkers, society hostesses, profiteers and every variety of wartime parasite. Yet when one looks at the citations for the first OBE awards, it is clear that the majority of recommendations were justified as reward for real bravery, usually in munitions factories, often in fires and frequently involving saving the lives of fellow workers. So what was it that gave the OBE a bad name? One aspect was the giving of the OBE to workers who stayed at their post in air raids. For cynical soldiers, a citation such as 'Ernest Stubley – For courage in remaining at his post in circumstances of considerable danger in order to safeguard the works' looked like a sick joke. Any soldier who didn't remain at his post in circumstances of considerable danger could be shot under military law and, of course, many of them were. Worse still was the citation for Samuel Hall Bennet, 'For courage in returning to work within an hour of breaking his thumb', or for Margaret Burdett-Coutts, 'For courage in that, after losing a finger and badly lacerating her hand in a circular saw, she went away quietly to have it treated, in order not to unnerve her fellow workers.' In the context of Passchendaele this seemed a fairly trivial definition of courage.

Yet one should hesitate before accepting such a harsh judgement. As the citation makes clear, what was impressive about Bennet's act was his age – sixty-nine. Likewise it is clear that Burdett-Coutts was rewarded less for what she did than for who she was, for as a member of a prominent and privileged family there were many easier, more prestigious and safer ways for her to see out the war than working as a machinist. Whilst it might be unfair that she was honoured for stoically bearing a fairly ordinary industrial injury (possibly caused by incompetence), which doubtless happened to many of her workmates unremarked, is it too much to suggest that there was something at least a little noble in the fact that she was there in the first place?[73]

The other side of the accusation, that trivial acts of obedience to duty by civilians were rewarded whilst the heroism of soldiers was unremarked, is manifestly untrue. These OBE citations follow many pages of military citations from the *London Gazette* which appeared daily in *The Times*. The assumption that military awards were rare and always well deserved, but that civilian awards were frequent and generally unearned, should not be taken on trust.

The condemnation of an award for 'Other Bugger's Efforts' catches nicely some of the dangers inherent in the pervasive language of sacrifice during the war. However much the concept of self-sacrifice as opposed to selfishness might appear to be attractive, it contained within it some very destructive possibilities. Sacrifice is insatiably demanding. This dynamic was neatly caught by a cartoon in *The Passing Show* in July 1917. An 'exacting patriot' is pointing at two young men in Khaki uniforms: 'Why 'ain't 'efty young fellows like them in hospital blue.' Michael Macdonagh recounts that a female friend with two sons in the Army had gone up to comfort another woman who had recently lost her only son. For her pains she received a diatribe: 'How dare you speak to me whilst your sons live.'[74]

Ultimately only the 'supreme sacrifice' could bring redemption. Furthermore, the greater the sacrifice, the greater the demand for further sacrifices until redemption occurred.

In response to the German 'peace offer' in December 1916, Eva Isaacs wrote: 'At last there is a glimmering of peace ahead and at last a chance that the boys will soon be coming home. In weak moments I feel "What is

Serbia to me" ... in comparison with my beloved.' The catch was that the German terms would appear to reward aggression: 'of course one realises the impossibility of such terms'. The war had become self-sustaining, actually fuelled by the casualties: 'I think most of us at home have but one idea, to get our men back, except those whose men are not coming back, they want to see vengeance for their dear ones; and I suppose that is what we really feel as a nation.'[75]

Failure to sacrifice sufficiently, more or less impossible for the living, deferred the redemption and incurred guilt. It was a short step from this to the search for scapegoats, the picking out of those who are sacrificing less and are therefore more guilty of delaying redemption.

Likewise the related demand for equity of sacrifice founders on an inherent impossibility. In reality the sacrifices being made by any two individuals were highly unlikely to be the same, and as each fell short of total self-sacrifice in certain respects, it invited judgement of the inadequacies of others' sacrifices. In this complex economy it was easy for those who were making certain personal sacrifices, for example separation from a loved one, to judge this to be the only sacrifice that mattered and to condemn shirkers. But the same individual might be relatively materially privileged. In turn, those suffering from material privations, even if protected from separation and danger, would fasten onto that aspect of sacrifice and describe the wealthy as hoarders or profiteers. It is easy to see the general acknowledgement of the language of equal sacrifice as a social cement, but it must be remembered that it tended to founder on observable social realities, ones that could be literally life and death. In those circumstances it became a bitter language of self-justification and condemnation.

Among the many ironies of the war was that in terms of the language of sacrifice soldiers and civilians had an identical understanding of moral hierarchy. Highest in the scale of the morally admirable were the soldiers. Their sacrifice was definitive, the blood tax which everyone else had to justify themselves against. Yet in the most enduring wartime writings by soldiers, this point is not only not acknowledged, it is explicitly denied. Civilians, all civilians, were callously ignoring the sufferings of the troops. They made no meaningful sacrifices.

Perhaps the civilians deserved it; after all civilians were constantly harping on the moral failings of *other sections* of the civilian population and contrasting it with the moral self-sacrifice of the troops. This self-righteousness was picked up by the great soldier poets and novelists and turned into a blanket condemnation of all civilians. But far from these failings indicating a failure to acknowledge the supremacy of the soldiers' sacrifice, they stem from a language that did exactly that.

Where did this language come from? A useful clue can be found in the writings of the war poets, particularly Siegfried Sassoon and Wilfred Owen. However much they rejected and mocked formal religion (and they did), their poetry is shot through with religious imagery and themes. The identification of the self-sacrificing soldier with Christ on the cross, suffering to redeem the world by example is, even when apparently rejected, unavoidable. This was no esoteric code, the Biblical imagery of these poets was their most directly populist aspect.

At a recruiting meeting on 10 October 1915, the Rector of Holy Trinity Church in Hove, justified what might have struck some as peculiar: 'it seems a strange thing to hold a recruiting meeting on a Sunday, but victory is only to be won by sacrifice and on this day of all days we think about sacrifice and what it means'.[76] It would be easy, but mistaken, to dismiss this on the grounds that no one listens to vicars. A series of articles by the Scottish clergyman Norman Maclean were first published in *The Scotsman* in 1914, then reprinted as a pamphlet *In Our Parish* in 1915 and finally as a book, *The Great Discovery*. The pamphlet version alone had a print run of 100,000. Maclean wrote: 'Under the Shadow of the Cross, self-sacrifice has become the only rock on which our feet can stand.'[77]

The language of sacrifice was at heart a Christian language. As such it created both a dangerous challenge and a possible opportunity for formal religion. How did it respond?

5   Redemption through war: Religion and the languages of sacrifice

Clad in glittering white

> Honour, Duty, Patriotism and clad in glittering white, the great pinnacle of Sacrifice, pointing like a rugged finger to Heaven.
>
> David Lloyd George, Queen's Hall Speech, 19 September 1914 [1]

An overlooked advantage of Lloyd George in his bid for power in wartime Britain was his bilingualism. He could talk the esoteric code of political intrigue, but, far more importantly, he was fluent in the language of sacrifice. It distinguished him from his colleagues and rivals. Asquith never could sound like a native speaker, and a notorious sceptic such as Balfour had trouble with even the basic vocabulary. As a son of the manse, Bonar Law should have been able to master it, but his Scots-Canadian Presbyterian accent sounded like a tin whistle compared to a full-throated orchestra rehearsed in Welsh revivalism. There was a little irony in this, because personally Lloyd George did not have to make the greatest wartime sacrifice. By 1917 much of the political elite had suffered the loss of a close family member to the war. The leaders of the main parliamentary parties suffered heavily. The Conservative leader Bonar Law lost two sons. Asquith, still officially leader of the Liberals, lost his beloved son Raymond on the Somme at much the same time that Arthur Henderson, leader of the parliamentary Labour Party, lost his son. In 1917, John Redmond, leader of the Irish Nationalists lost his brother, a close political ally. Although Lloyd George was very worried about the safety of his son serving at the front, he was spared. It might be precisely this which allowed him to continue to emanate conviction in his rhetoric, uncorroded by doubt.

This elevated language, 'high diction', rings hollow to modern ears. [2] We are told that it increasingly rang hollow at the time. But this shouldn't be taken for granted. The grammar and vocabulary of the language of sacrifice were deeply familiar to a Bible-reading and hymn-singing public. Even if Christian belief was declining, which is a proposition difficult to prove, and one which is more questionable than secularisation theorists suggest, this does not mean that the habits of thought and the unspoken assumptions had disappeared. In a sophisticated analysis of working-class Southwark in the early twentieth century, S. C. Williams delineates a pervasive informal religiosity in a borough widely perceived to be 'heathen'. She argues that 'popular religion' should not be assessed in terms of quantifiable measurements of churchgoing, but rather understood as a cultural system in its own right. There was an implicit ideal of 'Christian' behaviour which was widely shared. Wartime made these things explicit.[3]

This did not lead to a straightforward religious revival: Geoffrey Studdert Kennedy, the Army chaplain known as 'Woodbine Willie', who was a more sophisticated and even cynical thinker than his public persona suggested, commented that there was 'a run on the Bank of God' at the start of the war, but that it was short-lived.[4] In a formal sense this was true, but the war seemed to encourage theological exploration, sometimes from the most unlikely sources. Much of it was unintentionally surreal – the corpulent con-artist Horatio Bottomley donned the mantle of Pope Urban II and, in his modestly entitled *The Great Thoughts of Horatio Bottomley*, announced an indulgence for those who died in the holy war:

Every hero of this war who has fallen in battle has performed an Act of the Greatest Love, so penetrating in its purifying character that I do not hesitate to express my opinion that any and every past sin is automatically wiped out from the record of his life.[5]

Bottomley faced a certain amount of criticism over this. Prior to the war he had been an outspoken anti-clerical, and secularists attacked him for getting religion. He was sent a bust of the famous nineteenth-century atheist Charles Bradlaugh by a reader. With impressive chutzpah, Bottomley placed it on his desk and retrospectively claimed Bradlaugh for religion. In February 1915 he replied to comments in *The Freethinker* by stating 'Secularism has had its day ... Faith is grander than Christianity.' Bottomley continued to attack the clergy, particularly when they dared to suggest that the nation needed to repent its sins. He argued that the war called for a 'new religion'.[6]

He had competitors for the chair: H. G. Wells, in the most popular novel of the war, *Mr Britling Sees It Through*, appeared through his fictional alter ego to be undergoing a rediscovery of faith: 'Our sons have shown us God.' Coming from a notorious pre-war secularist, this raised a few eyebrows. Like Bottomley, Wells was challenged by secularist colleagues and admitted to Frederick Harrison in a letter that he was uncomfortable being 'cuddled by Bishops'. After the war, an embarrassed Wells would emphasise that his God was a metaphor for the 'Spirit of History' or some such concept.[7]

These were just extreme manifestations of a national hobby of the English at war, and perhaps to a lesser extent the Scots and Welsh; the motto of the country could well have been 'every man his own theologian'. The ever-valuable Harry Cartmell quoted a supposed French proverb: 'The English are a people of a hundred religions and one sauce.' Cartmell continued, 'I do not know about the sauce, but from knowledge gained on the Tribunal, I am not disposed to question the dictum about religion.'

The much-quoted remark about the soldiers in the trenches – that they had got religion, but apparently not Christianity – has been generally misunderstood as expressing a peculiarity of the war.[8] In fact, from an *orthodox* and particularly an Anglican point of view this is a perfectly good generic description of the English for at least three centuries, and indeed perhaps still is. Terms such as dogma and dogmatic were heavily laden with negative connotations in ordinary speech. This resistance to religious authority was a *reductio* almost *ad absurdum* of the Reformation. Many thought about God while at the same time absolutely refusing to be told *what* to think about God. In England at least, in 1914, the tradition of 'religious independence' dating back to the 1640s was still bearing strange fruit. Curiously enough, the validity of a highly personal reading of Scripture was the common ground between some of the war's strongest advocates and conscientious objectors. On occasion it led to a sense of kinship.

If a man argued, with deep conviction and learned coherence, that he could not join the Army because killing German workers on behalf of capitalists was wrong, he was likely to get short shrift. But religious arguments, no matter how bizarre, were often treated with great respect. Luckily for them, many socialist objectors had religious convictions as well and they were well advised to emphasise that aspect of their objection. Reuben Farrow in his appearance before the tribunal claimed 'Christian' grounds for exemption. He states that the panel knew him well and knew his objections to be genuine. The exchange was fascinating:

the Chairman however, claimed that they too were 'Christian' but the war had been forced upon them and they were compelled to deal with it as best they could. I agreed that they had a right to their conscientious convictions; and they accepted that I had a right to mine.

Farrow was conditionally exempted and went back to his railwayman's job, 'and to ILP anti-war activities'.[9]

Cartmell gives a similar picture from the other side of the bench: 'In regard to some of the objectors, we had personal knowledge. We knew them as men who appeared regularly in the market place, and in all weathers delivered themselves of the message with which they felt themselves charged.' With an affectionate irony and an obvious admiration he describes them as 'Timid souls, who might easily be crushed by the iron heel of military discipline. Though not prepared to fight the Germans, they had courage of the kind which in times past led men to the stake for their convictions.'[10]

It is worth pausing to consider why the Tribunals apparently took these men so seriously. It is likely that they were rather aware of their own precarious moral position, as Cartmell's testimony indicates. In a country where *Foxe's Book of Martyrs* still had some resonance, no one wanted to act the part of a Marian magistrate sentencing Protestants. Even more profoundly, there could have been few Tribunal members who did not, from time to time, think uncomfortable thoughts about Pontius Pilate.

The result was a desperate effort to judge the sincerity of the objector. This lead to tribunal proceedings which were a strange mixture of a *viva voce* in scriptural knowledge and the Spanish Inquisition, with the significant difference that a genuine heresiarch was likely to be spared. The power dynamics were peculiar. In important respects the advantage was with the objector. Resembling a tutor facing a serious undergraduate who has read the texts more recently, it is clear that arguments about the Gospels were often weighted towards the appellant. It was, however, vital that he had done his research properly. The conscientious objector in Preston who based his appeal on Christ supposedly having said 'I come not to bring a sword, but peace', was failed for perverse misquotation and dispatched to the Army. On the other hand, in a case where one of the Tribunal attempted to justify military service against Germany on the Old Testament endorsement of the *lex talionis*, 'an eye for an eye, a tooth for a tooth', he was contemptuously lectured by an objector who rightly pointed out that the response of Jesus to this had been to state that evil should be repaid with good. The Tribunal exempted him.

When dealing with members of small Christian sects, the Preston Tribunal would usually try to canvass the opinion of the sect's 'elders'. They often discovered that the man before them turned out to be a rather young 'elder' himself. A non-Christian variant of this became something of a national issue when a *kohen* claimed exemption on the grounds that, as a hereditary priest, he was unable to come into contact with dead bodies. It could be argued that this was soundly based in scripture, but of course many *kohanim* had already entered the Army. The Chief Rabbi was asked for a judgement. Whether motivated by patriotism, or by the morale of serving soldiers from the community or perhaps concerned about potential anti-semitism, he gave his opinion that the prohibition was not absolute. Whether the individual concerned acknowledged this ruling is unclear.

Religious objection to the war was the minority position; far more common was religious or quasi-religious justification. Harry Cartmell's wartime speeches as mayor were filled with religious images and idealism, explicit and implicit. He might have reacted to marketplace preachers with amused admiration, but there doesn't appear to be any irony in his hailing of Woodrow Wilson as a capitalist 'Prophet' on 4 August 1918. In the same speech he describes the League of Nations as embodying the 'yearnings of all Christian men'. In a speech on 17 May 1917 which argued against the growing demand for 'reprisals' he described German philosophy as 'a force which menaces Christian civilization'. Of course, the wartime language of sacrifice stretched far beyond the explicitly Christian, but the accumulated bulk of centuries of revivalism and internal evangelism lay beneath it. The idea of redemptive sacrifice was second nature to the population, whether they realised it or not.

The visual counterpoint to Lloyd George's speech was the most popular and reproduced print of the war, brought out for Christmas 1914. 'The Supreme Sacrifice' showed Christ taking a soldier in his arms. As the quotes from Wells and Bottomley demonstrate, patri-passionism, the redemption of the world through the blood of soldiers, was the informal civic religion of wartime Britain.

Indeed, by 1918 this amounted to a real problem for more traditionally minded Christians, because, strictly speaking, it was a heresy. W. J. Carey in a short book entitled *Sacrifice and Some of Its Difficulties*, wrestled with the problems involved: 'Prayer will be for the God-Like power to stick it out – that the boys will be faithful to death as Jesus was, that there may be no betraying the good in order to be spared sacrifice.' Sacrifice willingly endured was the essence of Christian unselfishness: 'the old prayers won't do, "Spare my boy and let others' boys die"; "Spare me and let other people perish."' In this criticism, Carey reveals what was doubtless the essence of many people's real wartime prayers by 1918. But Carey also draws back from patri-passionism – the imitation of Christ was an imitation, not the same thing: 'Let the Church preach sacrifice at all sorts of services, but let her – at any cost of numbers – keep the Holy Sacrifice as her central mystery and glory.'[11] Others were taking an even stronger line.

A halfpenny pamphlet entitled *The War and Sacrificial Death: A Warning* was circulated by the World's Evangelical Alliance in 1918.[12] The author found himself trying to tackle a difficult problem: how to insist on the singularity of Christ's sacrifice without belittling the deaths of the soldiers. He begins by condemning 'modern thought' which had run counter 'to the absolute necessity for the Sacrifice of Christ to redeem men from the consequence of their sin'. Unfortunately the 'present sad days of war' had exacerbated this and 'Christian men are to be found who unhesitatingly declare their belief that a soldier's glorious death can atone for the sin of his past life.' The author believed that 'Sufficient has appeared in print and in the press' to suggest that this view was held by many of both the laity and clergy. He condemned it as based on 'misdirected patriotism or misguided sentimentality'.

Such a statement obviously laid him open to a charge of anti-patriotic feeling. As a result he was at pains to indicate his approval of the soldiers' patriotism. 'It is a glorious deed to die for ones country ... Never was Britain more worthy than in this absolutely righteous war.' But, 'to substitute for the atoning death of Jesus Christ' (the one and only grounds of salvation) with the 'supposed atoning virtue of the death of a patriot' would be 'exchanging a foundation of rock for one of sand'.[13]

In the mood of 1918, this was a frank and rather shocking statement. Was the author prepared to suggest that the deaths of the soldiers had no redemptive purpose; that they were no more spiritually significant than the deaths of civilians? The argument ends with a sophisticated double move: individually the deaths do not lead to atonement, but they may have a providential purpose:

The men, who in days gone by, have recoiled from the plain statement of God's Word that 'without shedding of blood their is no remission of sin' should find this doctrine easy of acceptance in these days when our lives in this Nation, as the lives of those in the Nations allied to us, are being redeemed by the blood of our sons.[14]

This reconciliation of patriotism and orthodoxy is both clever and bathetic. In essence, having rejected the Bottomley formula, the author justified the death of hundreds of thousands as having saved the soul of H. G. Wells. If this was the best that orthodoxy could do, it was not surprising that the war gave a boost to heterodoxy.

The spiritual fate of dead soldiers was an obvious issue in wartime. By 1914 belief in hell and judgement had been reduced to a residual phenomenon and, in any case, the idea that a just God might consider punishing those who had died for the cause of righteousness was abhorrent to all but a small fundamentalist minority; but belief in a 'heavenly' afterlife was still very strong. Spiritualism was an active popular force in pre-war Britain and was seen by many as a 'scientific' alternative to traditional Christianity. The discovery of electro-magnetic forces was used to promote the idea of ethereal communication with the unseen: the medium could receive the message. It is tempting to see the growth in spiritualism in wartime Britain as a direct consolatory response to mass casualties, and this certainly played a role; but it should be noted that spiritualist interpretations of the war were promoted and becoming popular well before mass casualties. A 1915 book by William Tudor Pole, collecting his writings from the first months of the war, illustrates this. With eclectic references to Swedenborg and the 'Bahai revelation', the author set out to explain the 'deeper issues' of the war. The war was simply the earthly manifestation of a titanic struggle on a higher plane: 'It is difficult, if not impossible to write of the struggle between the forces of light and darkness in an intelligible manner', a proposition he amply demonstrates.[15] There is certainly a consolatory message to be gained from the book, albeit a bizarre one: 'I believe that the transient conditions of so-called death are becoming more harmonious than ever before.'[16] In a letter to his mother in 1914, the author assures her that heavenly mobilisation had been conducted with pleasing efficiency, perhaps unconsciously echoing press notices from the War Office and Admiralty: 'the arrangements on the other side for receiving those who pass over are wonderfully complete and working well'.[17] But the fate of the 'so-called dead' was obviously of secondary importance.

In reply to a letter from a mother asking how to protect her son at the front, Tudor Pole advocated meditation and the projection of positive energy, 'It may seem incredible that these spiritual weapons of defence can actually safeguard your son whilst he is fighting in the trenches ... *Yet it is a fact.*'[18] There is, one might think, a certain inconsistency in protecting someone from illusory death.

Was this charlatanry? The war was certainly a golden opportunity for mystical snake oil merchants to prey upon the vulnerable and the confused, but such activity is hardly confined to wartime – bizarre philosophies of a 'new age' always seem to find a ready market. The more important feature of this book was the congruence with broader currents of wartime thought. At the centre of the argument, if it can be called an argument, was the idea of the inauguration of a millennium through the conversion of human behaviour: 'selfish individualism, in the face of the tremendous issues before the country, is giving place to a broader view'.[19] From a radically heterodox writer, this was an almost perfect statement of wartime orthodoxy.

The background

Examination of the role of religion in Britain during the First World War needs to be situated in a much longer historical evolution. During the nineteenth century the problem of the 'godless masses' had in the first place produced a strong evangelical impulse amongst both laity and clergy. The realisation, hammered home by the mid-century religious censuses, that much of the working class had no knowledge whatsoever of Christian doctrine, was perceived both as a disgrace for the Church and potentially threatening to the social order. Furthermore the failings of the 'national' Church provided ammunition for denominational opponents, both Roman Catholic and nonconformist. The evangelical efforts of the Churches during the nineteenth century, particularly in education and church-building, were on the face of it rather successful. The Church of England had a better claim to being a national Church in 1914 than it had a century before. The major competing religious groups could also point to real successes.

Nonconformity, which by 1914 might be said to have finally come to include Methodism, had played an enormous role in shaping the society and politics of Victorian England. Admittedly the campaign for Church disestablishment in England had faltered (although by 1914 it had succeeded in Wales), and temperance had not triumphed despite a growing number of adherents; but there was still considerable vitality in the 'nonconformist conscience', as the civil disobedience surrounding the 1902 Education Act had demonstrated. Indeed the wartime history of Guildford notes that non-payment of rates was still occurring in the summer of 1914, until the outbreak of war brought an end to it. Roman Catholicism, underpinned by continual and massive Irish immigration, was buoyant to the point of triumphalism in 1914: the clergy were better educated and the creed far better inculcated than had been the case fifty years before.

Reports of the death of God in Edwardian Britian are much exaggerated. Jose Harris rightly points out that Continental observers were amazed by the religiosity of British life. Uniquely in Europe, neither socialism nor liberalism were strongly anti-clerical and irreligious creeds in the British Isles, indeed both were heavily influenced by religious idealism. The massive effort of all denominations to introduce Christianity on all levels meant that in some ways the generations alive in 1914, particularly among the working classes, had been exposed to greater religious influence than at any previous time.

But in the latter decades of the nineteenth century there was an increasing discontent within the clergy about the real significance of this apparent success. The pre-eminent difficulties were threefold. First, the evangelical insistence on preaching and scriptural knowledge as central to the enterprise of re-Christianisation was perceived as dangerous in the light of nineteenth-century 'higher' criticism and post-Darwinian scientific knowledge. There was a real danger that the foundations were being cut from under this form of belief. Second, the nature of the 'internal mission' provoked resistance. It could easily be seen as middle-class interference with working-class life, and was resented accordingly. Third, many Anglicans, in particular, were worried that nominal adherence to the Church was all that was being created. 'Real' Christianity, particularly a sense of fellowship in the taking of sacramental communion, was largely absent.

Within the established Church, the response was an emerging generation of energetic clergy who wished to tackle these problems head on. Their inspiration was largely drawn from F. D. Maurice, with a strong flavouring of nineteenth-century philosophical 'Oxford Idealism'. In churchmanship the predominant style was 'Catholic modernism'. The emphasis was heavily on placing sacramental communion at the centre of Church life. Foregrounding the aspect of incarnation and religious mystery would sidestep some of the dangers of scriptural criticism. It would also increase the sense of fellowship in the Church.

This connected directly to the predominant political tone of these younger clergy, which was Christian socialist. Through inner-city 'University Missions' (of which Toynbee Hall in the East End of London was by far the most important), many of these men had had sustained contact with the urban working class, and had become aware of the dangers of 'preaching down'. They wanted to adapt the Church to take into account working-class reality. The aim was to transcend class difference through fellowship. Christian socialist movements were widespread in early twentieth-century Europe, but the English variant was becoming increasingly left-wing in tone. Unlike most Christian socialist movements it had strong relationships with those inside the broader socialist movement. Many of the younger clergy were distinctly partisan in favour of the working class in industrial and social disputes.

The outbreak of war in 1914 was therefore perceived by many within the Church of England as an opportunity of unparalleled proportions to undertake the 'real' Christianisation of the 'masses' and social reconstruction of the nation. The evidence of many of the younger Army chaplains, notably Neville Talbot, that nominal Anglicans in the armed forces had only the most shaky grasp of doctrine and no experience of taking communion, underlined the urgency of the task.

Patriotism is not enough

The Dilemma.

> God heard the embattled nations sing and shout
> 'Gott Stafe England' and 'God Save the King'
> God this, God that and God the other thing
> 'Good God', said God, 'I've got my work cut out.'
>   J. C. Squire, in *The Survival of the Fittest* (London, 1919)

It is lawful for Christian men, at the commandment of the Magistrate, to wear weapons, and serve in the wars. (Articles of the Church of England No. xxxvii.) Quoted at the front of E. Blunden, *Undertones of War* (London, 1928)

I realise that patriotism is not enough. I must have no hatred or bitterness towards anyone. (The words of Edith Cavell to the Anglican chaplain at Brussels on receiving communion before her execution)

The widespread view within the Church was that the war represented an unparalleled opportunity. A long-standing desire to create a genuinely Christian nation led to a very optimistic interpretation of the national mood. At the centre of this was an interpretation of the war as in some sense demonstrating a 'sign of grace' in the English people. Before the war all the indications were supposedly of disaster: a disaster caused by materialism, selfishness and social division. The war had called forth a better nature. An altruistic willingness to sacrifice oneself for the cause of righteousness, as evidenced by the crowds at the recruiting stations, was a clear indication that people were ready to receive God into their hearts.

Before continuing, it is worth examining a partial exception to this view. Ralph Inge, the Dean of St Paul's, was the very model of an Anglican intellectual, with an interest in history and in matters ecumenical. He lectured on Plotinus, was a follower of Malthus[20] and, as the war progressed, he showed himself to be more sceptical.[21] From the very outset, Inge was worried that 'patriotism' could become a false ideal:

I preached in the Abbey, a sermon which was destined to get me into trouble. I chose as my subject 'Problems of Faith and Patriotism' and mentioned the coincidence that the day when war was declared the Jews everywhere were celebrating the anniversary of the destruction of their temple and the loss of their independence. I said that the Jews had chosen the lower instead of the higher patriotism, exhorted Englishmen to think more of the moral and spiritual greatness of our country than of material power.[22]

By 1917, Inge's private view was that the war had become a catastrophe. He said to Lord Haldane in November 1917: 'I cannot see the use of bleeding Europe to death.'[23] At a meeting of the League for Promoting International Friendship Through the Churches on 14 December 1917 he took the opportunity to tell them some unpopular truths:

We cherish three impossible hopes:
1. That we can destroy German militarism. We cannot; they will only live for revenge.
2. A restoration of the balance of power. This means a mad competition in armaments.
3. That we can force Germany to adopt the democratic system.[24]

Once again, he had made the mistake of speaking his mind, and noted in his diary on 17 December: 'The newspapers are attacking me more furiously than ever for my speech on the 14th, and I have had a swarm of abusive letters. One good lady says; "I am praying for your death, I have been very successful in two other cases."'[25] On the last day of 1917 he wrote: 'So ends another year of protracted nightmare. Whatever the end of the war, Europe is ruined for my lifetime and longer.'[26]

Inge was impressed by, but not hopeful about, the pacifist activities of Quakers and others. But what is most interesting is that he was in no respect a wild left-wing radical; indeed his politics were distinctly to the right. His objection to the war was that of Lord Lansdowne with a twist of concern about the dysgenic effect of warfare: 'Nearly one fifth of the Upper and Middle Class of Military age ... are dead. Our people, slow and reluctant to enter the war are mad with rage.'[27] His belief that there were too few of the middle classes, and already too many of the poor made the war appear a double catastrophe.

Ralph Inge was fairly isolated in Anglican circles in developing a straightforwardly catastrophic view of the war. But his earlier sermon about 'higher' and 'lower' patriotism was not far from the view of many of his contemporaries. The man most exercised with this problem was William Temple, at this time the Vicar of St James in Piccadilly. He was 33 years old at the outbreak of the war, the son of an Archbishop of Canterbury and clearly the rising star of the Church. Described, somewhat acidly, by his fellow Oxford clerical don, Ronald Knox, in 1912 'As Thinker, Usher, Statesman, and Divine',[28] Temple was an active pamphleteer from the start of the war, publishing *Christianity and the War* in 1914 and *The Holy War* in 1915. In 1915, he was one of the twelve men called upon by the Archbishop of Canterbury to produce a report on 'The Spiritual Call to the Nation and the Church'. This was the group that were to recommend 'a National Mission led by the Archbishops', to call the nation to repentance and to hope through 'the Living Christ'.

Temple was appointed as secretary to the central committee of the National Mission, and unofficially its chief ideologue. He contributed three of the first series of pamphlets. These were the very first pamphlet, *The Call of the Kingdom*, followed by *The Fellowship of the Holy Spirit* and *The Church's Mission to the Nation*. From these three pamphlets it is possible to reconstruct Temple's thinking about the significance of the war. In the beginning:

In 1914, God called us, as a nation, and we heard and obeyed His call. That is our starting point. There came to us a claim that we should make great sacrifices for righteousness and honour ... But though we answered God's call, it cannot be said we answered it as his.[29]

The war was a revelation of a 'Christian' instinct, but also of the weakness of the Church:

Few of us would have predicted that in the response to a great crisis a readiness so complete for service and sacrifice would be found. No doubt the Church may claim much of the credit for the existence of this spirit ... Yet we have to face the fact that the Church itself has never elicited this readiness to serve and share.[30]

The war had taught men new values: 'We have really learned that sacrifice is better than enjoyment and that to die for a just cause is better than to live for pleasure ... But as I have said we have been lifted to this new plane by causes which will pass.'[31] Once the war ended there was a danger of reverting to moral and social decadence as Temple claimed had occurred with the Regency after the Napoleonic War; therefore the time for repentance was now: 'We are called to repentance not because we are particularly bad, but, because for the moment we are especially good. In logic it may look as if repentance is especially appropriate at times of gross sin. So it is, only it is then unobtainable.'[32] The Church had to tell the nation 'that the evils from which it suffers are the result of our own sin; we are to trace our divisions, our party spirit, our love of pleasure and all the bitterness of classes that flow from these, to the nation's neglect of God'.[33]

These evils were at root because of the failure of fellowship: 'The life of fellowship is in fact what all mankind through all its history is seeking.'[34] For Temple, the whole effort of civilisation is an attempt to reach fellowship. Without fellowship the individual perceives themselves as powerless to change the world:

We can abolish slums and build decent houses ... We can remove from the Church the great scandal that endowments are tied up in such a way that you may have a post that is almost a sinecure richly endowed while close by great opportunities of work are left unused ... Here again is a question to which the individual can rightly say, 'I can do nothing.' The danger is that saying is true, but there is another saying equally true, and it is that other saying that we must learn to take on our lips, 'we' can do what is needed. 'I' cannot beat the Germans, but 'we' can and will. But 'we' can only do this if each plays his part. So 'I' cannot cure the evils of national life, but 'we' can, if 'I' and everyone else plays his part.[35]

The barrier to fellowship, to the empowerment of 'we' was materialism:

When we ask what is the root of this breach in fellowship, we find that it is materialism. It cannot be too often insisted that the devotion to individual ends will always lead to division and strife, because of material goods, at any given time, there is only a limited supply, so that the more one has, the less there is for others. But the spiritual goods are unlimited, the more love or joy or peace that there is in one man's soul, the more there will be in the souls of those who have dealings with them.[36]

9. The Roman Catholic Archbishop of Westminster addresses a War Loan rally. IWM (Q 54217).

The answer had to be to break out of materialism into fellowship. The war had demonstrated that this was possible, but to be sustained it had to be rooted in a free individual choice to embrace fellowship as a permanent way of life – for this only God could provide the means: 'It is in the absolute dedication of ourselves to the service of His Will, whatever that may mean for us, that we shall find our fellowship with one another.'[37] and only the Church could be the instrument: 'Our Fellowship is in the Holy Spirit ... And the pledge of our fellowship is in the service which we call the Holy Communion or Holy Fellowship.'[38]

Temple's Balliol background, in an environment permeated with debate about individual freedom and the common good which had been going on ever since T. H. Green, predisposed him to seek an answer in a free individual act leading to communal redemption. A strongly sacramentarian Christianity was to be the response to selfish individualism creating an unselfishness based on an individual relationship with God expressed through Christian fellowship. The war was a model, but ultimately a transitory and inadequate model. Invigorated by the sacramental model, a Christian nation could tackle the dire consequences of materialism and, in a sort of 'feedback' system, by being tough on the causes of sin, ultimately remove sin. Just as the nineteenth-century evangelicals had established a role for the Church in personal morality, the twentieth-century 'Catholics', through consent, would shape social morality: 'The right of religion in private life is now universally admitted, it still has to be won as regards public life.'[39] In the middle of a world war, it cannot be claimed that the Church lacked ambition.

The National Mission, 1916

George Sherston, the fictional alter ego of the poet Siegfried Sassoon, arrived wounded at Charing Cross Station, where he was presented with a leaflet by the Bishop of London, 'who earnestly advised me to live a clean life and attend Holy Communion'.[40] This image of the utter inadequacy of a revivalist message in the face of war reflects the intellectual disillusionment which Sassoon felt by 1917, and which had come to be widespread by the time of the publication of his fictionalised memoirs. Yet this is far from being the whole story of the National Mission.

Pamphlet B of the National Mission, *My Faith and Hope in View of the National Mission*, was by the Labour politician George Lansbury. From an 'ethical socialist' background, by 1916 he was a committed Anglican Christian socialist. Lansbury took up the challenge of the role of religion in public life. His target audience was middle-class Anglicans:

I write this pamphlet mainly for my fellow members of the Church of England and beg them to accept it as from one who ... feels it to be his duty as a follower of Christ to bear testimony at this supreme moment to the faith which has guided and controlled a fairly long life of service among men and women on whose toil and industry we all depend for our daily bread, who have given their sons without stint to fight and die, as they believe, in our defence.[41]

That the second pamphlet of the National Mission, addressed to a predominantly middle-class audience, was a stirring defence of the Labour Party, can be seen as radical in the political context of 1916. In middle-class circles there was deep distrust of the Labour Party in particular and the working class in general, widely perceived as shirkers, 'conchies' and even possibly traitors. Lansbury himself was a member of the Fellowship of Reconciliation, a neo-pacifist group, and editor of the *Daily Herald*, the Labour newspaper which provided one of the strongest dissenting voices in wartime. He was an opponent of conscription and personally assisted in sheltering those who wished to avoid military service.[42] Yet a pamphlet by Lansbury was appearing under the authorisation of the Archbishop of Canterbury (who admittedly had some misgivings about this).[43] The convergence between Lansbury's views and Temple's is clear in the pamphlet, but Lansbury is more outspoken. He begins with a critique of Church attitudes: 'I often wonder if those with leisure understand how impossible it is for business men and work people to participate in the daily services of the Church and how out of place a church bell sounds calling men and women to worship at a time when all sweat and labour has to be spent in working for the bread that perisheth.' But, like Temple, he sees the war as revealing an opportunity:

Since August 1914, we have lived through terrible days which have brought home to us all the futility of the mad scramble for material riches ... But if the futility of material things is being proved, there is something else also which we are all able to recognize. No one hates and detests war more than I do, yet out of it comes great, noble deeds which fill us with admiration and love ... The trenches call out this spirit of brotherhood and comradeship just because each is striving to do his best for all.[44]

For Lansbury the selflessness of wartime is the moral precursor of socialism:

We go to Sunday school and to church, we are confirmed and commence our adult religious life with our first Easter Communion ... There is a startling contrast between the advice of Bishops at Confirmation time and the advice we receive when entering into industrial or business life. Bishops tell us to find our highest joy in serving God and in striving to do his will. Our friends tell us that our first duty is to succeed ... I believe that to many people failure is the first sin against the Holy Ghost.[45]

This worship of material success was profoundly anti-Christian. Lansbury called upon an archetypal pre-war example to refute it:

When the Scott expedition failed ... the story of how one of their number walked out to die alone, in order, by the earlier sacrifice of his own life to give his companions a chance of living ... [this] will forever redeem the expedition from any stigma of real failure ... human nature, inspired by the example of the Lord, is even in this sordid, miserable time of competition and greed, capable of rising to the most supreme height of sacrifice and service in the love of others.[46]

The pursuit of material success was, as Temple argued, the source of sin, which was a social phenomenon. The moral disorder of the East End was a product of capitalism. Lansbury demonstrates this in (literally?) melodramatic terms:

Where I live, I am surrounded by people for whom life has very few gifts; I often see a girl fresh from the country ... start housekeeping full of joy of living, and in a year or two, when children come, find the same girl a prematurely aged woman, because trouble and difficulty in the shape of sickness and unemployment have fallen on the family, and driven her to drink and despair. Prostitution, with its attendant moral and physical degeneracy, is largely the outcome of bad social conditions, and is quite unnatural. Do we realise that we are failing in our duty to God and our Fellows while any of these evils flourish?[47]

The answer was Christian socialism, in an argument directed by Lansbury not at the working class, but to the middle classes for the salvation of their souls:

I have no doubt of the response if we preach our religion as one which offers nothing but service to its followers. For I am certain that in spite of all appearances, selfishness and seeking one's good at the expense of one's fellows is not the true expression of our nature ... Therefore let us all go to God for strength and inspiration to carry his message of Fatherhood and Brotherhood. I should like our private motto for the mission to be Mazzini's 'God and the People' 'No rights without duties' God grant that the whole Church of England, rich and poor, old and young, may be drawn together so that the class barriers that divide us may be broken down.[48]

Lansbury was invited to write this pamphlet because the explicit aim of the mission was to reach the working class.[49] It was felt that a Labour Party leader would be particularly effective in doing so. Lansbury's response, like Temple's, was that preaching down to the working class in traditional mission fashion was missing the real point. A Church which in itself lacked real Christian fellowship, could not hope to succeed.

The National Mission did not speak with a unified voice. This was not for want of trying. Even Dean Inge, in public, seemed prepared to endorse the view of the war as spiritual opportunity within the Temple paradigm: 'We have to thank God for such a spiritual awakening as few would have dared hope for ... If we can keep all this after the war, we shall be a great nation.' But at least he was honest enough to repeat his qualifications about patriotism:

But now comes the necessity for a grave warning. These spiritual gifts for which, when we see them bearing fruit all around us, we are thanking God, are not and never will be given to those who seek them for an ulterior end, even the greatness of their country, and they will not survive the present tension unless they are based on the firm acceptance of a Christian standard of values.[50]

This paragraph could be lifted directly from Temple. But the problematic relationship between patriotism and Christianity did not exercise the titular leader of the National Mission to the same degree, if it bothered him at all.

On the first Sunday of Advent 1915 in Westminster Abbey, A. F. Winnington-Ingram preached what might be regarded as the most infamous sermon in Anglican history:

Everyone who loves freedom and honour, everyone who puts principle before ease and life itself beyond mere living, are banded together in a great crusade – we cannot deny it – to kill Germans: to kill them not for the sake of killing, but to save the world; to kill the young men as well as the old, to kill those who have shown kindness to our wounded as well as those fiends who crucified the Canadian sergeant, who superintended the Armenian massacres, who sank the *Lusitania*, and who turned the machine guns on the civilians of Aerschott and Louvain – and to kill them lest the civilization of the world should itself be killed.[51]

This was the man charged with leadership in a campaign to bring the nation to God. A sense of Arthur Winnington-Ingram's own priorities might be derived from his biography: the chapter on the war years details at great length his tireless activity as the chaplain to the London Regiment and doesn't mention the National Mission once.[52]

It is tempting to condemn the Bishop of London as an over-promoted and jingoistic buffoon.[53] The principle witness for the prosecution would be Winnington-Ingram. His pamphlet for the National Mission, *The Nation's Call*, was intended as the keynote of the campaign. It begins in his inimitable style: 'I honestly do not think that it ought to be necessary to convince any man who gives the subject any amount of deep thought that it was to be expected that the Church should have a message to the Nation at this time.'[54] A little obligatory Hun-bashing and assertion of the 'chosen' nature of the British Empire develops the argument:

the Providence of God seemed picked out to preserve the most precious things that can be preserved in life, and, first of all, the freedom of our country. I can imagine nothing more calamitous that the home of freedom should become a German province. As I said going up and down the line last year, I would rather die than see the country a German province. But we are not only fighting for our freedom but for the freedom of the world … we are not those who glory in war; but how can war ever be averted and international peace secured unless one nation can trust another's word.[55]

With this masterly demonstration that the war would have to continue until the Germans could be persuaded to behave like gentlemen, Winnington-Ingram sets out his views on how the war will be brought to this desirable conclusion. The answer, of course, is patriotic commitment such as the troops show: 'I believe that we have to breathe that spirit into the nation. I greatly valued a word that was sent to me by a friend; I love to use it every time I can, I have it in big letters over the door at Fulham. It is "Fortitude."'[56] Civilians had a responsibility to show solidarity: 'Therefore I cannot help first of all asking some very plain questions … Do you sit up late at night writing to the men in the trenches? ... Do you make the women left behind feel that they have brothers and fathers and friends to look after them? It is said that some of these women drink very much.'[57] The Church could help with this:

As we have gone from diocese to diocese, we have tried to take all the ideas that have come to us from any parish or any deanery and pass it on. I know there are Rolls of Honour in churches. Do not be content with leaving them in the church; you might have them in the street as well. In such ways the Church must show people that it is supporting the men at the front ... when they die we die, when they win, we win.[58]

Prayer had an important role as well:

I have been told, and have received the intimation with some dismay, that the Intercession services have been dwindling away during this second year. It may be true or not. It may be true in some places and not in others. To all here, clergy and laity, I say, If it is so, what does it mean ... If we diminish our prayers we lessen God's power of acting through us. It is by these prayers He acts. If we are failing God, we are failing our sons, we are failing our fighting men ... some of you may remember in a rather famous publication a picture of a nun at her prayers. There she sat kneeling looking such a frail obstacle to oppose the sin of the world; but the eye of faith sees that from that slight figure there is radiating to every part of the world the power of prayer. If that is true of one single figure, what about the prayers of a united Church? They would simply radiate power throughout the whole world, power we cannot see, but which we are promised shall come down in answer to prayer.[59]

After this brief exploration of the power of prayer, the bishop returns to the war. In another long passage he stated, 'It is the Christian in us that makes us burn with indignation when we hear of children ill treated and women wronged in a terrible way,' but he was at least partially retracting his Advent sermon:

On the other hand we must never mix up the innocent with the guilty. I am thankful to think that in East London righteous indignation at the sinking of the *Lusitania* was shown, but when it took the form of wrecking innocent peoples houses, the Church protested and even sheltered some of those who were in danger, I believe the prayer, 'Father forgive them they know not what they do' covered the soldiers who, acting under orders, were crucifying the Son of God ... we must let the prayer cover in our minds those in the Zeppelins and submarines who are acting under orders and would be shot if they had not obeyed.[60]

Having played somewhat fast and loose with doctrine up to this point, the bishop begins to tumble into fully fledged patri-passionism. He quoted a poem by Katherine Tynan:

> Now Heaven's by Golden Boys invaded
> 'scaped from the winter and the storm ...
> The old wise Saints look down and smile,
> They are so young and without guile.

> Oh, if the sonless mother weeping
> The widowed girls could look inside …
> They would rise and put their mourning off
> Praise God and say, 'He has enough.'[61]

Warming to the theme, the Bishop praised 'this brighter view of death to the nation in war, if we have not shown that death is not the ultimate calamity and end of all', having clearly forgotten that one of the objectives of the Mission was to persuade the country that patriotic service in itself did not guarantee a heavenly reward, which in effect would render the Church irrelevant. Horatio Bottomley was attacking the National Mission on exactly this point in the pages of *John Bull*.[62]

Belatedly, about halfway through the pamphlet, the Bishop appears to remember that he is leading a call to repentance. He sets about it in fine Victorian style. Before the war:

Unless we repent of the national sin of drink, we are not following the call of repentance and therefore not of hope.

Take an even more difficult point to put before you, the ravages in this nation of lust … I for one am not going to stand by while this goes on. We are nothing if not a fighting Church. The Church is no mere debating society but really a fighting force. If people in London think I for one am going to sit down while I preach repentance and hope, while all the time there is an open moral sewer in London, they are making a great mistake. If music halls are still to be known as places of assignation, if we are going to allow things to be put before young people's eyes in cinema shows to injure their minds, then I for one have yet to learn what the good of the church is … I am trying negotiation first. If that fails I shall call upon the whole Church, the whole of London, to stand where I stand on the question and see whether we Christians are going to be masters in our own house.[63]

None of that new-fangled nonsense about materialism here: sin is sin, largely committed by poor people and to be preached against.[64] Even after more than eighty years William Temple's groans seem audible. Winnington-Ingram was not alone in his view that the National Mission should be used to promote clean living: in one of the stranger pamphlets, Capt. Douglas White, MD, RAMC, suggested that during the catechising process, doctors ought to be involved to warn young people of the dangers of promiscuity.[65] Nevertheless the run of pamphlets as a whole were far less obsessed with the sins of lust and drink than *John Bull* or Siegfried Sassoon believed.

Perhaps the most revealing pamphlet was that by Canon Streeter which indicated the low expectations of the mission among many in the church:

Unless my own experience is a very unusual one, it must be frankly admitted that the prevailing feeling in the Church about the National Mission is not at all optimistic.

Like other Englishmen in this hour of grim struggle, clergy and church workers are anxious to do their bit ... But along with all this readiness to serve is a deep and widespread despondency ... Firstly, the forces at our disposal are so inadequate – so many of the youngest and most vigorous of the clergy are away as Chaplains ... People are much too occupied with the war to take the slightest notice of the mission. Thirdly, we ask ourselves, what is the good of telling the nation to repent just now, when it knows that it is fighting for the cause of righteousness, and when it has shown an amount of heroism, sacrifice and discipline which neither our enemies, nor our friends, nor ourselves ever supposed it was capable of.

No doubt the nation has many sins to repent of, but is this the moment to insist on the fact?[66]

Streeter tried to refute these arguments, but the pessimists were absolutely right. Judged as a mission to reach the unchurched, the whole 1916 effort was a complete failure. Church attendance was not noticeably boosted and the working class remained as apparently indifferent as ever. The 'Woolwich Crusade' to munition workers in 1917 even saw claims that the workers were becoming actively hostile to the Church.[67] The Church took some comfort in the thought that this had been an unprecedented communal effort by the Church of England, and had gone some way to overcoming historical fissures within the Church and deepening laity commitment. But judged as a mission, it was a failure.

It is tempting to attribute the failure of the National Mission to leadership. An analogy with that other great national effort of the year, the Battle of the Somme, comes to mind: enormous effort, negligible results. The image presents itself of young clerical lions led by Episcopal donkeys.[68] Dick Sheppard, in a piece entitled *The Casual Correspondence of a London Vicar*, wrote:

I am convinced that for more than three years now the leaders of the church have displayed complete incapacity for effective and vigorous leadership, and a disastrous inability to realise that heroic days need and welcome heroic action.

   Does authority realise that there are thousands standing aloof from organised religion not because of what is worst in them, but because of what is best.[69]

But such an analysis should be treated with great caution. The fundamental vision of the Mission's greatest advocates was hubristic. The belief that they could bring the entire nation, particularly the working class, into a sacramental fellowship in the midst of a world war, was an extreme case of wishful thinking. As well as the obvious practical difficulties, it was based on a profound misunderstanding of popular religiosity, in particular what people actually wanted from their Church. A private letter from Rev. Lord William Cecil to the Revd George Bell, secretary to the Archbishop of Canterbury, made some obviously sound points:

I a little regret the pessimistic tone which runs through a great deal of the National Mission work ... religion is a thing of tradition not of personal conviction in most minds, and the alteration of that tradition is always a very slow matter ... What I feel strongly is wrong is to suggest that the normal state of the nation is that everyone should be a Christian and that therefore the Church that has to confess that a large amount of the population is only semi-Christian has failed ... let us remember that the sacramentarian Christianity, however true is not the only Christianity ... One cannot help feeling thankful for what Christianity as a whole has done. For after all what other country has raised four million recruits to the call of duty, where in the history of the world has such splendid sacrifice been shown. Whether sacramentarian or non sacramentarian, the thing is beautiful. We should all be proud that ninety per cent of the nation which has done such a wonderful thing call themselves Churchmen. It attributes to the Church the origin of the ideals, whose nobleness astonishes the world.[70]

This might seem complacent, but it is eminently plausible. Winnington-Ingram himself, although he admired the dedication of the young Anglo-Catholics, belonged, like Cecil, to a generation that did not define frequent communion as the essence of Anglicanism.[71] The emphasis of his approach – patriotic sermonising and patri-passionism, a bit of moralising and, in practical terms, a concentration on street shrines and intercession, writing to the troops, charity to families and so on – crude though it sounds, may well have been better judged than Temple's exhortations for Christian fellowship, or Lansbury's plea for the replacement of capitalistic selfishness. It might have been intellectually unsatisfying, indeed downright offensive, for a secular sceptic such as Sassoon, but Sassoon was not typical. It is worth remembering that Winnington-Ingram had a quarter of a century of experience of the religious challenge of London: at Toynbee Hall from 1888 to 1895, as Rector of Bethnal Green 1895–1898, Bishop of Stepney 1898–1901 and finally as Bishop of London for thirteen years. He had learned his trade at the sharp end. Unpalatable as it may be, he was probably the best judge of the popular mood of wartime London and perhaps the country in general. Indicative of this was his shrewd attempt at rapprochement with Horatio Bottomley, when *John Bull* attacked the mission as 'obsessed with drink and lust'. He invited Bottomley to tea and charmed him to the extent that Bottomley offered him space to write in *John Bull* for three weeks. Winnington-Ingram's intention to write a pastoral letter beginning 'Dear Brother' and confessing the sins of the Church was vetoed by the Mission Council. The Bishop regretted this: 'I wanted to reach the ordinary man in the street, while I am afraid that the mission has only reached, in the main, those who were already Church people.'[72] This was a very accurate judgement.

The 'failure' of the National Mission prompted a degree of soul-searching. Institutionally, the Archbishop's Committee of Inquiry would be the most important response. But this response was in part shaped by the actions of a pressure group within the Church which coalesced soon after the mission ended in 1917.

In March 1917, William Temple had a meeting with Dick Sheppard at the vicarage of St Martin's. The two men, almost exact contemporaries, were somewhat different in temperament and recent experience. Temple's heavy personal investment in the National Mission had apparently been in vain due to the institutional constraints of the Church. For an establishment golden boy, used to success, this must have been galling. By contrast Dick Sheppard, in maverick fashion, was having a rather successful war as vicar of St Martin's in the Field, a phenomenally successful church for soldiers in transit through London. The meeting was to draw on both men's conclusions to demand a new beginning for the Church of England. At Queen's Hall on 16 July 1917 they launched the 'Life and Liberty Movement'. Significant amongst the speakers was Maude Royden, a good friend of Temple's and a congregational minister. The issue of women's ministry, although not that of ordination, in the Anglican Church, had been raised by the National Mission. Preparatory to the movement's launch they had prepared a 'scandal sheet';

It is a scandal that the right to appoint a man to a cure of souls should be bought and sold ...

It is a scandal that there should be no place for women in the councils of the church.

It is a scandal that the church should have no power to alter her forms of service, according to need, and it is a scandal that the church should be unable to adjust her finances, which too often permit a great inequality of payment for services rendered.[73]

It would not be an exaggeration to say that the National Mission and the Life and Liberty response were the crucial events in setting the agenda for the Church of England for the rest of the century.

Chapels

A national war effort had obvious potential benefits for a national Church. Where did the war leave the chapels? Nonconformity had been ambivalent about the prospect of war, but the idealised and crusading aspects of the war, once begun, had at least some appeal in these circles. Chapels could act as a focal point for civilian volunteer activity. In Hartlepool, the Grange Road Primitive Methodists held regular 'socials' for servicemen which were attended by 12,000 during the course of the war, but this was dwarfed by the concerts of the St George Congregationalists which were attended by 122,000. The desire to provide a moral alternative to drinking and whoring for young men away from home drove virtually every chapel to attempt to provide this form of social service. This pious concern for the morals of the fighting man was much derided in *John Bull* and other populist newspapers who saw it as a slur.[74]

But there was also genuinely disinterested generosity, as when Hyde in Cheshire suddenly found itself host to 137 Roman Catholic refugees from Belgium. Of the 26 different groups which volunteered accommodation, no fewer than 9 were the local chapels, including all 3 Methodist denominations and the Congregationalists.[75]

In many urban localities the chapel was a powerful focus of identity. A defiant spirit forged in three centuries of political conflict with the 'establishment' could be turned towards a broader patriotism. J. E. Buckrose, in a fictionalised but plausible account of an East Yorkshire chapel meeting, described the response to an air-raid warning. Her aged female heroine insists that the congregation stays put: 'You're – You're not going to let Kayser think he's scared us Chigsby Primitives!' She begins singing:

the same miracle happened to every Yorkshire man and woman there. One by one they joined in; the volume of sound grew louder – louder – and when Mrs Briggs reached the final chorus: 'We are on the Lord's Side! We for him will go!' the very roof tree seemed to quiver in the blast of sound which burst suddenly from every straining throat. But it was not a hymn any longer. It was the battle cry of Holderness sounding through the ages.[76]

The appeal to those on the 'the Lord's Side' could become a specific inducement to patriotism. In the Caerphilly district the chapels joined the appeal for volunteers: 'We need not point out to you that this appeal is essentially a Christian duty. This war is a contest between our most holy faith and the brutal barbarisms of the modern school of German philosophy.'[77]

English Presbyterians were probably the 'dissenters' with the fewest qualms about warfare. The sermons of Alexander Connell, ex-president of the Free Church council and minister at Sefton Park Presbyterian Church in Liverpool, showed a particular crusading fervour. The outbreak of the war was 'Armageddon, surely the last madness of humanity. The pity of it and the horror of it'; but even though, 'we have loved peace', it had been pursued, 'to the verge of dishonour'. By 30 August 1914 his sermon was entitled 'A Moral Menace to Civilization'. Connell had no doubt that the war was a crusade: 'What have we to defend? Not our shores only, but also our shrines', and that the very fabric of decency was threatened: 'Not our rights only, but our freedom to perform life's common duties. Not our independence only, but also our charities ... Not our pride of race only, but also religion.' On the second anniversary of the war his sermon was entitled, 'The Sceptre of Ungodliness'. The congregation met 'this Sabbath morning to commemorate a woeful day ... A reckless hand unleashed the dogs of war, and the struggle that followed has soaked Europe in blood ... has held up, for a time at least the forces of progress.'[78]

By October 1916, in response to the National Mission, which the Free Churches did not participate in, but were sympathetic towards, Connell echoed the rhetoric of the Anglicans: 'this still more ominous fact may be asserted, that in a time of unexampled suffering and nameless sacrifice – the Cross of Christ – that supreme symbol alike of suffering and sacrifice, has not laid its spell upon us with new power'.

Connell identified what was, from a Calvinist viewpoint, a particularly offensive form of profiteering as being to blame:

It is impossible to resist the conclusion forced upon us from many quarters that there is a strain of unseemliness and even of obscenity appearing in our social life and amusements and it is nothing but sheer disgusting hypocrisy on the part of those who are making blood money out of the corruption and debasement of our youth to pretend otherwise.[79]

Commitment to the national cause broadened the respectability of non-conformity, but also weakened it. The very identity of dissent had been a product of conflict. Wartime ecumenicism was a double-edged sword. When a Unitarian minister could preach a sermon in a combined inter-cession service to a mixed congregation of Primitive Methodists, Wesleyans, Unitarians and Anglicans, ironically at Holy Trinity Church in Hyde, it appeared in many respects that dissent had finally attained full respectability. But at the same time it was a tacit acknowledgement of the centrality of the 'National' Church.[80] The rivalry of dissent with the establishment had frequently been the essence of local religious behaviour. If all Christians were united, what was the point of the chapels?

Internally the war was causing them problems as well. The demography of losses, with a particular focus on young men of the lower middle classes, had particularly worrying implications for the culture of the chapels. The stalwarts of the associational life of dissent were particularly vulnerable. While it is true that nonconformist idealism could act as a cultural resist-ance to the pressure to volunteer, as the recruitment patterns of rural Wales and Leicestershire might suggest, equally the volunteer ethic which was the lifeblood of the chapels was a powerful draw *towards* military service in many areas. The denominational 'rolls' from Hyde, an area of substantial religious diversity, illustrates this:

	Church of England	Roman Catholics	Methodists (all)	Other 'dissent'
Volunteers	c. 1028	207	446	324

Sidebotham, *Hyde*, pp. 141–6

Whilst the number of Anglicans volunteering outnumbers all the others put together, it should be noted that the Church of England was claiming everyone who wasn't demonstrably something else. The others included the non-denominational PSA and even nineteen members of the Socialist Church. It is clear that many of the dissenting laity who volunteered had been important and active chapel members; such comments are far less common regarding Anglicans.

Furthermore, the sacramental and priest-based hierarchies of Anglicanism and Catholicism, particularly the latter, could be maintained without a vigorously active male laity. The ultimate prospects for dissent were not as good, if key personnel disappeared during wartime. Connell sermonised on the impact of war on these men, 'I myself have heard a young man home on leave ... slip in the observation with the most natural air in the world, "I can tell you life out there makes you pray." On the other hand the cases are numerous where the opposite effect seems to be produced.' A second-hand anecdote told of a young man who claimed, 'the whole business shatters one's faith in religion'.

An aspect of British Protestantism had always been the visible rewards of the godly life. Among the ironies of the war was that the 'conscientious' volunteer was likely to suffer worldly pain, whilst the immoral apparently went unpunished. Although in a strict sense this had always been consistent with the religious message of Christianity, it took a certain strong-mindedness within the 'elect' to accept this on a huge scale.

The Rolls of Honour for the Baptist and Congregational Chapels in Hornchurch in Essex show one local case of disproportionate casualties amongst chapel volunteers:

	Baptist Chapel	Congregational Chapel
Served	30	19
Died	7	6
Death rate	23.3%	31.5%

Perfect, *Hornchurch*, pp. 264–5

These losses were equivalent to those suffered by the alumni of the public schools or the Oxbridge colleges. Such losses would have long-lasting implications for the life of the local chapel. Until there is a full-scale study of the impact of the war on nonconformity as a whole, this must remain speculative; but there is one clear indication that the war, either through death or disillusionment, hollowed out male nonconformity in Britain. The male war generation – men under the age of 25 in 1914 – were, *after* the war, conspicuously absent statistically in the call to ministry.

Age profile of serving nonconformist ministers

% of ministers between the ages of 31 and 40	1891	1911	1931
Wesleyan	27.7	22.3	13.8
Primitive Methodist	22.9	34.2	15.9
United Methodist	34.7	26.3	12.5
Baptist	31.6	26.5	11.5
Congregational	26.8	25.6	15.3

K. D. Brown, *A Social History of the Nonconformist Ministry in England and Wales*, Oxford, 1988, p. 230

In an already numerically declining ministry the 'war generation' were *further* disproportionately under-represented. A modest generational decline pre-war is replaced by a catastrophic post-war absence. This decline of younger men becoming ministers is specific to the war generation; for the *post-war* generation it is considerably less marked. It is not possible to say whether this is caused by the death of young men who would otherwise have found a calling, or by a rejection, conscious or unconscious, of deeply held faith on the part of the survivors. It could be explained institutionally – the men who would have trained for the ministry in 1914–1918 did not do so – but this still begs the question as to why they did not train after the war.

In retrospect it is clear that the historic peak of nonconformity was achieved in the first years of the twentieth century, contributing to the resurgence of the fortunes of the Liberal Party in 1906. The long decline had set in before 1914. But the war may well have contributed far more than is usually acknowledged. At the same time it should be noted that the long-term impact of nonconformist evangelicalism was still in various forms a crucial component of popular mentality, and one which helps explain the heterogeneous religiosity of wartime Britain.

Religion: the laity

THE PARSON'S JOB

> What do you want?
> Coming to this 'ere 'ell?
> Ain't it enough to know he's dead,
> Killed by a bit o' German lead
> What! Does the Lord mean well?
>
> I guess ye' are daft!
> He's one of the good 'uns Jim;

Nature's gentleman, rough but true.
He didn't know how to sin,
But what is that to you?

You make me sick.
Why should he die,
When forger Wright wins a V.C.
And criminal Kelly catches a spy?
That don't spell justice to me.

Get out, or I'll strike you down.
I'm carrying his kid
Do you call that fair? ...

I hate your religion
I don't want gold.
I only want my man.
What? It's in me to enfold
Jim in my babyland?

God bless yer, Parson,
I'll try to think right
upon my widowed way,
So Jim ain't quite out of sight
Teach me – ow – to pray.

Margaret Ida Bedford[81]

This condescending but not entirely unsympathetic view of 'cockney' religious attitudes encapsulates the view of some middle-class believers that the war was both a challenge and an opportunity for formal religion. London, and particularly working-class London, was an infamously irreligious city by British standards in the early twentieth century. Robert Saunders provides a sidelight on this with a pointed wartime joke:

A good story is going the rounds at the moment of a cockney who joined the army and at the end of a week's marching and drilling and being referred to as No 254 he found himself nodding at his first church parade. Rousing up he heard, 'No. 254, "Art Thou Weary" and promptly shouted 'Not Arf!'[82]

Although there is a danger of over-interpretation the choice of a cockney to be unfamiliar with the Anglican hymnbook and undeferential at church parade is revealing. But this should be seen within the contemporary British context. Despite theories of secularisation, religion was still a pervasive part of Edwardian life. National statistics help illustrate this. In 1914 there were 2,226,000 Easter communicants in the church of England, 9.2% of the adult population. Historically this was a very respectable figure, substantially better than for the middle of the nineteenth century. Secularisation theory is a blunt instrument. In the fifty years before the First World War some statistics indicate a rise in religious practice: Sunday Schools, Confirmation, Easter Communion and Baptism; some indicate a fall: adult Sunday attendance, church marriage, church burial. Rather than assume that urbanisation had led to a 'decline' in religion, it makes more sense to acknowledge that practices and beliefs were changing. Church attendance was no longer a pre-requisite of respectability by 1914 and the biggest *decline* in Sunday attendance was amongst the middle classes. But Britain in 1914 was not post-Christian, and neither was the Britain of 1918.[83]

Casual use of religious language and reference was commonplace in a society where exposure to the tenets of organised Christianity far outweighed formal churchgoing. Back-handed evidence of this can be found in the adaptation of hymn tunes for popular wartime soldiers' songs: 'Fred Karno's Army' was sung to a hymn tune and the song the 'Bells of Hell Go Ding a Ling' included the distinctly exotic Biblical adaptation, 'Oh death where is thy sting a ling, oh grave thy victory.'

Although these parodies might be taken as evidence of wartime rejection of religion they also stand as strong evidence of widespread familiarity with the tunes and language of hymns, unsurprising in a nation where acts of worship were compulsory in schools, and Salvation Army bands played outside pubs. According to Sarah Williams hymns were closely woven into the communal and family life of Southwark. If this was the case in an area where both chapel and church were weak in formal terms, it is likely to have been far more the case in areas of chapel vitality.[84]

Williams has also found a more general 'personal, familial and corporate familiarity with a series of religious images and symbols'. This is perfectly explicable. Sunday-schooling was a standard part of the formation of the war generation. Thompson and Vignes found this in their oral history interviews of working-class Londoners born between 1878 and 1908. Of forty-five people interviewed, *all* of them had attended Sunday school. Hugh Macleod's analysis of these interviews broke the families into three groups: thirteen of them were actively religious, fourteen indifferent or antagonistic, and eighteen in between. It is noteworthy that even the indifferent and the antagonistic were prepared to be bribed, by 'school treats', into sending their children for a religious education, and that a much larger group saw it as an important part of bringing up a child.[85]

The disparity between this near-universal childhood involvement and apparent adult apathy was much remarked upon by clergy: 'the children – so promising while quite young ... will one day casually leave us without saying a word. They have no support at home, "Father and mother don't go to church, why should we?"'[86] Church involvement was often seen as a phase in the lifecycle amongst the working classes, to be put aside on entry into work and adulthood. But as much as five years of Sunday school shouldn't be dismissed lightly – the Londoners of 1914 were not the 'ignorant heathens' of 1850; they had a grounding in Christian doctrine and often had a distinct, if idiosyncratic belief in 'Christian values'. London has been singled out as the 'worst case'. If the informal influence of Christian belief was still pervasive in the metropolis, where formal allegiance to the Church was weak, it seems reasonable to contend that elsewhere it was stronger still. In many other parts of England, formal religion in the form of church and chapel attendance was much stronger, in Wales stronger still and in Scotland there was a patchy picture of strength and weakness.

Religion probably held more personal significance than this would suggest. Letters to and from the front invoke God frequently, and it is quite clear that families regularly prayed for the safety of absent members.[87] Such sentiments were widespread. The Bishop of Stepney quoted a prayer composed by a 7-year-old girl for recitation during air raids:

> God is our refuge
> Don't be dismayed
> He will protect us
> All through the raid.[88]

That *some* individuals occasionally appeared indifferent to religion is illustrated by Elizabeth Fernside's comment, 'Last night we went to the pictures as being Good Friday, there was nothing else doing';[89] her occasional visits to Westminster Abbey or St Paul's appear to be purely sightseeing. But in other letters she refers to the local congregational church and its activities, and a Christmas circular from the pastor F. W. Bryan is enclosed in Fred Fernside's letter collection. This impression of religious indifference is deeply misleading. The Fernsides were keen members of the PSA, Pleasant Sunday Afternoons, a popular movement founded in the 1880s with some 50,000 members in London. Non-denominational and dedicated to 'rational entertainment' and high-minded discussion, the movement typified a reaction to the stifling solemnity of much evangelical culture. Indeed the Fernsides' religious tastes were apiece with their general lifestyle: a mixture of thoughtfulness and light-heartedness.

Ordinary parish and chapel activity continued throughout the war. A letter from the 8-year-old Mabel Farrier in Hornsey, to her father at the front, shows that Sunday school still functioned in introducing children to some basic religious elements, and that religion appears to have acted as a tie of sorts within the family:

Mum said that when we go to Sunday school we can ask Mrs Hardwick if she has got a hymn book with a stiff cover. The Bible that Uncle Rube sent me has got all lovely pictures in it about Eastern countries. I wish you could see it. But when you come home you will be able to see it.[90]

One family with a clearly active religious life were the Proctors of Sydenham. William Proctor's letters to his son are full of quasi-theological speculation: 'We shall none of us die until the time appointed to us & then nothing in the world can keep us alive ... so why bother about it ... when we leave this world of trouble and hypocrisy we may rest assured that the almighty is far more merciful';[91] and a call to prayer: 'I should like to think that you, like your Mother and Father, repeat the Lord's prayer morning and evening daily, not garbled like a mere spell, but earnestly & thoughtfully, if we believe in Christ we will certainly do our best to carry out his commandments.'[92] William Proctor combined this religious eclecticism with a strong moralising tendency:

One thing you can be thankful for my son and that is while being a poor working man you escape the temptations & trials that a moneyed man with leisure must inevitably meet with ... it has been my life's experience that if one doesn't drink spirits and rake the streets nightly, well he will not be troubled above all never get mixed up with a loose woman, they are poisonous and no good at all.[93]

Proctor's 'independent' religious views were 'Cromwellian' in another sense: he had no difficulty with the idea of a vengeful and partisan God. On reading of the outbreak of the Spanish influenza among German troops: 'with this wonderful disease creeping up amongst the Bosches, it looks as if the Almighty has said "thus far and no further"'.[94] Nor did forgiveness play much role in his personal faith: 'as for the objects [conscientious objectors] I would not be cruel, but certainly give them something to think about, as they object to help the community so the community should object to help them.' 'We don't want war, but, if forced, we must be like the Quaker & serve the Hun as he did, push him overboard, saying "Friend, thou art not wanted here"',[95] 'such men as talk about peace and don't be harsh to the "gentle German", those men should be interned and their goods confiscated.'[96] At the end of the war, he wrote:

Everyone appears to be clamouring for the head of the Kaiser and no wonder as in spite of the Lawyer's decision he ought to be tried & the men who defend him, lawyers and liars are the same & it is notorious that as the Scribes and Pharisees behave just as they did in our Saviours time, they are just as hypocritical and lying.[97]

The mixture of 'patriotism', religiosity, moralising and bigotry in William Proctor's letters is strikingly reminiscent of the tone of Horatio Bottomley's *John Bull*, as is the distrust of politicians and the praise for the common-sense of the 'little man'. Indeed Bottomley's articulation of working-class and lower middle class 'religiosity' may have been part of his appeal. Just as Bottomley clashed with the Anglican bishops over the issue of 'national repentance', so William Proctor has a similarly Manichean view of the war in which Germany embodies all evil.

His wife expressed her faith in a very different way, and it was her rather than William who was the regular churchgoer: 'Daisy & I went to Holy Communion this morning and there was a large congregation – as many as there is on Xmas or Easter Day, Poor old Fred came home Thursday & has been home since 11 this morning so D.V. we shall go to church together this evening.'[98] The abbreviation 'DV' appears frequently in her letters and must in the context stand for 'God Willing'. Her letters often mention her prayers for family members and refer frequently to God.

Edie Bennet also appears to have been a regular wartime churchgoer. Indeed church attendance appears to be almost the only thing that she regularly did outside the home.[99] Characteristically of her, it doesn't seem to have brought a great deal of comfort or reduced her sense of isolation:

It was very sad in the church on Sunday evening, the Reverend Lampen told all the congregation that he had received a special message from the Bishop that he wasn't to preach the sermon that he'd made out, but to kneel in prayer as while we were doing this our country was deciding its fate for future freedom justice and liberty ... speaking for myself, I felt rotten & choked up, was all on my own as usual and had the pew to myself.[100]

These cases catch something important about the war: it accelerated rather than originated the gendering of religious observance. Congregations were already becoming feminised before the war, but the absence of male churchgoers in the forces made the process even more visible. Church and chapel attendance did fall slightly through the course of the war, as male parishioners and chapel stalwarts volunteered or were called up. Overall adult 'membership' of the Church of England and 'other major Protestant' denominations fell from 5,682,000 in 1914 to 5,563,000 in 1918, although there was supposedly a slight rise in Roman Catholic 'membership'.[101] Such statistics conceal as much as they reveal. This drop of 120,000 is extremely modest, with more than half a million adult men dead by the start of 1918, and with more than 4 million absent on military service. Even if the church attendance rate among military-age males had been very low prior to war, which is quite probable, it is still clear that more women, probably far more, were directly participating in formal religious life in 1918 than had been in 1914. The feminisation of congregations was everywhere remarked upon. Given the intensifying strains of war – queuing for food and overwork – this represented a real effort. Yet the rationale is obvious and straightforward: in conditions of

10. Petition for a day of prayer. IWM (Q53987).

separation and anxiety, resort to prayer for the safety of absent men was
perfectly natural, and churches could provide an element of communal
support where women would be in the company of others faced with the
same situation.

Religion was far more important to individuals in wartime Britain than
is generally believed. Regarding the Church of England in particular, it
has long been suggested, following Charles Masterman, that one of the
greatest disappointments of the church in wartime was its failure to stand
above the melee, with Masterman writing that a sermon at Westminster
Abbey sounded like the activity of Wellington House.[102]

But it seems equally plausible to present the opposite view: that,
Winnington-Ingram notwithstanding, the balanced and judicious attempt
to combine 'just war' theology with a call to national repentance was too
even-handed for many people who wanted a more whole-hearted commitment to the 'right side'. The Archbishop of Canterbury complained in
1917, after he had come out against reprisal air raids, that he was the
'recipient of a continuous shower of protests, denunciations and virulent

abuse from every part of England, particularly London'. A polemicist in 1917 raged against the 'flabby-babby babble of Boche-defending Bishops'.[103] Uncomfortable as it is to admit, Winnington-Ingram had his finger on the popular pulse in his patriotism and it was the moderation rather than the extremism of Anglicanism which probably caused the greater discontent amongst churchgoers. Furthermore the Church was open to accusations of deficient patriotism in practice. Indeed, one of the most emotive issues, and a cause of some real anti-clerical sentiment, was the exemption of the clergy and theological students from military service. The Church was accused of providing an escape route for shirkers and Episcopal opposition to clergy conscription was seen as subversive and a useful stick for anti-clerical demagogues.

John Bull maintained a relentless anti-clerical assault during the war years, publishing attacks on nonconformist ministers and Archbishops alike whenever they showed any sign of Christian sympathy with the German people. Clerical exemption was fiercely mocked: 'I don't see why able-bodied psalm-smiters shouldn't lend a hand.' When the bishops opposed reprisals, Noel Pemberton-Billing was allowed to attack the Primate directly: 'Is the Archbishop of Canterbury ... to be permitted to stand between this country and the crushing of a nation which has outraged and devastated Europe.'[104]

Furthermore, to assume that the patriotism of the State Church somehow discredited it is to accept an exaggerated idea of widespread disillusionment with organised religion after the end of the war. This is questionable. It is worth noting that the historic peak of the *proportion* of baptism of newborn infants occurred in the 1920s, and while this was probably more indicative of respectability, sociability and 'folk religion' than deep religious commitment, it is nevertheless hard to reconcile with a deep disgust at orthodoxy on the part of the population at large.[105]

In many respects the precise position of the churches on the war was probably not greatly relevant. The churchgoing population was already used to the idea of listening selectively to the Church message. The eclecticism of British religious life meant that even the already 'broad' range of styles and opinions available within the churches could be supplemented on the part of individual believers from a range of other sources, some of them technically very unorthodox.

The real test for Christian orthodoxy in wartime was whether it could provide adequate consolation to the bereaved. For some families the faith of their upbringing was highly effective in this respect. The Baines family of Putney were devout Roman Catholics. Indeed, Ralph Baines was inducted into the Society of Jesus in 1918. The letters he received show

how their faith helped them cope with extreme pressure: Ralph lost two brothers on the Somme and a third in May 1917. The last case was particularly bad – George Baines, known as 'Dodo', had been reported as recovering before he died of his wounds. A letter to Ralph from his sister Betty stated that the only consolation was that their brother was now enjoying 'wonderful happiness'. Traditional structures helped as much as personal faith: their mother had Father Cooney of Wandsworth say a requiem mass. The nuns of Roehampton inscribed the names of all three brothers on a Calvary in their garden which was turned into a shrine. The root of the family's confident faith was in all probability the devout grandmother who reacted to the loss of a third grandchild with the words, 'God's will be done.' The ordination of Ralph, and his sister's insistence that her fiancé convert to Catholicism before they married, are clear evidence that the Baines family were not shaken in their beliefs.[106]

Catholicism maintained a strong sense of an ongoing relationship between the living and the dead. Praying for those in purgatory and to saints in heaven for their intercession were central requirements of the faith. For devout Roman Catholics, coping with war deaths involved extending civilian practices. Justification was less of an issue – the Pope had not endorsed either side and Roman Catholics were dying on both sides in pursuit of their patriotic duty. The war was emphatically not a crusade: the Baineses believed whole-heartedly in the justice of the British cause but hopes of heaven did not rest upon that.

As a national Church, the Church of England was inevitably caught in a much more difficult position. They could not formally provide the comfort of a 'crusade', an automatic remittance of sins to those who died in the war – the concept was archaic and, from an orthodox Augustinian position of redemption by faith alone, heretical. Neither the 'Catholic' wing, which was keen on reviving the concept of purgatory, nor the 'Protestant' wing, which wanted to stand fast to the purity of election, could countenance such a course, although Winnington-Ingram sailed dangerously close to the wind at times. This left a gap for self-professed 'Christians' such as Horatio Bottomley to assert automatic salvation without any doctrinal basis. But many were prepared to go further, claiming that the dead were not only in heaven, but actually accessible. The popularity of spiritualism in wartime is well known. The church might condemn it, but street shrines and a hope of eternal life with no guarantees looked weak by comparison with actual conversation with those who had 'passed over'. All parts of society got involved, most famously demonstrated in the publication of *Raymond*, a description by Sir Oliver Lodge of his contacts with his dead son through seances; but the appeal may have been greatest where the hold of orthodoxy was already tenuous.

George Lansbury was approached by Sylvia Pankhurst to protect from conscription a delicate 18-year-old boy, with conscientious objections that he was unable to express. Lansbury couldn't do it. The boy was duly enlisted in the infantry and reported missing presumed dead. In Pankhurst's words: 'The mother took to Spiritualist seances, in the hope of finding him and sought to obtain messages from a board the Spiritualists supplied. "Some have their boys; – has her board!" her sister said.'[107]

There were times when Christian socialism was not enough either.

6 The conditional sacrifices of labour 1915–1918

The industrial truce and its limitations

Three years ago, the war was popular, a thing for which people were glad to make sacrifices. At present as far as I can see, it is not. I doubt one could get a hearing at a working class meeting if one spoke of the principles at stake. One would get laughed down.

R. H. Tawney, December 1917[1]

The limitations of a language of sacrifice had been neatly anticipated by the *Daily Herald* in the first week of the war: 'The toilers may well be tired of sacrifices. All their life is a sacrifice.'[2] At the start, this newspaper, along with most of the Liberal press and much of the Conservative press was anticipating complete industrial collapse: there would be massive unemployment accompanied by shortages and inflation. August did indeed prove turbulent, but by September prices were stabilising, there were no widespread food shortages and a labour shortage in certain industries led rapidly to full employment. Although there was a good deal of criticism, the Prince of Wales Fund for the relief of distress sent a helpful signal to those suffering from economic dislocation that the middle and upper classes were not reacting with indifference to their plight. Yet even with these qualifications duly noted, the first half of the war saw a great deal of real hardship for the industrial workers. In these circumstances, the relative social peace of the first two years of the war came as a surprise. Part of the reason was the harnessing of trade-union and class consciousness to the national cause.

The two black spots in industrial relations in the first war years were strategically important 'peripheries', the South Wales coal fields and the Clyde. The strikes in these areas gave an impression of labour discontent, but were motivated by essentially local considerations which took on national significance as a result of Government action. Anthracite coal was essential to the Royal Navy; engineering and ship-building on the Clyde were of great general importance.

The South Wales valleys were the Wild West of pre-war industrial relations. Isolated mining villages were acutely aware of the intensity of exploitation at the hands of coal owners and a defensive trade-union culture was extremely strong. An unwillingness to give up hard-won peacetime gains was evident from the outset of the war. These early strikes are best interpreted as warning shots.

The fact that the principal customer for the coal was the Admiralty and that the civilian head of the Admiralty was Winston Churchill, the man widely although erroneously believed in the valleys to have ordered a violent police response to the Tonypandy strike did not help. This helps to explain the intervention of Lloyd George, who pulled out all the stops in using ethnic solidarity to try to soothe the miners.

Wartime arbitration and agreements could not remove the underlying bitterness. A confidential agent's report in August 1916 on the mood of the Welsh miners stated succinctly, 'As regards the relationship between coal owners and their employees, I have nowhere experienced such mistrust.'[3]

The Clyde was very different. Whilst discontent in South Wales was principally rooted in pre-war conditions, the revolt on the Clyde grew out of pre-war concerns, but took on a very specific wartime aspect. The housing crisis was the first manifestation, but this discontent quickly contributed to a more generally poisoned atmosphere. The formation of the Clyde Workers' Committee, which grew out of the housing crisis, became perceived as a threat by both employers and Government. The Committee was essentially defensive, but it was also extremely combatative.

Employers and employees alike contributed to the growing tension. This was a tension exacerbated by Government intervention and the uses to which it was put. The Balfour report on Clyde disturbances highlighted the extent of 'local friction'. A private memorandum in January 1916 by an informant spoke of the 'irritation on account of the Munitions Act'. A letter from Phillip McDevitt, a longstanding trade unionist, was more explicit. He wrote of 'the thousand and one pricks of petty tyranny'. He cited the misuse of leaving certificates by employers to control the work-force against the spirit of the Munitions of War Act and warned that 'All faith in the Ministry of Munitions is going.' This loss of faith would have serious consequences.[4]

From the other side of the bench, the employers were complaining of obstruction and absenteeism. In October 1915, 80% of the workforce were working less than the supposed norm of fifty-four hours. In February 1916 inspectors at Beardmore's stated that 260 of the workforce did not show up on Monday mornings. At Fairfield's a figure of 20% absenteeism was reported, and '20% of the men were hopeless wasters who ought to be taken into the colours'. Employers blamed high wages which encouraged alcohol abuse. The hawkish tone is as important as the supposed facts: the employers, with Ministry of Munitions backing, were gearing up for a fight. The absenteeism, which reflected a truculent refusal by workers to submit to new working conditions, could not be tolerated. It is also abundantly clear that the Clyde had been chosen for a confrontation on the vexed issue of dilution in munition factories.[5]

The explosion, when it came, began on the issue of trade-union approaches to new women workers. David Kirkwood, a tool-maker and shop steward at Beardmore's new Parkhead gun making plant, introduced himself 'uninvited' to new female arrivals on 29 February 1916, to the chagrin of the Lady Supervisor. He told them that as a shop steward they could approach him with complaints. She complained about the interference of 'unauthorised men'. After a colleague repeated the approach the next day, suggesting that the women really ought to join a women's union, the colleague was threatened with the sack and Kirkwood was warned not to leave his bench. When he attempted to do so in March he was physically prevented from leaving his shop. After a discussion with William Beardmore, Kirkwood resigned his position as shop steward. This was the signal for a strike at the plant that began on 17 March 1916.

The apparent triviality of the incidents that led to the strike were in serious contrast to the consequences. It is clear that both sides had determined on a showdown, and so had the Ministry of Munitions.

The Clyde Workers' Committee (CWC) aimed to block the development of what they saw as 'industrial slavery'. They suspected, rightly as it turned out, that the local representatives of the Ministry of Munitions were not even-handed, but biased in favour of the employers. Management wanted to assert its right to manage. William Beardmore was an aggressive employer, although he seems to have been genuinely motivated by a patriotic desire to increase production: he had complained that male workers were turning out less than half of what the new machinery was capable of. The ministry wanted to break the CWC to deal with the endemic problems on Clydeside, but most significantly they wanted to force the executive of the Amalgamated Society of Engineers (ASE) to condemn the nascent shop stewards' movement and uphold the national agreement. As a result a small local dispute escalated rapidly. The strike spread to a second plant on 21 March and on 23 March the Ministry got the repudiation from the ASE that it had desired. Exraordinary action was then taken: four shop stewards including Kirkwood were picked out for 'deportation' from the Glasgow area. This led to a walkout of 300 more men at another plant on 27 March, and threats from several others; on 29 March the Albion motor works joined the protest. The ministry toughed it out, the deportations went ahead and the strike collapsed. By the middle of 1916 the situation on the Clyde was seen as very satisfactory. Nevertheless the CWC survived and the shop stewards' movement was maintained. It also began to spread.[6]

What did it all signify? To a certain extent it was personal. In December 1915, Lloyd George had met a hostile reception when he had spoken to munition workers in Glasgow. This undoubtedly coloured the Ministry of Munitions perceptions. The personalities of Kirkwood and Beardmore contributed: neither was the type to back down from a fight. Ironically, they would subsequently develop an excellent working relationship as fellow patriots concerned with modernising and improving production. In 1918, the CWC was properly integrated into the drive for munitions production and turned the area into the most productive in the British Isles. The most exaggerated influence was that of the Marxist economics classes of John Maclean and the newspaper *Forward*. This gave a tinge of revolutionary rhetoric to the Clyde strikes and many of the shop stewards had attended Maclean's classes. But the basic rhetoric was not one of capitalist exploitation but a fear of Government-sponsored slavery eroding the freedom of skilled workers. As Kirkwood retrospectively put it, 'I was happy at Beardmore's as a free man. I resented being at Beardmore's as a slave.'[7]

By the summer of 1916 the first ominous signs were appearing that the industrial truce was breaking down in a more general sense. Some of the deported Clyde shop stewards, when asked where they wanted to be sent, suggested Sheffield. An innocent interpretation would be that this was an area of good wages and high employment for skilled men. A less innocent one was that it was an area where shop steward activity amongst skilled men was on the rise.

A Ministry of Munitions report investigating Sheffield picked out the reasons. Wages as such were not a problem. Sheffield was noted for high wages. The report gave average weekly earnings for skilled men:

Trade	District rate	Under District rate
Turners	£5 3/8d	£3 9/6d
Fitters	£5 2/8d	£3 2/10d

Nevertheless the skilled workers were demanding a 10 shilling rise. The rationale was not pure greed; nor was it an objection to dilution, the employment of female and unskilled workers having gone ahead rather smoothly. This was in fact the problem: skilled workers in Sheffield were arguing that the nature of their job had changed radically. Their role was now quite different: 'war conditions had placed burdens on skilled workers supervising the semi- and unskilled'. They were 'deprived of rest'.

The figures from the Thomas Firth munitions plant bear out this complaint. Shell fitters were working an average 77-hour week; tool fitters were working 63 hours ordinarily and 88.5 hours when on nights; turners 58 hours rising to 88.5 hours on nights. Shift work of that level of intensity in wartime conditions was grinding the men down. They wanted tangible reward, to 'save against the end of the war' when they feared demobilisation might lead to unemployment, the 10 shillings were to compensate for increased prices.[8]

This kind of reasoning, sensible enough within the confines of an individual factory, was being balanced against wider concerns. Many would argue that working the equivalent of nearly thirteen hours per day for seven days a week was a reasonable price to avoid the trenches, particularly for good money. Productivity rises ahead of wage rises from the working class were being demanded by the Government as a right. Taking an overview, a Ministry of Munitions report at the start of 1916 admitted that the cost of living had risen 40% whilst wages had risen 10%. It went on to argue that wages did not measure income. In reality the picture was extremely varied. In four large munitions establishments, average income had risen between 25% and 70%. On the contentious Clyde, fitters' income had risen 43%; although other groups had done rather less well, for example, joiners' income had risen only 18%. In iron and steel income had risen between 20% and 60%, and in coal mining between 20% and 35%. What the report did not make explicit was that most groups of workers had seen their real income diminish, and those who had stayed ahead of inflation had done so only by substantially increased hours. But it did moralise on the issue: 'It is reasonable to expect that the working classes should bear some part of the cost of the war and also that during the war they should be willing to make some change in their standard of living (except amongst the very poorest).' The expected change was clearly downwards. This was a crucial admission: in the name of fairness the Government had already allowed working-class living standards to be squeezed by rising prices and intended to continue doing so.

Workers were not to be allowed to exploit conditions of full employment to redistribute wealth, a point that was made explicitly clear.[9] The stage was being set for a wider confrontation which would lead to a dramatic reversal.

Industrial unrest

Monica Couzens, a middle-class munitions volunteer, published an account of life in a munitions factory in 1916. It was not devoid of a certain propagandist edge, but Couzens was an astute participant observer and had a strong sense of a mission to explain to her middle-class readers. She brilliantly evokes the grinding conditions and the rough edge of the factory. The first thing she sees on her first day is a fight between two women workers over a hat. At the end of the day she passes out from the fumes, to general amusement. She describes the harshness of the management on the issue of punctuality and the frequent minor accidents.

Where she is most revealing is in her comments on the press perception of wealthy munition workers and the practical realities. Piece-rate bonuses that could theoretically be earned were in practice unobtainable except at serious cost to health. When a fellow worker did earn them, she remarked that this new friend had reproached herself for stupidity. Earning the maximum was a recipe for 'overstrain'. Couzens found it 'difficult to believe that the preposterously high wages sometimes quoted' even existed. In reality average earnings for women appeared to be between a pound a week and just over two pounds depending on whether it was night shift work, which region and level of responsibility. Earning the higher end of the wages required a twelve-hour shift. Because of the deterioration in transport, the twelve-hour shift in her factory involved being away from home anything from fourteen to sixteen hours. The regular workers were being sustained by their patriotism, their workplace solidarity and their humour. But there were ominous signs. The Minister of Munitions was perceived as the 'universal bogeyman'. The switch from eight-hour to twelve-hour shifts had met with universal resentment. Couzens collected some of the comments: 'We get more money, yes, but its not worth it'; 'It's killing me'; 'It's too much for anyone.'

The culture of the shop floor resented management: 'They'd tike the toe-nails off you if they 'ad half a chance.' On the whole Couzens was optimistic, but the picture she paints of her fellow workers is one of deep weariness. A similarly oppressive picture was published for an American audience the next year. The author, 'a representative war worker', spoke of the cold and comfortless dark winter mornings, which were borne because 'thousands of men are out in the trenches'. But, it went on to suggest, 'The ordinary factory hands … lack interest in the work … they do not definitely connect the work they do with the trenches.'

The condescension of this view is mistaken: at the back of all workers' minds the trenches never ceased to matter. When a strike was threatened amongst women workers at Woolwich, Lilian Barker, the larger-than-life superintendent, addressed the workers who met her with a 'grim silence'. She played the trump card of wartime industrial relations: 'to strike in wartime was giving arms to the enemy'. The threat was headed off. But day-to-day strain was taking its toll and a sense of inequity was building up. In 1917 industrial relations would develop into a complex game of brinkmanship. Underlying everything was the rising cost of living.

11. Work gates at Woolwich Arsenal. IWM (Q 27901).

By the start of 1917 prices had clearly outstripped increased earnings
for the vast majority of the regularly employed pre-war working class.[10] To
state this so baldly is to enter into a complex issue. That 'real wages' for a
lot of workers were falling might have surprised a lot of wartime commentators. As early as May 1916 stories of outrageous wages at Woolwich
Arsenal were becoming proverbial; for example, it was claimed that a
small businessman who had been forced to close by the war immediately
found himself earning £14 per week as a munitioneer.[11] The popular
folklore of munition workers buying pianos was universal, although
Bernard Waites points out that it is very hard to reconcile this with the
simple fact that the loss of German mechanisms brought piano manufacture to a virtual halt in wartime Britain!

Supporting the view of wartime prosperity, demographic studies have
pointed to a marked improvement in the sensitive indicator of infant
mortality across the war as a whole. Local histories also point to indications of increased prosperity, and there is a great deal of retrospective
anecdotal evidence to the same effect. In the inimitable words of Arthur
Harding, small-time crook in the East End:

The First World War had made a great change to Bethnal Green. Before then it was practically impossible to find work, but with the war every firm was getting busy and the people they said was 'unemployable' became the people to fill the jobs. Even the people round the corner in Gibraltar buildings got jobs. People who'd been scroungers all their bloody lives.[12]

For Robert Roberts in Salford the war was the single greatest leap forward in working-class living standards that had ever occurred. His chapter on the war is famously entitled 'The Great Release'. Talking of the local 'casuals', he states, 'For the first time ever they had money in their pockets all week.' An earlier indicator were the complaints of the local pawn-brokers that business was dropping away. Women appeared better dressed, houses began taking newspapers. By 1916 'abject poverty began to disappear from the neighbourhood'. One woman worker noto-riously complained at Christmas to Roberts's father that their shop didn't have a very wide stock and suggested that they might try selling some tinned lobster. Lobster shortage notwithstanding, the Roberts family shop in the heart of 'the classic slum' saw takings boom on the back of the new prosperity.[13] It is therefore tempting to see the war as an improvement in working-class living standards. Certainly an optimistic view of this issue has become prevalent in the literature. Bernard Waites has no doubts that by the middle of 1915 the general picture was one of prosperity. He cites numerous reports by the Charity Organisation Society, Home Office Intelligence and the Central Control Board concerned with the liquor industry. There were certainly some spectacular improvements: malnu-trition rates amongst London schoolchildren fell from 9.4% in 1914 to 6.6% in 1915, and in Doncaster from 31% in 1913 to 5% in 1915. In the classic slum of Salford, the medical officer noted a definite rise in nutri-tional standards among children, and overall the number of schoolchil-dren being fed under the 1906 act fell from a peak of 422,401 in March 1915 to 64,613 in 1917.[14]

But, when disaggregated, the picture is rather different. Full employ-ment was having a huge and significant impact on the poorest section of the working classes, the pre-war casual labourers. For example in Swindon the labour market was so buoyant that vagrancy disappeared, and in Leicester in the winter of 1915 it was found almost impossible to find sufficient fit casual labourers to clear the snow from the streets. Waites is doubtless right to point out that full employment benefited other workers as well; that pre-war underemployment had been much more widespread than anyone realised. But the other contention, that full employment immediately strengthened the bargaining position of all workers, is more suspect. In fact the effects of full employment were being deliberately hedged against by Government in regard to the broader working class. Restrictions in labour mobility and the no-strike agreements were holding wages down more effectively than is sometimes acknowledged. Jay Winter provides a useful table of weekly wages in a range of occupations which can be compared with the cost-of-living index:

Index (1914=100)	1916	1917
Cost of living	146	176
Wages (all workers)	121	155
Coal miners	138	158
Skilled engineers	111	134
Railwaymen	120	155
Dockers	130	150
Cotton (earnings)	107	119
Compositors	105	120
Bricklayers	108	122
Iron and steel	133	148
Building labour	115	134
Agricultural	140	189

Winter, *The Great War and the British People*, Table 7.7, p. 233.
Coal miners figure for Durham and North Yorks; iron and steel for South Wales

Only the wages of agricultural labourers had caught up with inflation by 1917, in part because of a chronic shortage by 1917, in part because the Government intervened directly that year to raise them. From the point of view of industrial relations the most serious gaps between wages and prices were those affecting the pre-war trade-union triple alliance: dockers, miners and railways, and the straight wage gap affecting skilled engineeers. Of course any commentator would immediately add that apart from the figure for cotton, these figures are misleading in that they ignore overtime, and the possibilities of piece rates and bonuses.

In Birmingham, it is possible to see some of the difficulties involved in assessing both real wages and differentials. Until December 1916, the wages of workers in engineering appear to have fallen behind inflation. Through 1917 and 1918 a series of ad hoc bonuses were negotiated. In April 1917 all workers received a 5/- raise, in August a further 3/-; in October skilled workers received a 12.5% increase, in December a 5/- increase; in January 1918 piece workers received 7.5%; and in August 1918 all workers received 3/- 6d.[15] How did this determine what was actually in pay packets? In August 1914 a skilled fitter or turner expected to earn 38/- per week. In November 1918, the minimum wage for these skilled men was 46/- per week plus 16/6d in 'war bonuses', plus either

12.5% or 7.5%. Labourers in the same industry had earned 23/- per week in 1914; by 1917 they were earning 30/- week, soon raised to 36/- per week plus 26/6d in 'war bonuses', plus 12.5%. The point to note was that most of these gains were registered from April 1917.

The picture was always messy, but the middle-class idea of prosperous munitions workers had little foundation in reality in early 1917.

More generally, Pemberton Reeve, in her wartime budgetary analyses, was sceptical about the idea of newly wealthy workers:

Mrs P., whose husband is a railwayman used to get 27 shillings before the war and now has 33 shillings. She has a new baby, which brings the number of her children up to five. Her rent for three rooms was 7 shillings, it is now 8 shillings for four rooms. She always paid a shilling a week each to a clothing and a boot club and this she continues to do. Her 'gramophone' ('the women are all buying a piano or gramophone') appears to be that she now buys twelve loaves a week instead of seven and pays 4 shillings instead of 1 shilling 5½ pence for it. Her coal costs her 10½ pence, her meat 2 shillings more and the rest of her expenditure is about 1 shilling 10 pence more than it was before the war. She therefore has ceased to buy fish, bacon, eggs, cocoa, jam and cow's milk altogether and buys less quantities of pot-herbs, margarine and sugar.[16]

It was possible for families to keep pace, even to outstrip inflation, but it involved trade-offs. Either men had to work savagely long hours or women had to enter the workforce. The latter was not always welcome: the culture of the single male breadwinner was central to the culture of much of the respectable working class, both among men and women. Even if a double wage brought in by a married woman returning to work allowed a slight ability to stay ahead of inflation, this would often be perceived as a subjective decline in living standard. By 1917 the strain was definitely beginning to tell.

Food supply had been largely managed on laissez-faire lines. Although much criticised, it had worked fairly well in dealing with the feared famine threat, as price sensitivity had provided incentives for increased supply and had smoothed distribution, as high profits attracted supplies to areas of high prices. But by early 1917 public patience was running out. The perception that high prices were caused by profiteering was now widespread. Whatever the micro detail, the working-class perception was one of increasing poverty.

The 1917 Commission of Enquiry into industrial unrest identified two strands of discontent: the local and specific, and the general. Barrow-in-Furness had such specific problems that it warranted its own report.

In effect a 'company town' supporting the Vickers arms and naval works, the principal problem in Barrow was a chronic housing shortage.

The population had grown from 68,523 in 1913 to 85,179 in 1916. In the same period the number of houses had increased from 13,259 to 14,588, an increase of average inhabitation per house from 5.1 to 5.8. But these averages do not begin to describe the problem. Much of the accommodation in Barrow was small and substandard. The commissioners exclaimed that 'they could not believe that the facts we propose to set down could so long remain the actual conditions of domestic life'. They detailed 'nine persons in one room, sixteen in one small house'. A family of man, wife, two adolescents and two children were subletting a bedroom of 12 feet square.

Another local problem was drink. The populist press had been attacking wartime restrictions on the working man's beverage as a cause of discontent. Most Commission reports including Barrow mentioned beer shortages, as a contributory element in discontent; but only the West Midlands commissioners list drink difficulties as a major cause of trouble. They were 'frankly amazed at the strength of the objections to the liquor restrictions'. Later reports to the War Cabinet bear out this claim. In this case it is very possible that the difficulty was rooted in local political tradition. Working-class conservatism was strong in the area, and opposition to teetotal faddists had been a political rallying cry for a generation.

Regarding the general discontent, in all regions high prices headed the list. In the north west, people were 'made angry by the high cost of living' and the 'increase in the price of food in relation to wages'. This was expanded in detail: food prices had risen 102% and the overall cost of living on 'an economical basis' had risen 70%, whilst 'wage increases vary enormously, but probably the highest figures put before us showed an increase of earnings of something like 40 percent or 50 per cent on pre war rates'. In the Midlands, food prices were 'the chief cause of unrest'.

It was not just the high prices, but their perceived causes, which were leading to problems. The north east division pointed to the 'alleged manipulation of prices by unscrupulous producers'. In the north west, the public were 'led by newspaper articles to believe that the profiteer is the sole cause of high prices'. In the London and south east area the main headings of the report were:
1. Food Prices.
2. What is called profiteering.
3. Industrial fatigue.
4. Inequality of sacrifice.
5. Uncertainty as to the future.
6. Want of confidence in the Government.

The theme of distrust runs through the reports: in Yorkshire there was a 'universal distrust of the Trade Union Executives'; in the West Midlands, 'a universal feeling of mistrust'. The regulation of the Labour market had led to a deep-seated fear of the loss of freedom: in the north east, the requirement of leaving certificates was described as 'a state of slavery'; in the north west workmen 'chafe under the restraints upon individual liberty'. Taken together these were creating a dangerous perception of injustice. In London, 'Of the patriotism of the overwhelming majority of workmen and their families there can be no question', but 'since the beginning of the war there has gradually arisen a sense of injustice and a feeling that there is a tendency to treat them as though they were rather the instruments of the community than part of it'. The commissioners who took in large amounts of evidence and interviewed many witnesses generally concluded that underlying support for the war effort was strong, but that wartime conditions were threatening that support. The Barrow commissioners noted that 'extreme men … approached us in a kindly spirit' and 'made a great point of their loyalty to their country', but that there was a sense of being pushed beyond reasonable limits. In the north west, workers were asking themselves whether 'the sacrifices they are making are really necessary'.

Bernard Waites has highlighted the importance of a 'moral economy' in wartime. Waites suggests that whilst the perception of profiteering did not cause strikes, it greatly 'increased the propensity to strike'. According to Waites once the term profiteer re-entered the language in spring 1915, it was constantly re-iterated by the Labour press. Waites is partly wrong in terms of causality, because it was the other way round: it was the re-iteration of the term profiteer in the Labour press from 1 August 1914 that brought the term back into common use.

In March 1917, *The Herald* remarked that there was 'a great deal of war weariness abroad, especially amongst those who are known as the poorer classes'. At the end of the month it commented that although 'strikes in wartime are always deplorable' the blame should fall 'on those responsible for the conditions which induce strikes'. By April two definite strands were emerging: in munitions and the mines, manpower issues predominated, but more generally there was a loss of patience regarding living standards. The Northern Textile Trades Federation was demanding a 20% pay rise for its members 'to allow them to live a decent life at the present cost of living'. The history of pay rises in the textile industry of Todmorden show how workers in this industry were faring. It shows clearly a war of two halves. Up until the end of 1915 prices in the town had risen 40%, but wages were lagging far behind. The situation was little better in the spring of 1917:

Pay rises	Spinners	Weavers
June 1915	5%	
January 1916		5%
June 1916	5%	
January 1917		5%
February 1917	10%	
July 1917		10%
December 1917	15%	15%
June 1918	25%	25%
December 1918	50%	50%

Lee, *Todmorden*, p. 145

In the second half of the war, spurred by strikes, the Government acted to redress the balance.

Other complaints quickly fed in – for example, the sense of excess profits by some employers. *John Bull* in 1917 centred on this hatred of profiteering as the key grievance. There was a circularity to this: it was precisely the claims of profiteering published in the populist press that were fuelling the pervasive suspicion of profiteering. But rather typically it also claimed that an important cause of the unrest was the shortage of beer caused by the imposition of tyrannical anti-drink measures. Once again this reflected a particular obsession of an interested party, yet it should not be entirely dismissed; certainly some reports from employers in the West Midlands suggest that this was an important grievance amongst workers in heavy industry.[17] The defence of trade unionism in itself was also an issue. By 1917 there was a fear of a 'comb-out' of skilled workers which would break local union power.

The revolt of labour

Should strikes be interpreted as opposition to the war? An intelligence report from Major Labouchere in March 1917 sent to the Minister of Munitions had no doubt that industrial discontent was being stirred up by a 'revolutionary ring'. He identified the organisations which to a greater or lesser extent were involved in this. They were the No Conscription Fellowship, the Union of Democratic Control, the British Socialist Party, the International Workers of the World, the Socialist Labour Party, the Independent Labour Party, the Women's Social and Political Union, the Clyde Workers' Committee, the Central Labour College, Sinn Fein, as well as various anarchists and individuals with 'Enemy and Unfriendly alien associates'. There were 'numerous agitators touring the country'. Labouchere believed that this agitation was not caused by genuine grievances, but was 'essentially the product of political and social agitation', although he admitted that 'anything like a serious rise in the cost of food would immediately react disastrously on the situation'.

It is therefore something of a surprise that his first recommendation was that the Government tackle genuine grievances![18] Should this be taken seriously? The answer is emphatically that it shouldn't. Labouchere had absolutely no idea about labour conditions, a point which had been made before his appointment – his prior experience was in Indian political intelligence. A refugee from the Great Game, perhaps a supporting character from a John Buchan novel, he was entirely unqualified to assess what was occurring. His incompetence is demonstrated by his identification of the militantly *pro-war* suffragettes of the Women's Social and Political Union as subversive. Far from originating the discontent, the other organisations Labouchere identified were attempting to exploit it. A letter from E. D. Morel to C. P. Trevelyan in August 1916 remarked that the railwaymen were beginning to feel the pinch of increased prices and that rising prices might prove decisive in swinging the railwaymen and subsequently the entire 'Triple Alliance' behind the call for a compromise peace.[19] A slightly less unhinged assessment than Labouchere, but one which was still conspiratorial in its assessment, was made after the summer strikes. In a memorandum entitled 'Labour in Revolt', sent to the War Cabinet in August 1917, Professor E. V. Arnold gave his opinion of the phenomenon 'its supporters describe as the working class movement'. He claimed to base his assessment on reading the periodicals circulating, and from conversations with 'individuals who are promoting it'. Arnold claimed that this 'movement' was quite distinct from the 'pacifist movement' which was 'middle-class', and the 'revolutionary' movement which was confined to the lower class of the large towns, most vigorously in East London. He stated that 'Labour in Revolt' was a movement of 'well-paid artisans', but that these three movements were apt to combine in public demonstrations and so were confused in the public eye. The strongholds of the 'Labour in Revolt' movement were the South Wales mine fields, the dockers everywhere, the Clyde shipyards and the Manchester and Sheffield districts, with the latter two only recently involved – but that was precisely what was 'cause for alarm'. He characterised the movement as led by young men between the ages of 20 and 40, and as a result the trade-union leaders both held themselves aloof from it and could not understand it. Indeed they were 'of all people the least competent' to advise about it.

In Arnold's view:

a decided majority of the workmen are everywhere opposed to it, but nevertheless they are swept away by it. It has repeatedly brought them increases in wages and

12. Labour Conference 1918. IWM (Q 54004).

reductions of hours, for which they are grateful, but chiefly they recognise that the movement is strong and the government weak.

According to Arnold, the movement 'absolutely denies all patriotic ties'; for them, 'England is not their country and the war is not their war.' He believed the official reports on industrial unrest hopelessly underestimated the danger, and that only the one on South Wales took it seriously enough: 'Labour is stronger than parliament at the moment.' Furthermore, 'By keeping the Government continually on the jump, through fear of strikes, they are undermining confidence in lawful authority.' That final sentence is highly significant. The memorandum provoked a reply by Mr Mackintosh of the Workers' Education Association. He felt that Arnold was alarmist, that the main inspiration for unrest was a continuation into wartime of the pre-war 'Triple Alliance', and that if the grievances of miners and railwaymen were met, it 'would do much to relieve the present strain'. For Mackintosh, 'the demand for a greater degree of control over one's working life is a natural and commendable one in a free community'. The one danger he conceded was that some young men were being drawn towards 'dogmatic Marxism'. His, obviously disinterested, view was that the best response to this would be to encourage better education of workers through institutions such as the Workers' Education Association!

The sound of axes grinding in both these memoranda is fairly deafening, as it has been in most literature about the 'shop stewards' movement. Generalising about motivation is exceptionally difficult. The first strikes were probably triggered by a genuine sense within the organised working class that their living standards had been eroded in the first few years of the war, and that the regular leadership of the trade unions was behaving in a supine way.

A few strikes may have had a mild ideological component in favour of a negotiated peace. But the idea of an outbreak of revolutionary defeatism, or even any powerful sense of working-class consciousness is largely absent. It is worth noting that in 1917 and 1918 the days lost to strikes were a fraction of the pre-war figures. The alarmist rhetoric of Basil Thomson of Special Branch, claiming that there had been a 'sudden growth of Pacifism among the actual workers', was the paranoia of a secret policeman. His claim that 'the strikers are trying to hide their real motive under an elaborate camouflage of dissatisfaction about the 12%, food difficulties, victimisation etc.' is a classic of conspiracy-theory reasoning. In fact the strikes were genuinely about these things – it was Thomson who was pursuing a hidden agenda.[20]

Arthur Gleason claimed that the South Wales Miners' Federation knew with precision exactly how much coal was required by the Royal Navy, and that they timed their strikes in such a way that this supply would not be endangered. Gleason is not entirely trustworthy on this point, as he was an apologist for British labour and engaged in persuading an American audience of the resolve of the nation at large. Perhaps a better indication comes from the reaction of Winston Churchill to a Cumberland iron-ore miners' strike in August 1917. Churchill asked the economist Walter Layton to provide statistics on how many merchant ships could have been manufactured with steel which was not produced as a result of the strike: 'I believe I am right in supposing the fortnight's cessation of work has inflicted more damage on our shipping and food supply than all the efforts of the German submarines in the last 1, 2 or 3 months as the case may be.'

Layton calculated the loss as twelve ships, the equivalent of one month's German action. Churchill took these figures to a meeting on 24 August 1917 and argued that the strike would result in dearer bread, which would hurt all workers. He also listened to the miners' grievances. At the end of the meeting the miners agreed to return to work and formally recorded their thanks to the Minister of Munitions. This story is indicative on several levels. Churchill assumed that the strike would be strategically damaging, although he clearly had no idea to what extent, and asked a civil servant to prove this for him. He deployed that information as his central rhetorical appeal, but in a very specific way, arguing that the strike would be harmful to the working class in general. At the same time he did listen to specific grievances. The combination of responsiveness, cajolery and a patriotic appeal based on class solidarity worked. Of course, the argument that

50,000 tons of lost iron-ore production meant 50,000 tons of lost steel production, which in turn meant twelve ships not built, which would mean half a million tons of wheat not imported, was basically facile, a plausible fiction. Nevertheless the Cumberland miners accepted the fiction and went back to work.[21]

A snapshot of industrial unrest produced for the War Cabinet in February 1918 helps put the issue in perspective, and reveals the nature of wartime strikes:

January 1918	Strikers	Days lost	% total days lost	Days lost per striker
London and south east	7,199	19,283	7.7	2.7
South west	1,528	2,812	1.1	1.84
West Midlands	9,489	41,023	16.4	4.32
Yorkshire and east	14,212	63,023	25.3	4.43
North west	7,833	29,853	12.0	3.8
Wales	2,900	45,500	18.2	15.7
Northern	821(?)	7,853	3.1	9.5
Scotland	10,544	39,990	16.0	3.8
National	54,446	250,039		4.6

CAB 24: GT 3645, 'Notes on the Labour position in the Munition Industry', 12 February 1918. Statistical retrospect. Figures do not precisely balance

Three distinct patterns emerge. The south shows low levels of industrial unrest, both in total amount and intensity. Most of the country shows moderately large numbers involved, but for a fairly brief time. Wales and the north east show small numbers involved in prolonged disputes. Both Wales and Scotland suffered more days lost than their proportion of the workforce, but the patterns of unrest were distinctly different in each, and furthermore in January 1918 both were eclipsed by Yorkshire as trouble spots.

These figures need to be seen in terms of the total possible work days. Two hundred and fifty thousand days were lost out of a total of 67,600,000. This amounted to 0.37%. By January 1918 the worst was over; indeed, the report for the week ending 12 February 1918 claimed that 'as regards strikes the situation has rarely been better'.

Month	% possible work days lost to strikes
July 1917	0.05
August 1917	0.04
September 1917	0.13
October 1917	0.09
November 1917	0.76
December 1917	0.38
January 1918	0.37

CAB: GT 3645

13. A voluntary public kitchen. IWM (Q54564).

The Government was now embarked on a policy of domestic appeasement. It would no longer attempt to force the working classes to bear part
of the financial cost of the war. In part this was because the context had
changed and priorities were altering. The spectre of national bankruptcy
had been removed by the American entry into the war. But, at the same
time, the Russian revolutions had intensified fears as to where the discontent might lead. Furthermore the distribution of manpower had
become a more pressing concern than money. The Government needed
to direct skilled labour in the face of union hostility. The fruits of the
policy in this respect became apparent in early 1918. The ASE threatened
widespread disobedience to the policy of comb-outs, raising the cry of
'industrial slavery'. But the cry fell largely on deaf ears in the wider labour
movement. Despite a grim background of lengthening queues and bad
news on the battle fronts, massive opposition to the Government did not
eventuate. Whilst the intensified activity of the propagandists of the
National War Aims Committee helped, it was the background of food
subsidies, war bonuses and a cautious approach to the manpower problem
that defused tension. But it was a shift in policy that had been forced.

Seen in perspective, the strikes of 1917 and 1918 were modest affairs.
Fewer working days were lost to strikes during the entire war than had been

in 1912. Workers were in fact as open to patriotic appeal as anyone else. But by 1918 they were resorting readily to strike threats and short strikes to send a message. A comparison of 1912 and 1918 is instructive: in 1912 there were 834 stoppages and a total of 40.2 million working days lost; in 1918 the respective figures were 1,165 and 5.88 million. Strikes in 1912 involved the loss of almost ten times as many working days per strike as those in 1918. In 1918 the Government usually intervened and the strikers usually won their demands. The large number of disputes in 1918 is evidence of the perceived effectiveness of these blackmail tactics. But the precise timing is also important. The vast majority of strikes in 1918 came in the second half of the year, as military victory became first likely and then almost certain. When defeat seemed a real prospect the picture was quite different. At the supreme moment of crisis the labour situation was the brightest part of the picture. In summarising the week ending 10 April 1918, the Ministry of Munitions reported 'the magical disappearance of labour opposition'. In the week after the news of the opening of the German offensive a total of 2,733 working days were lost, and by the end of the week there were two strikes in the entire country involving 155 workers. By 8 April this had diminished to one strike. In all the number of working days lost were '1/36th of one percent'. This was far more than compensated by the voluntary extra days being worked. In Glasgow, 'instead of watching holiday football 100,000 men were at work in shipyards and factories'. It was appropriate that specific mention was made of the Parkhead Forge, where the electricians 'not only decided to forego their holiday, they resolved to contribute the day's pay to a charitable fund'. They did so 'to repudiate the feeling that they are indifferent to the sufferings of the soldiers in France'. The general report on the labour situation spoke of 'tranquillity' because 'the present crisis has resulted in the stimulating of the patriotism of the working classes'. The intelligence report on pacifism and revolutionary organisations showed a similar hardening of opinion. The political symptoms of labour unrest had vanished with it. Whilst the report felt that the German treatment of Russia and the offensive would naturally have had a profound effect, it conceded that it was still far greater than expected. 'There has been an almost entire cessation of public meetings to advocate an immediate peace.' Instead a mass meeting at Woolwich had pledged the engineers to fight 'until the German military machine is smashed'. Perhaps the most profound indicator was that among the miners and engineers who had been opposing comb-outs up to the middle of March, 'a considerable number of men are enlisting without waiting for their calling up notices'.

So, in 1918, rising wages and tightening control of the food supply combined with a patriotic recommitment of the working class to national war aims saw the Government through.

Duncan Tanner's assertion that, contrary to the view of some Marxist historians, 'Workers were not discontented with an oppressive state', needs to be heavily qualified. They were discontented, but not in every respect: not sufficiently to rebel against the war, not necessarily more so than other social groups and not to the extent that they couldn't be bought off.[22] The last point should not be taken as a complete endorsement of the views of Niall Ferguson. Ferguson has argued from a macro-economic comparison of the German and British war economies that the British war economy was inefficient, and that a principal reason for this was that real incomes of British workers fell less than the productivity of the economy as a whole. In essence the British working class were being paid too much for too little work. What Ferguson misses is the dynamic involved – one which his own figures make clear. Across the course of the war overall production fell in both countries and so did 'real wages'. Both fell more in Germany than in Britain.

But in 1915 the picture is precisely the opposite of Ferguson's conclusion. Real wages in Britain fell sharply, more sharply than in Germany, whilst production actually rose. In 1916 production in Germany fell more sharply than real wages, less sharply than in Britain, once again the opposite of Ferguson's conclusion. In 1917 the gap narrowed. Production and real wages were higher in Britain but the margin between them was much the same as in Germany. Finally in 1918 real wages rose sharply in Britain and fell sharply in Germany, while both sides suffered further declines in production. In other words Ferguson's argument rests on the final year of the war alone.

In fact, for the first half of the war, the British working class in aggregate was working harder and making greater material sacrifices than their German equivalents. In the middle of 1917 the situation began to reverse as strikes put pressure on Government and, in the second half of 1918, as Germany slid into defeat, British workers began to demand the fruits of victory. This corresponds with the general picture presented here. The other part of Ferguson's comparison – the strike record of the two countries – is equally misleading. The significance of a strike varied dependent on context. Germany from 1 August 1914 was effectively under martial law. Civil liberties in Britain had not been suspended to anything like the same extent. But does this mean that we should ignore the coercive power of the British state to suppress manifestations of dissent?

Brock Millman, in a provocative and massively documented study, has argued strongly that the British state was much more effective and ruthless in dealing with internal dissent than has usually been acknowledged. This challenge to the more 'whiggish' accounts of the home front is welcome. The emphasis of Millman's work is very different from the account presented here. Whilst this book has concentrated on the bases of consent to the war effort, Millman concentrates on the suppression of dissent. Although these two views might be seen as contradictory, they should more properly be seen as complementary.

This doesn't imply total agreement. Millman's emphasis on the analyses of 'revolutionary potential' does not allow sufficiently for the exaggerations intrinsic to such sources, and his use of the accounts of the dissenting minority does not account for just how small a minority they were. That the British home front was essentially solid was not simply a retrospective invention – a broadly patriotic middle ground certainly existed. But Millman is absolutely right to point to the fact that there was potential for dissent, and that it had to be actively managed.

From 1916 this management was conducted on three levels. The first and most important was that the Government controlled the overall level of sacrifice that the population was called upon to make. In both economic and military terms, the British Government, as far as was possible, protected the British people from the worst strains of war. With Russia collapsing and France approaching the end of its resources, the British Army was forced to take up a much greater share of the military burden; but even so the British Government was parsimonious in the release of manpower to the Army for fear of an unacceptable level of casualties. Economically the British people were uniquely sheltered – even in the darkest days of the U-boat campaign, bread rationing was avoided. In the second half of the war the standard of living actually began to rise for much of the population. The British people were never called upon to sacrifice themselves to the cause to the extent that had become routine in France and Germany, let alone the kind of martyrdom sustained by the Serbs. Whether the home front could have remained solid under those kind of pressures is a moot point.

Secondly the Government was increasingly active in manipulating opinion. All combatant nations conducted domestic propaganda, but the British Government may have been among the most effective in organising their appeal to the population. Millman emphasises the role of the National War Aims Committee (NWAC). The NWAC was a direct response to the discontents that manifested themselves in spring 1917. The original executive committee significantly represented the major British political parties: Lloyd George, Bonar Law, Asquith and George Barnes. Technically a non-governmental organisation, the NWAC was funded directly by the Treasury, to the tune of £1.2 million in eighteen months. Other funds were raised privately.

Despite the many strengths of Millman's analysis, it is flawed in taking the fears of dissent by the state surveillance and policing apparatus at face value. A good example is his citing of the chief constable of Weymouth asking permission of the Home Office to prohibit all meetings of socialist and Labour organisations in 1918. It is frankly difficult to imagine Weymouth in 1918, or at any other time, as a hotbed of revolutionary agitation. The Home Office refused the request, the official minuting that informal opposition to pacifist meetings would suffice.[23]

Millman considers 1918 as a year of 'counter-revolution' in the making. In this he is definitely close to the mark. Where he is probably wrong is in the extent to which he sees the process as initiated and encouraged by state agencies. Individuals in both the military and civil establishments certainly shared in the general paranoia and discontent of the middle and upper classes, and 'patriot' extremism was intermittently encouraged as an informal method of suppressing left-wing dissent. But it is doubtful that the highest levels of Government were genuinely planning for a 'white' coup, a pre-emptive counter-revolution. Millman's arguments about troop deployments in Britain, designed to be utilised against urban revolt, are not very convincing.

In reality the Coalition Government was still trying to walk a tight-rope, simultaneously appeasing labour and controlling and directing the middle-class backlash. They succeeded, but only by a narrow margin.

The potential revolt of the middle classes

Anticipating Ferguson by eighty years, Alf Bradburn, a volunteer machinist working in Bristol in 1915, had some harsh things to say about the working class in a letter to his brother Sam:

we are spending far too much money for the results we get. We 'bribe' the soldiers to fight and 'bribe' the men to work all at enormous expense ... the conditions of labour have advanced beyond all conception since I was a working man, they work less, are more independent and get more money.

These reflections had made him distinctly pessimistic:

Our methods of working will always be beaten by the German method.
Our men say, 'oh let them beat us' we will have tarriff charges to keep their goods out; we will do less work and get more money for it after the war. And all of this makes me feel that the war is useless, so far as we are concerned.[24]

By January 1916, his defeatism had turned into a visceral anger. Praising Belgian workers in his factory he contrasted them with the British: 'I sometimes hope that some of our workmen had a taste of what Belgium has had; they would wake up some & get on with work. I would shoot some of the S. Wales Blighters.'[25]

While a Bristol man desiring capital punishment for the Welsh might be unsurprising or even axiomatic, there can be little doubt that Bradburn's sentiments were starting to become widespread amongst the middle classes. Harold Cousins wrote of the same strike, 'their state of mind must be inconceivable'.[26] Macleod Yearsley wrote of Clydeside strikers, 'they are wanting in patriotism or they are being duped by German agents'.[27] Elizabeth Fernside wrote in May 1917, 'the engineers are on strike because they have paid £100 for their indentures & they are taking boys under military age and putting them to work with these bounders ... I wonder how many lads have had to leave work that had cost them far more to learn than that to join the army?'[28] Echoing Bradburn, Frederick Robinson expressed a desire that ringleaders on the Clyde should be shot.[29]

It should be pointed out that there is a difference between widespread and universal. Members of the middle classes who felt uneasy about pre-war hierarchy might welcome a degree of working-class empowerment, and some who were still close to a blue-collar background felt more sympathy than Bradburn did. Gunner Bennet's father was one such – he wrote to his son that the war would create a better world for working men, which he regarded with approval. Elizabeth Fernside still listened sympathetically to lectures on the 'new democracy', although she had doubts about the enlightened intelligence of those who would be enfranchised. Perhaps most remarkable of all was the apparently sympathetic reception in Sussex of an ILP speaker recounted in one of Robert Saunders' letters. Even Frederick Robinson, as hardline an opponent of trade unions as it is possible to imagine, remarked regarding 'industrial unrest' in March 1918 that it was really a demand for 'industrial rest', 'Work people ... are getting tired, they may earn good wages, but good wages to the working man mean good food ... which he can't get ... There is something to be said for this point of view.' [30]

The 'undermining of confidence in lawful authority', was, ironically, in the end a middle-class phenomenon. The strikes and threat of strikes had got results for industrial workers – in some cases remarkable results. By the winter of 1917 the average earnings of skilled munition workers were probably beginning to overhaul the average earnings of clerks, male and female alike. Figures for the Newlay munitions work in Leeds show the apparently modest effects of wage rises on average earnings by March 1918:

	Wages
Skilled men	£4 4s 2d
Unskilled men	£2 12s 6d
Unskilled women	£1 17s 6d

But it is made clear that the really striking feature was the money that could be earned by piece working. Skilled male turners were in fact earning £10 per week on average and female copper band turners £7.[31]

More alarming still for the lower middle class was that the *gap* between lower middle class earnings and unskilled labour was diminishing even more quickly. Discontent was becoming universal. A letter to Gunner Bennett, serving in Mesopotamia, from a female office colleague, gives a sense of one clerk's miseries: 'My "fed upness" has reached the limit ... They have given me 5/- extra this week which makes my salary up to £3 now, but believe me it only goes as far as 30/- . I travel by train now and this costs £ 1 2 /- 9d per month. It used to take me two hours to get home by bus ... In addition to that food and clothing is an enormous price.'[32] It should be remembered that this was mild compared with the constant litany of complaint Bennett was receiving from his wife, struggling to cope on a separation allowance.

Furthermore the mythic qualities associated with munitions workers' and miners' earnings exaggerated the situation. The cover of *The Passing Show* in November 1917 shows Lloyd George bowing to the threats of a hulking ogreish coal miner at the expense of 'John Citizen'.[33] The 1917 strikes coincided with intensifying casualties, an intensified comb-out of 'unbadged' men and the beginnings of intermittently severe shortages. A. H. Hudson, in a newspaper article published in the *National Weekly* on 26 May 1917, entitled 'Strikers, Shirkers and Conscientious Objectors', took the view that if men were exempted from military service because they worked in a reserved occupation, it could not be regarded as a matter to be left largely to their discretion 'whether they work at that occupation or refrain from doing so.' Engineers strikes were immoral: 'if it were not so monstrous it would be entirely farcical that while the best of England's sons, brothers and fathers are giving their blood to preserve their country ... these young wasters who are befouling the good name of Sheffield should be free'. He advocated drastic measures: 'A man who endeavours to prevent his fellows from working in a munition factory is just as much a traitor as a soldier would be who tried to keep his comrades from an attack, and should be dealt with in the same way.' This was a call for the type of industrial conscription that the strikers themselves feared. A pamphlet by a sergeant in the London Scottish published in 1918 expressed sympathy with workers' grievances: 'there are two sides to every strike' but 'there is no time to examine them now. Everyone must now be prepared to sacrifice, as the soldier sacrifices everything.' He proceeded to describe life at the front: 'Strikers you complain of excessive work. Have you in your worst moments ever done such work as this? You complain of the pay – the infantryman receives a shilling a day.' He appealed to the strikers on behalf of the soldiers' families: 'Can you see his parents, his wife, his children ... praying daily for his safety ... he knows that theirs is the harder part than his.' The soldiers would endure for their sake until there was 'peace on earth and war shall be no more', but in the meantime he demanded that workmen should support him fully.[34] This developing backlash is exemplified by *The Victory Book* by 'Daphne', actually Helen Stenhouse, an expatriate New Zealander. This little pamphlet, sold for two shillings and sixpence, 'proceeds devoted to winning the war', could be a serious contender for the award for the most generally offensive publication of 1918. In particular, the poem 'The Dauntless Three: An Episode of the Strike in Coventry', demonstrates smugness, prejudice and insensitivity on a scale which is far more genuinely epic than the flat appropriation of Macaulay:

> Now we add a modern story,
> A thrilling tale you'll learn,
> Of two loyal English roses,
> And a staunch New Zealand Fern.
>
> How they kept the old flag flying,
> When the crowd went out on strike
> For butter, *beans* and bacon
> A *demonstration* if you like.
>
> And 'fed up' with the success of this adventure bold
> The crowd went out on strike again
> Their power they extolled
> 'We're masters now' they proudly cried,
> 'We'll make all bend the knee,
> Unity is strength' and then they sighed
> There stood the dauntless three.

These heroic strikebreakers refuse to be intimidated by the mob:

> While fifty thousand idled,
> They came at break of day
> And hammered rivets gladly, to keep the Hun at bay.
> But some in the crowd grew fiercer,
> As they watched the dauntless three,
> And they whispered planning vengeance;
> They hated such loyalty
> Never a thought for the Homeland
> At deathly grips with the Huns!
> Never a cheer for the grand old flag
> Upheld by our noblest ones!
> But they ranted and sang of a *red* flag
> A revolutionary rag of the town,
> While with cowardly courage of numbers
> They let their country down.
> And they prated of their *rights* forsooth
> When their glorious *right* to-day

> Is to stand, aye to die, for freedom
> In the grand old British way
> To keep 'Hell out of England,'
> To protect the weaker lands
> To *war* for a *peace* that will last for aye,
> Fit work for many hands.[35]

It is not surprising that this crass, jingoistic, Antipodean tourist provoked the working people of Coventry into revolutionary rhetoric. One can only praise their restraint in declining to lynch her, although it would have been a service to English letters.

Before exploring these sentiments further, it is only fair to note an equally polemical piece of verse from 1918 which made the case for empathy and compassion. 'Britain's Defeat' by 'Bonavia' responded forcefully to the moralising and contempt increasingly apparent in middle-class circles:

> Forsake the folly of past years,
> Your vapid hopes and trivial fears ...
> If seven folk slept on your floor,
> If poverty surged round your door,
> If desperation your heart tore,
> You, vain girl, might be a whore.[36]

Or perhaps a striker. It was left to Walter Raleigh, a minor but competent literary figure, delivering an official lecture at Oxford, to put things in perspective:

I asked a friend of mine whose dealings are with the industrial North, what the work people of Lancashire and Yorkshire think of the war. He said, 'Their view is very simple: they mean to win it; and they mean to make as much money out of it as ever they can' ... before you judge them put yourselves in their place. There are great outcries against profiteers ... and against munition workers ... I do not defend either of them; they are unimaginative and selfish, and I do not care how they are dealt with; but I do say that the majority of them are not wicked in intention.

For Raleigh they were engaged in a natural attempt to 'better their position'. Their patriotism was undoubted: 'the bulk of these people would rather die than allow one spire of English grass to be trodden under the foot of a foreign trespasser', but 'their chief sin is that they do not fear. They think that there is plenty of time to do a little business for themselves on the way to defeat the enemy.'[37]

Yet now the effect of this successful blackmail on patriotic middle-class opinion by 1918 was threatening to undermine domestic peace.

7   Struggling to victory 1917–1918

The Christmas crisis

> Ever since August 1914, our capital, once the blithest and jolliest city in
> Europe has been in danger of being Prussianised ... not of course by the
> enemy, but by the scarcely less disagreeable Puritans in our midst.[1]

In the course of 1917 the strains of war were creating a widespread sense
of gloom. The journalist Charles Sheridan-Jones, in a book published that
year, complained of a 'plague of regulations under which the most harm-
less things had become "verboten" '. In the capital it had become impossible 'to get a whisky after nine-thirty or cigarettes after eight', and that
'the shopkeeper who sells you chocolate may face a ruinous penalty'.[2]

Small symbolic changes could indicate wider issues. Looking back,
Dorothy Peel remembered of the winter of 1917–1918, 'the world was
poorer for the disappearance of the muffin': an institution of her domestic
life had ceased to exist.[3] That winter was the winter of the queue: 'anyone
who penetrated the poorer neighbourhoods became familiar with the
queue'. Initially this was a burden which fell on the working class, but
soon, 'the middle classes who could not obtain servants also swelled the
queue'. By early 1918, 'women used to go from shop to shop trying to find
one at which they could buy meat or margarine'.[4]

The low point in public confidence was between October 1917 and
February 1918. The prospects never seemed bleaker.[5] The Bolshevik revolution and the subsequent peace negotiations at Brest-Litovsk eliminated
Russia from the war, and the Italian defeat at Caporetto briefly threatened to
remove a second ally. News of the bloodbath at Passchendaele, despite
positive representations in the press, reached the general public. The brief
exaltation over the breakthrough at Cambrai turned to an even more bitter
disillusionment. Only Palestine provided any good news, and Edmund
Allenby's 'Christmas present' of Jerusalem, although vital in providing
some cheer, was insufficient to dispel the gloom.

At home, an intensive night-bombing campaign spread fear and anger
in London and the south east. Although by the standards of later wars the

casualties were slight, civilian populations were not yet hardened to the idea of sudden and arbitrary death from the air. Above all there were the shortages and queues.

Statistics collected by the Ministry of Food illustrate the difficulty clearly. A survey of fat stock at fifty-nine British markets demonstrates both the long-term decline in supply of fresh meat and the drastic short-term acceleration of this:

Fat stock	Cattle	Sheep	Pigs
January 1916	18,509	68,923	17,329
July 1916	14,487	68,848	10,283
January 1917	16,234	64,462	14,283
July 1917	15,672	71,896	8,689
January 1918	5,725	48,427	4,162

Cab. 24: GT 3707, Ministry of Food Memorandum, week ending 20 February 1918

Whilst the shortage in January was partly caused every year by heavy purchases at Christmas, the year-on-year comparison was stark. Large-scale importation of meat covered some of the shortage, but not all of it. The combined consumption of meat fell sharply even on the fairly low level of May 1917:

May 1916	112
August 1916	108
December 1916	96
May 1917	100
August 1917	96
December 1917	79.5

Index May 1917 = 100

The consumption situation for other fats and proteins was even worse:

	Butter	Bacon	Cheese
October 1916	194	179	146
October 1917	100	100	100
January 1918	43	64.5	55.5

Cab. 24: GT 3707, Ministry of Food Memorandum, week ending 20 February 1918; Index October 1917 = 100

It is hardly surprising that food was becoming a public obsession. Even obtaining these reduced supplies was a time-consuming, tiring and demoralising business, a burden which fell principally on women. In the first three years of war the price of food had been one of the great talking points; this did not go away, but it was now supplemented with anger about queues and non-availability.

The Member of Parliament W. H. Dickinson wrote to the War Cabinet at the end of January 1918 regarding the situation in London. The shortage of meat was causing 'intense public anxiety and disturbance is likely to arise'. If the situation continued, 'public indignation will grow rapidly and events in London might even jeopardise the nation's prospect of success in the war'.[6] This may not have been hyperbolic. On 8 January 1918, Edie Bennett of Walthamstow wrote to her husband: 'we are slowly being starved out, we have to line up for everything now … tea, sugar, marg and a joint of meat is a thing of the past'. She continued in a vein that must have been deeply depressing to the recipient: 'What a life, to think it should come to this & our dear ones fighting so we should have it ok & we should have to line up in this bitter cold weather inches thick with snow, we wouldn't mind so much if we could see any prospect of the end.' On 15 January she wrote: 'I reckon we shall have to have peace at any cost soon or be starved to death.' A week later she queued for two hours with her mother-in-law for cheese only to find that the shop had sold out. 'Your mum & I were fed up and quite down hearted … It's the kiddies that worry you. They must live on something.'[7] Edie Bennett was a natural pessimist; Elizabeth Fernside of Fulham was a natural optimist. When she successfully obtained a joint of meat in December 1917, she was able to take an amused view of the scene: 'when I felt inclined to leave my purchase on account of the struggle, the butcher whispered "stay here, it is as good as the pictures" & he was correct, the pictures were nowhere in it'.[8] On 27 January H. E. Miles wrote in her diary: 'The food shortage is becoming very dreadful … we hope that with rationing things will get better.'[9]

The crisis was not limited to London. In Todmorden the climax came on 21 and 22 December 1917. A giant queue formed which never consisted of fewer than 500 people at any one time, and lasted from noon until 'late at night'.[10] Paradoxically, whilst the introduction of rationing for meat was popular, the *avoidance* of bread rationing was also good for confidence. Once again the danger point came in the first month of 1918, but there was a rapid recovery in most parts of the country:

Flour consumption	January 1918	February 1918
London	98	103.5
Newcastle	93.5	98.5
Leeds	93	98.5
Manchester	92	97.5

Nottingham	94.5	101
Birmingham	93.5	98.5
Home counties (north)	96	99.5
Home counties (south)	97.5	101.5
Cambridge	104	107
Bristol	96.5	99.5
Caernarvon	92.5	91.5
Cardiff	94	93.5
Glasgow	91	104
Edinburgh	95	95.5

Index 100 = Average July 1916 – February 1917, i.e. before unrestricted submarine warfare

Several comments are worth making about this. The maintenance of wheat supply was a major cause in itself of shortages of fats, because farmers were encouraged to concentrate on arable. The table also demonstrates that voluntary reduction in bread consumption was much less widespread at any point than civic histories claim. The very low figure for Glasgow in January rather confirms those who suggested that food shortages were an important component in the January strikes there, whilst the big increase in consumption in February coincides with a remarkable onset of peace on the Clyde. But above all there is the psychological significance of the February figure. In restoring pre-February 1917 levels of supply of breadstuffs, a crucial signal was being sent out: the U-boats had failed and the country would not starve. This was combined with the effect of meat, fat and sugar rationing, at first local, then national, which seems to have eliminated queues – and the temporary suspension of bombing. Hope was slowly being restored. This was just as well, because the British public now had to brace themselves for a terrible shock on the battlefield.

Moments from Ethel Bilsborough's war

There was no single experience of the war, but there were perhaps identifiable currents in the way middle-class opinion developed. The diary of Ethel Bilsborough at the Imperial War Museum both shows an individual variant and gives a sense of a broad chronology. On 15 July 1915 she wrote:

One little realised then what it was all to mean in the future for us, the appalling loss of life, – the sacrifice – the horror of it all! Yet it is now raging – no abatement of the cruel slaughter, it just goes on from day to day, increasing in venom and hatred and loss of life. Oh – that such a thing should be possible in these enlightened, civilised (?) days!

In a retrospective entry for May 1915:

Some of the tables are occupied by wounded soldiers ... a young fellow was calmly enjoying himself with the whole of his head bound up in a white bandage! Yet no one even glanced at him, though a year ago he probably would have been asked by the manager to vacate his seat.

A similar mix of indignation and horror is found in an entry for August 1915: 'War, war, war and our brave lads are being hacked and shot down every day.' At this point she places the entry facing a cartoon clipping of a shirker befriended by the Kaiser. Yet on 21 October 1915 she is grumbling about rather trivial impositions:

It is not often that one is touched personally by the war in comparatively small matters. But there is one way we are affected that is exceedingly annoying. It is when one receives a letter like this [encloses envelope marked opened by censor].
    To have strange prying eyes reading one's own letters that concern no one else is exasperating ... For some reason best known to those in authority, there has been an immense Universal Registration Act passed throughout the country & every man and woman has had to give their names and occupations. I've no use for the silly thing, & why did they put 'household duties' as my principal ocupation in life when they certainly constitute the least. Just as if I was some German Hausfrau or careworn 'Martha'!

In early 1916, she comments several times on conscription. On 5 March: 'Naturally every coward and slacker thinks fighting is "wrong" and the most ludicrous reasons are being put forward by men who want to get exemption owing to their conscientious (!) scruples.' In May she expresses frustration:

Our government does nothing but wangle and procrastinate; there has been a serious rebellion in Ireland ... just as if we did not have enough on hand with party politics and strikes ... They introduced conscription at first in a pitifully weak way ... but now all this is stopped and every man will have to do something for England provided he is not past the age limit – ie: 45 *(Thank goodness K is!)* [K was her husband, my italics.]

By 1917, food shortages and air raids begin to take up more space. In April she writes: 'Food is getting scarce ... But a great deal of nonsense is written by people saying that we must not give even our crumbs to the poor birds. Because we are fighting against brutes must we ourselves become brutes? Feeling strongly on the matter I wrote to "The Mirror".' By 4 November there are real indications of war weariness:

Poor old England is going through dark days just now and one cannot see the faintest prospect of peace in sight ... Women and children and old men and boys being ruthlessly murdered by these devils in the air is unspeakably horrible. But as someone said the other day, 'there are no civilians now, we are all soldiers.' ...

Prices of course are awful … Yesterday I wanted to buy a small tinned tongue which formerly cost 2/- to my consternation the man demanded 4/- 6d! I walked straight out of the shop with no tongue beyond what nature has blessed me with gratuitously and I used it freely!

Bilsborough remained committed to the war, but doubts were now apparent:

It is terrible to see how lengthy the list grows in the war shrine at church (even in a small place like this) for those who have laid down their lives for King and Country.

And it is hard for those who still struggle bravely on to put Patriotism before peace. But a peace now would not be an honourable or a lasting one…But how in heavens name will it end? And When?

On 19 January 1918, she wrote, 'it looks ominous for the future, and things are getting harder and harder, especially for the poor, and I think it is exasperating of Lord Rhondda to calmly accuse the people of being "greedy growsers"'. Her view of the war fluctuates for the next six months: on 19 June 1918 she comments more favourably on Rhondda but is still gloomy about military prospects:

Lord Rhonda [*sic*], the great food controller, has just died. Poor man, he had rationed himself too severely and when he got ill with pleurisy or something, he had no strength to fight against it. But he will be much missed. He worked out the problem of placing England under food rations with amazing skill … Things look about as gloomy as they possibly can … Our lines are broken badly at the front … Fortunately the thought of England conquered is unthinkable (which sounds rather a paradox).

In October she looks both forward and back:

It seems impossible to believe that the end is in sight at last. Is it really true that after four years of uphill fighting and grappling against tremendous odds, that we are finally going to win? No Englishman would ever admit it to himself, but I believe that there have been times in the war when the paralysing thought has flashed through our minds that we were going to get – well that we were not going to win!

On 11 November 1918, her relief is palpable: 'Today has been a truly wonderful day, and I'm glad that I was alive to see it.'

Bilsborough was a middle-aged housewife (despite her objections to the term), married to a man above military age, and childless, living more or less outside the line of raids in Chislehurst in Kent. To what extent did Mrs Bilsborough 'experience' the war? She did not belong to any of the much-studied groups – the war workers or the soldiers – and she had hardly any close connection with them. On the spectrum of participant/spectator she seems almost a pure spectator. But as her substantial diary/memoir indicates, she was a very *engaged* spectator and increasingly the war impinged on her life. Bilsborough never lost her belief that the war was a moral cause; her comments on German behaviour are consistent in their condemnation. Equally she never ceases to indicate that the war, particularly for the soldiers, was horrifying. But in 1917 and 1918 she did, briefly and reluctantly, doubt the likelihood of victory. 'War weariness' was setting in.

Nina Macdonald in the 1918 *War-Time Nursery Rhymes*, despite its title clearly aimed at an adult audience, shows the frustration that was mounting in middle-class circles at wartime sacrifices. Some are genuinely funny in their black humour:

> Little Bo-Peep had sold her sheep,
> She hated having to do it,
> And cried when told,
> That her pet had been sold
> To make Mutton cutlets and suet.

But others are filled with bitterness at the day-to-day frustration of diminished living standards:

> Matthew, Mark, Luke and John,
> Guard the dish the butter's on
> For we don't want a theft.
> Four coupons I have left
> One for sugar, one for fat
> And two for liver for the cat.
> Don't tell D.O.R.A 'bout the puss
> Or she'll make an awful fuss.

The resentment of popular pressure and regulation runs through the rhymes:

> Old Mother Hubbard went to the cupboard
> For bones for her dear little dog
> But she'd thrown them away
> Lest people should say,
> She was hoarding and call her food hog.

Sometimes the mood is mock stoical:

> How doth the little busy wife,
> Improve the shining hour.
> She shops and cooks and works all day,
> The best within her power.
> How carefully she cuts the bread.
> How thin she spreads the jam.
> That's all she has for breakfast now,
> Instead of eggs and ham.

In dealing with the tradesmen,
She is frightened at the prices
For meat and fish have both gone up,
And butter too and rice has.
Each thing seems dearer ev'ry week.
It's really most distressing.
Why can't we live on love and air,
It would be such a blessing.

In 'Sing a Song of Wartime' some of the frustration about relative deprivation boils over:

Life's not very funny,
Now for little boys,
Haven't any money
Can't buy any toys
Mummy does the housework,
Can't get any maid
Gone to make munitions
'cause they're better paid.

Macdonald still clings to a certainty in victory, but in the rhyme 'One, Two' there is a note of desperation:

One, two what shall we do?
Three, four, go to the war...
Seventeen, Eighteen, War abating
1920, PEACE AND PLENTY.[11]

As always, people wanted the war to end. But how to end it?

'The Tank Bank': deciphering the geography of patriotism in 1918?

The pattern of subscription to war loans cannot be reduced to patriotic sentiment. War loans were aggressively sold as a good investment. Nevertheless, used with a certain amount of caution, some of the details of war-loan subscription can help to illustrate levels of patriotic commitment in various regions. After all, even as an investment, war loans rested on confidence in the Government's ability to repay, and that meant winning the war.

The formation of local savings associations gives an indication of how much of the community was being drawn in. As well as town and village associations, they were formed in workplaces, churches and chapels, schools and clubs.

The first annual reports of the War Savings Associations, which were compiled in spring 1917, list by county the number of local associations. It is a crude measure but it does give some idea of the depth of involvement of local communities.

For England and Wales the ten counties with the largest number of associations on 1 March 1917 were:

County	War Savings Associations
Yorkshire (West Riding)	145
Lancashire	137
Cheshire	54
County Durham	44
Staffordshire	43
Hampshire	41
Kent	39
Lincolnshire	38
Northumberland	35
Devon	31

Broadly speaking these figures unsurprisingly mirror population, although some counties with smaller populations have larger numbers of associations reflecting dispersed settlement. However these figures cannot be reduced to a straightforward reflection of population. There are very conspicuous absentees in the top ten, most notably London, Middlesex, Glamorgan and Warwickshire.

At the other end of the scale most of the smallest numbers of associations likewise mirror size and population: none in Rutland, one in Merioneth, two in Montgomery, Anglesey, Huntingdonshire and Carmarthen. But once again there are other counties which by any standards are conspicuously under-represented: only four associations in Norfolk and five in Gloucestershire. Similarly, a swathe of 'home counties', Bedfordshire, Hertfordshire, Oxfordshire and Buckinghamshire, have fewer than ten associations. These distributions might be random, but this becomes less likely when the Scottish case is considered. The figures for numbers of War Loans Associations in the top ten counties in Scotland were remarkably different:

County	War Savings Associations
Lanarkshire	845
Midlothian	552
Renfrewshire	229
Fifeshire	181
Aberdeenshire	172

Ayrshire	172
Forfarshire	161
Stirlingshire	124
Roxburghshire	91
Dumfrieshire	71

In other words, eight out of the ten counties with the largest number of associations in the whole of the United Kingdom were Scottish. Lanarkshire had more associations than the top ten English counties combined, and indeed Roxburghshire had more War Savings Associations than the whole of Wales. Size was not everything. Shetland had nineteen War Savings Associations and Orkney had twenty-five. Even the most exaggerated view of the thrifty Scots would be forced to concede that this does seem to imply a remarkable level of willingness to organise the subscription of funds to national needs.

In an advertisement that appeared in the press in the second week of January 1918, the reciprocity of sacrifice is appealed to in a complex and subtle fashion. A picture of a soldier standing guard on a parapet is used to promote the purchase of war bonds. It is accompanied by a revealing textual appeal:

> Let your Bond help to bring my man back to me.
> For two long years he has been in the trenches. He is my husband – and he is living through Hell – for me and You ...
> Now and then, no letter comes for two, three, four days.
> And I – well the letter has always come. And I clasp my little one to me with a heartache you may never know.
> Is it too much to ask you to lend your money to your country at 5 per cent interest – Bonds save lives?
> Is it too much to ask you to tend your money on the safest security in the world?
> Go to the Post Office or the Bank. Put your savings – ALL YOUR MONEY – at least every penny you can – into National War Bonds – and help bring my man safely home again.[12]

The appeal is multi-faceted. First of all the loan could release a soldier from 'Hell', which he is suffering voluntarily for others, particularly the reader. Note that there is no minimisation of the soldier's suffering in this – the War *is* Hell. It is precisely because of this that his moral claim is paramount. But the soldier does not suffer alone; his wife also suffers – continual anxiety, constant uncertainty. She is suffering the pains of separation in the present and could, if victory does not come soon, suffer bereavement in the future. The reason to subscribe is not abstract patriotism, because ultimate victory is not in doubt. Indeed this is a second reason to invest, it is an utterly secure investment. The reason to invest is to speed victory and therefore relieve suffering, both of the soldiers and their relatives. In effect the war loan subscriber is being asked to make a sacrifice, which is no sacrifice, or rather one which leads to certain redemption, both spiritual and financial.

Did the public respond to this appeal?

War Loans in England and Wales: November 1917 – January 1918
Per-capita subscription per week over fourteen weeks (% of £)
(bold = 200,000 + population)

£1 or more per week per head
Newcastle 1.6, **Bradford 1.3**, West Hartlepool 1.03, Wisbech 1.02

15 shillings or more per week per head
Birmingham 0.98, Cardiff 0.97, **Manchester 0.94**, **Liverpool 0.79**

10 shillings or more per week per head
Newport (IOW) 0.65, **Leeds 0.58**, **Bristol 0.56**, Harrogate 0.53

5 shillings per week or more per head
Cambridge 0.476, York 0.474, Oxford 0.452, Bath 0.451, **Sheffield 0.43**, Newbury 0.416, King's Lynn 0.400, Wolverhampton 0.360, Winchester 0.350, Truro 0.316, **Hull 0.315**, Chelmsford 0.313, Tunbridge Wells 0.288, Maidstone 0.260

2 shillings or more per week per head
Scarborough 0.250, Surbiton 0.242, Worksop 0.220, Bedford 0.220, Bury (Lancs) 0.205, Wigan 0.200, Hartlepool 0.170, **Leicester 0.148**, **Nottingham 0.147**, **Portsmouth 0.146**, Dover 0.140, Preston 0.133, Newmarket 0.128

1 shilling or more per week per head
Great Yarmouth 0.090, Hitchin 0.090, **Stoke 0.080**, Luton 0.080, Watford 0.080, Folkestone 0.080, Swindon 0.077, Llanelli 0.071, Mansfield 0.070, Rhondda 0.060

Less than 1 shilling per week per head
Bishop Auckland 0.034, Tredegar 0.020, Ebbw Vale 0.012

(*The Times*, 15 January 1918)

The first point to note is that even at this moment of dismally low morale, the level of per-capita subscription to the war loan, over the fourteen-week period described, was remarkably high. The 'average' inhabitant of Bradford subscribed over £18 to the war effort in the period, and even the 'average' inhabitant of Stoke subscribed more than £1 (a week's wages for a pre-war labourer). It is hard to tell whether people subscribed to the war loan out of disinterested patriotism or from confidence that victory was certain and that therefore it was a secure and remunerative investment (or from both motivations). Either way it is a clear indication that popular morale was not as bad as the Government sometimes feared. Of course these 'average' figures could be and were blatantly distorted by high subscription from individuals and institutions. During Tank Week in Preston, when a total of just over £1 million was raised, more than £450,000 was raised from a dozen 'corporate' subscribers making investments of more than £10,000. Two of these subscriptions, from W. Birtwhistle and G. and R. Dewhurst were for £100,000; two more from North Lancashire Cotton Spinners and Horrockses were for £50,000. At the same time the 'Tank Bank' did attract popular support. The mayor describes men and women 'who had never made an investment before' subscribing to the loan. One man came with a fish basket full of coins and notes and a widow invested her life's savings. 'One working man produced a bag of gold coins – a rare sight in these times and bought war bonds for £110'; whilst another staggered to the Tank under the weight of two carpet bags filled with coppers. Not just companies but other collective institutions subscribed, Emmanuel Girls School bought £5 in bonds,[13] and two churches, presumably Roman Catholic given the names, subscribed heavily – St Ignatius invested £140 and English Martyrs £330. In all, by September 1918, Preston's War Savings Associations had 14,503 members, somewhat over 10% of the total population of the town.[14] If Preston was at all typical, it seems likely that the loan was raised in roughly equal proportions from 'large' and 'small' investors, but it is also highly probable that the balance in this respect differed greatly between towns. In Bristol during the whole war it was claimed that over £3,000,000 was raised from 'sixpences, shillings and half crowns' out of £14,000,000 total, but this understates popular support. In addition, to give some examples, the employees of Imperial Tobacco collectively subscribed for £38,000, the Tramway employees, £19,000, the Parish of Stapleton, £10,500, and Fairfield School, £4,400.[15]

At first sight the table of subscription per capita demonstrates no rhyme or reason. The disparities are striking: the highest rate of subscription is more than one hundred times greater than the lowest rate. There can be immense disparities even between two comparably sized towns which were geographically close together. For example, Wisbech in Cambridgeshire subscribed more than £1 per week per head, while the population of nearby Newmarket subscribed little more than a shilling.

In some respects this is itself very revealing. Even within urban Britain the energy and activity of local elites might make a huge difference; so might the intensity of domestic propaganda. The advertisement in *The Times* notes that several of the larger urban centres had not been visited by a tank – those that hadn't generally gave less. These tanks were widely

publicised as 'veterans' of the Battle of Cambrai, which had been celebrated by the ringing of church bells across the country. The evidence
from Preston strongly suggests that their visits were very important. The
mayor in his memoir of the war quotes Lord Salisbury: 'There is much
virtue in a circus' and states that prior to the visit of the tank, 'Egbert',
Preston had not subscribed enthusiastically:

> In the course of three months, a town, always more than usually loyal, responds
> with a contribution of something over £200,000, a sum considerably below its just
> quota, but with the consolation, if it be a consolation – of knowing that if it was no
> better, it was no worse than the rest of the country. A circus comes along as a
> means of arousing the *amour propre* of the town and in one week, the total is raised
> to £1,300,000.[16]

In response to the poor earlier performance of the capital, the tanks
returned to London in the spring of 1918. Elizabeth Fernside wrote to her
son Fred of visiting the tank in Trafalgar Square, where a large oil painting
hanging over the national gallery depicted Francis Drake going out to
meet the Armada, accompanied by 'the cheering legend' that '"Britain is
again threatened"'. The 'dirty, rusty old tank', 'Egbert', back from the
tour of the provinces, was doing 'a roaring trade'. The next week a tank
came to Fulham, and Elizabeth wrote to Fred that she intended 'spec-
ulating on 3 £5 bonds in your name'.[17] On the same day in Islington, the
mood surrounding the 'Tank Day' was carnivalesque: 'flags and streamers
were given full play and Holloway Road once again presented some of its
pre-war appearance'. The campaign motto was 'The Bond that brings
peace nearer'. This idea was sufficiently appealing to raise £204,750.[18]

Whilst the influence of 'the circus' was clearly important, the
per-capita subscription still raises questions. The most obvious point is
that the larger urban areas subscribed substantially more. This is rather
counter-intuitive: it is very peculiar that, for example, Bristol has a higher
per-capita rate of subscription than Bath, when per-capita wealth would
suggest a very different outcome. At the extremes it verges on the bizarre;
that Newcastle should subscribe three times more heavily per head than
Oxford is almost inconceivable.

There are however, some very plausible explanations. The first is that
this is a late loan. Wealthier areas might already have given to their
perceived limit. The second explanation is wealth redistribution in wartime. Areas of heavy involvement in war industry might well have had
more surplus cash floating around. A few large subscriptions by wealthy
individuals or a larger number of newly wealthy workers might radically
influence the picture. Associated with this is actual or perceived
middle-class impoverishment. Many of the middle classes might have
felt unable to subscribe in the straitened conditions of 1917–1918.

Finally there is simple distortion: how many of the inhabitants of the commuter belt, for example Tunbridge Wells or Surbiton, had subscribed to war loans in London rather than locally? This would be more convincing were it not for the extremely low initial level of per-capita subscription in London itself.

Broader economic influences also probably played a role. The strikingly low figures for Leicester and Nottingham might imply that the disruption of their peacetime industries had never entirely been overcome, although by some accounts the textile industries were doing rather well out of war contracts. Even more striking is the low figure for Stoke-on-Trent, markedly below the rate of subscription for major urban centres and quite possibly attributable to the same cause, in this case the limitation on the demand for pottery.

But economics cannot explain everything. It is difficult to explain why the South Wales towns of Ebbw Vale and Tredegar have a per-capita subscription level which is vastly lower than Sheffield. Nor is it easy to explain why Bury in Lancashire should have a rate of subscription more than double that of Luton. Above all West Hartlepool was not an obviously wealthy town.

The low figures for industrial Wales are blatantly obvious. It is difficult to avoid a degree of political interpretation. Ebbw Vale and Tredegar had been singled out as centres of growing pacifist agitation in Labour intelligence reports in August 1917. Curiously the supposedly troublesome Rhondda was somewhat better, although for an industrial area of its size it was not subscribing very actively. It is also worth comparing the figures for Rhondda with Bishop Auckland in County Durham. Mining areas were hardly suffering from unusual economic hardship in 1917–1918, yet their take-up on the loan was clearly poor. A sense of relative deprivation, tension over mine owners 'profiteering' and anger at the prospect of a conscription 'comb-out' may have played a role. Even this generalisation should be treated with a degree of caution: Wigan in Lancashire, partly a mining town, was comparable with other Lancashire towns, and Mansfield in Nottinghamshire, a mining town, subscribed more per capita than Nottingham itself. Likewise whilst the generalisation about low subscription in Wales seems sustainable, it needs to be qualified by the very high level in Cardiff. Furthermore Wales, particularly rural areas, later caught up to an impressive and indeed suspicious degree. In July 1918 Lampeter, with a population of 5,368, invested £103,608, with no single sum exceeding £1,000. Potadulais invested £80,000 from a population of 7,000 in June and Aberystwyth supposedly averaged an extraordinary £75 16s 2d per head. Even Merthyr caught up with a total of over £1 million during its Tank Week in the summer. But there was every difference in the world between subscribing in the grim mid-winter and subscribing in the summer when victory was beginning to draw near. These figures suggest an unseemly rush to secure excess profits rather than patriotism. It is worth noting that in the 'first three years' of the war, charitable giving in the principality had been very low: for example, £35,000 was raised by the Red Cross in the whole of Wales through to 1917. In a slightly longer period Guildford alone had raised £2,401, whilst Todmorden raised £2,583 in single appeal in 1916.[19] Wales aside, the most striking failure of the loan in the winter of 1917–1918 appears to be a belt of surprisingly poor performance in 'middle England'. The figures for Luton, Watford and Hitchin are less than impressive. This seems to be of a piece with the poor figures for small but wealthy towns throughout the country.[20]

It was above all the big regional centres that subscribed heavily. One possible reason is that the large towns were and had been an obvious target of air raids. This further explains the West Hartlepool paradox; indeed the civic history of the Hartlepools makes it clear that one of the reasons why the subscription to war loans was so high, ultimately the highest per capita in the country, was that money was invested from the annual 'thanksgiving offering' collected on the anniversary of the December 1914 raid. So in at least one case direct enemy action had led to intensified commitment. Even this must be heavily qualified: whilst some 'raided' towns, for example King's Lynn, subscribed more than would otherwise be expected, neither Scarborough nor Hartlepool proper are particularly high subscribers for their region or size, and Great Yarmouth and Dover, subject to rather frequent bombardment, did poorly. Folkestone, near the bottom of this table, suggests that very recent aerial bombardment could actually shake confidence in victory. There is a hint of this in Dover's civic history: 'The continued air attacks were a strain on the nerves of the people of Dover. Many who were free to change their residence at pleasure left for safer quarters.'[21] Not just raids, but persistent fear of raids, may have had an impact. In the three months after 1 September 1917, there were twenty-nine separate air-raid warnings in Dover, almost one every third day.[22]

Amongst the major provincial cities, Newcastle stands out, just as it had in the well-publicised recruiting contest of 'pals' battalions in 1914–1915. There seems to be a particular and peculiar Geordie patriotism being demonstrated which might conceivably have had its best counterparts north of the Anglo-Scottish border. The table published excluded Scotland, but in the next few weeks Scotland would demonstrate an extraordinarily high rate of subscription and participation.

The strongest correlation between high subscription and any other variable is size of the urban centre and a distinct sense of civic identity.

The extraordinarily high level of subscription in Cardiff compared with other parts of South Wales is a perfect illustration of this. Furthermore the subscription to the war loan was evidently competitive.[23] Because the 'Tank' loan had been launched in London, the major provincial centres had a target to aim at and exceed. They subsequently also competed with each other. A sense of this dynamic is provided by the story in *The Times* on 21 January 1918. Glasgow raised £14 million in 'Tank Week', breaking all records. This was compared with the figure of just under £3.5 million raised by London in the first 'Tank Week'. In reaction to this, the civic authorities in Manchester and Liverpool requested that the 'Tanks' be allowed to return, so that they could try to break Glasgow's record.

That Glasgow *could* set the record in January 1918 is noteworthy in itself. Less a case of 'Red Clydeside' than 'True Blue Clydeside'? It might be thought that the £14 million raised simply reflected the wartime profits of Clydeside manufacturers making safe long-term investments. Certainly the subscriptions to the loan included an anonymous one of £1 million, a £250,000 investment from the Clydeside Bank and £50,000 each from Sir Thomas Lipton, the Lyle Shipping Company and Nobel Explosives. But this still leaves more than £12 million to be accounted for in subscriptions of less than £50,000. To some extent it is plausible that the 'disloyalty' tag actually helped persuade Glasgow's 'patriots' to demonstrate conspicuous loyalty. In any case, the supposed revolt on the Clyde was always an ambiguous phenomenon, as indicated above. Amongst the ringleaders of industrial discontent in 1916–1917, only one, John Maclean, could honestly be described as anything approaching a 'Revolutionary defeatist'. By the winter of 1917 the majority of the prominent activists were in fact involved in local war production committees which were in the process of turning Glasgow into the most productive munitions centre in Britain.

Solidarity with local soldiers might also go some way towards an explanation. By all accounts Glasgow had a very high level of military participation. One count suggested that there was one Glaswegian in the army for every twenty-three Englishmen.[24] Finally there is the question of Scottish ingenuity in selling the bonds. The example of Edinburgh is instructive in demonstrating how widespread popular subscription was mobilised north of Hadrian's Wall. A letter to *The Times* illuminated the innovative method used:

I venture to write to you about an incident in the Tank Week in Edinburgh which, to my mind furnishes a very strong argument in favour of the Government adopting the issuing of premium bonds.

Personally, I should like to say that until now I have been old fashioned enough to object to the gambling element connected with these bonds, but what happened in Edinburgh has converted me. During the first two days the subscriptions to the Tank Bank were largely confined to banks, insurance and other large companies and private individuals with means. Then a few of our large and enterprising shopkeepers advertised that one in every 20 of the Tank issues would entitle the lucky buyer to a war certificate on presentation at their shops, whilst one generous donor gave £1,000 to be divided on somewhat similar lines. The effect was remarkable and instantaneous. In spite of biting winter weather a queue of one furlong long was immediately formed, additional premises had to be opened and in spite of this people waited patiently for hours to buy the bonds. The result is that Edinburgh, up to till now, has the largest number of small subscribers to the Tank of any city in the country. I think everyone must admit that, for the future no less than the present benefit of the country, it is most desirable that our working classes should be encouraged to invest in the funds of the State and if, as was proved in Edinburgh, a slight element of gambling assists this end, I think that the good effected would more than counterbalance the evil.[25]

The mixture of patriotism and self-interest is self-evident. Shopkeepers benefited from self-advertisement and also perhaps by deflecting charges of unpatriotic profiteering.

Working-class subscribers to the loan stood the chance of material benefit and also had the fun of a legitimate and socially sanctioned gamble. In an atmosphere where self-interest was usually contrasted with the common good, the citizens of Edinburgh had created a reconciliation of the two. In response to this letter, an English vicar from South Mymms endorsed the call for 'premium bonds':

It will be a matter of universal regret that there is to be no immediate issue. In this village, which is I suppose like most country places, we have by dint of hard work been able to save £200 by war loan certificates. These have been subscribed for by people who already save. The majority of the population has not been touched as yet and some are squandering the large wages they are earning. If these people had the chance of winning prizes of £200 to £500 with which to buy a cottage and land, they would quickly save that amount and convert the chance into a certainty. My experience is that of the clergy all over the countryside.[26]

It is a striking letter, albeit heavily biased towards a condescending conservatism. In January 1918, the English villages, the very ideal of so much wartime propaganda, were almost completely unresponsive to patriotic appeal, whilst demonised Glasgow was breaking all records.

Leaving aside the arguments of self-interest (important as they are, but complicated by the degree of willingness of individuals to merge self and public interest), the blunt figures of the 'Tank Loan' do suggest something important and counter-intuitive about the popular mood in early 1918. The obvious heartlands of traditional patriotic conservatism – the Home Counties, rural England, the commuter belt and London – were not responding particularly well. By contrast much, although not all, of provincial urban England and even that supposed hotbed of dissent, Glasgow, were subscribing heavily. Was it specifically 'middle England' that was undergoing a crisis in morale?

In one respect the answer is probably yes. The strain of prior sacrifices was being felt in the south east. Some caution should be applied to this. Stefan Goebel of the University of Kent has collated in impressive detail the subscriptions to the war loan occasioned by the *second* visit of the tanks to London.

Investments into Tank Banks (war bonds and savings certificates) in metropolitan boroughs and urban districts in Greater London, March 1918

Metropolitan borough/urban district	Population 1911	Population 1921	Investments (£)
City *	19,657	13,706	24,654,705
Trafalgar Square *	–	–	7,214,755
Holborn +	49,357	42,796	1,673,786
St Pancras	218,387	210,986	1,044,274
Shoreditch	111,390	104,308	444,291
Woolwich +	121,376	140,403	443,213
Finsbury	87,923	76,019	402,527
Islington +	327,403	330,028	370,182
Lambeth +	298,058	302,960	367,394
Croydon (Surrey)	169,551	190,877	360,000
Battersea	167,743	167,693	334,041
Stepney +	279,804	249,738	301,540
Marylebone	118,160	104,222	292,986
Southwark	191,907	184,388	281,826
Camberwell +	261,328	267,235	249,588
Lewisham	160,834	174,194	245,078
Ealing (Middlesex)	61,222	67,753	242,054
Chiswick (Middlesex)	38,772	40,942	232,879
Kensington	172,317	175,686	217,050
Wandsworth +	311,360	328,656	212,161
Hornsey (Middlesex)	84,592	87,691	210,000
Hampstead	85,495	86,080	205,021
Kingston (Surrey)	37,975	39,484	182,000
Bromley (Kent)	33,646	35,070	175,217
Hammersmith +	121,521	130,287	174,550
West Ham (Essex)	289,030	300,905	174,099
Chelsea	66,385	63,700	166,566
Hackney +	222,533	222,159	164,643
Wimbledon (Surrey)	54,966	61,451	153,215
Bermondsey	125,903	119,455	141,256
Acton (Middlesex)	57,497	61,314	134,129
Willesden (Middlesex)	154,214	165,669	133,050
Fulham	153,284	157,944	132,000
Greenwich	95,968	100,493	131,542

Paddington	142,551	144,273	130,035
Tottenham (Middlesex)	137,418	146,695	124,374
East Ham (Essex)	133,487	143,304	120,567
Walthamstow (Essex)	124,580	127,441	116,330
Stoke Newington	50,659	52,167	112,000
Ilford (Essex)	78,188	85,191	104,607
Poplar	162,442	162,618	104,462
Wood Green (Middlesex)	49,369	50,716	101,090
Bethnal Green	128,183	117,238	91,600
Enfield (Middlesex)	56,338	60,743	90,926
Deptford	109,496	112,500	81,976
Leyton (Essex)	124,735	128,432	34,410
Edmonton (Middlesex)	64,797	66,809	26,900
Greater London	6,111,801	6,202,419	42,941,197

Notes:
* One-week campaign.
+ Two-days campaign. The other boroughs one day only.
PRO, NSC 3/1, 'The Tank Campaigns', *War Savings* 2.7 (1918), p. 79; London County
Council, *London Statistics, 1920–21*, vol. 27 (London, 1922), pp. 26–9.

The very high levels of subscription for the City may well indicate that
many of the middle classes subscribed at 'the office', although it should
also be noted that the city figure was massively boosted by large 'corporate' donations. Aside from this, the variations between boroughs do not
follow any straightforward sociological pattern: some commuter suburbs,
for example Wimbledon, Acton, Kingston and Bromley subscribed heavily per capita and a lot of the variation would probably be explained by
chance and by local leadership. Furthermore the growth of pockets of war
industry in outer London make it difficult to be absolutely sure about class
compositions on a borough-by-borough basis. Nevertheless the surprisingly high levels of subscription in heavily working-class districts such
as Shoreditch, Lewisham, Southwark and Woolwich can be contrasted
with some very low levels of subscription in, for example, Leyton and
Edmonton.

These figures are from what was London's second, and maximum-
effort, war loans drive, made in conscious competition with the large
provincial efforts. They do modify the picture of middle-class disillusionment somewhat, but do not undermine it.

By 1917, high middle-class casualty rates, the erosion of middle-
class incomes through inflation and taxation, the tensions of food queues
and perhaps the fear of bombing created a generalised feeling that the
social order was being upset. The diaries of Frederick Robinson, of
Cobham in Surrey, show immense scepticism specifically about war

loans. In January 1917 he wrote of an earlier loan that the advertisements were 'objectionable' and in February he wrote of the plight of the middle classes who were being urged to invest all their available cash in loans but would then suffer from increased demands upon them as rate payers. It was not pleasant to be told 'if you don't subscribe your last farthing you are not only "unpatriotic" but a fool'. On 17 February 1917 he remarked that it was a relief that war loan advertisements had ended: it was unpleasant to be faced by advertisements accusing non-subscribers of 'shirking unpatriotism' who would let other people 'give their lives' whilst they refused to lend money.[27]

In September 1917 he remarked, 'the people who concoct these appeals ... don't seem to appreciate that it is as much and more than many can do to make ends meet, what with reduced dividends on the one hand and immensely increased cost of living on the other, coupled with a 5/- income tax'. Even more damaging was the fear that the Government was going to bow after the war to the call for 'the conscription of riches' and that the war loan subscribers would be robbed. At a shareholders meeting in the City, 'such a "possibility" was regarded as an absolute certainty'.[28]

Ironically, but perhaps appropriately, the very people who in 1914 seem to have had the fewest doubts about the war were now feeling the pinch. Furthermore, they feared that it would last a long time:

Boys and girls are being paid absurdly high wages for doing unskilled work that leads to nothing except to the formation of idle habits ... Those high wages can only be paid by piling up debt for all tax payers to pay and pay and go on paying, but after the war is over this cannot continue and at present it ought not to continue. People are not encouraged to *make sacrifices or lend money* merely to be wasted in demoralizing unskilled labour.[29] (My italics)

Does this indicate a growing unwillingness to make sacrifices? A cartoon in *The Passing Show* on 9 June 1917, saw 'the public' as a Christian martyr surrounded by lions. They were labelled 'Heavy taxes, Rising prices, Strikes and Unrest, Tobacco Profiteering, Restrictions and Beer Famine.' Emerging from a cage is a new threat, a lion cub which is labelled '33 Flag Days in June'. The *Islington Daily Gazette* on 22 October 1917 commented on the contrast between the charitable collection on 'Our Day' in October 1916 and that in October 1917. The area had raised £1,526 18/6d. in 1916; in 1917 this had fallen to £419 13/8d. The newspaper stated categorically, 'the big drop can only be attributed to a lack of lady helpers'. Whilst 'those who did come forward worked splendidly', the general response was disappointing. The fact that ladies were fast growing tired of flag days 'is not to be wondered at', but the paper expressed surprise 'that in the matter of helpers there was not a greater response of womanly sympathy'.[30]

More difficult to interpret is the pattern of wartime charitable giving in Guildford street collections.

Guildford Flag Days

Month	Cause	Amount raised
August 1915	Russia's Day	£50
October 1915	'Our Day'	£584
December 1915	Serbia's Day	£326
April 1916	Belgian Refugees	£332
June 1916	Prisoners of War	£425
July 1916	YMCA	£127
November 1916	'Our Day'	£438
April 1917	St Dunstan's	£200
May 1917	Sick and Wounded Horses	£396
August 1917	Italy's Day	£128
September 1917	'Our Day'	£663
October 1917	Red Cross	£726
May 1918	Prisoners of War	£200
May 1918	Red Cross	£382
August 1918	France	£214
September 1918	Sailors' Day	£500
October 1918	'Our Day' & Red Cross	£1,391*
November 1918	Queen's Regiment	£120

*Distorted by a single donation of £500

Apart from the disturbing implication that the good burghers of Guildford cared more in 1917 about horses than they did about blinded soldiers and Italian allies, this table doesn't provide a clear-cut picture. Even after inflation and 'compassion fatigue', the September and October Flag Days in 1917 were still successful. But there is an inference of difficulties in a striking absence. The *gap* between Flag Days around the low point in morale is easily the longest in the war since 1915. After a flurry in autumn 1917, the public were not approached again for six months. Was there a fear of embarrassment?[31]

In looking for dissent in 1917–1918, it is important to examine the increasingly shrill voice of populist middle-class protest. It is easily missed as a form of dissent because, paradoxically but logically, it manifested itself as hyper-patriotism, criticising the Government for weakness. The focus was seeking out the 'enemies within'. These groups wanted the war to end and quickly, but they wanted it to end with a clear-cut victory that would justify their sacrifices.

Enemies within

The Sussex schoolmaster Robert Saunders was far from being a classic 'jingo'. But at the height of the 'Gotha Summer' of 1917 he commented on anti-German riots in London: 'probably innocent people have suffered, but it will take very little to turn the intense anger of the people against the Government incapables ... I am afraid there will be trouble unless the Authorities recognise the danger in time.' In his view there was a growing conviction 'that the present Government has been in office too long & many of the members misrepresent the opinion of the country'. In particular, 'the Resolutions and Memorials' sent from areas that had been bombed, 'focussed public attention on the Government and their failings, especially in Reprisals'.[32]

Although anger at the intensified bombing in 1917 played a role in fuelling support for the radical right, the groundwork was laid in 1916. The return of the eccentric 'member for air' Pemberton Billing in the East Hertfordshire by election that year was a first signal that something serious was happening in the Home Counties. By January 1917, The British Empire Union (BEU), which merged with the Anti-German League, was becoming distinctly active in southern England. The branches which reported activity in December and January 1916 were: Bath, Brighton and Hove, Farnham, Haywards Heath, Balham, Ealing, Islington, Norwood, Streatham, Wandsworth and Putney, Welshpool, Portsmouth, Reigate, St Andrews, Teddington, Worthing, Bury St Edmunds, Kingston and Surbiton, Oxford, Liverpool, Walthamstow, Folkestone, Market Harborough, Chislehurst, Watford, Hampton in Arden, Roehampton.

Propagandists for the BEU were also listed as being active in attacking pacifists in South Wales, but no branches in the area are listed. This list is overwhelmingly skewed towards the London suburbs and the Home Counties. That there were active branches in neighbouring Brighton *and* Worthing, but apparently none in the Manchester metropolitan area or the whole of Tyneside, is revealing. A third of the active branches were in London suburbs.

Therefore in 1917–1918 the Governing Coalition was truly unfortunate in finding itself fighting a series of by-elections in London's inner suburbs. These resolved themselves into contests between the platforms of the right wing, the extremely right wing and the insanely right wing. The first of them, East Islington in October 1917 in the wake of a Gotha raid, saw Alfred Baker, treasurer of the Vigilantes, fighting under the slogan, 'Hinder the Huns, Paralyse Profiteers, Purify Politics. Win the War.' He gained 32% of the vote, easily outstripping the slightly less rabid candidate of the National Party. The hardline populist anti-alien candidates between them almost matched the Government electorate. In Clapham in June 1918, the almost certifiable H. H. Beamish of the Vigilantes, in the face of widespread Fleet Street hostility, garnered 3,331 votes to the Coalition candidate's 4,152, and might have done better still if the Coalition candidate hadn't himself adopted much of Beamish's persecutory programme.[33] The next Vigilante candidate, the unquestionably lunatic American expatriate, Captain Spencer, did less well in East Finsbury in July: there was a split in the vote caused by another populist right-winger Allan Belsher, and the actions of a Vigilante mob in attacking a meeting organised by Belsher backfired. Once again, the Coalition candidate stole the rhetorical clothes of the radical right. The result was that the right-wing dissidents 'only' took a third of the votes between them. The Government response to the extreme right was double edged. They began unleashing the forces of the state against them: National Party branches were raided in the summer and at the same time they cut the ground from under the platform by adopting most of it, systematic 'retaliatory' bombing was begun and a harsher new anti-alien internment law was introduced.

The changing pattern of anti-Germanism? From riots to associations

Manifestations against Germans in Britain began with the war. There were sporadic attacks on German businesses as soon as war was declared. The biggest and most widespread outbreak of 'racial' rioting and civil disorder in twentieth-century Britain were the *Lusitania* riots in May 1915. Contemporaries had three explanations: that the rioters were expressing personal hatreds, that the ideological atmosphere had been poisoned by the jingoism of the press or that the riots were essentially 'hunger riots' motivated by economic hardship. Panikos Panayi in his study of the riots comes down firmly on the side of an ideological justification.[34] Whilst it is clear that the anti-German temperature of the public mood had risen considerably by May 1915 for reasons discussed in Chapter 2, Panayi is overly hasty to dismiss the other two elements. The discussion of the riots as a straight either/or reflecting three competing ideological viewpoints rather misses the possibility of a more complex interaction. For example Panayi dismisses the idea that personal anger played a role in the severe riots in Liverpool, claiming that the magistrate's court report in the press states that 'hardly any' of the rioters had relatives on board the *Lusitania*. This is not conclusive. In a broader sense, anger at the loss of relatives in the war may have played a role in the riots that would be hard to reconstruct. Nevertheless there is some revealing specific evidence from the *Lusitania* riots in Hull. A witness questioned by police stated: 'the disturbance was initiated by four women who had spoken of sons who had been killed or injured in the war'. This may or may not be believed, but there is further evidence that the riots in Hull were premeditated: a letter delivered to Charles Hohenrein on 12 May stated, 'I belong to a secret gang ... I wish to warn you your shop is in danger.' The strongest evidence that the *Lusitania* incident was the occasion rather than the cause of anti-German anger in Hull, is found in the geography of rioting. The riots in May 1915 were closely confined to the Hessle Road area. The fishing community of this part of town had suffered heavily from the war: many trawlermen had been interned in Germany and others were daily facing danger from German mines and U-boats.

It is noteworthy that the rioting in May was confined to rough areas connected with fishing, and that the pubs on Hessle Road had a reputation for Saturday-night disturbances. By contrast, in June, after the first air raid on the city, rioting was far more ubiquitous and widespread.[35]

The weight of blame that Panayi puts on a specific and obscene editorial in the *John Bull* dated Saturday 15 May 1915, calling for a 'vendetta' against all Germans in Britain, is rather undermined by the fact that it would generally have appeared after the rioting had already finished.[36] There can be little doubt that the cumulative effect of press reporting of German behaviour helped stoke up popular anger and that the editorial rhetoric had become more inclined to stress the innate depravity of the German character, but it is worth noting that the specific areas which rioted were generally those which would have had a lower rate of newspaper readership.

Whilst overstating the centrality of specific inflammatory rhetoric, he is too quick to dismiss economic causality. His use of Arthur Marwick and Jay Winter to dismiss the possibility of working-class grievance, on the grounds that living standards were improving, is unsubtle and misleading. Even if by May 1915 full employment was leading to alleviation of working-class living standards, this was not necessarily universal at this stage of the war. Furthermore food riots, logically enough, are triggered by actual prices, not the relationship of prices to real wages. There had been intermittent attacks on shopkeepers, German and English, over the past six months, and there would be more throughout the war. The further argument on the diversity of the occupations of rioters is even less convincing. The presence of 'cabinet makers' or 'paper hangers' amongst the rioters does not disprove a possible economic motivation. Such groups, obvious losers in the transition to a war economy, actually strengthen the possibility of economic motivations. Likewise the mixed ages and sexes is not a disproof, indeed the presence of middle-aged women in the crowds might be taken as a marker of economic reasons playing a part.

Finally that looters charged in the later stages of rioting were predominantly charged with stealing things other than food proves less than nothing. The operative word is 'charged'. That the person who stole furniture or 'a crucifix' would be considered more worthy of prosecution than someone who had walked off with a loaf is clear. The June riots in Hull provide concrete evidence of this. Compensation claims demonstrate that eight pork butchers and an egg dealer were looted during the disturbances, but the record of prosecutions doesn't clearly indicate anyone charged for stealing food. The police prosecuted those whom they could demonstrate were in possession of stolen property. Looted food was, of course, quickly unavailable for use as evidence.[37]

Despite occasional specific denials, Panayi clearly demonstrates that food retailers were usually the target of these riots, bakers and pork butchers in particular. In some cases the looting spilled over to such businesses run by other foreigners, even, although rarely, towards the unambiguously English. Whilst Panayi is clearly right in dismissing the interpretation of the events as 'hunger riots', a view which was put forward by Sylvia Pankhurst at the time, this should not be taken as proving that material considerations played no part.

Ultimately economic and 'racial' motivations are not incompatible: the desire to punish small business 'profiteers' was never absent in the war, and the 'Hunnishness' of these businessmen allowed it to be done violently and with a feeling of clear moral righteousness which made looted sausages taste better.

One thing remains clear. Most of the rioting in 1915 was associated with working-class districts. This is less the case in London, but even in London the violence and intensity of looting was far greater in the East End. Panayi makes great play of the sporadic outbreaks in middle-class areas, but incidents in Tunbridge Wells, Winchester, Bury St Edmunds and Walton-on-Thames do not really bear out the argument that the rioting was a truly national phenomenon. The lack of rioting in such major centres as Glasgow, Cardiff, Bristol, Birmingham, Nottingham, Leeds and Newcastle is striking and rather damaging to the purely ideological argument. In general the outer suburbs and smaller towns seem untouched. A partial exception was Scotland, where there were riots in Greenock, Annan, Leith, Perth and Alloa. Catriona Macdonald believes that an analysis shows three particular features at work: economics, generation and casualties in these riots. In some cases local businessmen had deliberately targeted German rivals, 'bored youths' frustrated by wartime impotence saw rioting as entertainment and above all the specific areas affected had all suffered recent and heavy military casualties.[38]

In England, the poorer areas of some, but not all, big cities exploded in May 1915. What needs to be stressed is that this is a very different sociology and geography from the later manifestations of anti-Germanism. The striking thing is the lack of correlation between the main areas of rioting in 1915 and the areas of organised anti-alien sentiment in the last two years of the war. True, Liverpool did have an active BEU branch and so did Islington (where severe rioting broke out in 1917 as well), but Hull and Manchester apparently did not. Likewise places such as Brighton and Oxford with active BEU branches had not seen rioting earlier in the war. Anti-Germanism was becoming less visceral and more clearly ideological. It was also developing a clear class identity – middle-class anger.

The spread of hatred

Anti-Germanism was the focal point of wartime racism, but the rhetoric of the enemy within began to metastasise into a more generalised attack on unpopular minorities.

The correspondence files of Arnold White, the author of *The Hidden Hand*, show the process at work. After addressing a 1917 public meeting on the subject, members of the general public wrote to him. The letters make extremely unpleasant reading. Some of them show straightforward and vindictive anti-Germanism based apparently on personal grudges: E. F. Kernick, owner of the King's Arms Hotel in Godalming, denounces 'German' hotel owners, 'there are hardly any British hotels ... Four fifths of the Hotels of all sizes [are] Germany's hotels. Their managers – Foreign pro-Germans – all know one another ... All of them are Spies.' Miss Florence Hardy believed 'the Hidden Hand is at work in the education committee of the LCC'. She was horrified that 'At the recent July County Scholarship examination ... one successful candidate was found to be the daughter of a German father.'[39]

A long letter from Arthur Barley in North London informs White about his noisy and suspicious neighbours: 'I live in a semi detached house. The renter of the other half of this building has let his home, furnished and the present occupiers are an odd assortment of people, foreign speaking ... I gather that the neighbours are likewise suspicious.' Barley, whilst protesting his fair-mindedness, was waging a vendetta: he had already approached the British Empire Union and had demanded an investigation by Scotland Yard. This had been carried out: 'I was informed by a detective that he had thoroughly examined the occupants of the house; they are two Russian men and one woman, a Belgian Refugee, also a Russian. One man was wounded fighting for us, the other two have work which keeps them occupied all day.' Barley was unsatisfied, 'Sounds Ok, doesn't it. But why should the Russian tell my wife he was Australian? Why should people be asked who they are before the door is opened to them?' The obvious answer to the latter question, that caution is perfectly understandable when living next door to stupid bigots who denounce you to the police, did not occur to him. Although the probable Jewish identity of Barley's neighbours is only implied, other writers were less reticent. S. Cooke, a theatrical agent, wrote: 'might I venture a few details in connection with the Alien Jew in connection with my own case as a theatrical agent'; the rest is predictable. The usual suspects come under fire. An anonymous correspondent writes a long diatribe about the pernicious influence of the Standard Oil Company: 'The master mind, the "Unseen Hand", is a German-American Rockafeller [sic] and his principal chiefs are Jews and people of German extraction.' A Mr Browne who had been at a Queen's Hall meeting and been 'duly impressed', felt that White's suggestion of a Royal Commission was 'too slow. We want inter alia an "England for the English party" … In the Government office where I was previously working, I sat at a table with a German Jew.' Browne did not want to belittle the Jews: 'they are more clever than we, but they should not be put in power over Englishmen as in the case of the L.C. Justice'. He volunteered to help the 'movement': 'the press is too soft where the Jews are concerned. I have been a journalist & found myself too often against Hebrew influence.' The Lord Chief Justice was cited again in a letter from a Mr Wiseman: 'Haldane, Reading and Parmoor. I believe it will be no injustice to the trio to label them suspect.' The London doctor, Macleod Yearsley had his own 'hidden hand' suspects, citing the fact that 'Felix Cassell, a naturalised German is Judge-Advocate General of the armed forces & as such the last appeal for "tommy" when the latter is convicted of a military crime', before going on to denounce, 'Julius Meyer Bernstein', a doctor who had changed his name to Burnford and obtained a temporary commission in the Royal Army Medical Corps and 'is doing special work at the War Office'.[40]

Mrs Beta Forbes of Hove considered it her duty 'to inform you as a shareholder in the Metropolitan Supply co. that I charge a superintendent named Rowle or Rose, a Jew, with another named Weill … of working to the present day a system of secret telephone wireless … the underlying object being to sell this country to Germany'. The most extreme communication is an anonymous postcard sent from Italy in 1918. The provenance and precise date are unclear – it could be from an Italian anti-Semite – but the content and postmark suggests that it is most likely from someone serving in the British Army in Italy:

> "The Hidden Hand"
> Who are the pacifists, let's look at their noses ...
> They are <u>Jews</u>, they are <u>Jews</u>, They are Jews my friend
> And the <u>Jews of all countries</u> have planned this war
> As a revenge on <u>Christ</u>, Like the curs that they are ...
> No one would guess theirs was "The Hidden Hand"
> Whose spies cause disaster on sea and on land
> And who were to <u>crucify</u> Christian men on <u>the field</u>
> And to force Christian Women, to their bestiality yield ...
> The plan of the Socialist is a play on the name.
> Of its founder <u>Rothschild</u> who played the Revolutionary game
> By the net of Freemasonry, they have Englishmen caught
> And <u>Socialism</u> and <u>Sinn Feinenism</u>, <u>Labourism</u> taught
> Dissensions in Church, Discontent in State and on Land
> Every kind of rebellion, <u>The Jews</u> in secret have fanned.
> P.S. The Jews have another card to be played. Revolution. Englishmen
> Awake, don't let Socialism/Jews destroy England.

There will always be anti-Semitic lunatics, and it is not surprising that the correspondence files of a right-wing journalist are full of such things. But what is important about such writings is that they begin to tap into and merge with other wartime concerns. Increasingly, anti-German and anti-Semitic sentiments, which were never easily separable due to the Ashkenazi antecedents of most of the Jewish population, showed signs of merging. Furthermore it was tapping into a specific social stratum. With the exception of the last cited, all of this correspondence came from London suburbs and the Home Counties. This is not to suggest that areas which had been notable for political anti-Semitism prior to 1914, particularly the East End of London, with its large Jewish population, became any less anti-Semitic.[41] In June 1917 there was serious anti-Jewish rioting in Leeds involving 1,000 people, and in September another riot in Bethnal Green involving 5,000. These incidents latched onto the issue of 'alien Jews' being excluded from conscription, but were not confined to it – Jewish men in uniform were attacked.[42]

Historians of the Jewish community have been divided on the issue of wartime anti-Semitism, as they are by the issue of anti-Semitism more generally. At one extreme, David Caesarini has argued that the war 'savagely eroded the status of Jews in Britain'. William Rubinstein robustly denies this. He argues that the main focus of wartime hatred was 'Aryan' Germans; only by 'distortion' can the BEU be seen as anti-Semitic, and that the National Party had 'no populist base'.[43]

Whilst Caesarini may be exaggerating it is clear that Rubinstein is protesting too much. Demagogues such as White might not have used explicitly
anti-Semitic rhetoric, but they were clearly understood to be referring to
Jews. The incessant resurrection of the pre-war 'Marconi scandal' as the
exemplary case of improper financial manipulation, and the connected
accusations against Rufus Isaacs, Lord Reading, were the essence of
'hidden hand' accusations. It is disingenuous to claim that anyone was
unclear on the message when 'cosmopolitan financiers' were accused of
being the agents of Germany. Wartime anti-alien sentiment, as Colin
Holmes rightly points out, was frequently difficult to distinguish from
anti-Semitism.[44]

   This is not to argue that wartime anti-Semitism was a natural manifestation of a society imbued with popular anti-Semitism. Nor is it to argue
that by 1918 a fully fledged popular anti-Semitism had become pervasive
amongst the middle classes. It was present in an embryonic form, one of a
bundle of wartime fears and hatreds. The ability of anti-Semitism to
flourish was always dependent on its perverted ability to act as an explanatory framework for wider discontents, and by 1918 anti-Semitism was
beginning to latch onto concerns in other areas.

The hidden hand

This sentiment crystallised in the cause célèbre of 1918, the Pemberton
Billing libel case, a veritable compendium of wartime hatreds. In the
16 February 1918 edition of Pemberton Billing's newspaper *Vigilante*, a
small box paragraph appeared under the bizarre heading 'The Cult of the
Clitoris'.

   It publicised a private performance of Oscar Wilde's notorious play
Salome, the lead role in which was being played by the American actress
Maud Allan. It was accompanied by the comment that if Scotland Yard
were to attend they would obtain the names of several of 'the first 47,000'.

   The compounding of sexual impurity and spy accusations was meat and
drink to *Vigilante*. It had taken White's conceit of 47,000 highly placed
traitors and added its own explanation – that they were perverts who had
been blackmailed by the German high command. Encouraged by the
Attorney General F. E. Smith, Maud Allan sued for libel.

   Amongst the audience at one of Allan's performances had been Margot
Asquith. Her alleged lesbianism became the focal point of the trial. The
bad impression made by the Asquith family had been duly noted by
Neville Chamberlain in December 1917: 'their dress and general behaviour make the worst impression on our staid population'. They were
'painted', they smoked and they showed their knees. Cynthia Asquith

claimed in her diary that after the verdict, shop girls could be heard stating 'We always knew it of the Asquiths.'[45]

Billing's final address to the court demonstrated his sure grasp of his audience: 'Do you think I am going to keep quiet whilst nine men die in a minute to make a sodomite's holiday?' He claimed there was a hidden influence 'which seems to prevent a Britisher from getting a square job or a square deal'. Even as he spoke, 'there will be thousands of men who have "gone out" because of our "mistakes". I want to know why those mistakes have occurred.' He was acquitted by the jury and cheered from the court-room. Sexual corruption became hopelessly entangled with the politics of race. The rhetoric of 'degeneracy' had always connected the two.

Pemberton Billing was more of a general fantasist than a deep-dyed anti-Semite. Horatio Bottomley, presumably thinking that Jewish readers could be swindled just as well as others, occasionally condemned anti-Semitic comments in the pages of *John Bull*.[46] But an atmosphere of traitor-hunting, the shadow of Bolshevism, a condemnation of shirkers, profiteers and 'foreigners' in general, combined with a heightened 'Christian' rhetoric, and provided an environment in which anti-Semitism could flourish.

One of Pemberton Billing's witnesses had been the doctor J. H. Clarke. In 1917 he had published a pamphlet entitled *The Call of the Sword* which was unambiguous in its language:

When the son of a millionaire of alien blood who has ... put his hatred of Christ on such unmistakeable record as to cut off from his golden inheritance any descend-ant of his who should marry outside the synagogue of Caiaphas ... can climb to a foremost place in the British political machine without a breath of disapproval from Archbishop or nonconformist it is plain for all to see how little the interests of Christianity in Britain count in manning and steering the ship of state ... Britain's agony today is due to the measure in which the doctrine of Mammon has ousted the Gospel of The Christ from her land. The leaven of Mammon must have eaten deep into Britain's national life for the Shylock ideal to have so corrupted national aims.[47]

Superficially a long way from the National Mission message, it was not difficult to transmogrify the call for purification of morality to one of purity of blood, hatred of materialism into hatred of the classic usurer and attention to the sacrifice of Christ into persecution of his supposed tormentors. It was not unprecedented for crusade against an external enemy to be sidetracked into an assault on the Jewish enemy within.

The idea of a stab in the back could also latch on to a more conven-tionally deep-seated prejudice: anti-Irish sentiment. The increased sour-ing of English attitudes towards Ireland after the Easter Rising is illustrated by numerous hostile comments in diaries and letters. A 1916 poem by Jane Barlow, 'For Herself Alone (To Sinn Fein Ireland: Easter 1916)', indicates a strong sense of betrayal. Earlier in the war Barlow had written in praise of the Irish, and the tone is of disillusionment:

> Thy true sons, hearkening, left thee full many a heroes name.
> These all thou hast forgotten; by evil arts misled
> To thy bitter woe hast followed ...
> My heart's grief Ireland this bides ever thy shame
> That thy faith has been broken and hast betrayed thy dead.[48]

Delia Fox, a schoolteacher of Irish parentage, encountered some of this hostility when selling 'harp' badges in aid of Irish soldiers in Rochdale in 1917:

> I had a basket fine, with green silk it was lined,
> And across my chest a green sash told my trade.
> On my sleeve an armlet telling all the people I was selling,
> Irish flags for Irish lads of every grade.
>
> The ladies were the best, only pence they could invest,
> And a lecture on the Army they give free.
> On war they'd speak so long, you'd hum a ragtime song,
> And quickly turn to capture males you'd see.

A hint at the tension behind this verse is in Delia's description of 'one dame smartly dressed in fastidious first best', who dropped coppers in the tin but waved aside 'with scoff and empty smile' the Harp badge stating, a 'Crown she'd wear but not a Harp'. Delia Fox described this woman's attitude as cold hatred.[49] The failure to apply conscription to Ireland was an even greater grievance than 'Sinn Fein' disloyalty: *John Bull* commented in December 1917 that the country was a hotbed of shirkers, 'and we dare not apply conscription to it'.[50]

In April 1918 under the heading 'No Panic Call Up', Bottomley damned the Irish root and branch. He commented unfavourably on the new comb-outs of British men: 'You cannot justify calling up the men of England, Scotland and Wales of middle age while lusty young men of Ireland are living on the fat of uncouponed towns and drilling, not to fit themselves to fight the Hun, but to fight each other.' And continued: 'Is it fair and reasonable – is there any meaning to "equality of sacrifice", so long as these young fellows dodge their duty?'

Conscription was being demanded not simply for the men it would provide, but to send a message of fairness:

I know the British public, I know their sufferings and their sacrifices. They must be treated fairly; they will deeply resent anything like a humbugging scheme, which, while it makes a further and far reaching call on the manhood – and the middle aged manhood of this country, leaves Ireland for all effective military purposes the happy land of the neutral, free from every one of these restrictions which press heavily, if necessarily upon the homes of England and able to pursue that path of uninterrupted prosperity which without the money and support of this country they could never enjoy.

The implication of this was taken a stage further in the next issue, 'Ireland must remain in the United Kingdom – enjoying its privileges and sharing its burdens – or she must go out. She cannot have it both ways.'[51]

When it was reported that priests were supporting the opposition to conscription, Bottomley came very close to raising the old battle cry of 'No Popery'. In his opinion everything that was happening in Ireland had to have the approval of the Pope, and that this approval was forthcoming because 'Only by the victory of Germany and Austria ... can Rome regain her lost political and sovereign status.' But the British people 'will have no Pope's peace'.[52] A courteous complaint from the Roman Catholic hierarchy made Bottomley back off, and the opening of the Pemberton Billing affair shifted the target back to traitors in high places.

In December 1914, W. Holt White had claimed: 'Kitchener's Army is out of all proportion an "upper" class and middle class army'. He predicted 'those working men who could fight today and did not will have cause to remember the hour of the Army's return ... they will turn a deaf ear to the multitude of shirkers ... they will have given enough'.[53] This prophecy was never entirely justified or fulfilled, but the burden of military service did not fall evenly on the nation in 1914 or in 1918, and neither did the burden of the war economy or the 'blood tax'. In absolute numbers the majority of the dead and wounded were working men, but as a proportion of the pre-war workforce it was the middle classes that were suffering most. As the exemption of industrial workers was recognised as crucial to the war effort, and as trade unions resisted the extension of compulsion, it was the middle classes who were being swept up in the conscription net. The conscript Army was just as disproportionately middle class as the volunteer Army, perhaps even more so. Even in the first draft of 'Derby men' this became clear. A sample of occupations in a company of the 20th Royal Welsh Fusiliers shows that 51% of the attested men who reported for service came from commercial, clerical and professional occupations.[54] A letter from Walsall in the West Midlands forwarded to the War Cabinet voiced the complaints of small businessmen. The Butchers' Trade Association complained that since the beginning of the war they had lost over a hundred butchers and assistants to the Army, and there had been similar letters from the coal merchants, bakers, grocers, drapers, tobacconists, boot and shoe trade and dairymen. In Todmorden an association was formed to help small businessmen appeal against conscription. Almost inevitably these particular resentments took on a political shape. The Mayor of Bethnal Green pronounced: 'Men have to sacrifice their little business or their small factories to serve at the front, and neighbours of foreign extraction step into their places and reap the reward.'[55]

That the most war-weary section of the population became the fiercest and most intolerant patriots is, on the face of it, a paradox. Those who felt disproportionately burdened by the war – a double burden of declining living standards and actual or feared military losses – responded by demanding a more vigorous prosecution of the war and a campaign against the internal enemies who were preventing victory and, by extension, peace. Yet within an economy of sacrifice it made perfect sense. Those who felt they had already made the greatest sacrifices felt most strongly that those sacrifices had to be justified. Contemporary observers noticed that those who had lost children, particularly only children, in the war, were often much less willing to contemplate compromise peace than those who still had children in uniform. Only victory would be adequate recompense. A similar phenomenon can be observed in the trade-union movement. The trade union which developed the most chauvinistic and hyper-patriotic politics in wartime was the Seaman's Trade Union, led by Havelock Wilson. This was almost certainly the trade union that had suffered the highest proportion of casualties in the war. It was members of this union who refused to take British delegates to the Stockholm conference. Although they were tacitly encouraged in this by the Government, there can be little doubt that it reflected a genuine sentiment amongst merchant seamen. In 1918 this union actually broke with the TUC and a shortlived rival 'labour movement' began to emerge, committed to radical social change and fight-to-the-finish anti-Germanism.

A series of false syllogisms were gaining ground: that the war effort was being undermined by strikes and shirking amongst the working class; that this was the work of pacifist 'agitators'; that the agitators were supported by the Germans; that the Germans were operating through the 'alien' population; that the Jewish alien population was pro-German by inclination.

Ironically the Jewish middle-class population was paying a price as heavy as anyone else, perhaps even more so. For example, Merthyr Tydfil synagogue recorded thirty-four war deaths from a male military-age population that cannot have numbered more than a few hundred.[56]

Class antagonisms, never absent in British society, were sharpened in the latter years of the war, and fed into post-war politics. But extreme

14. Recruiting the Women's Army Auxiliary Corps. IWM (Q 31082).

right-wing politics, after a brief post-war flurry, remained marginalised. This was not because there was no incipient stab-in-the-back myth in wartime Britain. Far from it – the search for the 'hidden hand' was a pervasive feature of wartime culture in the latter years of the war. Blaming sinister forces for the frustration of the war effort had become a natural reflex. In autumn 1917, revelations of 'Boloism' in France, German-paid agitators funding pacifist newspapers, led automatically for a hunt for the British 'Bolos'. The tone of *John Bull* became increasingly rabid – Bottomley had predicted the war would end by Christmas, and when it became clear that it wouldn't he hinted darkly that the reason was treachery, possibly even including the Prime Minister.[57] The shocks of the spring of 1918 brought this interpretation to a head in the Pemberton Billing case. But the season for treason-hunting soon passed. With a rapidity that surprised everyone, Britain emerged victorious.

15. Flag day in aid of Indian soldiers. IWM (Q31081).

16. American troops in London. IWM (Q 53994).

In November 1918, a mass meeting was held at the Albert Hall. The list of main speakers reads like the leadership of an embryonic mass-fascist movement that never fully coalesced.[58] Addressing the crowd were Bottomley, Lord Charles Beresford, Arnold White, Ben Tillet, Havelock Wilson, General Page-Croft and Mrs Dacre Fox. One prominent figure was absent: Pemberton Billing's stock had fallen since the summer of 1918, due to infighting with other nationalists and a concerted effort to discredit him. But those who had called during the summer for the overthrow of parliamentary government were now stymied. They called for a harsh peace, but Bottomley's main act was to pass a resolution of unabated loyalty to the king. Being Bottomley, he added: 'provided there are no further Teutonic alliances, I see no reason why our constitution should not survive the present trial'.[59]

The week after the Armistice, he tried a final throw in *John Bull* asking, 'King George or Lloyd George?'[60] In the euphoria of peace and victory it was clear that that kite would not fly, and to save face Bottomley claimed that the Prime Minister had come around to his way of thinking. Bottomley was successfully elected on an 'Independent' platform in Hackney, beating the Coalition candidate, but his hour was over. His wartime scams caught up with him and his political career ended in disgrace and an overdue prison sentence.

It had been very different in May 1918 when *John Bull* had confidently published the headline 'Why Lloyd George Will Go'. It predicted 'the impending collapse of parliamentary government' because 'the politicians have sold the pass'.[61] Bottomley was a chancer and a confidence trickster, but the example of Mussolini suggests that an opportunistic populist journalist might be capable of leveraging himself to power on middle-class disillusion, with the inability of the parliamentary system to deal with labour militancy even in a nominally *victorious* nation. In the event of defeat it is perhaps even likely that this prediction would have been fulfilled.

8   The last war?

Remembering

In November 1917, Arthur Godfrey, the Chairman of Woking District Council, wrote to Sir Edward Carson complaining about the cursory nature of the death notices sent to bereaved relatives. His work for the Soldiers' and Sailors' Family Association and War Pensions Committee brought him into 'daily contact with the relatives of our soldiers and sailors'. He asked that a letter be sent in the name of the Prime Minister 'expressing appreciation of the government of the loyalty and self-sacrifice of the deceased and of sympathy with his family'. This was to be accompanied 'with an assurance that the Government is determined to carry the war through to a successful issue and satisfactory peace so that the sacrifices made shall not have been made in vain'. This would 'go a long way towards comforting and uplifting the bereaved – inspiring the people towards new courage and determination', and was required for 'strengthening the government and counteracting the poisonous and pernicious operations of the pacifists'.[1]

The need to comfort the bereaved was a wartime as well as a post-war imperative and from the very start official initiatives were as much about convincing the bereaved of the justification of the sacrifice as about simply giving comfort. Pembroke Wickes at the War Office commented on this proposal on the usefulness of sending 'a message of encouragement as an anti-toxin to Pro-German pacifist poison now being so freely scattered in stricken homes'.[2] Although there is no evidence that pacifists targeted the bereaved, the concern is apparent. Lord Derby decided to approach Rudyard Kipling for his assistance with wording the letter. Kipling was thrice appropriate, as a popular poet, as a strong supporter of the war and as a bereaved father. Kipling was doubtful about a letter from the Government, which he himself distrusted, and came up with an alternative proposal, suggesting instead that all bereaved relatives be awarded a special medal:

A medal and specially a brooch is a sign of distinction and (which is important) entails the wearer to look and to talk with contempt at people who have not given their sons. Also it shows they are together and makes a topic of united discussions. It would practically badge and brigade all relatives of the dead and might just turn the scale with people who thought they had grievances. People would soon learn to wear their medals. They would begin in villages where regular Sunday sermons are preached to the dead and by the time we go to making village and town memorials to the dead, pretty nearly they would be badged members of the order. I'd give it to the nearest male & female relatives and if both wife and mother remained I'd give it to both of them. I'd have big regular services for these people in the big cathedrals & churches from time to time (that's where the church would come in useful).

Kipling goes on to state that it would be a mistake to make this look as if it had been forced by 'public opinion' but rather it should appear as a 'mere notion' originating with the king.[3]

Kipling's idea of a marked, recognisable and exclusive community of the bereaved is distinctive and represents a road not taken. The reason is apparent in the letter: Kipling, bitter and self-recriminating over his loss, was aggressive in his attitude towards the majority who did not share it. The badge of bereavement would be a badge of reproach, a permanent reminder for others of the inadequacies of their sacrifices. It would be permanently divisive. A real community of the bereaved would be formed with clear boundaries and a moral superiority, constantly reminding others of their debt. But instead of Kipling's exclusive vision, the processes of official commemoration would diffuse and defuse the sense of loss, making it the property of the whole 'community', a fictional 'nation in mourning'. This idea of universal bereavement served a broadly political purpose by implying that everyone had participated in the 'ultimate sacrifice'. It would subsequently shape the way that the war was remembered with results that still shape our understanding of the war.

War debts

I am afraid we are going to see the pensions question very much to the front, especially at election times and few will have the courage to stand out against an abuse of the natural desire to deal liberally with men who have fought for their country. And things are made more difficult by the behaviour of the miners, railwaymen and others who perceive they can paralyse our war power and exploit the fact to their own selfish advantage ... Already there is bitter feeling amongst the discharged soldiers about those who have stopped at home on whatever pretext and it may be that presently we shall find the country divided into two hostile camps, the soldiers on one side and the civilians on the other. It is not a pleasant forecast. (Neville Chamberlain, letter to his sister Ida, 15 September 1918[4])

Despite the fact that the country was in the grip of a lethal influenza epidemic, the Armistice on 11 November 1918 was greeted with joy. The end of the war was far more genuinely popular than its beginning. Those who simply wanted peace and those who wanted victory had no argument when the firing stopped. Elizabeth Fernside travelled from Fulham to join the enormous crowd outside Buckingham Palace; her daughter Edie went back in to the town centre to join in the evening excitement and stayed out until midnight joining the street party with impromptu bands. In her letter to her son in Scotland, she wrote, 'I guess we shall have Peace signed soon.' Almost a week later she described the ongoing celebrations which were turning into near riots. One girl wrote that it was positively unsafe to go up Whitehall and the Strand: 'soldiers embraced every girl they met and vice versa'. In Sunderland impromptu fancy-dress parties were soon in full swing; in Blaina in South Wales 'practically every house exhibited a flag'. In Leith Street in Edinburgh, soldiers and sailors hijacked a beer lorry and broached a barrel on the pavement to the enjoyment of the crowd, although the inhabitants of Glasgow were described as exhibiting commendable restraint.[5]

There were those who viewed the whole thing with distaste, but it is clear they were a tiny minority. There were some who had good reason for sorrow and anger. Phyllis Illiff had lost her fiancé in action in June 1918; for her 11 November was 'the day when this war has ended that has wrecked my life and altered my own character and what does it mean to us who have lost our all in this fight, a fight which has not been won. It is wickedly unfair to our dead, you dear boy are the only one I think of.' Parenthetically it is worth noting that the implication of this is that Illiff did not feel that Germany should have been granted an Armistice at all. She went on, 'on the night where all are laughing and enjoying themselves, left alone I sit and think of what it would have been if you were not taken away and my heart were not slowly breaking. This night when "everyone is happy" as people say.'

It is well known that Wilfred Owen's mother received the telegram informing her of her son's death on 11 November. This case, tragic and much cited, should not lead us to overlook that this was the day on which several million mothers knew that their sons *would* be coming home. For an extraordinary week, to quote a *Daily Express* headline, London was in the 'throes of jubilation'. The lights, which metaphorically went out in August 1914 and physically were turned off in the winter of 1915, came on again.

The nation wanted to celebrate, particularly that vast majority of families whose relatives would now be returning. It is in this reaction that the impetus for post-war commemoration was born. The fortunate majority, and it cannot be stressed often enough that the majority *were* fortunate, could not help feeling a certain unease about their reactions. Robert Saunders had had six sons serving in the war – all survived. Statistically this was not unlikely, although it was fairly lucky for a man of his social class. Saunders wrote to his son in Canada on 16 November 1918, that during the war 'one's thoughts naturally turned to those in peril & try as you would, you could not help worrying ... It certainly appeared as though our feelings were blunted as regards those not directly connected with us, but specially sharpened as far as those near and dear to us were concerned.' Now that the war was over, proper consideration should be shown to others:

I think most people think that some time must elapse before we can celebrate peace, our feelings have been too much harrassed and our sympathies too often called forth. As I look back over the last 4 ½ years, I can see so many tragedies in families I know well & I can see so many of my old boys who are dead or wounded, or dying of consumption & recall them as boys at school where I used to urge on them the duty of patriotism, so that at present *it doesn't seem right that those who have escaped shall give themselves to joy days.*

Sunday we are having the proper Thanksgiving services, morning and evening, but I doubt if they will equal the one on Tuesday for feeling and enthusiasm. I have suggested to the Vicar that when our boys return we should have a special Reunion service of Thanksgiving for those who escaped death. He quite agrees and also wishes to have another memorial service for all those who have fallen, for although we have already had one, others of our Boys have fallen and *there is an almost universal feeling through the country that Honour should be rendered to the dead and sympathy shown to the bereaved.* (My italics)[6]

A careful reading of reactions to the Armistice show that this concern was widely expressed. An editorial in the *Accrington Observer and Times* suggested that the war had 'left upon too many hearths and homes its ineffaceable shadow' to permit wild rejoicing. In Nottingham, a beer shortage dampened spirits, but more importantly, 'bereavements caused by the war have been so terrible ... great as the relief experienced at its termination'.

It might seem logical that the institutions of commemoration which became so dominant in inter-war Britain were responses to the needs of the bereaved. Logical as this might be, it is a flawed logic. The near universal respect paid to the war dead cannot, in the first instance, have been dictated by direct family loss. The reason is simple: even by a very broad definition a considerable majority of families were untouched by the loss of a close relative. This statement, which will come as a surprise to many readers, clearly requires justification. It will strike some as distasteful demographic hair splitting, but it needs to be done if we are to properly understand the nature of commemoration. In his otherwise excellent book *Trench Fever*, Christopher Moore demonstrates how slack the thinking has been on this subject. He writes that in Britain 'at the outbreak of

Peace, 2 million parents woke up to the realisation that their sons had gone for ever'. This doesn't sound unreasonable until the reader thinks about it. A moment's reflection indicates that this figure would require every British soldier who died to have had 2.66 living parents in November 1918![7]

The highest conceivable number of those who lost an immediate family member by 1919 is 7.5 million. This is rather obviously based on 750,000 war dead and a multiplier of ten close relatives per death. It is undoubtedly far too high. Certainly the number of dead should be scaled up to account for those who died serving in the Dominion forces. But more importantly, the number of close relatives needs to be drastically scaled down. Most of the British war dead were unmarried and of the married, many would be childless. A disproportionate number of those killed would be only children, given the class biases in the death toll, and this meant no bereaved siblings. A fair proportion of the dead would have had one or no living parent. Finally, multiple bereavements within the same family would also scale down the number of bereaved. An average multiplier of six close relatives is far more realistic, even fewer is easily conceivable. If six is chosen, arbitarily, there were 4.5 million bereaved *close* relatives in Britain at the end of the war. This amounts, near enough, to 10% of the population. The long-standing assumption that every family 'lost someone' explodes in light of this, or at the very least has to be radically redefined.

The idea of universal bereavement remains true in a sense. Most families could point to an uncle, an in-law or a second cousin killed in the war. What weight we should place on this depends on the contemporary understanding of family in early twentieth-century Britain. It should be conceded that the evidence of letters and diaries suggest that while the war was in progress, extended family became more important.[8] But equally the basic and underlying understanding of the nature of 'family' was already a long way towards a familiar concept of a nuclear family. The loss of a more distant family member was sad, but it was not devastating in most cases. One exception, significantly, is Neville Chamberlain, who appears to have been profoundly and permanently distraught by the death of a cousin, but this should be treated as the unusual case that it probably was.

The main dynamic of post-war commemoration was not therefore a straightforward product of familial grief, but rooted in a concern for the proper acknowledgement of the losses of *others*. Indeed it has been argued that the whole effort to justify wartime sacrifice was utterly ineffective in consoling those who really *were* bereaved. Pat Jalland argues that in the cases of war bereaved families she studied, death in war was perceived as a 'bad death', the waste of a young life akin to a teenage suicide in the pre-war years. It would require a great deal of detailed work to prove or disprove this as a generalisation. It could be argued that Jalland's evidentiary base is very narrow and biased towards the elites. The analogy with suicide is clearly hyperbole. Is it seriously suggested that those who died in the service of the nation were perceived by their families in exactly the same way as those who had committed what was still seen, however residually, as a crime against God? War memorials and the Tomb of the Unknown Warrior might not have been very efficacious against grief, but they at least indicated public approval. There was never a 'Tomb of the Unknown Suicide'. Nevertheless, Jalland provides a salutary warning against simplistic functionalism: that these things were ostensibly meant to comfort the bereaved does not prove that they worked.

In a subtle and provocative article, Catherine Moriarty, perhaps the foremost expert on British war memorials, points out that representations and inscriptions indicative of individual experience were rare, and that instead we are faced with 'a collective statement, a collective solution to individual loss' and that 'they tell us virtually nothing about how people mourned or remembered away from these structures'. It is inevitable that historians have heavily studied the public and therefore accessible monuments and rituals, but in understanding the processes of individual grief these studies may be at best irrelevant and at worst actively misleading. Moriarty points out that family photographs were probably the most ubiquitous material of commemoration: a specific record of one individual frozen in a moment of life, without a clear message about the meaning of the sacrifice. The Imperial War Museum began to collect these photographs in 1917 and was forced to give up after collecting 15,000. The original intention to display these photographs was never implemented. There is no indication as to why the project was abandoned, but Moriarty suggests that it was more than logistics; such a display would have been too powerful and too disturbing – the 'ironic rescription' of men in life, however important in the individual home, would not have provided the safer and inclusive meanings required of public commemoration.[9]

To suggest that memorialisation was only 'ostensibly' for the bereaved might seem cynical. Some of those involved in creating the ceremonies and memorials were bereaved themselves, Rudyard Kipling being the most noteworthy and important. Despite the sentiments expressed above, Kipling was a key actor in the more universalist approach to commemoration that eventually developed, providing a wide range of epitaphs and most famously suggesting the inscription 'Their name liveth for evermore'. But Kipling, to say the least, was highly ambivalent about the whole process. Indeed, in support of Jalland's position, his almost frenetic commemorative activity does not seem to have worked particularly well as therapy for him. Most of the other key people in setting the tone of post-war commemoration at the national level – Mond at the Board of Works and main instigator of the Imperial War Museum, Curzon the impresario of commemorative ceremony, Lutyens as architect of the Cenotaph and prime mover in the design of war cemeteries, Fabian Ware as head of the Imperial War Graves Commission – were personally detached. It is revealing that although 'widows and mothers' were the archetypal bereaved in public rhetoric, only one woman played an important role in creating official commemorations, and she was not English – namely Mme Guérin, who initiated the sale of poppies for Belgian war charities before the British Legion adopted them.

Not only were official commemorations not created by the bereaved, rather 'on their behalf', but it could also be claimed that the extent to which they genuinely reflected their wishes is sometimes dubious. The two-minute silence, the poppy appeal, the Cenotaph and the Tomb of the Unknown Warrior gained massive popular support, much of this undoubtedly from the bereaved; but in at least one case, this is open to question.[10]

An illustration of how national commemoration could in fact manifestly overrule the wishes of the bereaved can be found in the controversy surrounding war cemeteries in 1919–1920.

The Imperial War Graves Commission had decided, as policy, not to allow the repatriation of bodies and to insist upon a basic uniformity to grave-markers. On the first point the Commission was soon receiving ninety letters per week requesting that bodies be returned to families. The Commission stood firmly behind the principle of equality: 'One could never explain why Lord and Lady This was able to have a body ... while plain Mrs Smith, a labourer's wife or widow could not.'[11] Admirable as this extension of wartime concepts of equality of sacrifice might be, it is important to note that it involved standing *against* the explicit and expressed wishes of bereaved relatives. Even more patent was the refusal to budge on the uniformity of headstones.

In 1919, Lady Florence Cecil appealed that crosses should be allowed as an alternative to headstones; she did so as a mother who had lost three sons in the war and in the name of 'thousands of heartbroken parents, wives, brothers and sisters'. She was not exaggerating: she presented a petition with 8,000 signatures, to which various remarks were added: 'three out of four soldier sons have given their lives'; 'only son'; 'four dear sons (out of five) have given their lives for their King and Country'.

The conclusion of the debate that the concept of uniformity of sacrifice should be upheld at all costs and that the cemeteries were not for use simply in the present, but for all time, showed that broadly ideological considerations called the shots.[12] A peculiar alliance of aesthetes, trade unionists and imperialists, in the name of a silent majority of the bereaved,

17. A war widow and her child presented to the King. IWM (Q 54012).

had overruled those who represented the vocal bereaved. That those who advocated customisation of headstones represented the more privileged section of society is probably true, but the advocates of uniformity had no real evidence at all that they represented the majority view. The artist Eric Gill fumed that the imperial cemeteries were 'an idea worthy of the Prussian or the Ptolemy', and that the widespread desire of relatives to have some control over the graves had been overruled by the desire to commemorate 'comradeship and common service' and that 'under the cloak of culture' mourners were to be denied 'even the unfettered choice of words'. Gill had his own aesthetic arts and crafts agenda, preferring the use of a diversity of stone masons and architects to imposed uniformity; nevertheless he had a point.[13] Although the Commonwealth War Graves have come to be seen as a quintessentially British (or perhaps English) aesthetic statement, the idea of uniformity is far removed from the individuality, disorder and downright eccentricity of a traditional British graveyard and even the more aesthetically controlled 'modern cemeteries' never went so far down this path.

The 'wishes of the bereaved' were always the rhetorical trump card in debates over commemoration, and these wishes were presented in such a way as to back up whatever a particular advocate believed appropriate. Thus, Armistice Day parties, which undoubtedly were popular amongst the more prosperous veterans of the war, were suppressed as offensive to the sensibilities of the bereaved. It is certainly possible that they were offensive, but the agenda of those who opposed them was driven strongly by egalitarian motives.[14]

The wartime economy of sacrifice continued to influence the post-war. Wartime rhetoric had come close to foundering on tangible inequalities. Not the least of wartime 'debt repayments' was the continued need for those who had not been directly touched by loss to at least appear to pay tribute to those who had. Undoubtedly the post-war did see a form of 'fictive community' in loss. But we would do well to realise that in important respects it was fictive in the sense of untrue. Depictions of Britain in the 1920s as a traumatised society, with a shattered sense of itself, should be understood for what they are: constructions to cover up a much more complex social reality of winners and losers, continuities and changes.

Sites of mourning?

Local memorialisation began very quickly and climaxed early. Of the 5,930 First World War memorial unveilings catalogued by the UK National Inventory of War Memorials at the turn of the millennium, no fewer than 5,151 had occurred by 1920. If anything this may understate the rapidity of commemorative enterprises, since the date of unveiling is more likely to be known for the larger and more elaborate memorials. In the UK the concept of memorial covered a much wider range than the classic picture of *monuments aux morts* in France. A survey of the most common memorial forms indicate that the memorial plaque or tablet was far and away the most common.

All memorials	38,213
Plaques	13,009
Crosses	4,781
Gravestones	2,117
Book of remembrance	1,779
Window	1,574
Obelisk	730
Pillar	441
Memorial hall	431
Battlefield cross	375
Gate	358
Reredos/screen	352
Figure of serviceman/woman	298

Amongst other memorials were 146 church organs or parts of church organs, 185 clock towers, 90 sports fields and 9 chalk figures. The comparative rarity of figurative commemoration is striking. In total only 2.2% of British war memorials are sculptural. The iconoclastic Protestant tradition, which would lead to controversies about 'crucifixes' in a number of villages, might be a partial explanation, but this cannot be the whole story given the boom in public sculpture during the nineteenth century. It is more likely that the comparative expense of sculpture, the difficulty in deciding on an appropriate image and, speculatively, a certain amount of anti-Victorian reaction, may account for this striking rarity. Equally striking is the fact that 57% of all memorials were sited in places of worship, slightly below the figure for the Boer War but still a clear majority. The diversity of British religious practice played a key role. Only the smallest hamlets would be without at least one nonconformist chapel in addition to the village church. Furthermore population change over the course of national history had led to a massive residual presence of Anglican parishes in counties of comparatively small population. This can be seen in the county totals for England and Wales:

Greater London	2,416
Greater Manchester	1,584
Humberside	1,232
West Yorkshire	1,517
Suffolk	1,076
England and Wales	38,213

Whilst the major urban areas dominate, they do not do so proportionately to their population or their losses. There are some massive anomalies: the urbanised West Midlands has a mere 307 memorials, compared with 856 in largely rural Hereford and Worcester, or a cumulative total of 367 for the offshore Isle of Wight, Isle of Man, the Scilly Isles and the Channel Islands. Somerset has 648 memorials compared with 388 for Tyne and Wear; Devonshire has 738 memorials compared with 497 for Durham. Wales is even more stark in its contrast, with a near-inverse relationship between population and density of memorials. The rural areas are heavily represented: Dyfed has 321, Gwynedd 286 and Clwyd 285. By contrast the industrialised counties are sparsely represented: West Glamorgan has 64, Gwent 167 and mid-Glamorgan 168. Even allowing for the fact that industrial workers were under-represented amongst the losses, it is highly doubtful that these figures honestly represent massive over-representation of rural casualties, particularly as these county totals take in the hard-hit suburbs of the major cities where the losses were worst of all. Neither the micro- nor the macro-geography of commemoration genuinely corresponds with the geography of loss.

Alex King rightly points out that the 'forms and location of memorials was rarely chosen to reproduce the symbolic sites of mourning associated with peacetime life'. The dead commemorated were fragmented in multiple locations as members of clubs, religious institutions, employees, citizens and units. They are given a principally institutional significance and their individuality is lost. Such sites seem poorly calculated to act as focal points for the regular processes of grief. The street shrine movement of the war years might have acted as an alternative model, coming closer to the physical location of the lives of the dead and their living relatives. In St Albans, through the initiative of the clergy, this did in fact occur, but this is exceedingly rare. The erection of memorials was determined by institutional and not personal imperatives. The role of mourner in chief, which on a large scale had been appropriated from the families by the 'nation' was appropriated locally by 'the community'.[15]

The wishes of the bereaved themselves were certainly not always paramount at a local level. In Stoke Newington the decision to limit attendance at a public meeting to discuss the memorial to those who had contributed to the memorial fund, led to a protest of 200 of the bereaved and ex-servicemen. At Cockermouth a petition by the bereaved for a memorial in the cemetery was overruled by a public meeting which insisted on a Station Road site.[16]

A detailed study of the memorial deliberations for Newport on the Isle of Wight during 1919 shows a less conflictual picture, but one nevertheless where the bereaved were somewhat marginal to the process. The first meeting was devoted to the discussion of the mayor's two possibilities – a cottage hospital or a memorial hall – in particular the relative costs, and a sub-committee was formed to study the cottage hospitals in Ryde and Cowes, and to produce an estimate of the total cost of building and maintaining a cottage hospital for Newport. It is clear from the amount of time the committee spent on each scheme that its members favoured the cottage hospital over the memorial hall; the sub-committee was also charged with producing an estimate for the latter for comparative purposes, but the majority of the meeting was taken up with discussing the feasibility of a cottage hospital. A vote was carried mandating the mayor to invite public subscriptions by means of an advert in the *County Press*, and various members of the committee pledged £50 each out of their own pockets.[17] This in itself demonstrates that the committee could not be described as representative of the island as a whole, as they acknowledged themselves.

Furthermore, Dr McKay pointed out that 'it has come to his notice that people outside were saying the present Committee was composed of people who had not lost relations in the war'.[18] Presumably this was a source of worry to the committee because they might be criticised if they picked a form of memorial which was not considered appropriate, due to not having direct knowledge of what the bereaved wanted. They did consider forming a new committee and inviting people who had lost relations to sit on it, but the vicar of Newport argued against this, saying that it would be too painful for the bereaved to have to go through this experience. In truth, it would probably have been too troublesome to have to reconstruct the committee at this stage.

It was clear, though, by the end of March, that there were significant difficulties with the scheme under consideration; when this report was considered, the response to the mayor's appeal for funds had been lower than expected, and the committee was forced to vote that a cottage hospital was too expensive. So precarious was the financial situation that even the memorial hall was not a safe bet, and the committee recommended it only on the condition that enough money could be raised, with another scheme to be considered if funds were not sufficient. These resolutions were put to a public meeting on 8 April. This meeting was not well recorded in the minute book, appearing after the meeting of 11 June had been minuted, but a column of the week's paper was devoted to it. Quoting at length from this article gives a sense of the public feeling in the town about the memorial scheme:

Mr Cousins, for the Discharged and Demobilised Soldiers' and Sailors' Society, said those he represented preferred a cottage hospital.

Mrs Spencer, who said she had lost three brothers in the war, and her husband had been wounded six times, expressed the view that those who had given their lives would prefer that a memorial should take the form of helping those who could not help themselves.

Mr McKinley, for the Comrades of the Great War, said the great majority preferred a cottage hospital, and failing that something in the way of public baths.[19]

Mr W. G. Sibbick supported the suggestion of public baths, which would be specially appreciated by soldiers who had returned from the front.

Miss George favoured a public swimming bath so that their young might learn swimming in safety, many having lost their lives in the river.

Miss Monk, B. A., suggested a memorial hall which, during the summer, might be used for a swimming bath for school children and others. It would be the very greatest benefit physically and morally, and raise the standard of cleanliness in the town.

Mr Chester said people could have a bath at home. He favoured a cottage hospital, and would give £2 towards it.[20]

It can be seen that the suggestions favoured by the general public did not necessarily match those of the committee. Later on in the article, it was recorded that the cost estimates produced by the sub-committee were criticised for being too high and not in keeping with the amount of money so far raised, which was not quite £700.[21] The mayor was eventually forced to rule that if the £14,000 to erect a memorial hall was not achieved, he would convene another public meeting to decide on an alternative scheme. The committee's recommendations were eventually carried by thirty-three votes to twenty-three. The minutes of the next committee meeting make at least the secretary's feelings on the matter clear: he wrote of the public response to the memorial appeal that it was 'poor', and later crossed it out and substituted 'inadequate' on the line above. Possibly this was on the request of Mayor Whitcher, whose statement the sentence records.[22] He then recorded that due to this poor or inadequate response, the meeting resolved that both schemes would have to be abandoned, and a sub-committee was formed to discuss turning the funds over to the Newport District Nursing Association. The Nursing Association expressed, after a meeting with members of the sub-committee, that it would be 'agreeable' to accepting the money, and for the first time evidence appears of the origins of one of Newport's existing memorials to the war.[23]

This suggests, and other local studies confirm, that although public interest at a local level was usually quite strong, those who became involved in the actual decisions about commemorative forms were usually a small minority drawn from the established social and political elites. In Leeds only twenty people actually showed up to hear Sir Reginald Blomfield present his plans for the civic memorial, and only sixty turned up for a similar meeting in Carlisle.[24]

The massive number of physical memorials may have inadvertently misled us to the principal ways in which the war was commemorated. As the defenders of monumental commemoration often remarked, a physical site would have the advantage of perpetuity and unambiguous reference to the war. But there is a serious gap in recent surveys of memorials in that the wide definition of 'memorial' in the UK is not fully reflected. There is no inventory of the charitable endowments, relief funds and scholarships that made up such a large proportion of commemorative activity, as indeed the Newport example demonstrates. This submerged section of the iceberg may have been the most important. For example the Royal Artillery Commemoration Fund spent the following sums between 1919 and 1924:

Relief grants	£31,872
Education	£21,794
Employment	£3,062
Administration	£16,698
Monument	£8,546[25]

In other words, the monument absorbed only 10% of the funding raised, and more than half of the money was spent on 'serving the living'. Such an ordering of priorities might suggest, to British eyes at least, an admirable pragmatism: rather than concentrating on monumental grandeur, the real practical needs of the victims of war were being addressed. But this would be to oversimplify. In some cases it is clear that the imperative towards expenditure on useful works represented an attempted diversion of funds towards socially worthy schemes which were deemed desirable anyway but which might not otherwise get funded. Thus at Wigton in Cumbria the decision to fund a recreation ground as a memorial was condemned by the British Legion as a manoeuvre by the local council to deliver a facility already promised but not delivered. In Islington, the Royal Northern Hospital claimed that a new wing would be 'a direct and tangible expression of sympathy for the bereaved', although it is difficult to understand why this was the case. In Enfield a specifically political division occurred with Liberal and Labour representatives wishing to re-endow the cottage hospital, while Conservatives held out for a Cenotaph. A writer to the *Carlisle Journal* was similarly critical of practical commemoration, suggesting that building civic improvements with money raised to commemorate the dead was not showing 'the same unselfish spirit' as that of the fallen. The suggestion of laying on electric light to the villages of Kirkoswald and Ravenstonedale was obviously open to the same criticism, although the provision of a rural nursing service to the latter was only marginally less self-interested. Burwell in Cambridgeshire did the same, although that scheme also included a memorial tablet to the local dead in the nurse's cottage. Of course, such pragmatism could be justified: in Carlisle it was stated that the dead would not have wanted a 'useless' memorial, but this was obviously speculative. It is clear that on many occasions the ex-servicemen's organisations did support utilitarian memorials, as indeed they had in Newport. The National Federation of Discharged and Demobilized Soldiers and Sailors, a left-Liberal grouping founded in 1917, seems to have often supported utilitarian memorials at a local level. In Bethnal Green, for example, they supported a maternity home. But perhaps more often they supported initiatives in the specific interests of ex-servicemen, a stance mirrored by the other veterans' organisations – the National Association and the Comrades of the Great War – which became more pronounced when the three merged to form the British Legion.

What is clear is that memorial funds could cover for failures in state action. The Dawson report of 1920 had identified the under-funding of voluntary hospitals as a serious problem, but expenditure cuts meant that the Ministry of Health was in no position to provide subsidies. The Conservative mayor of Islington argued that using memorial funds would prevent the charge of the hospital falling on the rates.[26] Such palpably self-interested arguments were rare, and met with opposition, but serve as a warning that high-minded rhetoric about honouring sacrifice should not always be taken at face value.

Supporting the living

That the symbolic appropriation of the dead might operate in disregard to the practical needs of their surviving relatives appeared to be illustrated as early as 1919. Jack Cornwall was one of the dozen or so personalised heroes of the Great War. At the age of 15 he died of wounds at the Battle of Jutland, remaining at his post when all around him were killed. He was mentioned in dispatches by Admiral Beatty and awarded a posthumous Victoria Cross. 'Boy' Cornwall was a perfect symbolic hero in many ways: as a heroic compensation for the ambiguous outcome of the Jutland battle which had dented the prestige of the Navy; as an exemplar for the nation's youth which was particularly attractive since his heroism could be celebrated in a way that was less easily available for the illegal under-age recruits in the Army; and as a hero of working-class London, his family living in poverty in East Ham. These symbolic significances were very apparent in commemoration: the cult of Cornwall was particularly encouraged by the Navy league, by the education system and youth movements, particularly the Boy Scouts, as Cornwall had been a Scout, and by the borough of East Ham. Large amounts of money were raised in Cornwall's name for various worthy projects. Yet in 1919 it emerged that his widowed mother was living in serious hardship working twelve hours a day at a Stepney hostel. This was scandalous enough, but the death of Mrs Cornwall that year and the realisation that the family lacked sufficient funds to pay for a decent funeral further emphasised the failure to repay the debt of honour on an individual level. The Cornwall case was in fact ambiguous. The fact that the neglect of Mrs Cornwall became a public scandal shows that some regard was paid to the material needs of the bereaved, at least rhetorically; but the post-war years saw a growing suspicion that those who had the greatest claim on public gratitude might find themselves sorely neglected.[27]

The dead represented the paramount sacrifice, but an equally pressing problem was the debt to the living. The two were often linked in rhetoric and practice: 'Honour the Dead, Serve the Living' was the slogan of the British Legion, and this was embodied in the manufacture of poppies by disabled ex-servicemen.

The official attempt to quantify degrees of sacrifice through the scale of disability pension ranged from 100% pension for the loss of two limbs or total loss of sight, to 50% pension for the amputation of the left arm below the elbow to 20% pension for the loss of two fingers on either hand.[28]

The place of the war-wounded in the general picture of sacrifice was more complicated than it first appeared. That there was a societal debt to these men was not generally doubted. But the honourable wound was ambiguous in the context of the First World War. It was well known amongst soldiers and probably amongst civilians that a 'blighty' wound had frequently been welcomed as the only secure method of escaping from the trenches. Whilst the severely crippled could still expect public sympathy, the less severely injured could appear to have traded a lesser sacrifice for the greater.[29]

This was even more true of those who were invalided out through disease. Every bit as devastating for the individual, but less conspicuously visible, disease casualties were less glamorous and somehow less worthy than those bearing obvious wounds. The Eugenics Education Society went as far as arguing against pensions for those invalided out due to illness.[30]

The story of provision for the survivors of the war began during the war itself. Pre-war pension provisions proved woefully inadequate in inflationary circumstances, and the Government moved slowly to address the issue. But the imminence of conscription meant that the issue took on great political importance and led to the setting up of a Select Committee on Pensions in 1915 and bringing in a Naval and War Pensions Bill in 1916. This Bill placed responsibility for pension provision under the aegis of a Statutory Committee of the Royal Patriotic Fund which was charged with the responsibility of setting up local committees to provide pensions, supplementary cash payments, rehabilitation and training for the wounded. In another case of the scale of quasi-voluntary activity required to underpin the war effort, 1,200 committees were created, involving 100,000 voluntary members. The initial attempt to foist a large part of the responsibility on voluntary fundraising and local taxation failed in the face of widespread resistance and a growing insistence that the central state had to take the lion's share of the responsibility; and with the arrival of the Lloyd George Government, a Ministry of Pensions was formed as part of the price for Labour Party support.[31]

But despite this apparent acceptance of state responsibility it soon became plain that voluntary action would continue to play a major role in discharging the societal debt to the wounded. For example, by the end of the war the work of rehabilitation and specialised employment for the severely wounded was carried on through voluntary organisations such as

18. Rehabilitation of blinded soldiers. IWM (Q 53979).

the Lord Roberts workshops, St Dunstan's, which dealt with blind service-men, Roehampton, which fitted prosthetic limbs, and settlements such as Enham and Preston Hall. These organisations rapidly proved formidable fundraisers: Roehampton raised £100,000 in 1917 though public sub-scription. Much of this money was raised from the traditional philan-thropic circles of the wealthy, but increasingly these appeals broadened their base in order to involve the general public. Thus the Jack Cornwall Fund raised £35,000 from some 7 million schoolchildren.[32]

At the end of the war there were 6,000 charities for the war-disabled registered with the charity commissioners – almost one charity for every 100 disabled men. In the context of the levels of self-mobilisation, and the importance of voluntary action in wartime under-pinned by a pervasive concern with economies of sacrifice, this is less surprising than it first appears. What is perhaps more significant is that 500 separate charities for the war-disabled were still operating in 1936 and spending some £6 million per year on various projects. Although this represented only about a tenth of state expenditure, this activity was in every respect more *visible*.

Where did the disabled serviceman stand in the post-war moral order? In the immediate post-war years there was certainly an idealisation, exemplified by the film 'Lest We Forget', which highlighted the ongoing debt to the wounded soldier.[33] But the general image of the wounded veteran in the post-war years is one of marginalisation and embitterment. How true is this? One thing is certain: the state authorities, particularly the permanent civil service, proved to be generally unsympathetic. In particular C. F. A. Hore, the principal Assistant Secretary at the Ministry of Pensions, saw his role as being more concerned with protecting the public purse than defending the rights of disabled servicemen. He was on record as believing that the Government had been mistaken in 1916 in accepting the bulk of the responsibility for assisting the wounded. Hore's position did have a principled element: he genuinely believed that civil society as a whole should take direct responsibility for the care of the disabled ex-servicemen and that the central state should minimise its own role, acting as a co-ordinator to voluntary and local efforts. But Hore within the Minstry of Pensions certainly acted as a powerful ally to a retrenchment-minded Treasury.[34]

The ethic of social solidarity promoted through the cult of voluntary action allowed the community as a whole to take credit for looking after the victims of war, and undoubtedly played a part in reducing the political tensions evident in Germany where this demand was placed upon a state that was unable to deal with the open-ended financial responsibility of moral debt. But before this is taken as an obvious case of the greater sense of responsibility of British civil society, it should be remembered that the British public were also the voters and taxpayers who supported a frequently mean-spirited and inadequate system of public support for war victims. Many of the criticisms that could be levelled at Victorian attitudes towards the relief of distress could equally be made of the public policy towards victims of the war – a self-congratulatory philanthropy but a lack of will to really provide fully effective relief. The British public wore poppies to remember 'their' dead and to conspicuously display compassion, but actual war victims frequently faced the reality of impoverishment. The rhetoric of a nation united in its grief overshadowed the persistent inequalities.

Redemption through victory?

Maybe it was a tragedy for you ... you failed; men died; so yes it was tragic because they died for a bad cause. But for us, the war was a noble sacrifice. (General Giap on the Vietnam War, quoted by Jonathan Mirsky in *New York Review of Books*, 25 May 2000, p. 56[35])

So much for debt; what of redemption? Initially the pay-off was fairly clear: the price had been paid and peace had been purchased. Peace through victory. Victory mattered and, in the end, nothing else mattered as much. All of the poisonous ingredients of extreme right-wing politics existed in Britain – particularly southern England by the end of 1918: middle-class grievance and resentment of both big capital and big labour, xenophobia including anti-Semitism, disillusionment with parliamentary government, conspiracy theories and even perhaps a tendency to reluctantly condone violence. The soup was ready, but no one turned on the heat.

Without a defeat, a stab-in-the-back mythology, which was clearly gestating by the summer of 1918, could not yet come to term. In some respects, during the crisis of summer 1918, Britain showed more signs of an embryonic Fascism than Germany. The search for scapegoats was gathering pace and would-be messianic leaders were sharpening their platform style. The stakes were very high, for had 'The Sacrifice' been 'in vain', it would have ripped the nation apart.

Only when the military tide turned was the threat seen to recede. Instead of revolution, or pre-emptive counter-revolution, Britain ended the war in a consensual celebration. Yet defusing the underlying tensions of the last year of the war would take time. Demobilisation was to prove a fraught process.

The speed with which soldiers redefined themselves as civilians and as a result demanded their rights as civilians caused a great deal of trouble. The Government decision to suspend conscription at the Armistice was probably inevitable, but it caused problems. The Army was still needed until a permanent peace was signed and indeed a military presence in Germany was likely to be required for quite some while. That such a force would be drawn from men who had signed up for the duration of the war, some of whom had already seen years of service, rather than recruited from those who had not already seen service, was a major grievance. Worse still were the wars after the war. For months after the Armistice there were unfortunate wartime soldiers who found themselves fighting and dying in Russia, Afghanistan and the Middle East.

The high expectations of national redemption were unfulfilled. But in a more modest way the war was still seen as an achievement. The suggested additional inscriptions for the permanent Cenotaph which were sent in by members of the public in 1920 give some idea of the interpretations current. Mrs Rimmer of Mosley Hill in Liverpool suggested:

Oh!, Ye who mourn in Ceaseless Pain,
Be comforted
They died for England; lives their name
Emblazoned on a scroll of fame.

Barry Poole wrote from West London:

> They've gone, but still a memory held dear
> By those who've lost remains.
> The battles won
> And those who lived through that great Hellish Sphere
> Return triumphant. But the men who've done
> As much, and died a soldiers death 'out there'
> We cannot thank except by humble prayer
> So one and all we thank you for your share
> And ever will remember – you were men.

Charles Damon of Woburn Place was more concise and more symbolic:

> The clods of battle-fields are red,
> With immortality, the Dead
> In their magnificence arise
> To shine before us through the skies.

William Simmons of the Royal British Institute of Architects chose prose and politics:

To the ever living memory of the (number) men and women who, in the late 5 years long war, begun and prolonged by the Germans in wanton lust of power and plunder and with bestial savageness and treachery till then incredible, victoriously sacrificed their lives for the life and honour of Britain and mankind; to each and all of them, in sorrow, and in gratitude and pride, we dedicate and consecrate this shrine.[36]

Having so obviously failed to find a previously mute village Simonides, the civil servants decided to leave the inscription unaltered. Nevertheless a great deal of the early commemoration was straightforwardly patriotic or even triumphalist. The massive memorial in Newcastle showed men dutifully marching off to war led by the figure of 'winged victory'.[37]

Yet overt triumphalism was not the usual order. The Leeds war memorial was altered so that the figure of victory, rather than brandishing a sword over its head, held the sword in front of it as a cross.[38] Indeed Simonides' famously laconic epitaph for the Spartan dead of Thermopylae was successfully appropriated for the title of the bestselling inter-war novel, Ernest Raymond's *Tell England*, published in 1922. Rosa Maria Bracco points out that in this and other immediately post-war novels, the righteousness of the cause and the validity of the victory was such an embedded assumption that it was in fact rarely explicitly stated. Thus H. F. P. Battersby wrote of the British troops that 'With everything on their side that might inspire heroism' the men were 'heroes for no reason at all'. Indeed explicitly patriotic rhetoric was treated with suspicion, not because it was untrue, but rather because it was unnecessary and diminished the inarticulate patriotism of the soldiers. Raymond was later to write that the British soldier would rather talk sedition than patriotism. Yet in the earliest war novels a concrete hatred of the enemy, not generally as individuals, but as an institution and an idea, makes clear what the war was for, it was a crusade against barbarism. Thus R. W. Campbell wrote in *John Brown: Confessions of a New Army Cadet*, that the peace-loving Britons 'home loving, shop-keepers in arms' had been dragged into the 'vile' and 'hellish' Western Front which was the sole creation of the Germans.[39]

In this context 'peace' and 'victory' should not be seen as competing interpretations but rather as complementary. The figure of winged victory at Finsbury was described as symbolising 'peace and victory'; a memorial at Ecclesfield near Bradford shows the figure of peace taking away the sword of strife whilst bestowing a victor's laurel wreath. The men of Bermondsey were, according to the speech at the unveiling of their memorial, 'men of peace, they had no wish for war', but they had endured.[40]

From the very beginning the war dead were presented not simply as military victors but as moral victors. Self-sacrifice had overcome not only the barbarism of Germany but the horror of war. As the former faded in popular belief, the latter became more important. But increasingly the idea of redemption was seen as provisional on the behaviour of the living. The rhetoric of commemoration was often enlisted to argue for social unity – the comradeship of the dead would be insulted by class conflict amongst the living. From the Armistice to the General Strike in 1926, industrial unrest was a more or less constant presence. At the unveiling of the memorial at Euston Station to fallen railwaymen in 1921, the company chairman gave a speech calling for forbearance on both sides in industrial disputes in order to 'prove ourselves worthy of the sacrifice these men have made for us'.[41] Such appeals were commonplace, but should not be seen purely as propaganda on the part of the economically dominant: the rhetoric invariably demanded restraint from employers as well as employed. Nevertheless such enlistment of the moral sacrifice of the dead was objectively conservative, and in many respects a continuation of the wartime appeal not to betray the men at the front with industrial militancy at home.

Redeeming the sacrifices of the dead was arguably less contentious, at least initially, when directed towards the sphere of international relations. From 1922 the League of Nations Union mounted a major propaganda effort timed to climax during the week around Armistice Day. In 1925 major rallies were held in Manchester, Hull, Grimsby and Derby and a house-to-house canvass was carried out in London.[42]

In the middle 1920s a peaceful order appeared to have been established in the world. The evolution of pilgrimages and tourism to the battlefields and cemeteries of the Western Front encapsulated the movement from the immediate aftermath of war, to a sense of a more peaceful world. In the immediate post-war years the overwhelming impression was one of devastation. Early Michelin guides in English to the battlefields in France and Belgium stressed the physical destruction to the architectural heritage of those countries, and these early guides were unambiguous in blaming the Germans for deliberately devastating the region.[43] Anger at Germany and a belief in righteous punishment were acceptable responses in these early years. But as the devastated regions were rebuilt, often with aid provided by local communities in Britain which had been 'twinned' by wartime military connections with French and Belgian communities, the visceral impact of the war in this respect diminished.[44] Faster than for the French and Belgians, a spirit of reconciliation arose, reinforced by the increasing presence of German veterans at the same sites. The publication in English of Eric Maria Remarque's novel *All's Quiet on the Western Front* humanised these German veterans, creating an increasing suspicion that they were in fact fellow-victims of the war. The 'discrediting' of wartime propaganda and the gradual impact of Keynes's condemnation of the peace treaties amongst political and cultural elites accelerated the process. But it should be remembered that this easing of opinion was not universal and, in as far as it did occur, was initially predicated on the luxury of victory and insularity.

In the end victory had itself made adjustment to loss easier, even when it ceased to be a major focus of the rhetoric. There were certainly ugly elements to the psychic reconstruction of the post-war period: some anti-Semitism and colour prejudice, anti-Irish sentiment, elements of gender backlash and class conflict, all of which were strong for a year or two after the war. But the main trend was not one of 'othering' or seeking the psychic consolations of Fascism – quite the contrary. The luxury of victory was that it minimised the searching for scapegoats and instead stressed universalism. The later 1920s saw a decline in sectarianism outside of Ireland, a more benevolent, albeit paternalistic, attitude to race within the Empire and perhaps a more conciliatory and in certain senses progressive outlook for gender relations. Class conflict climaxed in 1926, but although the peaceful nature of the General Strike has been exaggerated, the core narrative remains correct: the crisis passed peacefully by comparison with any other industrialised country, including the British Dominions and the United States. The 'wars after the war' were brief in duration and of low intensity.

The 1920s were thus a time of apparent paradox. On the one hand insular 'Englishness' was a cultural and political staple, but at the same time it was an Englishness that co-existed with rhetorical support for internationalism. The absolving of Germany from blame for the war was the logical climax of this, and also explains how the contradictions were resolved. Wartime propaganda had stressed decency and fair play as a contrast to German barbarism. These were the values for which the men had died. But redeeming the dead required that these values be extended, ultimately even to the enemy. Redemption required forgiveness. Yet this raised its own problem: if Germany had not been responsible for the war, what had the war been for?

Disillusionment?

I have never seen anything since 1918 that was worth the sacrifice. (J. B. Priestley, 'The Last Generation', 1930[45])

Most people, for one reason or another, came to doubt the value of the victory to a greater or lesser extent between 1919 and 1939. This should not be seen as simply a pacifist turn in opinion. Nor was it simply or even mostly a reflection on the experience of the war as such. The British public were regularly exhorted to think about the meaning of the war, but the way that they thought about it was heavily conditioned by contemporary circumstances.

Assumptions about the way that the war was remembered have tended to focus heavily on the 'canonical' literature of the war, in particular the works of Wilfred Owen, Robert Graves and Siegfried Sassoon. Although Owen was killed in the last week of the war, the collection of his poems edited by Edmund Blunden has often been seen as the definitive shaping force in the memory of the First World War, particularly as Blunden followed a distinctive editorial pattern designed to promulgate a definite interpretive stance. Sassoon's politicised poetry of satire was followed after the war with his fictionalised memoirs, which in turn overlap with Graves's memoir-fiction. To these leading figures can be added the other main authors of the 'disillusionment' school: Blunden, Henry Williamson, Ford Madox Ford and Richard Aldington. These authors are the main subject-matter of Paul Fussell's extraordinary work of literary criticism, *The Great War and Modern Memory*, which has triggered a quarter-century of debate about the cultural memory of the war in the English-speaking world.

Critiques of Fussell have followed three main arguments; these sometimes overlap, but they are in principle distinct. The first and most vehement critique comes from military historians. Their argument is ultimately less with Fussell the literary critic than with what they see, rightly, as Fussell's uncritical acceptance that his chosen authors were those who told the truth about the war. Corelli Barnett, John Terraine, Brian Bond and a new generation of British military historians, particularly Gary Sheffield, see the literature of disillusionment as a fundamental distortion of the war itself – a denial of victory which undermined the national achievement. A subversive tradition, beginning with Sassoon and Graves, reinforced in the 1960s by Alan Clark and the musical *Oh! What a Lovely War*, reinforced again by Fussell, and climaxing in *Blackadder Goes Forth* has, in their view, shaped a popular culture of rejection of the First World War, which acts as an obstacle to historical understanding of the real military achievement.

There is a certain truth in this, but it does represent an oversimplified cultural history. In particular it often assumes that Fussell's basic premise about the memory of war is correct: that these canonical figures dictated the terms on which the war was remembered during the inter-war period and that their 'pacifism' shaped the popular mood.

A powerful empirical critique to this view can be found in a second school of historical-literary criticism. This is represented by Martin Stephens, Hugh Cecil, Rosa Maria Bracco and to a certain extent by Samuel Hynes. They emphasise the mulitiplicity of literary interpretations of the war, pointing out that not all literature was literature of disillusionment, and that indeed some of the most popular literature of the inter-war period was affirmative of the war. Hynes is the closest in spirit to Fussell, but he also points out that what we now take to be the 'canonical' literary interpretation of the war emerged in specific historical circumstances and was heavily contested at the time.

The third line of critique is an attempt to contextualise and to some extent diminish the central significance of 'war books' to the construction of popular memory by pointing to the greater mass of memorialising activity which shaped the popular memory of the war. War memorials, veterans' organisations and acts of commemoration were at least as important as works of literature, and probably much more so in shaping popular memories, although literary works played a part in developing interpretations. Sometimes this took the form of a negative reaction. Tubby Clayton of the Christian veterans' organisation Toc H wrote in 1930 that the 'stains had to be taken off the War Memorial', because many boys could not look at them 'without thinking of the pestitential books that had got into their hands'. His own work in taking the young on pilgrimages to France had shown that when faced with the cemeteries he 'did not know of a single case of irony, shallowness or small mindedness among the thousands who had gone here as pilgrims'.[46]

This wider investigation, partly inspired by the broad comparative work on Europe by Jay Winter and George Mosse, has recovered what was perhaps inevitably a more conservative response to the war. The general conclusion of this research has been that responses to the war were more affirmative than was once assumed, but that at the same time there was a great deal of subtle nuance and variation over both time and space. The broad discursive parameters for talking about the war were being appropriated for specific purposes, leading to a memory that was continually contested and developing. It has become increasingly clear that in order to understand how the war was remembered it is imperative to get as close to the ground as possible, to look at memory in the locality and to examine how the 'myriad faces of war' were mirrored in everyday life.

Many places of work contained memorials that reflected as much pride as grief. The gas works in Beckton, perhaps inevitably, had a memorial which took the form of an eternal flame. In the company magazine a writer claimed that it had served as the model for French national memorial, despite the fact that the flame at the Arc de Triomphe predated it by two years:

What makes our memorial unique, in this country at any rate, is its perpetual lamp ... which has been copied by the French ... As most of our readers know there are many visitors at Beckton, and in going round the works, whether by train or by foot, a halt is always made at the memorial and many have been the tributes made.[47]

As late as 1939 it was still possible to find a residual redemptive value in the war.[48] The sacrifice had not been in vain, the folly of war itself had been demonstrated and it was surely impossible for the world to ignore the lesson. The wheel had come full circle. Just as in 1914, the bulk of British opinion had seen war as a criminal folly; so utilising the First World War as an example, war had once again become unthinkable.

Unfortunately the public was to discover once again that simply willing peace would not serve to preserve it. For the second time in thirty years the British were about to embark on a war that they had not wanted, and once again they would be sustained by their anger at this.

Hitler's wreath

By 1933 the processes of commemoration had been thoroughly nationalised, and the Cenotaph in Whitehall had become the focus of national attention. On 10 May 1933, Dr Rosenberg, the newly appointed German Ambassador to London, representing the new National Socialist regime, laid a swastika-shaped wreath at the Cenotaph on behalf of the new Government. Within hours it was removed by Captain James Edmunds Sears who unceremoniously dumped it in the Thames. Sears was no wild radical, as the manager of a building company and the chairman of the Aylsham branch of the British Legion. Charged with criminal damage, he stated in court that 'What I did was a deliberate protest against the desecration of our national memorial ... especially in view of the fact that the Hitler Government are contriving to foster those very feelings which occurred in Germany before the war for which many of our fellows suffered and lost their lives.' The magistrate was unsympathetic, describing the act as an 'improper and unmanly thing to do', and fining Sears forty shillings. Press comment was generally hostile to Sears's action. The *Daily Sketch* commented that the Cenotaph had to be kept sacred and was no place for political demonstrations, and Sir Ian Hamilton, head of the British Legion, moved a resolution at a Portsmouth meeting of Boer War veterans expressing 'regret that an ex-serviceman should break the sacred truce that had until now guarded the Cenotaph'.

Given the tone of this public comment, it comes as a surprise that all of the private correspondence received by the Board of Works about the event was strongly supportive of Sears's action. The St Pancras branch of the British Legion passed a resolution that no wreath likely to cause controversy and offence be placed at the Cenotaph, blaming the German Government for provocation. More striking were two letters from bereaved women, brimming with emotion. They are worth quoting at length. Mrs G. P. Davies wrote before the incident had occurred:

Re: The German wreath at the Cenotaph. My brother, the only brother I had in the world and one of the best lads the creator put breath into was blown to pieces by a German machine gun. Unless the wreath is removed from my brother's gravestone, I shall take the 9 am train from here next Sunday morning, remove the wreath and send it to the 'four winds' as they have served my brother.
   'God save the King'.[49]

Mrs Lydia Pellinghome wrote from Lynton in Devon to the Home Secretary:

As a mother who lost her only son in the war, I was grieved to read in the daily paper that a wreath draped in the German imperial colours and the Nazi emblem, the Swastika, was placed on the Cenotaph. That this should be allowed is an insult to all concerned. As I write, strange to say, 6pm news over the wireless that a man has been brave enough to tear this away- I am sure not only the mothers but the people of England (who suffered <u>and cannot forget</u>) will feel they owe this man a debt of gratitude, who would dare do this for the right, a noble action which should be chronicled in history, but who has been punished in an English court. Send Dr Rosenberg back to his master. 'Thin ends of wedges' are not required to be driven into our constitutional mechanism. The men (which the Cenotaph stands for) died fighting for peace, just the opposite thing which Dr Rosenberg and Hitler stand for.[50]

These powerful letters bring together many of the themes of this chapter. These women did relate to the 'sacredness' of the Cenotaph, but the raw nature of their grief, fifteen years after the war ended, was readily apparent. Any comfort they drew is fragile, and the meaning of the sacrifice was easily threatened. Clearly commemoration had not led unproblematically to the supposed final stage of mourning in the classic account, which is acceptance. Furthermore the political and the personal are inseparable. With shrewd foresight these women saw where the dynamics of a reborn German militarism would lead. To some extent they are unforgivingly re-fighting the last war, but they also desperately want to avoid the next. The bromides of an 'apolitical' commemorative sacredness collapse in the face of a real political threat. Undoubtedly in the context of 1933 these premature anti-appeasers are untypical, but they are untypical primarily in the clarity of their vision. The nation as a whole would come to have this clarity forced upon it. Martin Gilbert has written that the resolve not to drift into war was a prime determinant of the public support for appeasement, and Alex King has further commented that the 'pervasive representation of the war dead as martyrs for peace' was a powerful resource in supporting this opinion. But as King comments elsewhere, the symbolism of war remembrance was too open-ended to shape political opinion in a single direction, and the 'martyrs for peace' were available for a diametrically opposed purpose: opposition to resurgent German militarism.[51]

Armistice Day was cancelled in November 1939. There were good practical reasons for this: sirens could not be used to announce the two-minute silence, and the authorities did not want crowds gathering. But symbolically the cancellation was far more significant than mere practical considerations would imply. With the cancellation of Armistice Day, a meaningful interpretation of the First World War was cancelled as well. In his poem, 'To a Conscript of 1940', Herbert Read wrote:

> We think we fought in vain,
> The world was not renewed.

The two meanings of the war, victory and warning, were both dependent on peace. No peace meant no meaning. So the British people had to do it all over again. That they did so, reluctant and grumbling as they did, was the most eloquent evidence that the underlying values of 1914 retained some force. The last entry of voluntary nurse E. M. Selby's First World War diary was: 'one could hardly keep from crying – and when one thought of all the boys who would never be coming home.' She resumed the diary on 7 June 1940 in the midst of the Dunkirk evacuation, with four words: 'Another war. Same enemy.'

Of course Selby was not entirely right, the Third Reich and the Kaiserreich were not really the same enemy. But she was less wrong than our mythology of the 'bad war' and the 'good war' implies. The transcendental depravity of Nazism only became fully clear in retrospect; for the majority of the British people the war, particularly during the 'Finest Hour' of 1940, was against the undead spirit of German militarism and unprovoked aggression. The 'Last War' became the last war, lower case, when a new 'Last War' had to be fought.

Conclusion

She felt no rancour to these Huns; time had washed away from her any anger at the man, the regiment, the Hun Army, the nation that had taken Sam's life.

Her resentment was against those who had come later, and whom she refused to dignify with the amicable name of Hun. She hated Hitler's war for diminishing the memory of the Great War, for allotting it a number, the mere first among two. And she hated the way that the Great War was held responsible for the latter, as if Sam, Dennis and all the East Lancashires who fell were partly the cause of that business. Sam had done what he could – he had served and died – and was punished all too quickly with becoming subservient in memory. Time did not behave rationally ... she blamed it on 1939–45.

Julian Barnes, 'Evermore', in *Cross Channel* (London, 1996), p. 105[1]

War experiences

Subservient in memory. In many respects the British people of 1914–1918, soldier and civilian alike, have disappeared into our constructions of them, our collective memory. Like the character above I blame it on 1939–1945. The people of 1914–1918 were fully human, not crude abstractions. Absorbed in the writings of Robert Saunders, Edie Bennett, Harold Cousins, Andrew Clark, Harry Cartmell, Frank Lockwood, Elizabeth Fernside, Eva Isaacs and all the others, it is their humanity that strikes me. Isaacs coyly but clearly suggested to her husband that he should try to arrange his leave to avoid coinciding with her period. Cousins falls asleep exhausted, forgets to close the curtains and is fined for showing a light. Bennet was overjoyed to receive a gift for her beloved child from her sister-in-law's fiancé, who was stationed in Jerusalem; but a few months later, when the engagement is broken off, she dismissed him as 'unsuitable'. Fernside grows to hate the hit song 'A Perfect Day' which seemed to be playing wherever she went. There is a different history here, but one that is almost impossible to write. It would also perhaps be misleading. In the end they aren't entirely like me or the people I 'know', they belong in a subtly different world. Sometimes their attitudes horrify me, sometimes they make me laugh, but sometimes, indeed very often, I recognise myself.

In a privately printed volume, the wartime censors had this to say of the letters they had read: 'Men and women are simpler and truer, less bizarre and censorious than the novelist pretends and their attitude to life and the Government is much juster than that of the article writers in the news-papers.' Furthermore, the censors claim that in 'letters to and from the soldiers in the field, the writers, however illiterate, were moved by those strong and simple emotions upon which family life and the broad truths of religion rest'.[2] A slightly idealised view, but not an unjust one. These people entered into the war from a world both recognisable and significantly different. The challenge of very modern history is striking a balance between the familiarity and the strangeness of the recent past. It can reasonably be objected that throughout this book, because of a preference for contemporary written sources, rather than utilising the vast resources of oral history, I have been engaged in a collective biography of middle-class civilians. The objection is reasonable, doubly so in that ideas of class mattered a vast amount in wartime Britain. Any discussion of the world before the war, the world we have lost, must start from the realisation that Edwardian Britain contained not one, but several worlds within it.

Lost worlds

The most difficult imaginative leap is to comprehend the world of the working class.[3] The only way to visualise (let alone understand) the material conditions of much of the British population in 1914 is to summon up the image of a contemporary third-world slum. Ill health, insecurity, grinding poverty and resigned hopelessness punctuated by whatever escapism was cheaply available and occasional localised rebel-lion were the lot of much of the population in 1914. This is crucially important. No view of the horrors of the First World War can be complete without a sense of the horrors of the pre-war peace.

In 1913 the Fabian Women's Group published the results of a four-year survey of working-class life in Lambeth. The author stressed repeatedly that Lambeth was not a particularly poor district and that the families studied were not the poorest in Lambeth. The book that resulted, *Round about a Pound a Week*, should be required reading for anyone intending to write about the First World War. The death rate amongst the children of these sober, thrifty and generally employed working-class families was one in four. This is roughly double the death rate of adult males in the armed forces 1914–1918. Twenty-two out of the thirty-one families surveyed had lost a child.

Bread with a scraping of margarine, butter, jam or dripping was the sole article for two meals a day in most cases. Meat was a Sunday treat, principally for the man of the house. Eggs and milk were almost unknown. It is true that by contemporary third-world standards these people might count as well dressed, although the usual material for clothing children was the cheap and highly inflammable 'flannelette', which was very dangerous in an age of open flames. Their housing was generally damp, often under-heated or unheated, poorly ventilated and frequently infested with vermin. The average housing provision was three rooms for a family of eight. A family of eight usually possesed two beds, so they slept four to a bed, whether healthy or seriously ill. Medical care was practically non-existent.

This, it should be repeated, was not the 'abyss'; this was ordinary, everyday, *average* working-class poverty in 1914.[4] This was the quotidian nastiness of life for most of the population. Lambeth was only the first circle of the Inferno. For a sense of just how infernal working-class life could be, historians can turn to the experience of Sengennydd, probably the worst place in pre-war Britain. In 1913, in a single pit disaster, 440 men and boys of the village were killed. This was not far short of 10% of the total population. No British community suffered loss on this scale during the Great War. What makes this even more horrifying is that it was the second major disaster to hit the village in a generation: seventy-nine miners had died in 1901. Yet these were just the crescendos in a steady drumbeat of tragic death, inside and outside the mines. Sengennydd was in no way immune to the horrific childhood mortality of working-class Britain; in this too it was well above average. Over 200 children were buried in the Anglican cemetery of the village between 1900 and 1914, and in a predominantly dissenting community this was only part of the toll. Three Llewelyn sisters died in 1905, a son died in 1907; between the great pit disaster and the outbreak of war, three Morris children and their mother died. A smallpox epidemic tore through the village in 1902; in one month, March 1910, eight children died. Before the epidemic was finished twenty-seven children died in Grove Terrace alone.

Sengennydd was not spared the war: ninety men died, a figure in itself above the national average, but at least these men received a memorial. Ninety per cent of the premature deaths in the village in the years 1900–1920 were without the comfort of public recognition and public purpose.[5]

This world that we have lost explains much that would otherwise be inexplicable. The rawness of life prior to 1914 gave capacities for endurance on the part of working-class soldiers and civilians alike which are now hard to imagine. The men of Sengennydd who marched off to war in 1914 did not enter hell for the first time. From our perspective, hell was where they came from.

Like all such sweeping generalisations, this one needs some qualification: it didn't always seem that way at the time. Judging by early twenty-first-century standards, the lethal poverty of early twentieth-century Britain is a grim spectacle; but for those living in the early twentieth century the frame of reference would be less the future than the immediate past. In that respect things had been getting unsteadily better. Bad as the urban conditions were in 1914, they were better for most people than they had been for their parents or grandparents. The late nineteenth century had actually seen a dramatic rise in working-class living standards due to the impact of cheap food guaranted by free trade. Utilitarian sanitation measures had reduced the deadliness of British cities, and by 1914 the first hints of genuine state welfare were becoming apparent. Reading *Round about a Pound a Week*, or examining Sengennydd, one might be baffled as to why anyone would be willing to make a sacrifice to defend that way of life, but it has to be understood that it was a way of life which was felt to have been an improvement on what had gone before. Furthermore, even those with little to lose, perhaps particularly those with little to lose, didn't want to lose what little they had. As tales of the destruction wrought by the German Armies in similar slums in Belgium gathered strength, as the country was flooded with desperate Belgian refugees,[6] the determination for it not to happen here was strong enough. Remarkably a letter from a Sengennydd soldier stationed in France stated: 'Great Britain is fortunate ... It pains one to note the havoc in this country. This was an industrious place and the work of ages lies wrecked around us.'[7] Men would fight to protect even the worst places from the threat of worse fates.

Turning to the 'middle classes' we should be conscious of the plurality, covering as the category does all those who did not earn their living by dirty and dangerous manual labour, but were at the same time not obviously landed. This could include everyone from the most humble shopgirl to newspaper proprietors and the highest echelons of the professions. Middle-class life stretched over a vast amount of ground, from the dreary inner suburbs to the sybaritic pleasures of high society. The lower middle classes, whether the old self-employed shopkeepers or the new white-collar workers (the latter often the children of the former), lived lives that were lacking in amenities by modern standards. No cars and no refrigerators, generally no telephones, no radios or televisions. In those homes that fell below the level of affording servants, the burdens of cleanliness meant backbreaking work for the women of the house. Young men of this class rarely owned property before marriage and usually were highly mobile lodgers. Established families might own houses, but were still likely to rent. Yet these classes were aspirational and respectable and like the uppermost segment of the manual workers, with whom they overlapped, they lived above the level of mere necessities. They owned furniture, they enjoyed strong associational lives, they had various forms of recreation, cycling perhaps for the young, and of course possessed the ubiquitous piano. They were literate and they read, creating a demand for a cheap popular press and for a mass of 'middlebrow' literature.

The middle class proper began with the servantkeepers. Those who could afford to do so always hired domestic assistance. This is a difference in the world of 1914 which we would find striking: the regular presence of non-kin as part of the household. Class relations are often perceived in terms of factory work in the classic Marxist mode, but the real and visible interface between classes in Britain in 1914 was much more within the household and to a very large extent between women.

One of the striking things to a contemporary eye about the central core of the middle classes is the amount of leisure they enjoyed. Just as the employed working class appear to have worked terrifyingly long hours by modern standards, professional and commercial men, let alone upper middle class women of 1914, seem to have had a remarkably relaxed existence. One of the reasons why contemporary middle-class testimony is easier to find than that of the working classes is that, bluntly, they had more time to write letters and diaries.

At the top end of the best circles it overlapped with the world of the aristocracy, a diminishing, but by no means extinct force in British life. There was a degree of merger between social elites. Much of the aristocracy had shifted the basis of its wealth from rural estates to urban property and diversified investment; the successful professional middle classes aped the aristocracy with country houses, and they were bonded together by the public schools and the season.

These social elites have disproportionately shaped the popular view of Edwardian Britain, basking in the sunshine of an eternal Merchant-Ivory cinematic summer, with the black clouds of war slowly gathering on the horizon. Cultural history in particular has been vulnerable to their interpretation of the world. Whilst the importance of these groups in shaping the parameters of culture is undeniable in a society with such a strong implicit and frequently explicit sense of social hierarchy, it is vitally important not to let our view of the war be shaped entirely by the lamentations of the pre-war privileged. The war brought unprecedented loss and hardship to many who had not expected to see it in their lifetimes, but that was not the whole story. The end of civilisation in a country manor could be its beginning in a slum. What the First World War meant in people's lives was to a certain degree conditioned by these pre-war situations. In some cases this shakes the foundations of the myth of the war as universal catastrophe.

In *The Classic Slum*, Robert Roberts entitled his chapter on the war in working-class Salford, 'The Great Release'. Standing back and taking an overview, there can be little doubt that the working classes made relative gains in the war. Prior to the war, socialists had been fierce opponents of war as a potential catastrophe for the working class. In moral terms they hated the idea of workers slaughtering each other at the behest of the bosses, both industrial and political. In practical terms they believed that war would be an economic disaster which would deepen the poverty of the already poor, taking them over the brink to actual starvation. Neither view was unreasonable, nor did the actual war entirely falsify them. In the first months of the war, rising prices and falling employment caused very real distress. Intermittently throughout the war the very poorest did prove vulnerable. Likewise workers were indeed slaughtered. In absolute numbers the majority of casualties must have come from the working classes. Vast numbers of transport workers, miners, mill workers and labourers of all kinds died on the Western Front.

But ironically, the very poverty of the working class was for many their salvation. Childhood malnutrition had rendered a staggeringly high proportion unfit for frontline service. Furthermore, in an industrial war, industrial skills were in high demand. On the home front, clerks and lawyers, teachers and bankers were dispensable and replaceable, while miners and skilled metal workers were not. Less noticed is the degree to which this was also true of the armed forces. The Army was an increasingly complex organism with a great appetite for 'tradesmen'. Finally, working-class men were unlikely to rise to become officers. This was further protection from the disproportionately high death rates suffered by the junior officers of the army.

The experience of working-class men who did join is also not without paradox. Strange though it may seem, even the Army, even the horrors of the Western Front, could seem in certain respects an improvement on day-to-day civilian life. Many, perhaps most, soldiers were better fed in the Army than they had ever been in civilian life. To eat meat every day was a genuine novelty, even if it was the despised Machonochie stew or the somewhat less disliked bully beef. The lack of privacy and decency which were felt so deeply by middle-class men in the forces were no novelty to many working-class soldiers. Army life involved a great deal of hard monotonous labour, but for many men it also included more genuine leisure, as opposed to enforced idleness, than they had ever previously had. Even the omnipresence of death in the bad sectors of the frontline and the fear of death and maiming should be seen in pre-war perspective.

Miners in particular, the largest single component of the male workforce and a substantial component of the Army,[8] had already known a life when any minute could be their last. Other pit villages never suffered on the scale of Sengennydd, although the possibility was always present, but for fifty years before the war one miner had been killed evey six hours. Each generation of miners had suffered a long drawn out 'first day of the Somme'. If cave-ins, machine accidents and explosions did not kill them then occupational diseases would. Miners' experiences were extreme but not unique in their familiarity with industrial death and injury and occupational disease: fishermen, merchant seamen, building workers and metal workers lived in a world of high risk.[9]

This shouldn't be pushed too far though. The traumatic experiences of battle, the oppressive and savage nature of British Army discipline and the discomfort of outdoor living in sordid conditions (everyone hated mud), above all in most cases the emotional burden of separation from family, meant that on the whole Army service was still a negative experience.[10] Bad as Sengennydd was, the first day of the Somme represented fifty Sengennydds at once. The post-war mutinies which occurred when demobilisation appeared to be too slow are good evidence that most men were not particularly enamoured of the Army life as such. (Although the fact that more men wanted to 'stay in' than the post-war army could accommodate suggests that at least some of them were willing to tolerate it.)

Nevertheless, it is reasonable to suggest that many working-class men in the armed forces found their experiences less unusual and shocking than might be expected.[11] Logically enough, most of our canonical literary accounts come from middle-class men, either officers or 'gentlemen rankers'. It would be wrong to dismiss them as therefore oversensitive, but it is always worth bearing in mind that they were used to standards of comfort and security which had been unattainable to the bulk of the population before 1914.

Of course, even working-class soldiers soon became aware of their *relative* deprivation. Indeed those who had joined up because of the economic downturn in August 1914 may have found themselves bitterly regretting it. The principal impact of the war was labour shortage. Predictably this strengthened the economic bargaining position of male working-class civilians, individually and collectively. For some the war represented a transformation of fortunes – prior to 1914 the Roberts's family shop in Salford reflected the surrounding ocean of poverty. By the end of the war they were turning over £45 per week and his mother had saved £100. The Roberts family built this new prosperity on the back of the new disposable income of its customers. 'For the very poor this was a changed world indeed.' Best of all was the return of the ex-servicemen with gratuities of up to £40 in their pockets to spend – a year's pre-war wages. Even when the post-war depression began to hit home after 1921, the commonplace view in Salford was: 'Things are bad now, but nothing like before the war.'[12] This was the perception that was widespread during the war, but it was not unchallenged. Sylvia Pankhurst, for example, both during and after the war presented it as a period of intensified suffering and poverty for the working class. In reality the picture was complicated. Between July 1914 and January 1919 the cost-of-living index (itself a relatively new tool) showed that costs had just a little more than doubled over the course of the war. John Holford's calculation of 'real' wages in Edinburgh, expressed as a percentage of buying the trade council's 'minimum household budget', seems to demonstrate not only a narrowing of differentials, but a real decline in purchasing power between 1914 and 1918, followed by a post-war recovery:

Trade	1914	1918	1921
Painters	148	99	130
Engineers	143	109	129
Sheet metal workers	128	106	116
Compositors	131	103	112
Bakers	128	108	117
Warehousemen	75	72	83

J. Holford, *Reshaping Labour: Organisation, Work and Politics in Edinburgh in the Great War and After* (London, 1998), Table 3.6, pp. 34–5.

Unfortunately Holford's table deliberately omits 'war bonuses' from the 1918 figures. This means it would be dangerous to accept this conclusion completely. On these figures the content of the wage packets of the unskilled had roughly tripled, whilst the wages of the skilled had doubled. As prices had also roughly doubled, the former had advanced, and the latter had stood still. But, as the survey cited points out, the actual earnings of the skilled 'were considerably in excess' of this. These are the minimum figures. Skilled men 'normally' received wages higher than the minimum and these figures take no account of the considerable amount of overtime being worked.

The conclusion of M. B. Hammond in 1919 was the rather lukewarm view that if overtime, Sundays and holidays are taken into consideration, the economic position of working-class men and women had not deteriorated during the war, but they were working longer hours to maintain living standards.[13] This certainly puts middle-class and even perhaps soldiers' complaints about profiteering workers into perspective. But it also rather misses an important point: that during the war years the scourge of under-employment was temporarily solved and temporarily replaced with a problem of severe overwork.[14] Thus whilst average weekly wage rates fell slightly behind prices over the course of the war, average weekly earnings ultimately slightly outstripped the price rises.[15] If over-work allowed those who had been in full-time work in 1914 to just about keep pace with costs, the critical difference was that the unemployed, the casually and marginally employed, the short-time workers and seasonally or cyclically out-of-work segment of the population of 1914 – a very large percentage of the total – now also had full-time and more than full-time work. Physically exhausted men in their 50s and older, as well as the disabled, were swept into the workforce. So of course were a large number of married women and children.

So, were the working classes, particularly the unskilled, the economic victors? Demographic figures appear to be unarguable. The statistics for infant mortality are clear cut. Using 1911 to 1913 (incidentally the years of the Lambeth study cited above) as a baseline, the war years saw a clear decline in infant mortality in England and Wales:

	1911–1913	1914	1915	1916	1917	1918
North	121	110	112	96	97	102
Midlands	101	86	92	76	77	78
South	93	80	89	71	77	78
Wales	110	99	101	83	85	86
All	100	95	95	82	87	87

England and Wales 1911–1913 = 100. J. M. Winter, *The Great War and the British People* (London, 1985)

There was a small increase in 1915 and an even smaller one in 1918, but the aggregate figures all indicate a definite and substantial downward trend. Infant mortality declined overall by about 10% in four years of war. This is impressive enough in itself, but it should also be noted that the most dramatic gains were made in the poorest districts. Thus whilst in Hampstead, which had been the London borough of lowest infant mortality in 1914, infant mortality declined only 8%, in Shoreditch it declined by 33%. In wealthy Bath, infant mortality actually rose 2% during the war whilst in impoverished Burnley it fell 31%. In Scotland, in respectable Perth, infant mortality rose by 5% whilst for the Clydeside slum of Coatbridge it fell 27%.[16]

Infant mortality is traditionally perceived as the most sensitive indicator of general economic well-being. Though other explanations are possible, for example the declining wartime birth rate, or even the benefits of the lack of medical intervention caused by a wartime shortage of doctors (this is a serious point – cross-infection caused by doctors probably caused a proportion of infant deaths), the most likely explanation is the improved nutrition of children and mothers. War was good for babies and young children.

The same improvement can be seen in much, but not all, of the adult female population. Mortality rates amongst women between the ages of 30 and 34 dropped 16% between 1912 and 1918, between the ages of 50 and 54 they fell 6%, between the ages of 60 and 64 they fell 12%, and between the ages of 70 and 74 they fell 10%.

The picture in this regard is much more uneven than that regarding infant mortality. All of these groups saw moments of rising mortality in wartime as well as overall decline. The mortality of all women under the age of 30, apart from babies, actually rose in wartime. The cause was twofold: increased tuberculosis mortality and the Spanish influenza outbreak of 1918. The latter, a global demographic disaster, was not purely a result of the war. More importantly and paradoxically it did not discriminate against the malnourished and vulnerable; in fact the opposite is probably true. The terrifying nature of the epidemic was that it primarily killed those with good immune systems, particularly young healthy adults. The epidemiology of tuberculosis is complex, but the key issue is whether poor nutrition of women was to blame, implying a decline in living standards. The probable answer is no. The war did increase susceptibility to the disease, but the likely reason is the movement of the young female population into munitions work.

Demography does not fully answer the question of working-class well-being and neither does the data on real wages. Total family income rather than the abstraction of real wages was the actual determinant of well-being in wartime. This was likely to be determined by highly contingent features. Margaret Powell, the young daughter of a painter/decorator living in Hove remembered that, when her father was called up in 1916, 'the separation allowance was terrible. It really was. Starvation money, that's all you could call it.' For several months the family faced severe hardship. Then relief came: 'the best thing that happened to us in the war on our street was when they billeted soldiers on us ... I don't know what the money was, but I noticed that there was a change in our standard of living ... It made a big difference. All of a sudden everybody sprouted out with new things. Even the tally man got paid.' The arrangement was not without problems: Powell's mother was an attractive woman and her father in France was not happy at the presence of two strange men in the house while he was away, yet Margaret remembered the experience in a positive light 50 years on.[17]

Of course this cuts both ways: some families gained a billeting allowance, meanwhile others lost the income generated by a lodger. The extent to which the war was good or bad for poor families would be determined by a host of variables. The loss of a steady male worker who had conscientiously handed over his wages for the family benefit was obviously far more severe than the loss of the workshy or incompetent worker, or a drunk who neglected his family. For some women a separation allowance was 'starvation', for others it was more money in hand than they had ever seen.

Not only income but the balance of expenditure was shifted by wartime conditions. For example, it was argued at the time that drinking restrictions were in themselves a major contribution to family welfare and it would be wrong to dismiss this as conventional prejudice. In a minority of working-class households it is highly likely that expenditure on alcohol had indeed been a cause of poverty.

Nevertheless, middle-class comment on such changes in family income and expenditure amongst the working classes was frequently highly negative if it was too conspicuously for the better. In September 1917 a working-class woman in Kingston found herself in court. It was revealed that she was receiving £3 in Army separation allowance, was earning a similar amount for working in an armaments factory and was in receipt of a further £2 from her 13-year-old son, also employed in armaments. The reaction of the Mayor was: 'Four hundred pounds a year. It sounds like a fairy tale.' It is the reaction that is most significant, and the fact that it was reported in the national press. That a working-class family, which by any measure was contributing significantly to the war effort, could be in receipt of £400 a year, was treated as absurd. Yet by professional middle-class standards this sum represented a bare minimum that anyone would consider sufficient to guarantee a minimum level of comfort and decency in 1917.

The overall effect of the war, with all qualifications acknowledged, is that the poorest of the British people became less poor. A rather self-congratulatory and whiggish view has emerged which sees this social progess as a product of the superiority of British representative government which was responsive to the needs of the population at large. This is not entirely false: David Lloyd George had been the principal politician determining the nature of the war economy, whether as Chancellor of the Exchequer in 1914, Minister of Munitions in 1915 or Prime Minister from December 1916, and he was a talented populist politician aligned to the progressive movement in pre-war politics. But from the end of 1915 the bulk of the British political leadership was drawn from Conservative circles which had been very resistant to redistributive politics and would prove to be so again in the future.

That people gained a sense of entitlement in wartime is doubtless true, that even Conservative politicians could grasp and support the idea is also true, but any gains made by the poorest in the war had to be fought for and defended.

The main weapon of working-class self-defence was the traditional one; the withdrawal of their labour. Increasingly this had to be done informally or even illegally. But in wartime, when this labour was utterly indispensable and irreplaceable, it was a highly effective weapon. Some accounts of the First World War which have emphasised the extent of British patriotic consensus have rather skated around the very high levels of strike activity. It has taken the provocative work of Niall Ferguson to hammer the point home:

Year	Strikers (Britain)	Days lost (Britain)	Strikers (Germany)	Days lost (Germany)
1914	326,000	10,000,000	61,000	1,715,000
1915	401,000	3,000,000	14,000	42,000
1916	235,000	2,500,000	129,000	245,000
1917	575,000	5,500,000	667,000	1,862,000
1918	923,000	6,000,000	391,000	1,452,000

The disproportion is staggering. Even in 1918, the year of the 'German Revolution', Britain had more than twice the number of strikers and more than four times the number of days lost.[18] On several occasions during the war British trade unionists put their employers and the Government over a barrel. Still it should be noted that the number of strikers in 1918 represents less than a quarter of the total trade-union membership. The workers were not really unpatriotic. Even Ferguson, who is highly critical of British industrial performance, cannot hide the fact that production in Britain was maintained at high levels throughout the war.[19] Furthermore hardly any of the British strikes took on the political and anti-war nature that some of the strikes in almost every other European nation possessed.

In the face of often fierce middle-class hostility, members of the working classes fought a modest war within the war, in the first instance to prevent an intensification of exploitation and secondarily to claw a modest amount of benefit from the situation.

Although many of the strikes and strike threats came from the more comfortable members of the working class striking in defence of 'differentials', many others came from the poorest and most marginal. Trade unionism spread rapidly during the war: by the end of the war, one in three workers was unionised.

In the East End of London, the classic and definitive epicentre of pre-war poverty, almost every conceivable variety of worker fought for and won pay rises. The wonderfully named Military Cork Headdress Trade Union demanded and got a 7.5% rise from their employers, Charles Owen and Co. of Bow.[20] In October 1916, the 500 employees of Schneider's in Whitechapel, a clothing firm which was probably the most important Government contractor in the East End, walked out. The firm quickly settled. In many, perhaps most, cases it was not even necessary to strike: workers simply stopped working for the most exploitative sweatshops. In a situation of full employment they held all the cards. The Government, as is well known, responded with 'leaving certificates' for military-age males and with no strike agreements with the trade union leadership. The effect was limited. Skilled men were unimpressed by the threat of conscription; they were needed in war industry and they knew it. The Government could not hold back the tide. All forms of labour were needed: older men, women and adolescents could not effectively be prevented from going where the money was. To take only the most noticeable example, there were 400,000 fewer women in domestic service at the end of the war than there had been at the start, and those who stayed on knew that they could leave for better-paid work at any time, which strengthened their bargaining position no end. The 'servant problem', so widely discussed amongst the middle classes, was not just or even mainly about the supposed shortage of servants, it was about a shift in power relations.

For the middle classes, top to bottom, the war seen in general terms was a radically different experience. In broad terms, the greater the wealth and status of an adult male in 1914, the greater his chance of dying in the war.[21] Young middle- and upper-class men were the most conventionally patriotic component of the population in 1914, and they paid a heavy price for it. There was a big disparity in the percentage of enlistment of industrial workers compared to those in middle-class employment: 28.3% of the employed men in industry had joined up by February 1916; by comparison 40.1% of men in commerce and finance had joined; and 41.7% in the professions. Whilst it is true that employers of labour were probably slightly less likely than average to join up, this is in part a product of age structure – many of the heirs to businesses doubtless did join. The disparity did not end there. Middle-class men were more likely to meet the health criteria for frontline service and much more likely to become officers. The latter rank was particularly dangerous. The roll of honour of Westminster and Parrs Bank show that 15.7% of those enlisted were killed in the war (somewhat above the national average) and that, of those killed, a staggering 43% were killed after becoming officers. On average, those who had not been manual labourers were perhaps twice as likely to serve in the war and then perhaps 50% more likely to be killed than their working-class counterparts once in uniform. These odds were worst in the highest strata. Twenty-nine per cent of those serving in the war who matriculated at Oxford between 1910–1914, and 26% of those who matriculated at Cambridge, were killed between 1914 and 1918. These figures are substantially more than double the national average. Given that enlistment rates were similarly more than double, the likelihood of an Oxford or Cambridge student in 1914 being killed in the war was at least five times higher than his manual worker contemporaries. This was mirrored in less extreme forms throughout the middle classes. Amongst the battalions massacred on the first day of the Somme were many battalions composed of miners and textile workers, but there were perhaps equally as many with impeccably middle-class pedigrees. The 1st London Rifle Brigade (LRB), a unit so exclusive that it had still been charging an entry fee in 1915, suffered 36% fatalities on 1 July 1916. Although it is true that very few of these were members of the original battalion (16% of the total deaths) the vast majority were still the respectable office workers who had deliberately joined 'The Finest Regiment God Made' (as it was described on posters on the London underground).

The LRB was far from unique. The very names of many battalions which were shot to pieces indicate their social aspirations: Belfast Young Citizens, Hull Commercials, Civil Service Rifles. As John Keegan has rightly written, these units are poignantly resonant of the world of H. G. Wells novels, whole battalions of Kipps and Pooters.

For those men of this class who did not or could not go into the Army, the war would be a difficult if less deadly experience. Not the least of their problems must have been psychological. A fit young man in factory work had the advantage of a social milieu where the expectation of enlistment could be to some extent counter-balanced by an element of workplace solidarity. For an office worker, part of an ever diminishing minority of males in the workplace, the sense of exclusion must have been intense, regardless of fitness or legitimate reason for not joining. Furthermore the economic pressure was mounting as the war progressed. Male salaries fell substantially behind the increase in prices by 1916. The need for 'economy' in wartime seems to have obsessed middle-class households.

Although there was a fall in living standards, it was probably not as bad as it was believed to have been: the middle classes still remained immeasurably better off, on average, than manual workers. What seems to have bothered them most was a sense that the gap, so important to their self-esteem, was closing. It was less proletarianisation than fear of proletarianisation which drove their complaints and of course created the ideal conditions for a post-war political backlash.

Most ambiguous of all was the position of middle-class women. In some respects war can still be seen for this group in traditional terms, as a dramatic emancipation. Dramatic is certainly not too strong a word when considering a case highlighted by Gleason. A young woman he knew, working at the War Office in 1917, who came from a good family that had fallen upon hard times provided him, at his request, with a series of schedules from her earlier career. In what was admittedly the worst case, she had worked as a 'lady help' in a house where 'no servant was kept'. She had risen at 6.30 a.m., made and taken up tea at 7 a.m., dressed the children, made breakfast and swept and cleaned downstairs by 9 a.m., swept and cleaned the bedroom and emptied the toilet in the morning, looked after the children all day, cooked lunch and supper, washed up and looked after the children, including making their bottles until 11 p.m., spent all night sharing a room with a child who slept badly and whom she had to attend and make bottles for throughout the night, before getting up in the morning to repeat the routine. For this she was paid an *annual* salary of £12 on top of bed and board. In 1917 she earned 27 shillings a week, roughly £70 per annum, with far better hours and more independence. Gleason concluded that this 'showed why she would not return to her old job after the war'. Unfortunately she might, as it turned out, have had little choice.

Young respectable unmarried women did gain a degree of potential freedom during the war that was unusual prior to 1914. Yet women of this class had to carry a double psychological burden: both the anxiety about loved ones in uniform and the sense of guilt about exclusion from equity in their sacrifice with the men in uniform.

This raises the vexed question of gender. Seen as a discursive category this is difficult enough. By definition non-combatants, women were very largely excluded from making the 'Supreme Sacrifice'.[22] But at the same time propaganda stressed heavily and repeatedly the invaluable contribution, the 'small case' sacrifices, women were making to the national effort.[23] Even if it were possible to state conclusively that their exclusion from military service reinforced the patriarchal subjection of women or that their acknowledged importance for the war economy was potentially emancipatory, then it would still be of limited use in telling us how the war actually impacted on women's lives and how this language was used to shape experience.

In discursive terms a woman may just be a woman.[24] In reality her life exists at the intersection of many other identities as well: regional, class, occupational, religious and ethnic. It is not self-evident that patriarchy was a more central form of oppression and subordination in the Britain of 1914 than class hierarchy. Women may well to some degree have identified with other women and against men, but they also identified with men of the same class and against women of other classes.

But even this does not come near to grasping the complexities of lives as they were actually lived. Women were also positioned on a series of other polarised axes: married/unmarried, old/young, mothers and those without children, respectable/disorderly. Finally, even within groups with apparent common experience, once the superficial unities are interrogated, the subjective and significant differences become overwhelming: women with husbands in the Army and those without, those whose husbands were safe and those whose husbands weren't, those at risk from air raids and those who were relatively safe, and so on. This is not to be taken as a dismissal of gender history as such.[25] Far from it. The impact of ideas drawn from it ought to be apparent throughout this book. All of these women lived within a world where experience was interpreted through a gendered language. Rather, the meanings of that language, which was a language amongst other languages, should be applied cautiously and with a real sense of context when applied to the working-out of language in experience.[26]

What can be said of women ought to be said of the experience of war as a whole. We desperately need to problematise the whole issue of war experience, to think carefully about what we mean by the experience of 40 million people, each with their own hopes, fears and beliefs and with wildly different experiences of what the war was to them, in order to avoid falling into the trap of assigning it a single clear-cut meaning. Yet at the same time we have to acknowledge the powerful impulse to simplify and give the war a single consensual meaning, both while it was being fought and afterwards. That the war was interpreted as 'sacrifice' has been a central argument of this book, but we cannot forget that the interpretation of the word was relational and even individual.

So was the war conservative or radical in its social and cultural results? Neither and both. Britain went into the war a complex mix of conservative and progressive elements, and came out with a slightly different mix. Besides, the very concepts conservative and progressive are historically contingent, the 1960s assumption that the wartime growth of the state represented progress now seems archaic to many, but in fifty years' time it may once again seem credible. The emphasis on maternal and infant welfare which is now frequently read as a retrograde imposition of biological determinism, may in the future once again be perceived as enlightened. North American and Australasian historians frequently write about Britain as an appallingly class-bound and conservative culture; but are sometimes fooled into mistaking rhetoric for practice, as the British frequently use traditional forms precisely in order to gloss over radical change. Nostalgia in Britain, whether in the 1920s, the 1950s or the 1970s is sometimes most intense in the midst of upheaval. Myths of the past have contemporary uses.

The myths of war experience

George Mosse, in a polemical and brilliant study, presented us with the concept of the 'myth of war experience'. For Mosse this is a political claim expressed in cultural terms. It is the claim that the experience of combat provides the most fundamental insight into the human condition, a transcendent wisdom which uniquely qualifies the soldier to guide his nation's affairs. The quasi-religious nature of patriotism is emphasised; the cult of fallen soldiers empowers their living representatives to assert their superiority over mere civilians. It is the basic grounding of Fascism.

Mosse's model, which assumes a glorification of war itself, seems to work poorly when applied to Britain after the First World War. Politically, British Fascism was a marginal phenomenon: stifled by popular conservatism, soldiers were not given a particular right to assert their power over civilians, and war per se was not glorified.

But in the long term, the cultural claim of the myth of war experience has triumphed in Britain, albeit in a peculiar form. The 'meaning' of the war has been defined by the view from the trench parapet. Paul Fussell, in what remains the most brilliant single extended essay on the war, exemplifies this. In the afterword to the twenty-fifth anniversary reissue of *The Great War and Modern Memory* he states that he spent months in the Imperial War Museum reading first-hand accounts of the war. He read many personal accounts from the Army, mostly the infantry, on the Western Front. He deliberately *did not* read accounts of the air war, the Navy or documents left by civilians. Leaving aside whether Fussell's view of these soldiers' attitude is accurate, which is itself much disputed, this selection is highly revealing. Fussell confined his reading to a sample of the war experiences of less than 5% of the British population. That was his right, but the meaning of a war which had involved, to a greater or lesser extent, the entire population cannot be defined in that way.[27]

Whilst it is inevitable that the misery and terrors of trench warfare should hold a particular fascination, such a fixation is dangerous on two counts. One is that the best-known representations of this war experience are in fact highly subjective and selective accounts, which to some extent misrepresent that aspect of the war. The other is that this experience is a part and not the whole of the experience of war and should not be given the power to determine the meaning of the war as a whole. That it has been allowed to do so is, curiously, a by-product of wartime mentalities themselves. The centrality of the sacrifice of the soldiers was an acknowledged part of the language of civilian life in wartime. Far from being indifferent to the lives of the soldiers at the front, as the 'myth of war experience' implies, civilians were obsessed with it. It was the determinant touchstone of all other sacrifices. The devaluing of civilian war experiences in many respects began within the civilian population.

The greatest war poets followed their example only too well. Siegfried Sassoon's poetry reeks of hatred for civilians and implied violence towards them. From 'Blighters':

> I'd like to see a tank come up the aisles
> Lurching to ragtime tunes and 'Home Sweet Home'.

From 'Fight to the Finish':

> I heard the yellow press men grunt and squeal
> And with my trusty bombers went
> To clear the Junkers out of parliament.

There is a perfect one-word description for these sentiments and it isn't pacifist: these ideas are indistinguishable from Fascism. In British school history classes this rhetoric is associated with Nazism and is condemned, whilst in literature classes it is held up as noble.

Is it possible to return the First World War to ordinary history? An indispensable prerequisite is to dispose of our sense of the war as a rip in the fabric of national life, and view it as a typical and perhaps archetypical British war. The British, like most people, prefer to think of their historic wars as just ones. In reality a very high proportion of wars fought by Britain before 1914 were morally dubious at best, and many were the most naked aggression. But only the First World War is widely pilloried as wrong. To a large extent because of 1939–1945, the First World War has been reconstructed as an unjustifiable war.[28] This is mistaken on almost every count. By the classic standards by which a just war would be judged, 1914–1918 stands up rather well from a British point of view. Intervention could be justified on the basis that the failure to act was likely to endanger the nation – in that sense it qualifies as a necessary war. In moral terms it was a war against unprovoked aggression and the violation of international treaties, to which Britain was a signatory. This moral case was about as clear cut as a war can ever be. In terms of fighting the war, the British Government tried reasonably hard to maintain a sense of humanity, legality and proportion and, although it failed, as it was bound to do in a war of that scale and desperation, it should also be noted that it failed far more often and more seriously in the Second World War. The British war effort of 1914–1918 did not contain a policy of blatant inhumanity comparable with the bomber offensive of the Second World War.[29]

Only the liberation of the death camps in 1945 and the clear evil of the Nazi regime gave the war of 1939–1945 an obvious moral superiority to that of 1914–1918, and we should be aware that although this is not irrelevant, it is partly retrospective and partly spurious for understanding why the British fought that war at the time.[30] The British did not go to war in 1939 to liberate Belsen, although both going to war and liberating Belsen are things that the nation can and should remain proud of.

Finally there is the issue of the peace. Was the outcome of the war just? Versailles was harsh, but it was nowhere near as vindictive as subsequent legend suggested. The harshness of the treaty was neither inexplicable nor unjustifiable. Germany's territorial 'losses' were predominantly of areas in which the population did not believe itself to be German. The demand for reparations was perfectly understandable from nations that had had a terrible and extremely costly war forced upon them by German government policy, and had suffered enormous material damage, which Germany itself had largely escaped. Some of this damage can only be classed as vindictive and spiteful. Furthermore reparations were based on clear precedents, not least the policy which the German Government itself had pursued in the past fifty years whenever the boot was on the other foot. The demilitarisation of the Rhineland and the limitation of German armaments were equally understandable.

Versailles was not in any real sense a Carthaginian peace but rather precautions on the part of national governments which wanted to prevent a war of revenge. To see what a real Carthaginian peace would have looked like it is only required to look at the way Germany was treated after the Second World War. In 1945, Germany was humiliated, partitioned, truncated, controlled, plundered and her surviving political leaders were tried and in some cases executed by a tribunal of victors. But few really condemn that peace, mainly because no one has been able to construct a false causality by which it was blamed for starting another war.

The causality by which Versailles is held responsible for Hitler's war is phoney. It wasn't Versailles that caused the Second World War. Bodged treaty as it was, Versailles could have guaranteed European security. It was the failure to defend and enforce Versailles that led directly to the Second World War. Responsibility for that war rests less with those who imposed the treaty than with those who passively accepted and even connived in its rejection.

The implications of the First World War being a just and justifiable war are actually very disturbing, far more disturbing than the attempt to marginalise it as an aberration and a catastrophe. If the war, in the words of Trevor Wilson, really was one of 'Freedom's battles';[31] if as I have argued it was undertaken reluctantly by a people who quite genuinely believed in the value of peace and not by a crazed jingoistic mob, then it becomes more rather than less of a challenge to our ideals. If the war was sustained by the high moral value of self-sacrifice, by the language which puts the common good above individual self-interest and which was the central pre-condition of maintaining the war effort, then this implies some very dark conclusions. If so much misery and waste, hatred and intolerance was a product not of our worst instincts, but the 'better angels of our nature': the desire to serve a cause, our capacity for moral indignation, a willingness to stand up for core beliefs, our sense of social solidarity and trust in civilised values, then what hope is there? Dismissing the war as an error doesn't help; it wasn't an error. The British went to war in 1914 to curb and to punish German aggression in order to achieve a lasting peace. They pursued this goal with terrifying single-mindedness and in 1919, with a few dissenting voices, they believed they had achieved it. Many of the British public still think the same way, rightly or wrongly: the urge to act in 1914 was the same urge that led the British nation to war in the Falklands, the Gulf and the Balkans.[32] In 2003 the Prime Minister used similar language to justify military operations in Iraq. In this case there was substantial dissent, much of which was based on reflexive hostility to the United States and the Bush Administration, but there was also substantial quiet support – much more than is now admitted as the war has proved intractable. The same urge to support military interventions will be present until war is renounced, either through a genuine conversion to absolute and unconditional pacifism or a self-centred decision to forego any military action whatsoever on the grounds that it cannot serve our interests or, most hopefully and perhaps least likely, through the establishment of an orderly world in which aggression has ceased. Then and only then we can finally state with justified confidence that we have fought the last war.

Notes

INTRODUCTION

1. Cited in J. M. Winter, *Remembering War: The Great War between Memory and History in the Twentieth Century* (New Haven, CT, 2006), p. 46.
2. W. Schivelbusch, *The Culture of Defeat* (London, 2004), explores this idea in depth.
3. For a trenchant critique of this view, see G. Sheffield, *Forgotten Victory* (London, 2001). For a subtle dissection of how it came to be constructed, see D. Todman, *The Great War, Myth and Memory* (London, 2005).
4. Likewise the 1999 film, *The Trench* (screenplay by William Boyd), which is, in many ways, an excellent and understated film, about the lead-up to 1 July 1916. It ends, inevitably, with the death of all the main characters. In actuality, over 20,000 British soldiers died that day and 40,000 more were wounded. What follows may sound like a demographer's quibble about the logic of fiction, but there is something misleading about this insistence on near 100% death rates. Of the British soldiers who went into action on the first day of the Somme, one in six was killed and half were wounded. Bad enough, but why is it that in fictional accounts of the war, it seems that *no one* ever comes through unscathed, or gets a 'blighty' wound?
5. N. Ferguson, *The Pity of War* (London, 1998), p. 462. Nevertheless, Ferguson's willingness to take on his peers and provoke academic debate is laudable.
6. *The Times*, 11 November 1996, p. 15.
7. J. Grigg, 'Nobility and War: The Unselfish Commitment?', *Encounter* 74 (1990), pp. 21–7. I would like to thank Professor Brian Bond for drawing this article to my attention and Patrick Porter for tracking it down. Some of the lines of analysis in this book mirror Grigg's comments.
8. Would the result have simply been the Kaiser's European Union? Possibly, but it would have been a European Union with a peculiarly bad attitude, led by a notorious Anglophobe with a huge army and navy. I would imagine this ought to give even hardened Eurosceptics pause for thought.

CHAPTER 1

1. G. P. Gooch, *The History of Our Time: 1885–1913* (London, 1913), pp. 248–9. Gooch went on to edit the documentary collection of British documents relevant to the coming of the war. Such views were commonplace in Europe in 1913: see P. Wust, *Crisis in the West* (London, 1931), pp. 41–2.

2. R. Roberts, *The Classic Slum: Salford Life in the First Quarter of the Century* (Manchester, 1971; reprinted London, 1990), p. 186. For reasons that will quickly become apparent, I have tended to treat the testimony of reminiscences with great caution. But Roberts's testimony is worth stating at the outset, precisely because it contradicts the usual assumptions about the public mood at the outbreak of war. By common consensus, Roberts's is one of the best evocations of Edwardian life in that it avoids nostalgia and sentimentalisation. Although Roberts was only 9 years old at the outbreak of the war and although some of the chronology in his account is clearly dubious, it is still a useful and rare insight. Another observant child of about the same age in 1914 was A. J. P. Taylor, living in Buxton. He remembered 'no demonstrations, no crowds in the streets, no animated discussions in the family'. His major memory was his grandfather remarking, in the fine tradition of Lancashire Liberalism, 'Can't they see as every time they kills a German they kills a customer.' A. J. P. Taylor, *A Personal History* (London, 1983), p. 27.

3. A. Marwick, *The Deluge: British Society and the First World War* (London, 1965; 1989), p. 309.

4. It is interesting to reflect on a straw poll conducted by the US Senator for Indiana, Albert Beveridge, in the early spring of 1915, which suggested to him 'the middle classes are unaroused, the so-called lower classes divided between those who are sullenly indifferent and patriotically interested … Only the aristocracy was "eager, united and resolved".' A. Beveridge, 'War Opinion in England – Some Contrasts' (1915), reproduced in H. E. Straubing, *The Last Magnificent War* (New York, 1989), pp. 44–53. This is not to argue that Beveridge was correct; only that a contemporary observer could draw a very different conclusion.

5. Quoted in G. M. Thompson, *The 12 Days: 24 July to 4 August 1914* (London, 1964), p. 188.

6. B. Russell, *The Autobiography of Bertrand Russell: 1914–44*, vol. 2 (London, 1968), p. 16.

7. The classic text remains J. A. Hobson, *The Psychology of Jingoism* (London, 1901). See also C. F. G. Masterman (ed.), *The Heart of Empire* (London, 1901), a compendium of Liberal views. In point of fact most Liberal dissidents in 1914 were reacting to a well-established 'script' which assumed that the 'mob' would react enthusiastically to war. For criticism of the assumptions of turn-of-the-century mass psychology, see C. McPhail, *The Myth of the Madding Crowd* (New York, 1991) and for a study of their origins, see R. Nye, *The Origins of Crowd Psychology: Gustav Le Bon and the Crisis of Mass Democracy in the Third Republic* (Beverly Hills, CA, 1975).

8. The opponents of the war were quick to impute a psychological disorder to their opponents. The classic statement of this can be found in I. Cooper Willis, *England's Holy War: A Study of English Liberal Idealism during the Great War* (New York, 1928), pp. 159–68. Willis, using the then-fashionable psychological analysis, argues that the Liberals who supported the war effort were not motivated by reason but by emotion, and that their 'reasoning' was in fact rationalisation to overcome an inner conflict.

The arguments in Willis can equally usefully be turned back on Liberal pacifists in 1914.

9. D. Lloyd George, *War Memoirs* (London, 1938), vol. 1, p. 39.
10. For accounts, see Thompson, *The 12 Days*, pp. 166–72, 179–81.
11. In particular, J. J. Becker, *1914: Comment les Français sont entrés dans la guerre* (Paris, 1977). In a series of excellent local studies, German historians have questioned the existence of *Augustgemeinschaft* in Germany. There is now a first-rate overview of the state of research, and one which provides a compelling interpretation: J. Verhey, *The Spirit of 1914: Militarism, Myth and Mobilization in Germany* (Cambridge, 2000).
12. K. O. Morgan, *Rebirth of a Nation: A History of Modern Wales* (Oxford, 1981), p. 159.
13. I am very grateful to my student Rhodri Jones for exploring the Welsh dimension, particularly those parts inaccessible to a linguistically ignorant Anglo-Saxon. This section is entirely based upon his very original research. R. Jones, 'Wales and the Outbreak of the First World War', unpublished BA dissertation, Oxford, 1999.
14. See P. Simkins, *Kitchener's Army* (Manchester, 1988).
15. C. Benn, *Keir Hardie* (London, 1997), pp. 326–7, 330.
16. C. Pearce, *Comrades in Conscience: The Story of an English Community's Opposition to the Great War* (London, 2001), pp. 25, 70.
17. *The Globe*, 3 August 1914, p. 5.
18. To get a flavour of a 'normal' Bank Holiday crowd, see the description by A. St John Adcock, published in *Living London* in 1903. The normal rowdiness, social intermingling and enthusiasm of a Bank Holiday weekend is difficult to distinguish from classic descriptions of 'war enthusiasm'. See the reprint of this article in E. Sims (ed.), *Edwardian London*, vol. 2 (London, 1990), pp. 218–24.
19. Willis, *England's Holy War*, pp. 14–15. My italics. This testimony, like Playne's cited later, is important precisely because it comes from a severe critic of the war and a believer in mass irrationality. Although published in 1928, this paragraph was written, according to the author, in November 1918.
20. *South London Observer*, 8 August 1914, p. 6.
21. A potentially useful line of inquiry might be to consider how far the genuine mass enthusiasm at the end of the war was subsequently confused with reactions to its start. Many of the Liberal commentators on war enthusiasm were equally critical of the outbreak of jingoism on 11 November 1918. But celebrating the end of a war is obviously rather different in its meaning from celebrating the start.
22. *Hampstead Record*, 7 August 1914, p. 2. For similar comments regarding South London, see *South London Observer*, 5 August 1914, p. 5, and *Kentish Mercury*, 7 August 1914, p. 6.
23. *Manchester Guardian*, 3 August 1914, p. 8.
24. *Woolwich Herald*, 7 August 1914, p. 2.
25. *Islington Daily Gazette*, 4 August 1914, p. 2.
26. *Evening Standard*, 3 August 1914, p. 4.
27. *Daily Chronicle*, 3 August 1914, p. 6.

28. *Daily Herald*, 3 August 1914, p. 3; 4 August 1914, p. 2.
29. See *Daily News*, editorial by A. G. Gardiner, 'Why We Must Not Fight', 1 August 1914. For background see S. Koss, *Fleet Street Radical: A. G. Gardiner and the Daily News* (London, 1973).
30. Cited in Pearce, *Comrades in Conscience*, p. 229.
31. *John Bull*, 1 August 1914, cover and p. 11.
32. Cited in P. Esposito, 'Public Opinion and the Outbreak of the First World War: The Newspapers of Northern England', unpublished dissertation for MSt in Historical Research, Oxford, 1996, p. 17.
33. *Oxford Chronicle*, 31 July 1914, p. 7.
34. The derogatory term used for Liberal newspapers such as the *Daily News*, which were seen as promoting an unpatriotic agenda, derived from their proprietors' Quakerism. The split nature of the national press is brought out well in Thompson, *The 12 Days*, pp. 157–8.
35. For a full discussion of the complexities of the local press in Northern England in early August, see Esposito, 'Public Opinion', pp. 23–33. In 1915 the right-wing journalist Arnold White investigated this advertisement. The editor of the *Yorkshire Post* responded: 'I should certainly not have inserted the advertisement of the Neutrality League, had the decision rested with me. I have not the least idea who those responsible for it were, but as you remember there were a good many people in this country, up to the declaration of war, who took the view expressed in the advertisement.' Arnold White correspondence, letter dated 20 October 1915, WHI/117, National Maritime Museum.
36. Well illustrated in the papers of C. P. Scott, editor of the *Manchester Guardian*. Scott was first approached by J. A. Hobson to join a neutrality committee on 3 August; by 9 p.m. on the same day, Hobson admitted that war was now a fait accompli and suggested that the committee be reworked as a reconciliation committee. See T. Wilson (ed.), *The Political Diaries of C. P. Scott* (London, 1970), pp. 94–5. See also footnote comments on Norman Angell and the Neutrality League in Thompson, *The 12 Days*, pp. 193–4.
37. *Liverpool Post*, 4 August 1914, p. 7.
38. See H. Weinroth, 'Norman Angell and the Great Illusion: An Episode in Pre-1914 Pacifism', *Historical Journal* 17 (1974), pp. 551–75.
39. *Liverpool Daily Post*, 30 July 1914, p. 5.
40. *Eastern Daily Press*, 3 August 1914, p. 6.
41. *Leicester Daily Post*, 3 August 1914, p. 5.
42. *News of the World*, 2 August 1914, p. 10.
43. Diary of 'Anonymous London Woman, July–September 1914', Imperial War Museum.
44. W. H. Scott, *Leeds in the Great War* (Leeds, 1923), p. 6. Letter to *Yorkshire Post*, 4 August 1914, p. 4.
45. The frequently asserted opinion that the British people expected the war to be over by Christmas has very little foundation in contemporary sources. Prognostications on the war's length are actually quite rare in July and August 1914, either in public or in private; the few that do exist suggest that

the war was generally anticipated to last at least until the next year. For example, Harold Cousins's diary entry for 9 August 1914 reads: 'England now being involved in what will probably be known as the First World War of 1914 – probably 1915.' H. Cousins, diary, Microfilm, Imperial War Museum.

46. Pamphlet, *Bottomley's Battle Cry* (London, 1914).
47. *The Star*, 15 September 1914, p. 4.
48. *Abingdon Free Press*, 7 August 1914, p. 5. The following week an even older historical memory was evoked by the centenarian Emma Boyd, who 'spoke feelingly of the suffering that it would occasion, recalling the suffering that was rife during the Crimean Campaign'. *Abingdon Free Press*, 14 August 1914, p. 4.
49. *Hackney Spectator*, 7 August 1914, p. 1.
50. *Liverpool Daily Post*, 3 August 1914, p. 3.
51. *Hull Daily Mail*, 3 August 1914, p. 3.
52. *Cambridge Daily News*, 4 August 1914, p. 4.
53. R. L. Sawyer, *The Bowerchalke Parish Papers: Collett's Village Newspaper 1878–1924* (Gloucester, 1989).
54. *Islington Daily Gazette*, 6 August 1914, p. 5.
55. *Banbury Advertiser*, 6 August 1914, p. 6.
56. *Banbury Guardian*, 13 August 1914, p. 5. See also *Cambridge Daily News*, 4 August 1914, for Cambridge and District Free Church Council resolution against the war. *Yorkshire Post*, 4 August 1914, p. 7, carries a report of the Beeston Hill Baptist Men's Own Brotherhood resolution that they 'view with horror the terrible outrage to humanity and menacing challenge to Christianity involved in a European War'. It would be repetitious to cite the whole range of nonconformist churches, working men's clubs, trade union branches, friendly societies and so on who passed anti-war resolutions that weekend. On the same page of the *Yorkshire Post* for example is a resolution of the Kingston Unity of Oddfellows meeting in Ripon calling for reconciliation.
57. K. W. Clements, 'Baptists and the Outbreak of the First World War', in *Baptist Quarterly*, April 1975, pp. 74–92. J. M. McEwen (ed.), *The Riddell Diaries* (London, 1986), pp. 87–8, entry for 3 August 1914.
58. *Leicester Daily Post*, 3 August 1914, p. 6; *Daily Herald*, 1 August 1914, pp. 1, 7.
59. Pearce, *Comrades in Conscience*, p. 66.
60. *Birmingham Daily Post*, 3 August 1914, p. 3.
61. *Sheffield Daily Telegraph*, 4 August 1914, p. 5.
62. A. Bullock, *The Life and Times of Ernest Bevin*, vol. 1 (London, 1960), p. 45.
63. Pearce, *Comrades in Conscience*, p. 68.
64. *Islington Daily Gazette*, 5 August 1914, p. 4; *Daily Herald*, 3 August 1914, p. 3.
65. D. Boulton, *Objection Overruled* (London, 1967), p. 33.
66. *Kentish Mercury*, 7 August 1914, p. 7.
67. Strike call, *Daily Herald*, 29 July 1914, p. 5. Recriminations, 5 August 1914, p. 4.
68. A. Wiltsher, *Most Dangerous Women* (London, 1985), pp. 16–17, 22–3. See also M. Bondfield, *A Life's Work* (London, 1949), p. 142.
69. Wiltsher, *Most Dangerous Women*, p. 27.
70. There are numerous examples. One of the best is a letter from A. Simpson to the *Yorkshire Post*, 3 August 1914, p. 12: 'Russia stands for brute force; any

dominance by her in European affairs would be a setback for all the ideals of humanity.' Ben Tillett probably deserves the award for Russophobia when, on the platform of the Trafalgar Square Peace Meeting, he said, 'The whole career of the Russian Tsar is one of sordidness. Nero himself was never a worse destroyer than this man.' *Daily Herald*, 3 August 1914, p. 1.

71. *John Bull*, 8 August 1914, pp. 6–7. The full editorial is extraordinary: Horatio Bottomley clearly began writing it on or around 2 August 1914. The first half is a Catoesque call for the total destruction of Serbia, 'Serbia must be wiped out.' Halfway through, he changes tack to call for a pre-emptive strike to destroy the German Navy. He then ends (and bear in mind this edition of *John Bull* appeared after the declaration of war) with 'To Hell with Servia – God Save the King'.

72. Even the pro-war *Pall Mall Gazette* editorialised on 1 August 1914:

> There remains Germany. There have been times during recent years when the two nations have been full of rancour and suspicion towards each other. It is a cruel stroke of fate that they should have been brought face to face at the moment when ill-will appears to have abated … We believe that the Emperor WILLIAM and his advisers have laboured ardently for peace. If, as seems probable, their efforts have been overborne by forces beyond the control of man, why should we utter a word of bitterness towards them? We will not. If doomed, with heavy heart, but with firm and determined mind, to draw the sword, we will fight like gentlemen, respecting and honouring a knightly foe.

73. *Daily Herald*, 5 August 1914, p. 4.

74. This would not be surprising. When public opinion first started to be directly surveyed in the late 1930s in response to the Munich crisis, the gender division is firmly established. Women were twice as likely to favour appeasement than were men.

75. M. Stocks, *My Common Place Book* (London, 1970), cited in J. Marlow, *Virago Book of Women and the Great War* (London, 1998), pp. 23–4.

76. W. G. Gates, *Portsmouth in the Great War* (Portsmouth, 1919), p. 17; F. W. Longbottom, *Chester in the Great War* (Chester, 1920?), p. 2.

77. J. W. Rowson, *Bridport and the Great War* (London, 1923), p. 15.

78. J. H. Kennedy, *Attleborough in Wartime* (Norwich, 1920), p. 16.

79. *The Globe*, 5 August 1914, p. 5.

80. *Daily Herald*, 7 August 1914, p. 7.

81. Diary of Mrs Robb, Liddle Personal Experience Archive, Leeds University.

82. *East London Advertiser*, 22 August 1914, p. 3.

83. H. Cartmell, *For Remembrance* (Preston, 1919), p. 25.

84. *Eastern Daily Press*, 6 August 1914, p. 6.

85. *Woolwich Herald*, 7 August 1914, p. 2. This newspaper's political affiliation was Conservative.

86. *Daily Herald*, 7 August 1914, p. 5. See an interesting speculation on these lines regarding France in J. Cruickshank, *Variations on Catastrophe: Some French Responses to the Great War* (Oxford, 1982), pp. 7–8. Cruickshank draws on work by J. J. Becker and A. Philnonenko, *Essais sur la philosophie de la guerre* (Paris, 1976).

87. Scott, *Leeds*, p. 9.

88. Longbottom, *Chester*, p. 2; W. D. Bavin, *Swindon's War Record* (Swindon, 1922), p. 24.
89. *Daily Herald*, 6 August 1914, p. 1.
90. Bedfordshire County Record Office, SJ V II; Reports by Inspector Walter Parser, 7 November 1914, 10 February 1915; Anonymous letter, 15 February 1915.
91. *Daily Herald*, 10 August 1914, p. 5; 11 August 1914, pp. 5, 6.
92. *Daily Herald*, 10 August 1914, p. 5.
93. J. A. Lee, *Todmorden in the Great War* (Todmorden, 1922), p. 4. F. L. Carsten, *War against War: British and German Radical Movements in the First World War* (Berkeley, CA, 1982), pp. 26–8.
94. MacDonald wrote to the American socialist Laidler in November, 'there is nothing chauvinist or sordid about our intentions. It is a war for liberty and democracy as far as the man in the street is concerned.' Cited in Carsten, *War against War*, p. 29.
95. Thompson, *The 12 Days*, p. 214.
96. Cartmell, *For Remembrance*, p. 31.
97. R. Asquith, *The Volunteer and Other Poems* (London, 1916).
98. See A. Gregory, 'Lost Generations: The Impact of Military Service on Paris, London, and Berlin', in J. L. Robert and J. M. Winter, *Capital Cities at War, London, Paris, Berlin 1914–1919* (Cambridge, 1997), pp. 57–103.
99. Silbey, *British Working Class*, pp. 82–103.
100. For reporting and reaction see M. J. Farrar, *News from the Front: War Correspondents on the Western Front* (Stroud, 1998), pp. 17–22.
101. Louisa Harris Diary, Liddle Personal Experience Archive, Leeds University.
102. M. Pottle (ed.), *Champion Redoubtable: The Diaries and Letters of Violet Bonham Carter* (London, 1998), pp. 6–7. Her brother Raymond did enlist and was killed in 1916.
103. Both the facts and the interpretation presented here are drawn from Peter Simkins's magisterial and definitive account of voluntary recruitment. P. Simkins, *Kitchener's Army* (Manchester, 1988).
104. *Hackney Spectator*, 28 August 1914, p. 3. H. M. Walbrook, *Hove and the Great War* (Hove, 1920), p. 3.
105. A. Clark, *Echoes of the Great War: The Diary of The Reverend Andrew Clark 1914–1918*, (ed. James Munson Oxford, 1988), pp. 10–11.
106. E. H. Barkworth, Diary, Liddle Personal Experience Archive. Cricket enthusiasts seemed particularly prone to this. J. N. Pentelow, assistant editor of *The World Of Cricket* later remembered 3 August 1914 as a day 'tense with expectation, waiting to know the best or worst', and he was relieved when Jack Hobbs made 226 against Nottinghamshire. He had 'never a thought of the war'. N. Young, '"A Splendid Response"? County Cricket and the First World War', *Imperial War Museum Review* 12 (1999), pp. 36–47. The notebooks of Frank Lockwood at the Imperial War Museum show a similar spirit: a brief mention of the outbreak of war followed by a return to the serious business of chronicling the fortunes of the local cricket and bowls leagues.
107. *Islington Daily Gazette*, 31 October 1917.

108. E. Miles, *Untold Tales of Wartime London: A Personal Diary* (London, 1930), pp. 13–15. Children parading and playing war was unsurprisingly a common sight.

109. Ada Reece, Diary for 1914, Ada Reece papers, Liddle Personal Experience Archive, Leeds University.

110. *Eastern Daily Press*, 2 September 1914, p. 3. A similar incident involving a woman, whose son had been killed at Mons and who got drunk and threatened to kill the Kaiser, was widely reported in October. She was unrepentant before the magistrate: 'When I have killed the Kaiser I will give over drink', *The Scotsman*, 28 October 1914, p. 5. The role of alcohol in 'patriotic manifestations' is worth exploring. Some examples: a man was charged with being 'drunk and disorderly' on 11 August 1914 for climbing a statue in Leverington, according to *The Isle of Ely and Wisbech Advertiser*, 12 August 1914. At Hampstead Magistrates on 6 August 1914, a prisoner was fined for being 'drunk and incapable' after he got in a brawl, 'arguing the point about this here mobilisation', *Hampstead Record*, 7 August 1914. 'Quite a number of drunken charges came before the magistrates in which the prisoners pleaded they were seeing friends off to join the colours', *The Islington Daily Gazette*, 6 August 1914. The comments about drunken sendoffs for friends were widespread in accounts of mobilisation, and of course led in 1915 to the 'no treating order'. An exchange of letters between the Archbishop of Canterbury and Lord Sanderson, a church layman involved in temperance, provides more detail: Randall Davidson commented that he had had reports of public drunkenness, and also 'others to the effect that there has never been a time when the send off of regiments was so markedly sober'. Sanderson replied that both sets of accounts were correct: the formal sendoff of regiments had been 'quiet, orderly and self-controlled', but that the departure of individual reservists and Territorials to their depots had not.

> each one is at the centre of a group of relatives and friends and the leavetaking is marked by what in Scotland is called 'coviviality' ... and the impulse to patriotic jolifications strong ... One occasionally meets such parties in the street ... the result is that the father of the family has a bad headache and that the mother has to pawn the spare boots.

Sanderson nevertheless believed that, 'even of this there is less than on previous occasions', presumably meaning the Boer War. Cantuar to Sanderson, 17 August 1914; Sanderson to Cantuar, 18 August 1914: Davidson Papers 374/5, Lambeth Palace Library. The journal of C. R. Ashbee states on 7 August 1914, 'Patriotism manifests itself in the usual drunk way – Rule Britannia in Public Houses.' Ashbee is himself a good example of distinct lack of enthusiasm, his reaction on 5 August 1914: 'I woke this morning sobbing – or dreaming that I was sobbing – about the war with Germany. The whole thing is too horrible for words.' Ashbee Journals, King's College, Cambridge.

111. C. Playne, *The Pre-War Mind* (London, 1928), p. 381.

112. *Islington Daily Gazette*, 6 August 1914, p. 3.

113. Justin McCarthy, 'Armageddon', *War Songs from the Daily Chronicle* (London, 1914), p. 32.

114. *Daily Herald*, 10 August 1914, p. 5; 15 August 1914, p. 4.
115. M. Ceadel, *Thinking about Peace and War* (Oxford, 1987).
116. Wilson, *The Political Diaries of Scott*, p. 95.
117. Cited in S. E. Cooper, *Patriotic Pacifism: Waging War on War in Europe 1815–1914* (Oxford, 1991), p. 188.
118. *Evening News*, 29 July 1914, p. 4.
119. Ponsonby Papers, Bodleian Library, MS. Eng. Hist. C.661, Letter from Barbara Hammond to Arthur Ponsonby. Ponsonby's papers are full of Liberal criticism of his anti-war stance. A constituency meeting on 26 October 1914 reported by William Donaldson shows how isolated Ponsonby was, even within his own core support, 'there was no sympathy expressed with your views regarding the current crisis'. Even more damning is a letter from Vaughan Nash on 6 December 1914: 'It isn't pleasant to have been hopelessly wrong in one's judgements and to have to own up that the Daily Mail and the Music Halls were in the main right.' Ponsonby did not accept that, and, as will be shown in the next chapter, he would get his revenge.
120. Cited in Willis, *Holy War*, p. 179.
121. Letter to *The Times*, 10 August 1914. My attention was first drawn to this by S. Wallace, *War and the Image of Germany* (Edinburgh, 1988), which is full of similar examples. Most of the academic signatories of the neutrality appeal quickly renounced it once the war had broken out.

CHAPTER 2

1. R. Sidebotham, *Hyde in Wartime* (Hyde, 1916), p. 95.
2. The full story of the 'blackening' of British propaganda would require a chapter, perhaps even a book in itself.
3. See H. Lasswell, *Propaganda Technique in World War* (Cambridge, MA, 1927; 1972), p. 80. Northcliffe's incessant pre-war Germanophobia made him an obvious target. The degree of hatred Northcliffe generated in Germany is hard to overstate. Baron Von Jagow, the German Secretary of Foreign Affairs, considered him responsible for the war and wanted him shot. See S. J. Taylor, *The Great Outsiders* (London, 1992), p. 143.
4. Some worth mentioning are: N. Hiley, 'Sir Hedley Le Bas and the Origins of Domestic Propaganda in Britain', *Journal of Advertising History* 10 (1987), pp. 30–46; A. G. Marquis, 'Words as Weapons: Propaganda in Britain and Germany during the First World War', *Journal of Contemporary History* 13 (1978), pp. 467–98; N. Reeves, *Official British Film Propaganda during the First World War* (London, 1986); M. L. Sanders and P. Taylor, *British Propaganda during the First World War* (London, 1982); D. G. Wright, 'The Great War, Propaganda and British Men of Letters 1914–16', *Literature and History* 7 (1978), pp. 70–100.
5. Unsurprisingly, as it turns out, there is no such diary at the Imperial War Museum. When Philip Knightley inquired about it, the museum supposedly told him that they thought it might have been in a box of intelligence materials which was taken back 'on second thoughts'. P. Knightley,

The First Casualty (London, 1975), p. 106n. It is equally likely that it never existed.

6. A. Ponsonby, *Falsehood in Wartime* (London, 1928), pp. 102–13. Given the propensity of this book to 'disappear' from libraries, I am very grateful to Dr John Stevenson for lending me his copy. The Charteris denial is actually rather credible; certainly more credible than the American press accounts.

7. S. Sassoon, *The War Poems* (London, 1983), p. 54.

8. Diary of Harold Cousins, 12 July 1916, Microfilm, Imperial War Museum. This can be further pushed back as far as 1914: a report in *The Scotsman* on 9 November 1914, reprinting a story in the *Telegraaf*, states that the bodies of German soldiers in 'bundles of four' were being sent to Louvain for cremation. A process of continual elaboration is clearly occurring.

9. Indeed a cartoon of German corpses being used for the manufacture of glycerine appears in Louis Raemakers, *Cartoon History of the War*, published in 1916. This story also appears in *John Bull* in July 1916, after Cousins had written his entry.

10. For the sake of completeness it is necessary to mention a rather bizarre contribution to this debate by S. Rubinstein, *German Atrocity or British Propaganda. The Seventieth Anniversary of a Scandal: German Corpse Utilization Establishments in the First World War* (Jerusalem, 1987). Rubinstein contests that the 'corpse exploitation' establishments *did* exist. He traces the origin of the Charteris story to an article by Bertrand Russell in a volume: F. H. Hooper (ed.), *These Eventful Years* (London, 1924). Rubinstein asserts that Charteris was referring to this accusation anecdotally in his speech the next year. The absence of *any* reliable evidence from the German side to support the idea that these establishments were real, completely undermines Rubinstein's claim. We will never know how the story got started. My best guess is based on the workings of the 'trench mind': a world of rumour. One possible explanation is based on the timing of Cousins's testimony. The disturbing disparity between visible British corpses after the first day of the Somme, and the near absence of German dead on many parts of the front, would clearly have bothered the troops. A folkloric explanation as to where the German bodies had gone was a way of dealing with the disastrous mismatch.

A second possibility was suggested by C. E. Montague in his book, *Disenchantment* (London, 1922). He recounts in 1918 entering a German dugout where the British bombardment had killed the inhabitants and the blast had led to the bodies ending up in a 'Field Cauldron'. Such a scene might well have been witnessed earlier in the war.

A third possibility is that this was an example of black humour amongst German troops which somehow got transmitted to the British. It is not difficult to see how grumbles about exploitation and ersatz products could give rise to such a story.

It could also have been started by an angry Belgian or French civilian to demoralise the German soldiers, or by an unknown and rather sick 'satirist' in the British Army. The story could also originate with a combination of several of the above. Once it started, its transmission could be guaranteed both amongst those who believed it and those who didn't (like Sassoon), but who enjoyed telling it.

11. R. Graves, *Goodbye to All That* (London, 1929), p. 61. Graves in turn becomes a 'source' (in a way that doubtless would have amused him). Some of the most influential academics writing on the war have accepted this story. Jay Winter cites the story from Graves: see for example J. M. Winter, *The Experience of World War One* (London, 1988), p. 168. See also J. Terraine, *The Smoke and the Fire* (London, 1980), p. 32, and P. Fussell, *The Great War and Modern Memory* (London, 1975).

12. The full story of this invention can be found in J. Morgan Read, *Atrocity Propaganda* (New Haven, CT, 1941), p. 25. This author was clearly not a particular sympathiser with the Entente cause, but he maintained academic scruples in checking the veracity of well-known atrocity stories on all sides.

13. Ponsonby, *Falsehood in Wartime*, pp. 25–6.

14. I have concentrated my description on the most notoriously Germanophobe (and biggest-selling) daily newspaper which has, unthinkingly, been assumed to be the worst atrocity-monger. There may well be a case for arguing that when it came to atrocities it was in fact the *Liberal* press which was worst. It was the *Daily News* which printed the story of the 'Foulest crime in three centuries', of a 2-year-old child being bayoneted and carried away impaled, on 13 May 1915. For this and other gruesome examples from the same paper, see Terraine, *The Smoke and the Fire*, p. 30. Ponsonby conspicuously does not mention examples of such stories carried in the Liberal press, his allies by the mid-1920s. The nastiest rhetoric, if not the worst stories, came from the gutter press of the time, in particular *John Bull*. Bottomley tried to popularise the term 'Germ-Huns'.

15. The contemporary and literal translation of the German term *Shrecklichkeit*. To a modern reader 'frightfulness' sounds rather twee. To understand the way it was used at the time, it is useful to substitute the term 'terrorism'.

16. A. Kramer and J. Horne, *German Atrocities in 1914: Meanings and Memories of War* (Cambridge, 2000), p. 20. Horne and Kramer use both Belgian and German testimony throughout.

17. The Belgian Government had explicitly instructed civilians not to take up arms against the Germans.

18. Knightley, *The First Casualty*, p. 83. Knightley certainly does not apply these excuses to American troops in Vietnam. At its worst in 1914, the German Army anticipated its behaviour in the Second World War, and indeed the advancing German Army in the West in 1940 actually behaved *better* than it had twenty-six years previously.

19. For obvious reasons of access, the British press did not take the lead in reporting these stories.

20. See B. Nasson, *The South African War 1899–1902* (London, 1999), for a balanced discussion. P. Scholliers and F. Daelemans, 'Standards of Living and Standards of Health in Wartime Belgium', in J. M. Winter and R. Wall (eds), *The Upheaval of War: Family Work and Welfare in Europe* (Cambridge, 1988), pp. 139–58.

21. Caroline Playne, *Society at War* (London, 1931), p. 286.

22. Cate Haste, *Keep the Home Fires Burning* (London, 1977), pp. 83–4.
23. For an entertaining account of the background, see S. J. Taylor, *The Great Outsiders: Northcliffe, Rothermere and the Daily Mail* (London, 1992).
24. *Daily Mail*, 6 August 1914.
25. *Daily Mail*, 12 August 1914, p. 3.
26. Even Taylor, who is rather pro-Northcliffe, slips up here, stating that early reports of German atrocities in the *Daily Mail* would 'all turn out to be false'. Taylor, *Great Outsiders*, p. 146.
27. Ten Belgians reported shot, *Daily Mail*, 14 August 1914; 'Outrages by Uhlans' reporting the massacre of eighteen civilians, *Daily Mail*, 17 August 1914.
28. *Daily Mail*, 22 August 1914.
29. 'The recoil of the mailed fist: Psychological secret of German Brutality', *Daily Mail*, 24 August 1914.
30. Robert Roberts's childhood impression was that 'the first atrocity stories appeared in the second week'. *Classic Slum*, p. 188.
31. 'German Savageries', *Daily Mail*, 26 August 1914. Stories of deliberate sadistic mutilation are probably generally untrue (although occasional incidents should not be ruled out). Misinterpretation of the results of accidental civilian casualties suffering the terrible wounds inflicted by modern weaponry may lie behind some of these stories. Rape is perhaps a more contentious issue. Post-war investigation uncovered very few cases of rape committed by the German Army in 1914 (although it should be noted there were some 'confirmed'). But a certain degree of caution should also be ascribed to the validity of 'post-war' investigation. Rape is notoriously an under-reported crime. The assumption that every woman raped by a German soldier in 1914 would willingly give evidence to that effect *six years afterwards* seems deeply flawed, particularly in a country with a strong socially conservative and Roman Catholic ethos. Thus whilst accounts of rape in 1914 are almost certainly much exaggerated, it seems likely that the incidence of rape measured after the war would be prone to understatement. Some of these methodological problems were already apparent in 1914. On 5 October 1914, the *Daily Mail* quotes from the Belgium Commission:

In Aerschot as everywhere, many assaults on women and girls have taken place. But on this particular point, any inquiries met with great difficulties as the victims pointed out by public rumour and their relatives generally oppose complete silence to any question put to them.

In 1914 the choice was to believe the rumours. After 1920 the rumours were discounted. But the issue highlighted remains. Men at war commit rape. Angry soldiers in a hostile country faced by apparent civilian resistance are even more prone to do so. It would be incredible if there weren't a significant number of cases in Belgium in 1914. The report from Aerschot of the murder of civilian males is substantially correct.

32. *Daily Mail*, 5 September 1914.
33. See also, *Daily Mail*, 1 December 1914: 'Human life to them is nothing and animals are worse than nothing. At Louvain I saw a motor car with two

German officers in it run over a dog. The officers did not so much as look round.' The Hun at his most evil. Curiously, later in the war the *Daily Mail* would take up cudgels against the over-indulgence of dogs in wartime and meet a good deal of popular resistance. For example one of Northcliffe's wartime bulletins on 1 December 1916 read: 'The most important item of war news today is the opening of the pet dog show at Lambeth Baths ... It is a sin to have a dog show in wartime. The dogs will consume 500lbs of meat a day. The whole thing is a waste of time.' Northcliffe Bulletins, 1 December 1916, Mss Eng. Hist. Bodleian Library d. 303.

34. Pictures could be and were faked (or recaptioned). Because they were so much in demand, there was every incentive to do so. We will probably never know how many photographs of natural disasters such as the Messina earthquake or 'Balkan war' were recycled in August and September 1914. I do not believe that the *Daily Mail* deliberately foisted fake photographs on the public, but it clearly had quite a number foisted upon it. A letter on 12 October 1914 from an indignant reader points out that a photograph of a 'Zeppelin Bomb' was a pirated pamphlet photograph of his own design!

35. Much later in the war, Elizabeth Fernside would reach for this analogy to minimise the impact of a Gotha raid in a letter to her son: 'lorries loaded with broken glass ... it is *marvellous* to me how they miss every time & only do what the suffragettes were laughed at for doing, smash windows.' Elizabeth Fernside to Fred Fernside, 22 October 1917, Imperial War Museum. The Suffragettes were laughed at, but their 'vandalism' was also taken seriously.

36. In reality 'only' 12% of the buildings in Leuven were destroyed. The spelling 'Pompey' rather than 'Pompeii' is original.

37. The distant origins rest in a speech given by the Kaiser on despatching troops to deal with the Boxer Rebellion urging them to leave behind a memory in China like the 'Huns of old'.

38. An image that would be echoed precisely in Kipling's poem, 'For all we have and are'.

39. It was the destruction of Louvain which was the specific occasion of Kipling's poem.

40. Although the Dirk Bouts altarpiece 'The Last Supper' survived. Ponsonby makes great play of the false claim that it was destroyed, crediting the Germans for saving it. An appropriate analogy might be King's College Chapel being deliberately burnt down and praising the culprits for saving the Rubens. A. Ponsonby, *Falsehood in Wartime* (London, 1928), p. 83.

41. N. Maclean, *The Great Discovery* (Glasgow, 1915), p. 39. Louvain had a specific, albeit ambiguous, resonance for the English as it had been a centre of operations for Roman Catholic missionaries directed against Reformation England. As such it had a particular place in the heart of English Catholics. (But also, by implication, a particular place in the demonology of hardcore Protestants.) This raises some interesting questions. One feature of the war was the reinforcing of a rapprochement with Catholicism amongst intellectuals. (Already evident in some cases prior to 1914.)

42. Much of this is drawn from M. Derz, 'The Flames of Louvain: The War Experience of an Academic Community', in H. Cecil and P. Liddle (eds),

Facing Armageddon: The First World War Experienced (London, 1988), pp. 617–29. Also, S. Wallace, *War and the Image of Germany* (Edinburgh, 1988).

43. For an interesting discussion of this issue, see N. Lambourne, 'First World War Propaganda and the Abuse of Historic Monuments on the Western Front', *Imperial War Museum Review* 12, (1999), pp. 96–108. Lambourne demonstrates that many photographs of Rheims gave a misleading impression of the destruction by foregrounding destroyed houses in the vicinity of the Cathedral. Taylor points out that the photograph of Rheims Cathedral before 'destruction' was the first ever whole-page picture printed in the *Daily Mail*. See Taylor, *Great Outsiders*, illustration facing p. 146, p. 150.

44. *Daily Mail*, 21 September 1914. Note the translation of *Kultur*. The *Daily Mail* had an editorial policy against unfamiliar foreign words. It presumably begins to appear untranslated when it was deemed to be familiar.

45. A. Clark, 'English Words in Wartime', Bodleian Library, Oxford, Eng. Misc. Mss. 266, 267.

46. The real 'falsehoods' perpetrated by the *Daily Mail* at this time are the reprinting of wildly over-optimistic official communiqués about the course of the fighting.

47. To use a contemporary journalist's example:

> Investigators said survivors suffer severe stress and often unconsciously overestimate the size of crowds and number of bodies. In Rwanda far fewer victims than survivors described were found in graves. Some exaggeration is conscious.
>
> Several Muslim men interviewed for the book appeared to have made up accounts of atrocities or exaggerated them. None of their stories were used. Hurem Suljic, Mevludin Oric and other survivors may have overestimated the number of victims, but the overwhelming amount of physical evidence found at the sites corroborated the account of a mass execution. (D. Rohde, *A Safe Area. Srebenica: Europe's Worst Massacre since the End of the Second World War* (London, 1997), p. 348)

At the time of writing Rohde reports that 650 bodies had been found out of 7,079 missing Bosnian men. This is a good example of the problem. The perpetrators are hardly going to facilitate investigation in such cases, the verifiable death toll independent of refugee testimony is very small, but refugees exaggerate.

48. The reference is specifically to the village of Tamines. In the graveyard at Tamines there are 384 gravestones inscribed '1914: Fusilés par les Allemands'. See B. Tuchman, *August 1914* (1962; reprinted London, 1994), p. 307.

49. The actual figure for Dinant alone was 612. The chronology was more or less correct.

50. The most manifestly untrue statement about German atrocities in Belgium appeared in the American press on 3 September 1914: the famous declaration of five prominent American journalists (Roger Lewis, Irwin Cobb, Harry Hansen, James O'Donnell Bennet and John McCutcheon), after they had been given an escorted tour by the German army. 'We are not able to report

one case of undeserved punishment or measure of retribution. We are neither able to confirm any rumours as regards maltreatment of prisoners and non-combatants.' To which one is tempted to reply: 'Of course not, you weren't supposed to.'

An indication of the standards being applied in this shameful statement should include: 'A citizen was shot in Merbes-le-Château, but nobody could prove his innocence.' That a citizen of a nation which had just undergone an unprovoked invasion could be shot if he was unable to prove his innocence to the occupying army demonstrates the extent to which these journalists were repeating the official German line. This is cited (inevitably) by Ponsonby, *Falsehood in Wartime*, p. 130.

Philip Knightley states that none of these journalists ever retracted the story and then, without noticing the blatant contradiction, states that Irwin Cobb gave it as his opinion that only about 10% of atrocity stories were true. Knightley, *First Casualty*, p. 120. In any case it is not strictly true that there were no retractions. Harry Hansen later stated: 'Ironically enough, it became my task weeks later to report the shooting of civilians at Tamines and various acts of violence ... although I helped provide the Germans with a choice bit of propaganda for neutral countries, I never believed in their complete innocence.' *New York World*, 8 February 1929.

51. *Daily Mail*, 18 September 1914.
52. *Daily Mail*, 8 January 1915.
53. 'When the Germans Invade: By a Belgian', *Daily Mail*, 3 November 1914.
54. *The Passing Show*, 20 March 1915, p. 12.
55. J. M. N. Jeffries, *Front Everywhere* (London, 1930), pp. 124–5. This can be contrasted with the Ponsonby story of 'The Baby of Courbeck Loo', the supposed story of a *Daily Mail* journalist inventing an orphaned child and the *Daily Mail* collecting donations for it, which as far as I can see is another complete fiction.
56. Jeffries, *Front Everywhere*, p. 124.
57. E. M. Bilsborough, 'Diary, partly written up later', Imperial War Museum. By contrast, Harold Cousins cynically noted: 'The newspapers are full of the seasoned narratives of eyewitnesses. Most of the casualties seem to have been caused by people coming out into the streets to see the fun.' H. Cousins, Diary, 17 December 1914, Imperial War Museum.
58. *Evening News*, 19 December 1914, p. 4.
59. *Daily Mail*, 17 December 1914.
60. *Daily Mail*, 17 December 1914. It goes on to give five motives.
61. F. Miller, *The Hartlepools during the Great War* (Hartlepool, 1920), p. 88.
62. Miller, *The Hartlepools*, pp. 88–107.
63. Pope is remembered, if at all, as the bête noire of Siegfried Sassoon and Wilfred Owen later in the war. Pope's versification was frequently dire, but as a guide to popular mentality, bad poetry is often better than good.
64. Cited I. Willis, *England's Holy War* (London, 1928), p. 186. There was a noticeable increase in recruiting after Scarborough.
65. In reporting the Battle of Dogger Bank just over a month later, when one of the German battle cruisers that had shelled the east coast was sunk, the *Daily*

Mail editorial was entitled 'Rout of the Babykillers': *Daily Mail*, 25 January 1915.

66. *Daily Mail*, 27 March 1915, p. 5. Even on 9 July 1915 the *Daily Mail* has a small headline, 'Refugee English women well treated by Germans.'

67. See *Daily Mail*, editorial on 25 September 1914: 'As we have had frequent cause to complain of German misconduct on land and sea, it is satisfactory to be able to state that German cruiser captains have behaved to their victims as officers and gentlemen should.'

68. This was not hypocrisy: the view was consistent. Commenting on the use of a false flag by the German raider *Emden*, it was noted that 'The use of a false flag is a ruse distinctly permitted.' *Daily Express*, 31 October 1914, p. 4.

69. It is no coincidence that one of the most heated debates in the autumn of 1914 was whether 'German' music should still be publicly performed. Concert-goers frequently pointed out that without German composers the musical repertoire would be distinctly second-rate.

70. *Daily Mail*, editorial, 4 February 1915.

71. *Daily Mail*, 13 October 1914. It is worth noting that the raid being commented on saw the deaths of three French non-combatants, all of whom were in fact adult males. The association of non-combatant with 'women and children' was reflexive. Was this the whining of a technologically inferior power? Would the British have used similar methods if they had been able to? In one case we can answer reasonably confidently in the negative. The British did have aircraft capable of dropping bombs on Germany. British air raids in 1914–1915 were emphatically not directed at civilians. The submarine question is unanswerable, since the British simply had no need or real opportunity to use these methods against German shipping at the outset. However, in the summer of 1915, British submarines began operating against German merchant shipping in the Baltic. It appears that these British submarines operated by 'cruiser' rules; in other words surface attacks with proper warning. Neutral shipping was stopped and searched, and taken as prizes if carrying contraband. See P. Halpern, *A Naval History of the First World War* (Los Angeles, CA, 1994), pp. 202–3.

72. *Daily Mail*, 26 April 1915.

73. The most famous book about the *Lusitania* is C. Simpson, *The Lusitania* (London, 1972). Underwater archaeology has to some degree extended our understanding. The liner clearly split apart and sank very quickly. Was this a boiler room explosion (as many believed at the time, including the U-boat commander), or a secondary explosion of an additional secret load of munitions, as Simpson argues? Attention has tended to focus on this issue, which in my view is a red herring. See below. See also T. A. Bailey and P. B. Ryan, *The Lusitania Disaster* (New York, 1975).

74. The principal defence of the German action has been that the *Lusitania* was carrying munitions and sinking it was therefore justifiable on the grounds that the action saved the lives of German combatants. There is a real danger of anachronistic confusion here: this argument, which was essentially the argument for the destruction of whole cities by bombing during the Second World War, climaxing with Hiroshima and Nagasaki, was not deemed morally

acceptable in 1915 by any nation other than Germany. It is however flawed on other grounds. One is proportionality. The precise munition load of the *Lusitania* was deliberately obscured. But even on the crudest utilitarian level the action would only be 'justified' if the *Lusitania* was carrying enough munitions to kill more than 1,200 German soldiers. This is immensely unlikely, bordering on impossible. (By 1915 the quantities of munitions required to kill a single soldier were very large.)

75. *Daily Mail*, full back page, 1 January 1915. Entitled 'The wonders of science'. Perhaps the most 'classic' propaganda image that the paper ever printed. P. M. Yearsley in 'The Home Front' refers to it as the *Daily Mail*'s finest cartoon and that 'the only adverse comment I heard upon it was that it was unduly harsh on the chimpanzee'. P. M. Yearsley, 'The Home Front' Imperial War Museum, Misc/17, p. 50. Yearsley, writing up his account in the 1930s, was still a firm believer in 'Hun atrocities' despite 'Germanophiles who have denied them'.

76. *The Passing Show*, 15 May 1915, p. 13.

77. F. W. Wile, 'The German Murder Instinct'. His figures are: Germany (1897–1907), 350 murders, 9,381 rapes, 178,115 illegitimate children; England (1900–1910), 97 murders, 218 rapes, 37,041 illegitimate children. Although not total nonsense, the figures are seriously decontextualised. Ironically one of the major long-running stories in the paper at the time was the coverage of the trial of the notorious English serial-killer George Joseph Smith of 'brides in the bath' fame (see for example the *Daily Mail*, 2 July 1915, p. 2). Is an acid bath intrinsically less shocking than a sausage machine?

78. *The Passing Show*, 15 May 1915, pp. 10–11.

79. In a search for ironies, the diminution of atrocity stories in significance from the summer of 1915 should be noted. It was precisely at this time that the worst single atrocity of the war was being committed by the Central Powers: the Armenian genocide undertaken by the Turkish governement. The result of a year of demonising Germany was that this event was underplayed and fundamentally misunderstood. It was presented as a German-instigated (or -inspired) atrocity, which it wasn't. The British Goverment did encourage an official inquiry, which for all its propaganda use, is still a fundamental document of the genocide, and the Armenian events were noted in passing. But the shock value of systematic extermination was clearly lessened by earlier atrocity stories.

80. Ada MacGuire to Eva MacGuire, 6 October 1914, Imperial War Museum. Eva had clearly been reading the accusations and counter-accusations in the American press.

81. Ada MacGuire to Eva MacGuire, 11 October 1914, Imperial War Museum. Clearly a story was doing the rounds in Cheshire: in a speech in Hyde on 28 September 1914, Dr Hulme referred to mutilated children and raped women, 'recounted by an actual eyewitness'. Sidebotham, *Hyde*, p. 15.

82. A. Clark, *Echoes of the Great War* (Oxford, 1988), p. 26.

83. Clark, *Echoes of the Great War*, pp. 32–3. On 8 December 1914 Clark recounts another atrocity story: 'Metcalf brought some items of war gossip. Mr Metcalf does dentistry for Belgian convalescents. Other Belgians have told him that

over and over again they have passed the decapitated bodies of children lying by the roadside.'

84. Terraine, in a discussion of atrocity stories, states: 'Generally speaking, such effusions gain credibility with distance from the battle front.' But, he continues: 'Nevertheless it was a soldier who perpetrated one of the most blood-curdling stories of all.' Terraine goes on to detail a story of a little girl mutilated and hung from a butcher's hook, which was told in a 1916 account of the retreat from Mons by Major A. Corbett-Smith of the Royal Field Artillery. Terraine, as an historian of the retreat, was well aware that no town was retaken by the British Army on 26 August 1914 as Corbett-Smith claimed. Similar examples can be found in a Leicester soldier's letter cited in F. B. Armitage, *Leicester 1914–18* (Leicester, 1933), pp. 78–9, and one from a Todmorden soldier in J. A. Lee, *Todmorden in the Great War* (Todmorden, 1922), p. 113. Where I would differ from Terraine is in his trust in the soldier's general truthfulness; unfortunately for his case, his evidence that soldiers did not believe in atrocities rests heavily on Graves's recounting of the Antwerp story. See Terraine, *The Smoke and the Fire*, pp. 31–3. For contrasting evidence see the gleeful recounting of the 'corpse-rendering' story in the *5th Gloucester Gazette*.

85. *Evening News*, 3 October 1914, p. 3.

86. *Wartime Tips for Soldiers and Civilians* (London, 1914), p. 73.

87. 'Saml. Pepys Jun. esq.', *A Diary of the Great Warr* [*sic*] (London, 1918).

88. Marshall Steele, 'Those Russians', *War Songs of the Daily Chronicle* (London, 1914).

89. Many thanks to my student Thomas Boghardt for this information.

90. W. L. B. Towers, Diary, Imperial War Museum.

91. Another example can be found in Yearsley, 'The Home Front', p. 27 and p. 33.

92. See, for example, J. Lee Thompson, *Politicians, Press and Propaganda: Lord Northcliffe and the Great War 1914–1919* (Kent, OH, 1999), pp. 29–32.

93. See M. Macdonagh, *London during the Great War* (London, 1935), pp. 21–2. Macdonagh (a journalist working for *The Times*) published an edited version of his wartime diary.

94. The Angels of Mons are another good case in point. The 'origin' of this story is usually attributed to the short story by Arthur Machen, 'The Bowmen', published in the *Evening News* a month after the battle. See A. Machen, *The Bowmen and Other Legends of the War* (New York, 1915). But Machen's claim of 'authorship' was disputed in 1915 by Harold Begbie. See H. Begbie, *On the Side of the Angels* (London, 1915). See the discussion, making a slightly different point, in J. M. Winter, *Sites of Memory, Sites of Mourning* (Cambridge, 1995), pp. 67–8. But note the comments on this by Terraine. In a letter included in the memoirs of Brigadier General Charteris (once again), it is stated that the story of 'Angels' was already commonplace in the BEF by 5 September, three weeks before Machen's story was published. A story of friendly ghostly horsemen appears in the *Evening News*, two weeks before Machen's story. Terraine believes that it was a story which was generated as reassurance amongst the exhausted men of the BEF. See Terraine, *The Smoke and the Fire*, pp. 17–19.

95. There are some good examples in Ponsonby, *Falsehood in Wartime*, pp. 152–60. But Ponsonby draws the moral, 'As the public mind is always impressed by anything that appears in print, the influence of the Press, in inflaming one people against the other must have been very considerable', p. 160. The idea that the public were misleading the press is too uncomfortable for him!

96. T. Wilson, *The Myriad Faces of War* (Oxford, 1986), pp. 190–1.

97. Gary Messinger in his discussion of Bryce seems to be in two minds about this. He extends Wilson's contextualisation argument much further with biographical speculation about Bryce and his motives. But he concludes: 'Whether by intention or by accident, the report disseminated half truths which all participants knew in advance would accrue unfairly to the advantage of the British cause.' This seems a mild condemnation compared to what follows: 'In any case, they were either unwilling or unable to acknowledge, let alone apologise for, the huge untruths they nurtured with aid from the vast resources of the state.' It is strange how half-truths become huge untruths in the space of a paragraph. Messinger's book is both interesting and flawed. He does a very good job of examining the motivations of individual propagandists involved in 'state propaganda', but this very framework replicates the traditional errors in understanding. There is an over-emphasis on lying and invention in the deliberate actions of individual agents and a massive overestimation of the role of the state. See G. Messinger, *British Propaganda and the State in the First World War* (Manchester, 1992), pp. 70–84.

98. Ponsonby, *Falsehood in Wartime*, p. 18. Ponsonby's argument, probably unconsciously, reflects precisely the German wartime position: killing civilians is morally superior to lying about civilians being killed.

99. A favoured defence on this point is that the British blockade was silently starving German children at the same time. This would require a very long exegesis. Certainly German propaganda made the claim, although it was notoriously inconsistent in claiming simultaneously that the blockade was barbarously starving non-combatants and that it was utterly ineffective. The basic fact is that in 1915 the infant mortality rate in Germany did not increase significantly. Later in the war the impact of blockade almost certainly did kill children, and the continuation of the blockade after the Armistice in 1918 to force Germany to sign the peace could certainly be described as at the least a severe humanitarian failing, even as an atrocity. But it can be said with some confidence that, at the moment the torpedoes slammed into the *Lusitania*, the Royal Navy had not killed any German babies. A similar point could be made about bombing and bombardment. The argument has been made that the 1915 and 1916 bombings of Karlsruhe, when large numbers of German civilians including children were killed, demonstrates moral equivalence. This misses the point that the raids on Germany, then and in 1918, were retaliatory. Attacks on civilian targets had been carried out by the German armed forces from the first days of the war. By the time that Karlsruhe was first raided (actually by the French), 183 British civilians had been killed by German bombardments and 705 wounded. (And of course more than a thousand had been killed at sea.)

It would have been far better for the twentieth century if the degeneration into 'total war' had been avoided; if Britain had decided to stick to the moral high ground regarding the murder of non-combatants. But the German military were the initiators of the process.

100. Another implicit misconception is that evil press barons were inventing lurid stories in order to boost circulation and therefore profits. The truth is that the press was a desperately unprofitable business in wartime with escalating costs (reportage, paper, labour) and declining advertising revenues. Furthermore Northcliffe at least saw his wartime activities as genuinely patriotic rather than profiteering. By 1917, as the paper shortage was biting, he was actually trying to reduce the circulation of his newspapers. One of the most fascinating comments in press history can be found in an in-house memo of 17 March 1917 from Northcliffe to his staff: 'The sale continues to be obdurately too high.' Northcliffe Bulletins, Mss Eng. Hist. d. 303, Bodleian Library.

101. Clipping, *Evening News*, 10 October 1914, p. 2. Comment, Clark, 'English Words in Wartime', vol. viii. Bodleian, Eng. Misc. Mss e. 272.

102. Equally the Lord Chamberlain's office prevented negative portrayals of the Kaiser on the London stage until August 1915. In the end popular pressure lifted the rule. L. J. Collins, *Theatre at War* (London, 1998), p. 196, p. 199.

CHAPTER 3

1. *The Passing Show*, cover, 5 June 1915.
2. *The Passing Show*, 15 May 1915.
3. G. Moorehouse, *Hells Foundations: A Town, Its Myths and Gallipoli* (London, 1992), p. 86.
4. *Evening News*, 10 October 1914, p. 4. M. Macdonagh, *London during the War* (London, 1935), Diary entry 16 December 1914, p. 44.
5. Cited in G. DeGroot, *Blighty: British Society in the Era of the Great War* (London, 1923), p. 228; W. H. Scott, *Leeds in the Great War* (Leeds, 1923), p. 23.
6. D. Birley, *Playing the Game: Sport and the British 1910–45* (Manchester, 1995), p. 72.
7. See C. Veitch, '"Play Up! Play Up! and Win the War!": Football, the Nation and the First World War', *Journal of Contemporary History* 20 (1985), pp. 363–78.
8. See N. Oliver, *Not Forgotten* (London, 2005), pp. 232–4.
9. Birley, *Playing the Game*, p. 74, pp. 96–9. J. Fuller, *Troop Morale in the British and Dominion Armies 1914–1918* (Oxford, 1991), pp. 85–92.
10. See Birley, *Playing the Game*, pp. 68–9. Longbottom, *Chester*, p. 7.
11. L. J. Collins, *The Theatre at War* (London, 1998), pp. 5–32.
12. The largest was the Indian Army 1939–1945.
13. For a revealing description which makes this analogy, see C. Kernahan, *Experiences of a Recruiting Officer* (London, 1915). For extensive discussions of motivation for enlistment, see P. Simkins, *Kitchener's Army* (Manchester, 1980), and D. Silbey, *The British Working Class and Enthusiasm for War* (London, 2005).

14. Speech on 4 January 1915, Sidebotham, *Hyde*, p. 23.
15. H. Bottomley, 'The Art of Recruiting', *John Bull*, 27 March 1915, pp. 6–7.
16. R. Farrow, Undated letter, Imperial War Museum.
17. For example, P. G. Simmonds and F. H. Keeling described in C. Playne, *Society at War* (London, 1930), pp. 60–3.
18. Clark, 'English Words', Bodleian Library, Eng. Misc. Mss e. 266, p. 1011. Clark's handwriting is a little unclear – it might conceivably read 'feminines'. The comment appears to have been written in 1915. See also, Macdonagh, 6 October 1915, pp. 79–80, which is equally scathing.
19. Clark, 'English Words', Mss e. 278, under a clipping: '5 questions to those who employ Male Servants'. Clark himself employed a gardener whom he was reluctant to release.
20. H. Cartmell, *For Remembrance* (Preston, 1919), p. 40.
21. Cartmell, *Remembrance*, p. 43.
22. *The Scotsman*, 7 December 1914, p. 11.
23. K. W. Mitchinson, *Gentlemen and Officers: The Impact and Experience of War on a Territorial Regiment* (London, 1995). Bottomley criticised the recruiting advertisements for the 'clerks company' of the 8th Battalion Northamptonshire Regiment: 'Snobbery is not yet killed or even scotched.' *John Bull*, 22 May 1915, p. 4.
24. P. Ward, *Red Flag and Union Jack: The Left, Patriotism and the First World War* (London, 1998), p. 124.
25. H. W. Fowler, *A Dictionary of Modern English Usage* (Oxford, 1965; revised by Sir Ernest Gower), Preface to the revised edition, pp. iv–v.
26. *The Passing Show* had fun with a misprint regarding this battalion when it was stated that they had marched out led by 'popers'. The comment was 'It was a gratifying sign of the unity and toleration produced by the war that no one seems to have cried "No Popery".' *The Passing Show*, 24 July 1915, p. 15.
27. A thorny problem. Under a 1917 agreement, Jews of Russian citizenship had a 'choice' between volunteering for a British Army unit or facing deportation to Russia to be conscripted into the Russian Army.
28. 'The Anti-Semitism of the Present Government', Memorandum by the Secretary of State for India (E. Montagu), PRO: CAB 24, GT1868, August 1917.
29. David Silbey argues that, when properly weighted, working-class voluntarism 'rivalled, perhaps exceeded, that of the middle and upper class'. This is a complicated argument – the majority of the Army was drawn obviously from the majority of the population: the urban working class. Yet the barriers of health and increasingly of 'badging' vital workers meant that the proportion of middle-class men in the Army was higher than that in the population as a whole – a significant over-representation.
30. Cited in E. W. Macfarland, 'A Coronach in Stone', in E. Macfarland and C. M. M. Macdonald (eds), *Scotland and the Great War* (East Linton, 1999), pp. 1–11.
31. For the building trade, see P. Dewey, 'Military Recruiting and the British Labour Force during the First World War', *The Historical Journal* 27 (1984), pp. 199–223, p. 217. C. Harvie, *No Gods and Precious Few Heroes: Scotland*

since 1914 (Edinburgh, 1981), pp. 13–14. Gwynedd statistics: C. Hughes, 'The New Armies', in I. Beckett (ed.), *A Nation in Arms* (Manchester, 1990), pp. 100–25, p. 121.

32. I. Wood, '"Be Strong and of Good Courage": The Royal Scots Territorial Battalions', in Macfarland and Macdonald (eds), *Scotland*, pp. 103–24.

33. *The Scotsman*, 8 January 1915.

34. P. Reese, *Homecoming Heroes: An Account of the Reassimilation of British Military Personnel into Civilian Life* (London, 1992), p. 85. Admittedly Pamela Horn cites the case of Tingewick in Buckinghamshire which, with 18% of population enlisted, is actually higher than this, although her 'typical' English case, Childrey in Berkshire is slightly lower. P. Horn, *Rural Life in England in the First World War* (New York, 1984), p. 184. It is very doubtful that the typical figure was in fact that high: the sectional enlistment rate for agriculture in July 1918 was 35% of the men of military age. This makes it unlikely that the average rate of rural enlistment by population was more than 10%. See Dewey, 'Military recruiting', p. 216, Table 9.

35. J. M. Robertson (ed.), *The War Book of Turriff and Twelve Miles Round* (Turriff, 1926), pp. 467–8.

36. *The Scotsman*, Letter from Isabel Burton Mackenzie, 26 September 1914, p. 7. Some newspaper reports should be read with caution. It was claimed in early 1915 that 1,000 men had enlisted in Denbeath, part of Asquith's Fifeshire community, out of a total population of 2,500. This is total demographic nonsense. *John Bull*, 6 February 1915.

37. Horn, *Rural Life*, pp. 80–1. This was noted at the time, and led to a vicious article in *John Bull* by A. H. Hale entitled 'What is Wrong with North Wales?' It claimed that there was not one volunteer where there should be fifty. The blame was placed firmly on the nonconformist ministers, the 'Mad Mullahs' who hated the Army. It was claimed that 80% of the volunteers from the region were Anglicans and Roman Catholics. Axes were grinding in this: the 'teetotal pumpuritans' were a favoured target of *John Bull* – labelling them unpatriotic was very useful. See *John Bull*, 18 September 1915, pp. 6–7.

38. More than 70% of the Scottish population were nominally Presbyterian in some form. T. C. Smout, *A History of the Scottish People* (London, 1987), p. 191, Table 9.

39. S. J. Brown, '"A Solemn Purification by Fire": Responses to the Great War in the Scottish Presbyterian Church', *Journal of Ecclesiastical History* 45, No 1, January 1994, pp. 82–104, p. 91.

40. Poetry is a different story. The work of 'Hugh McDiarmid' provided some of the most consistently powerful and savage indictments of the war.

41. J. Reith, *Wearing Spurs* (London, 1966). See comments in the Foreword by Robert Lusty.

42. See G. Urquhart, 'Confrontation and Withdrawal: Loos, Readership and the First Hundred Thousand', in Macfarland and Macdonald (eds), *Scotland*, pp. 125–44. Urquhart claims that even today any second-hand bookshop in Scotland will have at least one copy of the book.

43. K. Jeffrey, 'The Post War Army', in Beckett (ed.), *A Nation in Arms*, pp. 212–34, p. 219, Table 8.2.
44. T. C. Smout, *A Century of the Scottish People* (London, 1987), p. 264. For rather pious praise of Scottish anti-militarism, see W. Kenefick, 'War Resisters and Anti-Conscription: An ILP Perspective', in Macfarland and Macdonald (eds), *Scotland*, pp. 59–77.
45. Reith, *Wearing Spurs*, p. 25.
46. The spirit of Glyndwr was evoked with regularity in Wales as the functional equivalent of Wallace and Bruce. See, M. Lieven, *Senghennydd: The Universal Pit Village* (Llandysul, 1994), p. 284, and A. Gaffney, *Aftermath: Remembering the Great War in Wales* (Cardiff, 1998), pp. 10–11. Lloyd George evoked 'Glendower' in his Queens Hall speech. The image of these national warriors for freedom was useful ideologically, but the scale and intensity was far greater in Scotland.
47. Smout, *Scottish People*, p. 146.
48. D. Jones (ed.), *Rural Scotland during the War* (London, Oxford, Newhaven: 1926), p. 20. Similarly the roll of honour for Selkirk reprints at the end the words and music for 'Flowers of the Forest'.
49. Robertson (ed.), *The War Book of Turriff*.
50. D. Kirkwood, *My Life in Revolt* (London, 1935), p. 82.
51. J. Holford, *Reshaping Labour: Organisation, Work and Politics in Edinburgh in the Great War and After* (Edinburgh, 1988), p. 152. I. G. C. Hutchinson, 'The Impact of War on Scottish Politics', in Macdonald and Macfarland (eds), *Scotland*, pp. 36–57, p. 49.
52. Fred Karno was the most popular music hall entertainer of the age; Charlie Chaplin began his career in Karno's troop. Some of the English volunteers may have had a literal claim to be in his army: in 1915 Karno lent the grounds of his home for a successful recruiting meeting, see *John Bull*, 26 June 1915, p. 3.
53. Specifically, the hymn 'The Church's One Foundation'. Still it should be noted that the Scots were not without ironic self-mockery. The marching song of the volunteer regiments of Cameron Highlanders was:

> Why did we join the Cameron men?
> Why did we join the army?
> Why did we come to Aldershot?
> Because we're bally [bloody] well barmy
> Skilly and duff, skilly and duff,
> Because we're bally well barmy.
>
> Noted in 'Marching songs' article, *The Star*, 2 October 1914

54. Once again excepting McDiarmid.
55. Some might question this. Sassoon's loyalty to the fighting soldier is self-evident. But Sassoon was committed solely to the men already in the Army, the purposes of Mackintosh and Sassoon in their polemics seem rather different.
56. Inserted in Clark, 'English Words', vol. viii, Eng. Misc. e. 274. (p. 206). Clark is highly critical of this appeal, which he misattributes as official.
57. God is the more polite version. The printed version in *The Star*, 2 October 1914, has heaven, which is even more euphemistic as it doesn't scan.

58. F. B. Armitage, *Leicester 1914–18* (Leicester, 1933), pp. 30–1, 84–6. For the boot trade, See Simkins, *Kitchener's Army*, p. 109.
59. Sidebotham, *Hyde*, pp. 103–9.
60. J. Lee, *Todmorden in the Great War* (Todmorden, 1920), pp. 84–6.
61. Clark, 'English Words', Eng. Misc. mss, 266.
62. Cited, Collins, *Theatre*, pp. 29–31.
63. Dewey, 'Military Recruiting', pp. 208–9.
64. Ada Macguire to Evelyn Macguire, 9 October 1915, Imperial War Museum.
65. H. Cousins, Diary, entries for 2 October 1915, 13 November 1915, 13 January 1916.
66. Cousins, Diary, entries for 19 March, 13 April, 26 April, 2 May, 11 May, 20 June, 6 July, 8 July, 11 July, 20 July, 21 July, 9 August 1916.
67. Cousins, Diary, 2 February 1917.
68. Cousins, Diary, 14, 15 February 1917.
69. See J. Tosh, *A Man's Place* (New Haven, CT, and London, 1999) for some middle-class ideas of responsibility towards family as a defining feature of masculinity. Tosh argues that the ideal of the Victorian paterfamilias was in decline by 1914 in comparison with a new male sociability outside the home. If this is the case, then the war appears to have revived a version of the older ideas. Smillie cited in Macdonagh, *London*, p. 232.
70. *John Bull*, 13 February 1915, p. 14.
71. Cited by Simkins, *Kitchener's Army*, p. 199.
72. *The Scotsman*, 2 September 1914, p. 7.
73. Perfect, *Hornchurch*, p. 227.
74. Scott, *Leeds*, pp. 255–8.
75. I. Hutton, *Memories of a Doctor in War and Peace* (London, 1960), p. 130.
76. Cantuar to Kitchener, 23 October 1914, Davidson Papers, Lambeth Palace, Dav. 374/42. See also *The Times*, 3 October 1914 and 14 December 1914.
77. Cantuar to Willesden, 26 February 1915, Dav. 374/159.
78. Memo from George Bell to Cantuar, 1 April 1915, Dav. 374/243.
79. R. J. Campbell to Cantuar, 5 April 1915, Dav. 375/54.
80. Draft Resolution, 6 April 1915, Dav. 375/62.
81. F. Briant to Cantuar, 19 April 1915, Dav. 375/78.
82. Cantuar to Croydon, 26 April 1915, Dav. 375/91.
83. Scott, *Leeds*, p. 35.
84. Markham to Robert Fox, town clerk of Leeds, 6 March 1917, in H. Jones (ed.), *Duty and Citizenship: The Correspondence and Papers of Violet Markham* (London, 1994), p. 84.
85. Lady Randolph Churchill (ed.), *Women's War Work* (London, 1916), pp. 37, 56.
86. Robertson (ed.), *War Book of Turriff*, p. 465.
87. Local Government Board for Scotland, *Charities Registered under the War Charities Act 1916* (Edinburgh, 1917). F. D'Aeth, *Liverpool Social Workers' Handbook* (2nd edn, Liverpool, 1916), pp. 271–4.
88. G. F. Stone and C. Wells (eds), *Bristol and the Great War* (Bristol, 1919), pp. 161–7.
89. *Common Cause*, 14 August 1914.

90. J. de Vries, 'Gendering Patriotism: Emmeline and Christabel Pankhurst and World War One', in S. Oldfield (ed.), *This Working Day World* (London, 1994), pp. 75–88. Parallels between this view of 'Prussianism' and later feminist analyses of 'Fascism' are striking.

91. I. Bet-El, *Conscripts: The Lost Legions of the Great War* (London, 1999), pp. 29–30. Oddly enough the one example she gives of this 'passivity' undermines her argument: a man who appeared before Tribunals not once, but twice, and did gain a postponement.

92. Almost incredibly they are not seriously considered in R. J. Q. Adams and P. Poirier, *The Conscription Controversy in Great Britain 1900–1918* (Columbus, OH, 1987). This work, the standard authority on the subject, barely acknowledges their existence. Yet the operation of Tribunals became *the* conscription controversy in the public mind after January 1916.

93. In his study of Huddersfield, Cyril Pearce, who is principally interested in the conscientious objectors, makes very little of this point.

94. Pearce, *Comrades*, p. 314

95. H. Cousins, *Diary*, Imperial War Museum. Macdonagh, *London*, pp. 98–9.

96. Pearce, *Comrades*, p. 314.

97. Scott, *Leeds*, p. 47.

98. F. T. Lockwood Diary, 15 March, 3 April 1916, Imperial War Museum.

99. Scott, *Leeds*, p. 35. Sidebotham, *Hyde*, p. 27.

100. R. C. Self (ed.), *The Neville Chamberlain Diary Letters*, vol. 1: *The Making of a Politician, 1915–20* (Aldershot, 2000), p. 110. Neville Chamberlain to Hilda Chamberlain (sister), 29 January 1916. C. Repington, *The First World War*, volume 1 (London, 1920), cites diary for 12 January, 19 May, 3 August 1916, p. 105, p. 203, p. 297.

101. Sidebotham, *Hyde*, p. 29.

102. Repington, *First World War*, vol. 1, 13 January 1916, p. 105.

103. Bedfordshire CRO AT/1.

104. The summary is from Pearce, *Comrades*, p. 158. For some negative views, see T. Kennedy, *The Hounds of Conscience* (Fayetteville, AR, 1987) p. 104; D. Boulton, *Objection Overruled* (London, 1967), p. 124. John Rae is more generous: J. Rae, *Conscience and Politics* (Oxford, 1970).

105. Cartmell, *For Remembrance*, pp. 70–2.

106. Cartmell, *For Remembrance*, pp. 74–6.

107. Solicitors' files: Imperial War Museum, Misc. 133, 2051.

108. Cartmell, *For Remembrance*, pp. 84–5.

109. Cartmell, *For Remembrance*, p. 86.

110. Self (ed.), *Neville Chamberlain Diary Letters*, vol. 1, Letter to Ida Chamberlain (sister), 23 January 1916, p. 109.

111. Cartmell was critical of press coverage which tended to focus on 'amusing or abnormal' cases. Cartmell, *For Remembrance*, p. 86.

112. F. T. Lockwood Diary, 16 April 1916, 28 October 1916, 3 March 1917.

113. A. Geddes, 'The Theory and Practice of Recruiting', PRO: CAB 24, GT 1484, July 1917.

114. Pamphlet included in Davidson Papers, Lambeth Palace. Dav. 375/293. Italics as in original.

115. *John Bull*, 10 April 1915, p. 17, p. 20; 24 April 1915, p. 6.
116. *The Passing Show*, 24 July, cover.
117. E. Isaacs to R. Isaacs, 28 January 1917, Imperial War Museum.
118. Gerard De Groot is critical of upper-class complacency on this issue. See De Groot, *Blighty*, pp. 226–7. The evidence he presents is slender and contentious.

CHAPTER 4

1. Sermon, 'Precious Blood' in Rev. F. T. Woods, *War Watchwords from Bradford Parish Church* (Leeds, 1914), pp. 47–8.
2. Letter, Eva Isaacs to Rufus Isaacs, 7 February 1917. Papers of the Marchioness of Reading, Imperial War Museum.
3. 'The Separation Allowance', in A. Reeve, *Lays of a Labourer* (London, 1916).
4. M. Armstrong, *War Poems* (Truro, 1916).
5. See Collins, *Theatre at War*, pp. 18–19. Includes a reproduction of the advertisement.
6. The reference is to a poem of Kipling's at the time of the Boer War.
7. These figures were compiled from the very long appendix in H. Keatley (ed.), *Croydon in the Great War*.
8. G. F. Stone and C. Wells (eds), *Bristol and the Great War* (Bristol, 1919), pp. 237–9.
9. *Grimsby War Work* (Compiled 1919? Reprinted Grimsby, 1994). It should be remembered that the chance of being wounded at sea was much less.
10. W. Turner, *Accrington Pals* (Preston, 1986).
11. W. Rye, *Recruiting among Farmers (North and East Norfolk)* (Norwich, 1917).
12. Rye, *Recruiting among Famers*, p. 2.
13. Horn, *Rural Life*, Appendix 1, p. 240. There is an 80,000 increase in the category of nursery men, market gardeners etc. which complicates this picture further.
14. C. Macintyre, *How to Read a War Memorial* (London, 1990), p. 41; *Windermere Parish Roll of Honour and War Record* (n.p., n.d.), *Hatfield Roll of Honour* (Hatfield, 1919).
15. J. H. Kennedy, *Attleborough in Wartime* (Norwich, 1920).
16. J. Davies, 'The World War One Dead as Commemorated on the War Memorial. St Saviours Church Tetbury', Unpublished paper, History of Tetbury Society, 1989. For comparison, the Wiltshire village of Broadchalke was reported as having suffered eighteen deaths out of ninety men who served, a death rate of 20%: C. Dakers, *The Countryside at War* (London, 1987), p. 210.
17. B. Bushaway, 'Name Upon Name: The Great War and Remembrance', in R. Porter (ed.), *The Myths of the English* (Oxford and Cambridge, 1992), pp. 136–67, p. 147.
18. Robertson, *Turriff*, p. 10, *Roll of Honour of the Burgh and Parish of Selkirk* (Edinburgh, 1921), *John Menzies Roll of Honour* (Glasgow?, 1921?). One possible explanation is the popularity of the Mounted Yeomanry regiments amongst John Menzies employees.

19. For example, an examination of the chronologies of deaths of two widespread surnames on the Aberdeen Roll of Honour shows a wildly divergent pattern with no clear underlying reason:

	1914	1915	1916	1917	1918	1919–
Robertson	0	15	17	12	11	6
Macdonald	3	6	7	27	15	4

Only a few months of the war show a consistent pattern of high loss associated with both names, April 1917 being the main one.

20. F. B. Armitage, *Leicester 1914–18* (Leicester, 1933).
21. T. Manson, *Shetlands Roll of Honour* (Lerwick, 1920).
22. A point of clarification: in British practice a Regiment was an administrative not a tactical unit. But it was fairly common practice for battalions of the same Regiment to serve together tactically.
23. *23rd London Regiment 1798–1919* (London, 1936), p. 24.
24. C. Asquith, *Diaries 1915–1918* (London, 1968), pp. 62, 90–1, 218. See also D. Cooper, *Old Men Forget: The Autobiography of Duff Cooper* (London, 1953), pp. 49–50, 54, 69–70.
25. A. Gleason, *Inside the British Isles* (London, 1917), p. 34.
26. For example, on 31 October 1914, *John Bull* had called for Alfred Mond as a 'German born subject' to be hanged in retaliation for German atrocities. Bottomley apologised for the slur on 14 November 1914 but attacks on Reading and Mond continued throughout the war.
27. *John Bull*, particularly 2 January 1915, p. 1, and 11 September 1915, pp. 6–7.
28. Gleason, *Inside the British Isles*, p. 36.
29. Scott, *Leeds*, pp. 39–40.
30. Self (ed.), *The Neville Chamberlain Diary Letters*, vol. 1, pp. 143–4, 145.
31. D. W. Williams, *Heroic Circumstances: An Account of the Sacrifices of the Men and Women of Ruthin District* (Ruthin, 1997). Williams's account of Ruthin is particularly valuable as he tracked down twenty-nine additional deaths as well as the seventy listed on the memorial.
32. Cooper, *Old Men Forget*, p. 66.
33. F. Robinson, diary 1914–1918, vol. 4, p. 166, Imperial War Museum.
34. Gleason, *Inside the British Isles* (London, 1917), pp. 205–6.
35. Cousins diary, 9 February 1916, Imperial War Museum.
36. Lady M. Sackville, *The Pageant of War* (London, 1916).
37. Roberts, *Classic Slum*. This memory is sufficently vivid and circumstantial to be believed. Anon, *Remember* (Cambridge, 1915).
38. 'Memorandum on Soldiers and Sailors Pay', September 1917, PRO: CAB 24 GT 2046. An accessible account of what was being valued at twenty shillings can be found in Edward Vaughan Campion's diary, with its ghastly description of the cries of men drowning in shell holes.

39. A. Crosley (ed.), *Chin-wag: Being the War Records of the Eton Manor Clubs* (London, 1930), p. 35. In the preface the editor states that the youngsters of the club were earning very good wages by the middle of the war.

40. F. W. Longbottom, *Chester in the Great War* (Chester, n.d. 1920?), p. 5.

41. *Daily Herald*, 31 July 1914, p. 1; 1 August 1914, cartoon, p. 11.

42. *Daily Herald*, 12 August 1914, p. 5.

43. *Daily Herald*, 14 August 1914, p. 7.

44. *John Bull*, 30 January 1915, p. 2, cartoon p. 17; 6 February 1915, p. 5.

45. *John Bull*, 27 January 1917, p. 5; 7 April 1917, p. 6; 28 April 1917, p. 12; 19 May 1917, p. 6; 9 June 1917, p. 12, p. 15; 23 June 1917, p. 12.

46. *The Passing Show*, 13 November 1915, p. 5; 17 June 1917, p. 6; 7 July 1917.

47. Ministry of Food Memorandum, August 1917, CAB 24 GT 1616.

48. Ministry of Food Memorandum, week ending 29 August 1917, CAB 24 GT 1919.

49. Ministry of Food Memorandum, week ending 5 September 1917, CAB 24 GT 1994.

50. CAB 24 GT 1691.

51. M. Lieven, *Senghennydd: The Universal Pit Village 1890–1930* (Llandysul, 1994), pp. 294–5.

52. Gleason, *Inside the British Isles*, p. 322.

53. By contrast, in the Second World War, when the labour movement was incorporated into Government much more fully and industry far more controlled, the merest hint of this language could meet with draconian Government action. The 'price of petrol' cartoon in the *Daily Mirror* of 1942 which roused ministers to fury, was nothing compared with press representations of profiteering between 1915 and 1918.

54. Horn, *Rural Life*, pp. 56–7.

55. Horn, *Rural Life*, p. 62.

56. Farm profits did drop in 1918; nevertheless the overall picture for the war was very good. See P. E. Dewey, 'British Farming Profits and Government Policy During the First World War', *Economic History Review* 27 (1984), pp. 373–90. Dewey estimates that the average net income of farmers rose more than threefold, which meant that farmers were about 50% better off as a group even if inflation had the same impact on them as on the rest of the population. Overall profit on capital in 1917 was somewhere in the range of 10.2 to 14.3%. He concludes that supernormal profits were certainly achieved and that in the first two years of the war conditions for making high levels of profits were 'almost ideal'. Dewey rightly points out that profits were not uniform within farming: the gross income from dairy farming only doubled.

57. Cartmell, *Remembrance*, pp. 166–8.

58. Cartmell, *Remembrance*, p. 163.

59. *The Passing Show*, 12 May 1917, p. 9.

60. *The Correspondence of H. G. Wells*, vol. 2: *1910–1918* (London, 1998), pp. 451–5, p. 453.

61. *The Passing Show*, 22 April 1916, p. 15.

62. C. Lucas, *The Call of the War* (London, 1917), pp. 11–14. Corelli named in Ministry of Food Report, week ending 9 January 1918, CAB 24, GT 3322.

63. 'War Economy', in J. E. Buckrose, *Wartime in Our Street* (London, 1917), pp. 133–45, p. 136.

64. H. M. Walbrook, *Hove and the Great War* (Hove, 1920), p. 121.

65. *The Passing Show*, 26 May 1917, p. 5.

66. J. Melling, *Rent Strikes: People's Struggle for Housing in West Scotland 1890–1916* (Edinburgh, 1983).

67. Melling, *Rent Strikes*, p. 60, p. 63, pp. 64–6, and photograph. See also *John Bull* for the use of the term 'Hun' to describe landlords: 'Homer the Hun', referring to a Dorset case, 13 March 1915, p. 8; the eviction of a soldier's wife in Partick, 3 April 1915, p. 11.

68. R. J. Morris, 'Skilled Workers and the Politics of Red Clyde', *Journal of Scottish Labour History* 19 (1984), 6–17.

69. Lieven, *Senghennydd*, pp. 291–2.

70. Money (pounds, shillings and pence).

71. Cited in E. S. Turner, *Dear Old Blighty* (London, 1980), p. 224.

72. Turner, *Blighty*, pp. 219–24. The phrase 'Other Bugger's Efforts' is still widely used of the award.

73. OBE citations, *The Times*, 9 January 1918.

74. *The Passing Show*, 7 July 1917, p. 9.

75. E. Isaacs to R. Isaacs, 16 December 1916.

76. Walbrook, *Hove*, p. 4.

77. N. Maclean, *The Great Discovery* (Glasgow, 1915), p. 77.

CHAPTER 5

1. Cited from, D. Lloyd George, *Through Terror to Triumph* (London, 1914). This is one pamphlet version of the many versions of this speech which were circulated.

2. See P. Fussell, *The Great War and Modern Memory* (London, 1976); S. Hynes, *A War Imagined* (London, 1988).

3. S. C. Williams, *Religious Belief and Popular Culture in Southwark, c.1880–1939* (Oxford, 1999). See also J. Cox, *English Churches in a Secular Society: Lambeth 1870–1930* (Oxford, 1982). Cox is subtly different, seeing religious belief as powerful but more residual, whereas Williams insists on the vitality of folk religion.

4. Although books of homilies tapping into the language appeared throughout and after the war. See R. M. Wills, *The Sacrifice of Prayer* (London, 1916); E. Tyrell-Green, *The Sacrifice of the Best* (London, 1919).

5. Studdert Kennedy and Bottomley, both cited in E. S. Turner, *Dear Old Blighty* (London, 1980), p. 72.

6. Bottomley did make a point of criticising the papal peace note in 1917 and giving his own judgement!

7. H. G. Wells to Harrison, n.d. 1917, in *The Correspondence of H. G. Wells*, p. 535.

8. D. S. Cairn (ed.), *The Army and Religion: An Enquiry and Its bearing upon the Religious Life of the Nation* (London, 1919).

9. R. W. Farrow, 'Recollections of a Conscientious Objector', unpublished memoir, p. 291, Imperial War Museum.

10. Cartmell, *Remembrance*, p. 91.
11. W. J. Carey, *Sacrifice and Some of Its Difficulties* (London and Oxford, 1918).
12. The pamphlet has no author marked, but is attributed to John Proctor. J. C. Proctor, *The War and Sacrificial Death: A Warning* (London, 1918).
13. Proctor, *Sacrificial Death*, pp. 3–5.
14. Proctor, *Sacrificial Death*, p. 6.
15. W. Tudor Pole, *The Great War: Some Deeper Issues* (London, 1915), p. 9.
16. Tudor Pole, *The Great War*, p. 14.
17. Tudor Pole, *The Great War*, p. 69.
18. Tudor Pole, *The Great War*, p. 57.
19. Tudor Pole, *The Great War*, p. 15.
20. To the extent that he acquired Malthus's sobriquet, 'the gloomy Dean'.
21. Adrian Hastings's judgement that Inge was 'a gifted amateur' and 'rather silly' seems to be based on political distaste. A. Hastings, *A History of English Christianity 1920–1990* (London, 1991), p. 177.
22. W. R. Inge, *Diary of a Dean* (London, 1949), p. 31. Entry for 8 October 1914.
23. Inge, *Diary of a Dean*, p. 35, Record of private conversation, 27 November 1917.
24. Inge, *Diary of a Dean*, p. 42.
25. Inge, *Diary of a Dean*, p. 42.
26. Inge, *Diary of a Dean*, p. 43.
27. Inge, *Diary of a Dean*, p. 43.
28. Hastings, *History of English Christianity*, p. 85.
29. W. Temple, *The Church's Mission to the Nation*, National Mission Pamphlet T, 1916, p. 6.
30. W. Temple, *The Call of the Kingdom*, National Mission Pamphlet A, 1916, p. 1.
31. Temple, *Church's Mission*, p. 7.
32. Temple, *Church's Mission*, p. 7.
33. W. Temple, *The Fellowship of the Holy Spirit*, National Mission Pamphlet G, p. 1.
34. Temple, *Fellowship of the Holy Spirit*, p. 1.
35. Temple, *Church's Mission*, p. 7.
36. Temple, *Church's Mission*, p. 7.
37. Temple, *Fellowship of the Holy Spirit*, p. 10.
38. Temple, *Fellowship of the Holy Spirit*, pp. 8–9.
39. Temple, *Church's Mission*, p. 12.
40. S. Sassoon, *Complete Memoirs of George Sherston* (London, 1937), p. 448.
41. G. Lansbury, *My Faith and Hope in View of the National Mission*, National Mission Pamphlet B, p. 1.
42. See S. Pankhurst, *The Home Front* (London, 1932), pp. 294–5.
43. 'We talked about Lansbury as a possible member of the council … my own notion is that Lansbury has become so unbalanced in different ways that he might be a source of peril, feeling it for example, his duty to raise some big question publically which would cross our mission purposes like a red herring across the trail … I think your wise course would be to consult with William Temple who would take a reasonable view, and probably knows Lansbury well.' Davidson to Winnington-Ingram, 28 Febuary 1916, Lambeth Palace, Davidson Papers, vol. 360.

44. Lansbury, *Faith and Hope*, pp. 2–3.
45. Lansbury, *Faith and Hope*, p. 4.
46. Lansbury, *Faith and Hope*, p. 5. Lansbury had editorialised to this effect in the *Daily Herald* when the news of the expedition was first received.
47. Lansbury, *Faith and Hope*, p. 6.
48. Lansbury, *Faith and Hope*, p. 11.
49. The National Mission poster was drawn by Eric Kennington: 'In the foreground is the figure of Christ facing a great crowd of people in a modern manufacturing town, whose chimneys belt out smoke in the background. In the crowd are a soldier, a sailor, airman, Red cross nurse, workmen, clergy, beggars, women and little children.' Bulletin of the National Mission of Hope and Repentance, No. 6, 15 August 1916.
50. Dean of St Paul's, *The Call of Hope*, National Mission pamphlet L, p. 8.
51. As cited in A. Wilkinson, *The Church of England and the First World War* (London, 1996), p. 217. By the time this sermon was preached, London had suffered 70 dead and 180 wounded in air raids. The bishop's sermon probably expressed the general mood in the Diocese. This doesn't excuse it.
52. S. C. Carpenter, *Winnington-Ingram* (London, 1949). Winnington-Ingram's papers in the 'Fulham' collection at Lambeth Palace do not include the war years.
53. He certainly wasn't perceived as a major intellect. The *Church Times* had commented upon his appointment to London: 'We have no desire to see the College of Bishops recruited from the ranks of the unlearned and undignified, but we cannot help thinking that the Church has greatly suffered in the past from the selection of men whose learning and dignified bearing removed them from all sympathy and fellowship with humbler folks.' Carpenter, *Winnington-Ingram*, p. 82. This shows more Christian charity than 'thick as two short planks'.
54. Bishop of London, *The Nation's Call*, p. 1.
55. *Nation's Call*, p. 2.
56. *Nation's Call*, p. 3.
57. *Nation's Call*, p. 4.
58. *Nation's Call*, p. 4.
59. *Nation's Call*, p. 5.
60. *Nation's Call*, p. 6. It seems likely that this may reflect a stern Archiepiscopal lecture, since Randall Davidson would not have approved of the Advent sermon. Even so, the bishop's idiosyncratic interpretation of Scripture remains apparent. The injunction to 'forgive those who trespass against us' clearly does not include the sub-clause referring to the Nuremberg defence.
61. The full poem is longer and even more awful.
62. Geoffrey Studdert Kennedy (Woodbine Willie) in his chaplaincy at the front developed an effective riposte. 'Bottomley says you are all Saints, Eyes Left, now look at your neighbour.'
63. *Nation's Call*, p. 8.
64. On the face of it this language of assault on popular pleasure would be repellent to the masses. But one can never be sure. In the popular mind, Church people were expected to do this – the tolerance that by 1914 was

extended to the temperance preaching of the Salvation Army by pubgoers might be taken as an example. Besides which this language was well chosen to appeal to the moralising minority in all social classes who were probably the representative churchgoers.

65. D. White, *The Sex Instinct and Confirmation*, National Mission pamphlet Q.
66. Canon Streeter, National Mission pamphlet M, p. 1.
67. *Commonwealth*, November 1917, p. 325. Cited in Wilkinson, *Church of England*, fn. 60, p. 317.
68. Alan Wilkinson doesn't specifically endorse this view, but he quotes a number of contemporaries to this effect. Wilkinson, *Church of England*, pp. 77–8.
69. C. Stott, *Dick Sheppard* (London, 1977), p. 90.
70. Cecil to Bell, Bell Papers 190/ 84–92, Lambeth Palace.
71. Carpenter, *Winnington-Ingram*, pp. 194–6.
72. Wilkinson, *Church of England*, p. 75.
73. Quoted in Stott, *Dick Sheppard*, p. 93.
74. Miller, *Hartlepools in the Great War*, p. 258.
75. Sidebotham, *Hyde*, p. 13.
76. J. E. Buckrose, 'Lights Out', in *Wartime in Our Street* (London, 1917), p. 13, pp. 14–15.
77. Cited Lieven, *Senghennydd*, p. 285.
78. A. Connell, 'The Breaking of the Storm', 9 August 1914, p. 3; 'A Moral Menace to Civilization', 30 August 1914; 'The Sceptre of Ungodliness', 6 August 1916, p. 1, in A. Connell, *War Sermons* (Liverpool, 1919).
79. A. Connell, 'Returning to God', p. 3, in Connell, *War Sermons*, vol. 2 (Liverpool, 1919).
80. Sidebotham, *Hyde*, p. 174.
81. In C. Reilly, *Scars upon My Heart* (London, 1981), p. 8.
82. R. Saunders, letter to his son, 11 October 1914. Imperial War Museum.
83. The classic exposition of the secularisation thesis is R. Currie, A. D. Gilbert and L. Horsley, *Churches and Churchgoers* (Oxford, 1977).
84. Williams, *Religious Belief*, pp. 149–54.
85. Williams, *Religious Belief*, p. 147, also pp. 155–9.
86. *St Silas, Annual Report*, 1913, p. 2.
87. See Williams, *Religious Belief*, pp. 146–9. There are various good examples in the admittedly pious autobiography of the Wesleyan minister, William Lax. See W. H. Lax, *Lax of Poplar* (London, 1927), pp. 202–5.
88. Bishop of Stepney, *Record of the Raids* (London, 1918), p. 2. Maclean believed prayer had replaced the sermon at the heart of the Church of Scotland. I. Maclean, *Great Deliverance* (Glasgow, 1915), p. 13.
89. Elizabeth to Fred Fernside, 15 April 1916. Imperial War Museum.
90. Mabel Farrier to her father (n.d. 1917?). Imperial War Museum.
91. William to Arthur Proctor, 4 June 1917. Imperial War Museum.
92. W. to A. Proctor, 2 August 1917.
93. W. to A. Proctor, 2 August 1917.
94. W. to A. Proctor, 7 July 1918.
95. W. to A. Proctor, 14 June 1917.
96. W. to A. Proctor, 2 August 1917; 11 August 1918.

97. W. to A. Proctor, 1 December 1918.
98. Mother to Arthur, 4 August 1918; 8 September 1918. The fourth anniversary of the war saw a particularly large amount of religious activity.
99. E. Bennet to Gunner Bennet, 29 July 1918. Imperial War Museum. In this letter, Edie Bennet gives her weekly schedule. Sunday involved visiting her mother-in-law and going to church. She also attended additionally at Christmas and Easter.
100. E. Bennet to Gunner Bennet, 17 April 1918.
101. Currie, Gilbert and Horsley, *Churches and Churchgoers*, p. 31. These figures, particularly for Roman Catholicism, are deeply problematic. Guesswork aside, there is some evidence of an increased rate of attendance *after* the war amongst Roman Catholics. Stephen Fielding gives figures for Hulme in Lancashire which show a rise from 47% to 60%: S. Fielding, *Class and Ethnicity: Irish Catholics in England 1880–1939* (Buckingham, 1993), p. 50.
102. The conventional view of this is well expressed by A. Marwick, *The Deluge* (London, 1965), pp. 297–8. See also A. D. Gilbert, 'All the Churches Lost Ground during the First World War', *The Making of Post-Christian Britain* (London, 1980), p. 77. But, as even Gilbert admits, the pace of decline in churchgoing does not really accelerate until the 1930s. The causes of this are almost certainly more complex than either 'urban secularisation' or 'wartime disillusionment'.
103. Wilson, *The Myriad Faces of War*, pp. 742–3.
104. *John Bull*, 3 March 1917, p. 16; 14 July 1917, p. 5.
105. W. S. F. Pickering, 'The Persistence of Rites of Passage', *British Journal of Sociology* 25 (1974), p. 64.
106. D. Scarisbrick, *My Dear Ralph: Letters of a Family at War* (London, 1994), pp. 103, 106, 126, 134, 145.
107. Pankhurst, *Home Front*, pp. 295–6.

CHAPTER 6

1. Cited in J. M. Winter, *Socialism and the Challenge of War* (London, 1974), p. 170.
2. *Daily Herald*, 8 August 1914, p. 3.
3. Anonymous agent's report from Cardiff, 30 August 1916, Bodleian Library: C. Addison Ms. 88, pp. 44–6.
4. Lord Balfour's Report on the Clyde Disturbances, Bodleian library; C. Addison Ms. 87, p. 7; Private anonymous memorandum dated 5 January 1916, forwarded by Thomas Jones, Addison Ms. 87, pp. 18–22, Letter from McDevitt, 27 January 1916, Addison Ms. 87, p. 370.
5. For the Clyde, see G. Rubin, *War, Law and Labour* (Oxford, 1987).
6. Addison Ms. 87.
7. D. Kirkwood, *My Life of Revolt* (London, 1935), p. 101.
8. Report by Commission investigating skilled men in Sheffield, Addison Ms. 77, pp. 403–20.

9. Briefing in response to visit from TUC Delegation 22 June 1916, Addison Ms. 77, pp. 254–9.
10. Retail prices reached an index figure of 143 in 1916 (1913 = 100) compared with a weekly wages index of 118 and an average weekly 'earnings' index of 133. See P. Dewey, *War and Progress: Britain 1914–45* (London, 1997), p. 41.
11. *John Bull*, 20 May 1916, p. 11.
12. Cited R. Samuel, *East End Underworld: The Life of Arthur Harding* (London, 1981), p. 236.
13. Profiteering?
14. B. Waites, *A Class Society at War* (Leamington Spa, 1987), p. 163.
15. *Birmingham and the Great War*, p. 143.
16. Cited in Gleason, *Inside Britain*, p. 332.
17. For example the letter from Lord D'Abernon, 9 August 1917, CAB 24: GT 1677.
18. Labouchere, 'Intelligence Report', 7 March 1917, Bodleian Library, Ms. Addison dep. C.88.
19. Cited in C. Wrigley, *Lloyd George and the British Labour Movement* (Brighton, 1976), p. 181.
20. B. Thomson, 'Memorandum to War Cabinet', 2 January 1918, PRO, CAB 24: GT 3424.
21. D. Hubback, *No Ordinary Press Baron: A Life of Walter Layton* (London, 1985), pp. 47–8.
22. D. Tanner, *Political Change and the Labour Party 1900–1918* (Cambridge, 1990), p. 351.
23. B. Millman, *Managing Domestic Dissent in First World War Britain* (London, 2000), p. 239.
24. A. Bradburn to S. Bradburn, 13 November 1915. Imperial War Museum 95/16/1.
25. A. Bradburn to S. Bradburn, 16 January 1916.
26. Cousins diary, 9 January 1916, Imperial War Museum.
27. P. Macleod Yearsley, 'The Home Front', p. 59, Imperial War Museum. Cites his contemporary diary for 1915.
28. E. Fernside to F. Fernside, 16 May 1917, Imperial War Museum.
29. Frederick Robinson Diary, 7 April 1916, Imperial War Museum, vol. 2, p. 132.
30. Bennett Letters, 25 June 1918.
31. Scott, *Leeds*, p. 177.
32. Anonymous Letter of 1 November 1918 from female colleague (signature illegible), Bennett Papers, Imperial War Museum.
33. *The Passing Show*, 3 November 1917.
34. A. H. Hudson, 'Shirkers, Strikers and Conscientious Objectors', in A. H. Hudson, *The Call of the Nation and Other Essays* (London, 1917), pp. 58–9; H. V. Holmes, *An Infantryman on Strikes: An Appeal to the Workers of Great Britain* (London, 1918), p. 13, pp. 18–19.
35. 'The Dauntless Three' in 'Daphne', *The Victory Book* (London, 1918).
36. 'Bonavia', *Britain's Defeat* (London, 1918).
37. W. Raleigh, *Some Gains of the War* (London, 1918), pp. 13–14.

CHAPTER 7

1. C. Sheridan-Jones, *London in Wartime* (London, 1917), p. 1.
2. Sheridan-Jones, *London*, pp. 1–2.
3. C. S. Peel, *How We Lived Then 1914–1918* (London, 1929), p. 95.
4. Peel, *How We Lived*, pp. 97–8.
5. For a good description of the situation at the turn of the year, see M. Brown, *The Imperial War Museum Book of 1918: Year of Victory* (London, 1998), pp. 1–18.
6. CAB 24: GT 3614, 'London's Food Supply'.
7. E. Bennett to Gunner Bennett, 8 January 1918; 15 January 1918; 24 January 1918, Imperial War Museum.
8. E. Fernside to F. Fernside, 19 December 1917.
9. H. E. Miles, *Untold Tales of Wartime London* (London, 1930), p. 142.
10. Lee, *Todmorden*, p. 148.
11. N. Macdonald, *Wartime Nursery Rhymes* (London, 1918), pp. 31, 38, 47, 53, 65.
12. War bond advertisement, *The Times*, 10 January 1918. It is interesting to compare this with the famous poster for a later German war loan, with its idealised and steely-eyed stormtrooper staring into the middle distance and the blunt slogan 'Help us win'.
13. Similarly in Leighton Buzzard, at St Andrews (Girls) School, a War Savings Association was formed by the 'first class girls' in October 1917 after a visit and talk by J. L. Fishwick who urged them 'to help their country by purchasing war savings certificates'. St Andrews Logbook entry for 19 October 1917, Bedfordshire County Archives, Leighton Buzzard, St Andrews 2.
14. Cartmell, *For Remembrance*, pp. 144–51.
15. *Bristol and the Great War*, pp. 318–19. See numerous illustrative examples of popular support in Gleason, *Inside Britain*, pp. 208–12. On 14 February 1917, Eva Isaacs wrote to her husband, regarding an earlier loan, that she had bought £10 worth of certificates for each of the servants and discovered to her surprise that the cook already had 'large sums invested'. Eva Isaacs letters, Imperial War Museum.
16. Cartmell, *For Remembrance*, p. 145.
17. E. Fernside to F. Fernside, 6 March 1918; 12 March 1918.
18. *Islington Daily Gazette*, 12 March 1918, p. 2.
19. I. Nicholson and L. Williams (eds), *Wales: Its Part in the War* (London, 1919), pp. 175–7, p. 185; Lee, *Todmorden*, p. 189.
20. It may be significant that on 29 January 1918 there were significant local protests against the Food Committees in Bedford and Luton; the former saw 10,000 munitions workers protesting. B. Waites, *A Class Society at War* (Leamington Spa, 1987), p. 230.
21. J. B. Firth, *Dover and the Great War* (London, n.d.), p. 91.
22. Firth, *Dover*, Appendix, p. 130.
23. Cartmell notes this, describing how each 'Tank Week' became a focus for civic rivalry. Liverpool went first, followed by Manchester which was the first city to beat London's total, with Birmingham then aiming to outstrip Manchester and succeeding by more than £2 million. Even so, everyone

was stunned when Glasgow *doubled* Birmingham's total. Cartmell, *For Remembrance*, p. 144.

24. E. S. Turner, *Dear Old Blighty* (London, 1980).
25. Letter from Robert Usher, *The Times*, 17 January 1918.
26. Allen Hay, South Mymms Vicarage, Letter to *The Times*, 21 January 1918.
27. Frederick Robinson Diaries, Imperial War Museum: 13 January 1917, 11 February 1917; 16 February 1917; 17 February 1917; vol. 3, p. 33, p. 100, p. 114, p. 117.
28. Robinson Diaries, 28 September 1917; 7 December 1917; 21 December 1917; vol. 3, p. 586, p. 745, p. 772.
29. 'N. R.', Letter to *The Times*, 7 January 1918.
30. *The Passing Show*, 9 June 1917, p. 7. *Islington Daily Gazette*, 22 October 1917, p. 3.
31. W. H. Oakley, *Guildford in the Great War* (London, 1935), p. 141.
32. R. Saunders, Letter to his son in Canada, 8 July 1917.
33. Beamish would show up after the war in Munich to congratulate Adolf Hitler on his grasp of the Jewish problem.
34. P. Panayi, *Enemy in Our Midst* (Oxford and Providence, RI, 1991).
35. D. C. Woodehouse, *Anti-German Sentiment in Kingston upon Hull: The German Community and the First World War* (Kingston upon Hull, 1990), pp. 37–9. For June riots, see pp. 44–9.
36. This is technically rather complex. *John Bull* would have been on sale somewhat in advance of 15 May 1915. Nevertheless it is probable that most copies would be sold on the Saturday. It is highly unlikely that many, if any, had been sold and read on the day that the rioting began, 10 May.
37. Woodehouse, *Anti-German Sentiment*, Appendix 2 and 3.
38. C. M. Macdonald, 'Race, Riot and Representations of War', in Macdonald and Macfarland, *Scotland*, pp. 146–69.
39. Arnold White papers, Letters E. F. Kernick to White (n.d), F. Hardy to White, 4 March 1917, WHI/109–110, NMM.
40. Letter from Macleod Yearsley, March 1917. This is the same Yearsley whose home front memoir is at the Imperial War Musuem.
41. Various boroughs in the East End passed anti-alien resolutions at this time. Fielding notes that in Manchester vicious gang attacks on Jewish youngsters escalated after the Battle of the Somme. S. Fielding, *Class and Ethnicity* (Buckingham, 1993), p. 68.
42. C. Holmes, *Anti-Semitism in British Society 1876–1939* (London, 1979), pp. 131–6.
43. D. Caesarini, 'An Embattled Minority: The Jews in Britain during the First World War', in T. Kushner and K. Lunn, *The Politics of Marginality* (London, 1990), pp. 61–81; W. D. Rubinstein, *A History of the Jews in the English Speaking World: Great Britain* (London, 1996), pp. 197–200.
44. G. Searle, *Corruption in British Politics 1895–1930* (Oxford, 1987), pp. 244–5. Holmes, *Anti-Semitism*, pp. 122, 138.
45. N. Chamberlain to H. Chamberlain, 15 December 1917, in Self, *Chamberlain*, p. 239.
46. This didn't stop him making a dubious remark during his December 1918 election campaign. When asked about his view on the 'Jewish National Home'

he supposedly supported it on the grounds that 'Brighton should be relieved'. This was probably more of a tasteless joke playing to the gallery than a real opinion.

47. J. H. Clarke, *The Call of the Sword* (London, 1917).
48. In J. Barlow, *Between Doubting and Daring* (Oxford, 1916).
49. In J. Fox, *Forgotten Divisions* (Winslow, 1994). John Fox, Delia's great-nephew, suggests that she was being paranoid. I'm not so sure: symbolically this seems pretty unambiguous, since the Harp was, after all, the symbol of the 16th Division. The woman was clearly indicating that as a patriot she would give money for soldiers, but that Irish symbols were marks of disloyalty.
50. *John Bull*, 8 December 1917, p. 9.
51. *John Bull*, 13 April 1918, pp. 6–7; 20 April 1918, p. 6.
52. *John Bull*, 25 May 1918, pp. 6–7.
53. *John Bull*, 5 December 1914.
54. Hughes, 'New Armies', in I. Beckett (ed.), *A Nation in Arms* (Manchester, 1995).
55. CAB 24: GT 1632, National Service Memorandum August 1917. Mayor of Bethnal Green cited Gleason, *Inside Britain*, p. 244.
56. A. Gaffney, *Aftermath: Remembering the Great War in Wales* (Cardiff, 1998), p. 19, n. 44. The total Jewish population outside Cardiff in South Wales was fewer than 3,000, and was served by nine synagogues.
57. *John Bull*, 10 November, 1917, p. 11; 24 November 1917, p. 12.
58. Two of the speakers, Page-Croft and White, would become important figures of the extreme right in the inter-war period. See M. Pugh, *Hurrah for the Blackshirts: Fascists and Fascism in Britain between the Wars* (London, 2006).
59. *John Bull*, 9 November 1918, pp. 6–7.
60. *John Bull*, 16 November 1918, pp. 6–7.
61. *John Bull*, 4 May 1918, pp. 6–7.

CHAPTER 8

1. Arthur Godfrey to Edward Carson, 14 November 1917, PRO: WO 32/4841.
2. Pembroke Wickes to Ottley, 18 November 1917, WO 32/4841.
3. Kipling to Derby, 20 November 1917, WO 32/4841.
4. Self (ed.), *Chamberlain Diary Letters*, p. 284.
5. E. Fernside to F. Fernside, 13 November 1918; 19 November 1918, Imperial War Museum. P. Liddle, 'Britons on the Home Front'.
6. R. Saunders, Letter to son, 13 November 1918, Imperial War Museum.
7. Similarly, Neil Oliver describes his own family as a 'lucky family' that lost no one in the First World War. This is of course a reasonable point, but it lacks the sense that this may have been a common experience. See N. Oliver, *Not Forgotten* (London, 2005), pp. 131–2.
8. For an example, see J. Watson, *Fighting Different Wars* (Cambridge, 2004), pp. 146–82 for a discussion of the Beale family.
9. C. Moriarty, '"Though in a Picture Only": Portrait Photography and the Commemoration of the First World War', in G. Braybon (ed.), *Evidence, History and the Great War* (New York and Oxford, 2003), pp. 30–47.

10. Those few readers familiar with an earlier work of mine, A. M. Gregory, *The Silence of Memory: Armistice Day 1919–1946* (Oxford and Providence, RI, 1994) will have spotted a partial change of viewpoint in this section. I have grown increasingly sceptical about a direct line between grief and commemoration, and I am now more drawn to a view which is latent but underdeveloped in that book, that commemoration was *about* the bereaved rather than *for* them. I always assumed someone would legitimately challenge some of my arguments. It might as well be me.

11. P. Longworth, *The Unending Vigil* (London, 1985), p. 47.

12. See also J. Bourke, *Dismembering the Male: Men's Bodies, Britain and the Great War* (London, 1996), p. 226.

13. Cited in Moriarty, 'Picture Only', pp. 32, 39.

14. See Gregory, *The Silence of Memory*. On a personal note, while visting the Museum of London's exhibition on 'London in the Jazz Age', I was struck by the reaction of two other visitors to a poster advertising a fancy-dress party held by the Ypres League in the early 1920s. It was one of utter incomprehension and disgust that such a 'terrible thing' could be commemorated in that way. Yet such events were initially commonplace.

15. A. King, *Memorials of the Great War in Britain* (Oxford and Providence, RI, 1998), p. 219.

16. King, *Memorials of the Great War*, p. 91.

17. Ken Inglis's listing of the Cambridgeshire memorial committee reveals a similar pattern among its members: heads of Cambridge colleges, the Dean of Ely Cathedral, the Mayor and Deputy Mayor of Cambridge, and some notable local employers. K. S. Inglis, 'The Homecoming: The War Memorial Movement in Cambridge, England', *The Journal of Contemporary History* (1992), pp. 583–602, p. 588.

18. Newport War Memorial Committee, minute book, 11 March 1919.

19. Representatives of both the above-named ex-servicemen's societies were included on the committee.

20. *Isle of Wight County Press*, 12 April 1919.

21. The County Medical Officer wrote to the *County Press* when the figures were made public, testifying that he thought a cottage hospital could be built for much less than the £9,000 allotted for construction costs; he quoted hospitals built for £2,000 before the war, and even with inflation he believed it would not cost as much as the sub-committee's report suggested. *Isle of Wight County Press*, 8 May 1919.

22. Isle of Wight Memorial Committee, minute book, 20 May 1919.

23. I am indebted to my student Abigail Broom for this account, which is drawn from her unpublished MSt thesis on memorialisation on the Isle of Wight.

24. King, *Memorials of the Great War*, p. 100.

25. Annual report for 1924 attached in Works 20/151.

26. King, *Memorials of the Great War*, pp. 68–9, 77–82, 86–102.

27. M. Connelly, *The Great War, Memory and Ritual: Commemoration in the City and East London* (London, 2002).

28. Ministry of Pensions leaflet cited in Bourke, *Dismembering the Male*, p. 66.

29. Bourke, *Dismembering the Male*, p. 62.

30. Bourke, *Dismembering the Male*, p. 59.
31. D. Cohen, *The War Came Home: Disabled Veterans in Britain and Germany* (Berkeley, CA, 2001), pp. 18–25.
32. Cohen, *War Came Home*, pp. 31–5.
33. Bourke, *Dismembering the Male*, p. 56.
34. Cohen, *War Came Home*, pp. 41–6.
35. J. Mirsky, 'The Never Ending War', *New York Review of Books*, 25 May 2000, pp. 54–63. Fifty-six thousand Americans died in Vietnam; the Vietnamese suffered around a million deaths in the 'second war'. Giap was both military genius and a butcher to put Douglas Haig in the shade. One could argue that he has no authority to speak for the bereaved of Vietnam or knowledge of their feelings. The only point I want to make is that 'trauma' is not simply a product of the scale of casualties. Which language did Giap use? The probability is French.
36. All references PRO: Works 20/139.
37. G. Robb, *British Culture and the First World War* (Basingstoke, 2003), p. 215.
38. King, *Memorials of the Great War*, pp. 176–9.
39. R. M. Bracco, *Merchants of Hope: British Middlebrow Writers and the Great War* (Oxford and Providence, RI, 1993), pp. 64–75.
40. King, *Memorials of the Great War*, pp. 175, 179–80.
41. King, *Memorials of the Great War*, p. 197.
42. King, *Memorials of the Great War*, p. 202.
43. D. Lloyd, *Battlefield Tourism* (Oxford and Providence, RI, 1998), pp. 116–17.
44. These local links await their historian.
45. J. B. Priestley, 'The Lost Generation', Society of Friends pamphlet of 1930, cited in Robb, *British Culture*, p. 233.
46. Lloyd, *Pilgrimages*, p. 173.
47. *Co-part Magazine*, July 1922, p. 21, cited in M. Connelly, *The Great War, Memory and Ritual*, p. 77.
48. See Gregory, *Silence of Memory*.
49. 11 May 1933, PRO: Works 20/255.
50. Undated, but clearly 12 May 1933. Works 20/255.
51. King, *Memorials of the Great War*, p. 212.

CONCLUSION

1. As with all fiction, whose is the voice here? The invention in *Cross Channel* is complex and superb. The nominal narrator of this piece is a middle-aged Jewish woman in the 1950s. At the end of the book she is revealed as the invention of a writer crossing the channel by train in 2020 (who passes the war cemeteries). Furthermore this narrator is in some respects a thinly disguised projection of the real author, Julian Barnes, into the future. An author imagining a character in the future, imagining a character in the past: time not behaving rationally.
2. *The London Censorship 1914–1919* (privately printed, London, 1919), p. 9.
3. A brief autobiographical excursus: growing up with grandparents who were born before the First World War, in a terraced house in south east London with

no inside bathroom or lavatory facilities, I once imagined I could grasp this. I have slowly come to the realisation of how distant it is. I don't think I had realised how far my grandparents themselves belonged to the uppermost and respectable segment of the class, indeed my grandmother would probably have seen herself as middle class to some extent.

4. The abyss existed and justified the term. In 1902 Jack London wrote of the hundreds of thousands at the bottom of society in London: 'How do they live? The answer is that they don't live. They do not know what life is. They drag out a sub-bestial existence until released by death.' J. London, *The People of the Abyss* (London, 1903, 1999), p. 85.

5. J. Brown, *The Valley of the Shadow* (Port Talbot, 1981), and Lieven, *Senghennydd*, pp. 156–7.

6. More or less every civic history has a section on 'our Belgian guests'.

7. Letter William Fisher to *Caerphilly Journal*, November 1915, cited in Lieven, *Senghennydd*, p. 279.

8. By February 1916, 25% of the pre-war workforce in mining and quarrying had joined the armed forces.

9. The likelihood of a miner being killed in his working life in the mines was approximately equal to the likelihood of a member of the British Expeditionary Force on 1 July 1916 being killed in battle on that day. To take the comparison a little further, in the post-war period 1919–1924, when safety standards had improved somewhat, there were 2,385,766 industrial injuries in Britain as opposed to 1,693,262 men wounded in the war. Whilst it is true that 'only' 20,263 of the proletariat were *killed* at work (again roughly the same as the fatalities on 1 July 1916), it indicates fairly clearly that familiarity with machine-inflicted violence was a normal part of both pre- and post-war working-class life. Cited G. Griffiths, *Women's Factory Work in World War 1* (London, 1991), p. 8.

10. Even here a certain caution is needed. The war was something of a lottery for the men on military service. It was quite possible, indeed not uncommon, to spend the war in a 'cushy billet', for example home service where the main problem was boredom. Once overseas, a very large proportion of soldiers never got near a trench or a bullet.

   There were whole battalions of infantry who spent the war on policing duty in India, others which never got anywhere near the Western Front and found themselves contesting instead with flies, heat stroke and malaria in Mesopotamia, Palestine or Salonika. War experience could mean a chance to see the Pyramids, Jerusalem or Venice or it could mean patrolling an increasingly hostile Irish countryside which was uncomfortable, but not very dangerous. It might involve guarding Gibraltar with heavy guns or building aerodromes in the Somme Valley. For much of the Royal Navy the war was rather a non-event, while for many supposed non-combatants in the Merchant Navy it was deadly serious and very dangerous. At any given moment only a tiny fraction of Britain's armed forces were 'in the line' as we understand it. On 11 November 1918, the mobilised strength of the United Kingdom was approximately 4.25 million. The total combatant strength of the Army on the Western Front (including Dominion and

Imperial forces) was 1.2 million. Even by a generous definition it is unlikely that more than a quarter of this number was in or near combat, and this at a time when the whole British front was unusually active. It is strange to read some of the letters in the Imperial War Museum and realise that for some in the armed forces, the First World War was quite close to 'a good war'.

11. Ilana Bet-El in her book, *Conscripts* (Stroud, 1999), maintains that the war and army life was a shocking experience to all regardless of background. The problems with this view are twofold. One is that her written sources, like all written sources, are skewed towards the articulate, therefore she over-rates the complaints of the 'respectable' segment of the working class and the middle classes. The second is a matter of assumptions: 'Food, clothing and cleanliness: the basic facts of everyday life. To a civilian such matters are automatic.' In the context of 1914–1918 this is an error. For most of the civilian population of 1914 these things were precisely not automatic, they were matters of everyday concern and anxiety. Working-class soldiers grumbled continuously about conditions; so did working-class civilians. It doesn't prove that quotidian life in the Army was a massive drop in usual standards.

12. The more contemporary evidence of Harry Cartmell regarding Preston is practically identical. He too mentions the pressure on pawnbrokers and the newly varied diet.

13. M. B. Hammond, *British Labour Conditions and Legislation during the War* (Oxford, 1919), p. 201.

14. On average male workers worked ten hours' overtime per week, female workers seven hours'.

15. C. Feinstein, *National Income, Expenditure and Output of the United Kingdom 1855–1965* (Cambridge, 1972), Table 64.

16. These illustrative examples are drawn from J. M. Winter, *The Great War and the British People* (London, 1986) pp. 147–55. An incautious reading of the figures for Perth and Bath might suggest a rise in middle-class infant mortality; a more likely explanation is the dispersal of war industry bringing poorer families into the boroughs.

17. M. Powell, *Below Stairs* (London, 1968), pp. 24–6.

18. My interpretation of what this means has similarities with Ferguson's, and at the same time profound differences. I would agree that at the core of British Government in these years was a deep-seated desire to appease labour and, like all appeasement, this encouraged aggression. But context does matter. British labour negotiated by strikes because it could. In Germany it was far more difficult. The other side of the coin of negotiating living standards is food riots. These were much worse and more frequent in Germany. In the end it is a question of perspectives. Ferguson states, almost in the tone of the Conservative press of 1918, that the engineers 'unbelievably' went on strike with the Germans at the gates of Paris in 1918. To which one might ask, 'When better?'

The Government, as the strikers doubtless guessed they would, folded instantly. The net result was a small increase in the cost of munitions, to be passed on ultimately to taxpayers. There is no evidence that the actions of strikers in Britain ever materially disadvantaged the British Army in France. In the first year of the war there was a shortage of munitions, but this had nothing to do with industrial militancy. Strike action and, even more, the desire to forestall it, increased the cost of the war, probably significantly. This cost would be met by current or deferred taxation in one form or another. In other words, working-class 'greed' was opportunistic redistribution of wealth. In effect the poorest people in the country forced the Government to bribe them to continue supporting the war by making the burden of sacrifice fall more severely on the comfortable. Given the nature of poverty pre-1914 this strikes me as perfectly rational, maybe even laudable. In essence it was what happened in 1939–1945 as well. I am not sure that from the relative comfort of a professional income in the early twenty-first century I would want to condemn it.

19. See N. Ferguson, *The Pity of War* (London, 1998), table 27 and pp. 271–2. Using 1914 as an index German production fell to sixty-nine by 1918, while British production fell to eighty-seven. This table doesn't seem to argue what Ferguson claims it does.

Ferguson argues that real wages in Britain fell less quickly than production, therefore the British were 'overpaid' relative to output. In 1918 this appears to be true, but this is presumably complicated by the relative impact of victory and defeat. Real wages recover sharply in Britain in 1918, in part because the Government is put under pressure when victory becomes apparent, for example in the police strike. Likewise German output falls precipitately in the chaos of defeat.

For the rest of the war the story is rather different. In 1915, British production actually *rose* whilst real wages fell faster than in Germany. In 1916 production in Germany had fallen *more* sharply than real wages while the opposite was true in Britain. In 1917 in both Britain and Germany real wages were substantially behind the production index (by about the same margin). Only in 1918 does Ferguson's argument work. The key point to note is this: real wages (and therefore living standards) *and* production both fell more sharply in Germany than in Britain. Germany was becoming even more of a low wage / low productivity economy than it had been before the war. And then they lost. Even leaving aside my left-wing tendencies to celebrate rises in real wages (how exactly is the 'Nation' better off if its people are poorer?), Ferguson's argument is not backed up by his own figures.

20. J. Bush, *Behind the Lines: East London Labour 1914–1919* (London, 1984), p. 142.

21. With one important qualification: logically enough, the amount of time spent in the front line was the single most important variable in determining mortality. A regular soldier of 1914 stood far more chance of being killed than a conscript of 1918. The ordinary soldiers of the regular Army were overwhelmingly drawn from the bottom social strata, and many of them reverted to this position when they left the Army to join the reserve. On the London County Council Roll of Honour, the most dangerous single occupation was school caretaker, with a death rate of 17.3%.

22. Once again an important qualification is required here. Uniquely amongst combatant nations the British generated a significant heroine during the war.

It is true that much of the image of Nurse Edith Cavell stressed traditional femine stereotypes – woman as victim of enemy male aggression, woman as nurturing carer – but it would be obtuse not to notice that Cavell died a heroic and in some respects soldierly death. Although Cavell famously stated 'patriotism is not enough', she was undoubtedly a patriotic icon. The classic statement of the war (and indeed all wars) as being at its core an expression and reinforcement of gendered hierarchy can be found in M. R. Higgonet (ed.), *Behind the Lines, Gender and the Two World Wars* (New Haven, CT, 1987).

23. The most optimistic interpretation of war as emancipation can be found in A. Marwick, *Women at War* (London, 1977).

24. The dangers of this approach are seen at their most reductionist in S. K. Kent, *Making Peace: The Reconstruction of Gender in Interwar Britain* (Princeton, NJ, 1993). Although this is technically a book about the post-war period, it puts the war at the centre as a negative force which set back the emancipation of women. The biggest difficulty is a highly proscriptive idea of what 'Feminist consciousness' ought to be. Having created a rather idealised view of feminist consciousness attached to the pre-war suffrage movement, Kingsley Kent bemoans its 'demise' and blames the war. This is flawed in many ways, not least in its underestimation of the extent to which the achievement of limited suffrage in 1918 inevitably took the wind out of the pre-war agenda. Most feminist political activity of the interwar period is dismissed as having sold out to the dominant patriarchal conceptions of society rather than being assessed on its own terms.

25. Gender history has proved immensely constructive in thinking about the war. Interestingly some of the best results have been achieved by applying the category to thinking about men at war. For a stunning example, see Bourke, *Dismembering the Male*. There is much more that could be done on these lines: the frequent slippage of non-combatant to mean female, which is observable in contemporary language, raises some fascinating issues about the experience of the non-combatant majority of males.

26. For a much more sophisticated and theoretical discussion of the same point, see D. Thom, *Nice Girls and Rude Girls* (London, 1998), pp. 201–8. The title of the book is a clue to the approach adopted: 'Nice' and 'Rude' should not be taken merely as terms derived from a patriarchal discourse of policing female behaviour, but they carried a powerful freight of class assumptions as well.

27. See J. Watson, *Fighting Different Wars* (Cambridge, 2003), for an extended discussion of this.

28. For a corrective, it is both shocking and refreshing to read Christopher Moore's memoir of his First World War obsession. The book is a tribute to his grandfather who participated in the breaking of the Hindenburg line. 'Fiction doesn't do it for me any more.' Instead he recreates the life of a man who fathered six children, bought his own house, fought the German Army to a standstill and remembered Leicester City's FA cup semi-final victory in 1949 as the best day of his life. Moore states, in a way that shows more imaginative empathy with the people of 1914 than any number of histories and novels: 'War is bad. Peace is good. But sometimes you have to fight.' C. Moore, *Trench Fever* (London, 1998), pp. 4, 9, 138.

29. This is simply a statement of fact, not a comment on the justifiability of that offensive. The blockade policy of 1914–1918 was directed at disrupting civilian life in Germany, but its purpose was not to kill civilians. Technically the same could be said of the 'dehousing' policy of Bomber Command, but in the latter case the distinction was far more obviously semantic. The massive use of incendiary weapons against German cities could have no other outcome than massive civilian casualties. Civilians under blockade at least theoretically have the option of pressuring their government to surrender, incinerated civilians do not.

    One moral advance of 1939–1945 over 1914–1918 was the absence of the use of poison gas. But this should be seen in perspective. The British began using poison gas in 1915 because it had first been used against them. In 1939–1945 the use of poison gas was frequently discussed and retaliation would have been massive and instant had it ever been used against British forces or civilians.

30. Obviously this is sensitive ground. Just as they had in 1914 the British people generally accepted the war as a justified one against a morally abhorrent opponent. It is probably fair to say that most people to some extent felt more abhorrence towards the Third Reich than people had felt about the Wilhelmine Reich. But the difference was probably not as large as it appears to us retrospectively. The British did not go to war in 1939 to save the Jewish population of Europe (had they done so then the war would have to be judged a failure); they went to war because Adolf Hitler was a serial treaty-breaker who appeared to threaten their security. The Polish guarantee was actually in many respects more dubious than the defence of Belgian neutrality as a *causus belli*, and the real threat to Britain may, arguably, have been less in 1939.

31. T. Wilson, *The Myriad Faces of War* (London, 1988), p. 853.

32. See for example the half-cynical, half-serious comment about intervention in Sierra Leone in *The Observer*, 14 May 2000, R. Dowden, 'Britain's Only Mission is to Protect Imperilled Humanity.' Despite the self-evident irony of the title, this was a pro-intervention argument.

Index

Aberdare, 12
Aberdeen, 327n19
Abertillery, 138
Aberystwyth, 226
Accrington, 127, 128, 252
Active Service League, 98
Aerschot, 50, 168
Afghanistan, 267
agricultural wages, 195
air bombardment, 46, 60, 227, 234
Albion motor works, 189
Aldington, Richard, 271
Allan, Maud, 241
Allenby, Edmund, 213
Alloa, 237
Alvah, 121
Amalgamated Society of Engineers (ASE),
    189, 204
Amritsar massacre (1919), 46
anachronism, 1
Angell, Norman, 18, 19
Angels of Mons, 67, 314n94
Annan, 237
anthologies, 134–5
Anti-German League, 234
anti-Germanism
    1930s, 274
    anti-semitism and, 241
    atrocities in Belgium, 42–55, 280
    atrocity mongering, 63–7
    changing pattern, 235–8
    construction of Huns, 52, 57–63, 147
    Daily Mail, 47–57
    extreme right, 234–5
    lies and half-truths, 40–4
    post-war, 270, 271
    propaganda, 67–9
    riots, 234, 235–8
    spread of hatred, 238–41
anti-Irishness, 242–4, 270
anti-semitism, 125, 155, 239–41, 242, 270

Antwerp, 19, 42–3
appeasement, 275
Arbroath, 123
Armenian genocide, 168, 313n79
Armistice (1918), 14, 250–2
Armistice Day (1939), 275
Armistice day parties, 257
Armstrong, Moira, 113
Arnhem, battle of (1944), 4
Arnold, E. V., 200–1
Arras, 128
Asquith, Cynthia, 124–5, 241–2
Asquith, Herbert, 32, 96, 110, 152, 207
Asquith, Margot, 241
Asquith, Raymond, 31, 125, 152
atrocity stories. *See* anti-Germanism
attestation, 72, 93, 94
attitudes to war, 37
Attleborough, 26, 120
Aubers Ridge, 46, 123

Bach, J. S., 59
Baden-Powell, Robert, 71
Baines, Betty, 185
Baines, George, 185
Baines, Ralph, 184–5
Baker, Alfred, 234–5
Baker, Kenneth, 4
Balfour report, 188, 191
Balkan wars, 296
Banbury, 21, 101
Bannockburn, 85, 86
Baptists, 21, 176
Barker, Lilian, 192
Barker, Pat, 3
Barkworth, E., 33
Barley, Arthur, 238–9
Barlow, Jane, 243
Barnes, George, 207
Barnes, Julian, 277
Barnett, Corelli, 272

Barrow-in-Furness, 196–7, 198
Bath, 223, 225, 234, 285
Battersby, H. F. P., 268
BBC, 83
Beaconsfield, 75
Beamish, H. H., 235
Beardmore, 188, 189
Beardmore, Wiliam, 189, 190
Becker, August, 62
Becton, 273
Bedford, 104, 223
Bedford, Margaret Ida, 177–8
Beethoven, Ludvig van, 59
Begbie, Harold, 145–6
Beith, Ian Hay, 84
Belfast, 127
Belgium
    German atrocities, 42–55, 68, 270, 280
    German invasion, 24, 36, 37
Bell, George, 171
Belsen, 295
Belsher, Allan, 235
Bennet, Samuel Hall, 149
Bennett, Arnold, 38
Bennett, Edie, 182, 215, 277
Bennett, Gunner, 209, 210
Benson, A. C., 67
Bentwell, 28
bereaved
    commemoration as therapy, 254–5, 275
    material support, 263
    participation in commemoration, 254–7,
        259–60
    remembrance, 249–50
    sites of mourning, 257–63
    statistics, 251–3
Beresford, Lord Charles, 248
Berlyn, Alfred, 142–3
Bernstein, Julius Meyer, 239
Bet-El, Ilana, 101
Beveridge, Albert, 298n4
Bevin, Ernest, 22
Billing, Pemberton, 234, 241–2, 244,
    246, 248
Bilsborough, Ethel, 55, 216–19
Birmingham, 22, 73, 95, 101, 102, 128,
    195–6, 223
Birtwhistle, W., 224
Bishop Auckland, 223, 226
'black legend', 44–7, 49
Black Watch, 123
Blackadder Goes Forth, 3, 272
Blaina, 251
Blair, Tony, 296
Blatchford, Robert, 79

blighty wounds, 264
blockade, 58, 59, 315n99
Blomfield, Reginald, 261
blood, value, 112–13
Bloomsbury, 108–9
Blunden, Edmund, 161, 271
Boer War, 10, 11, 19, 258, 274
Boloism, 246
Bonavia, 212
Bond, Brian, 272
Bonham Carter, Violet, 32
Bottomley, Horatio, 19, 69, 76, 137, 138,
    145, 153, 157, 170, 172, 181–2, 185,
    242, 243–4, 246, 248
Bourne, Cardinal, 96, 97
Bowerchalke, 21, 127
Boy Scouts, 263
Bracco, Rosa Maria, 268, 272
Bradburn, Alf, 208–9
Bradford, 88, 112, 127, 223
Bradlaugh, Charles, 153
Brassens, George, 2
Brathchell, E. G., 95
Briant, Frank, 97
Bridport, 26
Brighton, 234, 238
Bristol, 22, 74, 99, 101, 102, 115, 223,
    224, 225
British American Tobacco, 115
British Empire Union, 234, 238, 240
British Legion, 262, 263, 274
British Red Cross, 98
British Socialist Party, 199
Brown, Davis, 118
Brown, K. D., 177
Bruce, Robert, 85, 86
Brundrett, Whitmore and Randall, 106
Bryan, F. W., 180
Bryce Report, 46, 67–8
Buchan, John, 200
Buckrose, J. E., 144, 174
Bugden, J. H., 118
Burdett-Coutts, Margaret, 149
Burke, Edmund, 80
Burnham, Lord, 75
Burns, Robert, 85
Burwell, 262
Bury, 71, 123, 223, 226
Bury St Edmunds, 234, 237
Bush, George W., 296
Butchers' Trade Association, 244

Caesarini, David, 240–1
Cambrai, 213, 225
Cambridge, 52, 223

Campbell, R. J., 96–7
Campbell, R. W., 269
Cardiff, 139, 223, 226, 228
Carey, W. J., 156
Carlisle, 139, 261, 262
Carson, Edward, 249
Cartmell, Harry, 77, 95, 105–7, 142,
    154–5, 156, 277, 331n23
Cassell, Felix, 239
casualties, 7
    See also sacrifice
    chronology, 122–31
    civilians and soldiers, 131–6, 293–4
    class, 124–7, 130–1, 253, 282
    Croydon, 113–15
    demography, 175
    economy of sacrifice, 245, 257, 265
    farmers, 117–22
    numbers, 251–3
    occupational breakdown, 113–17
    Oxbridge men, 290
    Passchendaele, 129–30
    social elites, 124–7, 130–1, 289–90
    Somme, 127–8
    support of disabled, 263–6
Catholic Church, 159, 176, 182, 185, 244
Cavell, Edith, 161, 339n22
Ceadel, Martin, 37
Cecil, Florence, 255
Cecil, Hugh, 272
Cecil, Rev. Lord William, 171–2
Cenotaph, 255, 267–8, 273–5
Central Control Board, 194
Central Labour College, 199
Chamberlain, Neville, 95, 103, 107, 128,
    241, 250, 253
charities
    charitable giving, 227, 232–3
    war disabled, 265
Charity Organisation Society, 194
Charles Owen & Co., 289
Charteris, Brigadier General, 41–2, 314n94
Charteris, Yvo, 124–5
Chelmsford, 223
Cheshires, 78–9
Chester, 26, 28, 72, 137
Chester, Mr, 260
Chesterton, G. K., 36, 37
Chislehurst, 234
choices, 2
Chorley, 127, 128
Christianity. *See* religion
Christmas crisis (1917), 213–16
Church of England
    See also religion

1914 context, 159–60
clerical exemption from military
    service, 184
National Mission (1916), 165–73, 175
pre-war line, 20–1
sacrifice, 112
volunteers, 176
war and, 160–5, 183–4, 185
Church of Scotland, 83
Churchill, Winston, 57, 188, 202
Civil Service League, 99
civilians, soldiers and, 131–6, 293–4
clans, 86
Clark, Alan, 272
Clark, Andrew, 33, 52, 64, 66–7, 69,
    77, 277
Clarke, J. H., 242
class
    antagonisms, 245–6
    casualties and, 124–7, 131, 253, 282
    conscripted army, 244
    post-war conflicts, 270
    recruitment and, 72, 78–80, 82
    significance, 278
    war enthusiasm and, 25
    war experience and, 278–91
Clayton, Tubby, 272
Cleethorpes, 20–1
Clyde shipbuilding, 187, 188–91, 209
Clyde Workers' Committee,
    188–90, 199
Clydeside Bank, 228
coal mining
    casualties, 283
    profits, 140
    Sengennydd, 279, 280, 283
    South Wales, 187–8, 200,
        202, 208
    war loans, 226
Coatbridge, 285
Cockermouth, 259
cocoa press, 17
Colchester, 120
collective punishment, 45
Collet, Reverend, 21
commemoration
    1930s, 273–6
    contextualising, 272
    disabled support, 263–6
    dynamics, 253–4
    participation of bereaved, 254–7,
        259–60
    politics, 274–5
    post-war, 249–57
    rhetoric, 4

commemoration (cont.)
  therapeutic value, 254–5, 275
  war memorials, 254, 257–63, 267–9,
    272, 273–5
Commonwealth War Graves, 256
Companions of Honour, 148
Comrades of the Great War, 260, 262
concentration camps, 45
Congregationalism, 173, 174, 176
Connell, Alexander, 174–5, 176
conscientious objectors, 91, 101, 109, 122,
    154–5, 186, 217
conscription
  appeals, 101–8
  introduction, 93
  Ireland, 243–4
  Military Service Tribunals,
    101–8, 155
  reserved occupations, 210, 289
  rural tribunals, 122
  suspension, 267
  temporary exemptions, 102, 103
consent to war. See war enthusiasm
contemporary voices, 6
contraband, 58
Cook, George, 22
Cooke, S., 239
Cooney, Father, 185
Cooper, Duff, 126, 131
Corelli, Marie, 144
Cornwall, Jack, 263
corpse-rendering, 41–2
costs of war, 2
counter-revolution, 208
Cousins, Harold, 42, 92–4, 102, 133,
    209, 277
Cousins, Mr, 260
Couzens, Monica, 191–2
Coventry, 211, 212
Cromwell, Oliver, 181
Crooks, Will, 23, 75
Croydon, 101, 102, 113–17
Crudie, 120
crusading, 37, 168, 173, 174–5, 185
Curzon, Lord, 255
Cust, Henry, 72

Daiches, Samuel, 20
Daily Mail
  Belgian atrocities, 47–55
  dilemna, 68
  home destruction, 55–7
  photographs, 51, 56, 61
Damon, Charles, 268
Darwinism, 159

Davidson, Randall, 96–7, 326n43
Davies, G. P., 274
Davies, John, 120
Dawson report, 262–3
De Vries, Jacqueline, 100
death notices, 249
defencism, 37
Delmira, 57–8
demobilisation, 267, 283
demography
  female mortality rates, 286
  infant mortality, 193, 278, 279, 285–6
Denbeath, 318nn36
Derby, 88, 269
Derby, Lord, 72, 249
Dewhurst, R., 224
Dickinson, W. H., 215
diet, 279, 286
Dinant, 53
disabled, support, 263–6
disillusionment, 271–3
dissent, suppression, 206–8
distrust, 198
Dixon, Arthur, 128
dockers, 200
doggerel, 6
Dolan, Patrick, 147
Doncaster, 194
Dover, 223, 227
Doyle, Arthur Conan, 33
Drake, Francis, 225
drink restrictions, 197, 199
Dunstable, 29
Durham, 258
Dyson, Will, 62

Eagar, Aimee, 133–4
Easter Rising (1916), 45, 217
Ebbw Vale, 223, 226
Ecclesfield, 269
economy, war economy, 206
Edinburgh, 86, 98, 228–9, 237, 251
Edinburgh Territorials, 82
elites
  casualties, 124–7, 130–1, 289–90
  mobility, 281
  popular view, 281–2
Emden, 58
employment. See industrial relations
Enham, 265
Enlightenment, 85
enlistment. See volunteers
enthusiasm. See war enthusiasm
ethnicity, recruitment and, 79–80
Eton College, 124

Eugenics Education Society, 264
experiences. *See* war experiences

Fabian Women's Group, 278
Fabians, 142
Fairfield, 188
Fairstead, 33
Falklands War, 296
farmers, 117–22, 141–2
Farnham, 234
Farrier, Mabel, 180–1
Farrow, Reuben, 76, 154
Fascism, 293, 294
Fearnought, 98
feminism
    pre-war positions, 23–4
    volunteers, 99–100
    white feathers and, 77
Ferguson, Niall, 3, 206, 208, 288
Fernside, Edie, 251
Fernside, Elizabeth, 133, 180, 209, 215,
    225, 251, 277, 309n35
Fernside, Fred, 180
Field, Guy, 128
Field, Harry, 128
Flanders, 5
Folkestone, 40, 223, 227, 234
food prices, 18, 28–9, 139, 197, 200, 210,
    215, 218, 220
food supply, 122, 196, 214–16, 217
football, 71–2
Forbes, Beta, 239
Ford, Ford Madox, 271
Fore Stree Warehouse Company, 140
Forres, 98
Forward, 190
Fowler, Henry, 79
Fox, Mrs Dacre, 248
Fox, Delia, 243
Foxe's Book of Martyrs, 155
France
    Boloism, 246
    civilisation, 59
    cultural trauma, 2
    exhaustion, 207
    German atrocities, 52, 54, 270
    monuments aux morts, 257
    press, 51
    sacrifice, 207
    socialists, 23
    war memorials, 273
    war outcome, 2
Fry's, 115
Fulham, 215
Fussell, Paul, 271–2, 293

futility of war, 3–4
Fyfe, Hamilton, 49

gains of war, 1–2
Gairloch, 82
Gallipoli, 4, 46, 123
gamekeepers, 119
Gardiner, A. G., 16
gas, 46, 59, 60–1, 62, 63, 68
Gayton, 119
Geddes, Auckland, 108
General Strike (1926), 270
geography
    patriotism, 220–33
    rioting, 236–8
    volunteering, 81–90
George V, 95–6, 97, 98
George, Miss, 260
Germany
    See also anti-Germanism
    1870 quick victory, 20
    1930s, 273–6
    1945 position, 295
    atrocities in Belgium, 42–55, 68
    audience crowds, 13
    British post-war presence, 267
    Cenotaph wreath (1933), 273–6
    constructing the Hun, 52, 57–63, 147
    culture, 58–9
    destructions in UK, 55–7
    disabled support, 266
    invasion of Belgium, 24, 36, 37
    militarism, 276
    November criminals, 3
    peace offer (1916), 149–50
    pre-war attitudes, 25
    pro-war crowds, 14
    propaganda, 43, 315n99
    reparations, 295
    sacrifice, 207
    socialists, 23
    territorial losses, 295
    trauma of defeat, 2–3, 267
    war crimes, 45, 49
    war economy, 206
Giap, General, 266
Gilbert, Martin, 275
Gill, Eric, 256
Gilson, Cary, 128
Gladstone, William, 84
Glasgow, 29, 86, 127, 205, 216, 228, 229,
    230, 251
Glasgow rent strike (1915), 146–7
Glasgow Tramways, 82
Glasgow Women's Housing Association, 147

Glasier, Bruce, 84
Gleason, Arthur, 101, 125, 126, 132–3, 140, 202, 291
Godfrey, Arthur, 249
Goebel, Stefan, 230–1
Goether, Johann von, 59
Goetz, Karl, 61
Graham, Stephen, 78
Graves, Robert, 3, 43, 271, 272
Great Leighs, 127
Great Western Railway, 115
Great Yarmouth, 223, 227
Green, T. H., 164
Greenock, 98, 237
Grenfell, Billy, 124, 125
Grey, Edward, 21
Grigg, John, 4
Grimsby, 116, 269
guerillas, 45
Guérin, Madame, 255
Guildford, 128–9, 159, 227, 233
Gulf War (1991), 296
Gunn & Co., 139

Hague Convention, 45, 52, 57
Haldane, Lord, 161
Hales, A. G., 138
Hallam, Councillor, 22
Hamilton, Ian, 274
Hammond, Barbara, 38
Hammond, M. B., 284
Hampton in Arden, 234
Hardie, Keir, 12, 84
Harding, Arthur, 193–4
Hardy, Florence, 238
Harris, Jose, 159
Harris, Louisa, 32
Harrison, Frederick, 153
Harrogate, 223
Hartlepool, 40, 55, 56, 60, 173, 223, 227
Haste, Cate, 47
Hatfield, 130
hatred
    See also anti-Germanism
    anti-catholic feeling, 244
    anti-Irishness, 242–4
    anti-semitism, 125, 155, 239–41, 242, 270
    class hatred, 244–6
    culture of hatred, 6
    homophobia, 241–2
    spread, 238–48
Hay Beith, Ian, 84
Henderson, Arthur, 96, 152
Herald League, 29

hindsight, 1
Hiroshima, 61
historiography
    continental revisionism, 11
    home and war front, 7–8
    military history, 271–2
    revisionism, 272–3, 292–3
Hitchin, 28, 223, 227
Hitler, Adolf, 5, 273–4, 295
hoarding, 28
Hobson, Charles, 22
Hodgson, Radnor, 18
Hohenrein, Charles, 236
Holford, John, 284
Holland, Frank, 138
Holmes, Colin, 241
Holocaust, 295
holy war, 153
home, sanctity, 51
home destructions, 55–7
home front, memory, 5–8
Home Office Intelligence, 194
homophobia, 241–2
Hore, C. F. A., 266
Hornchurch, 95, 130, 176
horse racing, 72
hostages, 45
housing, working class, 279, 280
Hove, 32–3, 131, 144, 151, 234
Huddersfield, 13, 22, 101, 102, 108
Hudson, A. H., 210
Hull, 88, 223, 236–7, 238, 269
Hulme, 329n101
Huns, 52, 57–63, 147
Hussey, Dyneley, 135
Hutton, Isabel, 95
Hyde (Cheshire), 40, 75, 81, 89, 103, 174, 175–6
Hyndman, Henry Mayers, 15
Hynes, Samuel, 272

illegitimacy, 62
Illif, Phyllis, 251
Imperial Tobacco, 115, 224
Imperial War Graves Commission, 255
Imperial War Museum, 254, 255, 293
India, Amritsar massacre (1919), 46
industrial relations
    Clyde shipbuilding, 187, 188–91, 209
    full employment, 194–5, 236, 285
    limited industrial truce, 187–91
    middle classes, 208–12
    munition workers, 191–3, 196, 198, 209, 210, 212
    post-war, 269

reserved occupations, 210, 289
revolt, 199–208
strikes, 199, 202–11, 288
suppression of dissent, 206–8
unrest, 191–9, 288
wages, 190, 191, 195–6, 206, 209–10
Welsh miners, 187–8
infant mortality, 193, 278, 279, 285–6
inflation, 140, 191, 192–3, 196, 197, 218, 282
influenza, 250, 286
Inge, Ralph, 161–2, 167
Inglis, Ken, 334n17
injustice, 198
Inter-Parliamentary Union, 37
International Metal Trades Federation, 22
International Women's Suffrage Association, 23
Iraq War (2003), 296
Ireland
    anti-Irishness, 242–4, 270
    conscription, 243–4
    Easter Rising (1916), 45–6, 217, 242–3
    volunteers, 81, 91
Isaacs, Eva, 110–11, 112, 125–6, 133, 277
Isaacs, Rufus, 125, 126, 241
Italy, Caporetto defeat, 213

Jack Cornwall Fund, 265
Jalland, Pat, 253–4
Jeffries, J. M. N., 48, 54–5
Jellicoe, John, 67
Jellicoe, Lady, 67, 96
Jenkins, Hubert, 147
Jerusalem, 213
Jews
    See also anti-semitism
    Jewish Brigade of Royal Fusiliers, 80
    middle class casualties, 245
    patriotism, 161
    pre-war mood, 20
jingoism, 1914 myth, 9–11
John Menzies, 121
Johnston, Tom, 147
joint stock companies, 140–1
Jones, Rhodri, 299n13
just war, 183, 185, 294–6
Jutland, battle of (1917), 67, 263

Karno, Fred, 86, 179
Kaufman, Herbert, 57
Keegan, John, 290
Keen, Thomas, 104
Kennedy, Geoffrey Studdert, 153
Kennington, Eric, 327n49

Kent, S. K., 339n23
Kernick, E. F., 238
Keynes, John Maynard, 109, 270
King, Alex, 259, 275
King's Lynn, 223, 227
Kingston, 234
Kipling, Rudyard, 51, 249–50, 254
Kirkoswald, 262
Kirkwood, David, 86, 189, 190
Kitchener, Lord, 30, 62, 71, 79, 96
Knightley, Philip, 45, 311n50
Knolly, Henry, 72
Knox, Ronald, 162
Kultur, 58–9, 60

Labouchere, Major, 199–200
labour. See industrial relations
Lampen, Reverend, 182
Lampeter, 226
Lancing, 124
Lange, Christian, 37
Langton, Cecil, 112
Lansbury, George, 165–7, 172, 186
Lansdowne, Lord, 126, 162
last war, 5, 275
Law, Andrew Boanr, 152, 207
Layton, Walter, 202
Le Queux, William, 47, 62, 83
League of Nations, 156
League of Nations Union, 269
Lee, J., 199
Leeds, 18, 28, 72, 88, 95, 98, 101, 102, 103, 119, 209, 223, 261, 268
Leicester, 22, 88–9, 194, 223, 226
lesbianism, 241
Lest We forget, 265–6
letters, 278
Lewis, Edwin, 147
Lewis Methyr, 140
lies, half-truths and, 40–4
Life and Liberty Movement, 173
Limerick, Lady, 98
Linthwaite, 102–3
Lipton, Thomas, 228
Litman, S., 141
Little and Ballantyne, 139
Livermore, Vernon, 40
Liverpool, 17, 18, 98, 99, 139, 174–5, 223, 228, 234, 235, 238
Liverpool Rifles, 80
Liverpool Scots, 79–80
living standards, 191, 194, 207, 236, 280, 284
Llanelli, 223

Lloyd George, David
  Bottomley on, 248
  cartoons, 210
  German invasion of Belgium and, 24
  National War Aims Committee, 207
  nonconformists and, 79, 96, 109
  Pankhursts and, 100
  petitions to, 21–2
  public order, 86
  rhetoric, 152
  Scottish labour relations, 190
  South Wales coal mining, 188
  Wales and, 11
  on war enthusiasm, 10, 13
  war role, 287
Lockwood, Frank, 102–3, 107–8, 277
Lodge, Oliver, 185
Lody, Karl, 65
London
  ambivalence, 34, 35–6
  anti-semitism, 240
  Armistice Day, 251
  August 1914, 10, 13–16
  casualties, 127, 130, 131
  charitable giving, 232–3
  Christmas crisis (1917), 215
  extreme right, 234–5
  feeling of injustice, 197, 198
  infant mortality, 285
  irreligious city, 178, 180
  malnutrition rates, 194
  Military Service Tribunals, 102, 103
  night-bombing, 213–14
  outbreak of war, 26–8
  pay rises, 289
  pre-war mood, 18, 22–3
  recruitment, 30, 31–2, 73
  religious life, 179
  riots, 237, 238
  war loans, 225, 226, 228, 230–1
  war memorials, 262, 269
  war profiteers, 139
  working-class life, 278–9
London, Jack, 336n4
London County Council, 116, 123
London Rifle Brigade, 78, 290
London Territorials, 123
Long, Walter, 104
Lonsdale, Lord, 26
Loos, 84, 113, 133
Lord Roberts workshops, 265
lost generation, 127
Louvain, 50–2, 55, 57, 62, 67, 168
Lucas, Charles, 143–4
Lusitania, 40, 46, 58, 61–2, 168

Lusitania riots, 235–8
Luton, 104, 223, 227
Lutyens, Edwin, 255
Lyle Shipping Company, 228

McCarthy, Justin, 36
McDevitt, Phillip, 188
Macdonagh, Michael, 67, 71–2, 102, 149
Macdonald, Catriona, 237–8
MacDonald, James Ramsay, 30, 84, 88
Macdonald, Nina, 219–20
MacGuire, Ada, 63, 92
MacGuire, Rho, 63
McKay, Dr, 259–60
Mackenzie, Isabel Burton, 318nn36
McKinley, Mr, 260
Mackintosh, Ewart, 87
Maclean, John, 190, 228
Maclean, Norman, 52, 151
Macleod, Hugh, 179
Maidstone, 223
Malines, 57
Malthus, Thomas, 161
Manchester, 200, 223, 228, 234, 238, 269
Manners, Diana, 126
Manning, Frederick, 78
Mansfield, 223, 226
Marconi scandal, 241
Marin, Harry, 128
Market Bosworth, 107–8
Market Harborough, 234
Markham, Violet, 98
Marnoch, 127
married men, 92–4
Marston, 119
Marwick, Arthur, 9, 236
Marxism, 281
Masterman, Charles, 22, 183
Maurice, F. D., 160
memorials. See war memorials
memory. See popular memory
mentalities, 6
Merthyr Tydfil, 12, 245
Messinger, Gary, 315n97
Methodists, 21, 159, 173, 174, 175
middle classes
  casualties, 289–90
  conscripted army, 244
  leisure, 281
  living standards, 290–1
  oral v. written sources, 278
  potential revolt, 208–12
  pre-war experience, 280–2
  shrill protest, 233
  war experience, 289–91

Midlothian Campaign, 84
Miles, Mrs Eustace, 33
Miles, H. E., 215
militarism, 37, 276
Military Cork Headdress Trade
    Union, 289
Military Service Tribunals, 101–8
Millman, Brock, 206–8
mines, 46
mobilisation, 25–30
Mond, Alfred, 255
Monk, Miss, 260
Mons, 32, 113
Mons Despatch, 66
Montagu, Edwin, 80
Montagu, E. S., 119
Montague, C. E., 306n10
Moore, Christopher, 252–3, 339n28
moral economy, 198
moral indignation, 1
Morel, E. D., 200
Morgan, Kenneth, 11
Moriarty, Catherine, 254
Morrell, Ottoline, 10
Mosse, George, 272–3, 293
munition workers, 191–2, 196, 198, 209,
    210, 212
Munro, John, 86
Murray, Charles, 87, 121–2
Murray, Gilbert, 37
music hall, 72–3
Mussolini, Benito, 248
mutinies, 283
myths, 6, 9–11, 293–6

Napoleonic wars, 1, 12, 163
National Association, 262
National Federation of Discharged and
    Demobilised Soldiers and Sailors,
    260, 262
National Federation of Women
    Workers, 23
National Mission, 162, 165–73, 175
National Party, 235, 240
National Union of Women's Suffrage
    Societies (NUWSS), 23–4, 99
National War Aims Committee, 204, 207
naval warfare, 58–62
Nazism, 294, 295
Neutrality League, 17
Neuve Chapelle, 113
Nevinson, Christopher, 142
Newbury, 223
Newcastle, 88, 127, 223, 225, 227, 268
Newlay, 209

Newmarket, 223, 224
Newport, 223, 259–61, 262
Nicholas II, Tsar, 95
Nicoll, William Robertson, 21–2
No Conscription Fellowship, 199
Nobel Explosives, 228
nonconformists, 21–2, 79, 84, 96, 109,
    159, 173–7
Norfolk farmers, 117–18
Northcliffe, Alfred Harmsworth, Lord, 17,
    34–5, 40, 41, 47, 54, 62, 316n100
Northern Textile Trades Federation, 198
Norwich, 18, 22, 27
Nottingham, 88, 223, 226, 252
novels, 278
nutrition, 194, 279, 286

Offer, Avner, 76–7
Officers Family Fund, 99
Oh! What a Lovely War, 3, 272
Oldham, 88
oral history, 6, 278
Oramnel, 50
Order of the British Empire (OBE), 148–9
Orders of Chivalry, 148
Orkney, 27, 222
Owen, Wilfred, 3, 151, 251, 271
Oxbridge casualties, 290
Oxford, 52, 223, 225, 234, 238
Oxford Union, 71

pacifism, 9–10, 17, 37, 40, 41, 43, 84, 162,
    202, 226, 234, 272
Page-Croft, General, 248
Palestine, 213
pals battalions, 78–9, 127, 227
Panayi, Panikos, 235–7
Pankhurst, Christabel, 99–100
Pankhurst, Emmeline, 99–100
Pankhurst, Sylvia, 99, 186, 237, 284
Parkhead Forge, 205
Passchendale, 4, 129–30, 149
paupers, 74
Pawson and Leaf, 140
peace insurance, 19
Peace Society, 29
peace treaties, 270, 295
Pearce, Cyril, 13
Peel, Dorothy, 213
Pellinghome, Lydia, 274
Pemberton-Billing, Noel, 184
Pennell, Catriona, 9
Perfect, Charles Thomas, 176
Perth, 237, 285
Pettingell, Frank, 90–1

Philippines, 45
photographs, 51, 56, 61, 254
pianos, 193, 196
Playne, Caroline, 35, 47
Pleasant Sunday Afternoons (PSA), 180
Ploegstreet Wood, 128
poison gas, 46, 59, 60–1, 62, 63, 68
Pole, William Tudor, 157–8
politicians, family casualties, 152
Ponsonby, Arthur, 9, 38, 41–4, 55, 67, 68
Poole, Barry, 268
Pope, Jessie, 56–7
poppies, 263, 266
popular beliefs, 5, 19
popular memory
    bad war, 4, 294–6
    futility of war, 3–4
    historical understanding, 1–5, 272
    home front, 5–8
    stupidity version, 3
Portsmouth, 25–6, 223, 234
post-war
    1930s, 273–6
    commemoration, 249–63, 267–9
    disillusionment, 271–3
    living standards, 284
    redemption, 266–71
Potadulais, 226
poverty, 278–80
Powell, Margaret, 286–7
Presbyterianism, 83, 174–5
Preston, 27, 31, 77, 95, 105–7, 155, 223,
    224, 225
Preston Hall, 265
Priestley, J. B., 271
Prince of Wales Fund, 98, 145, 187
prisoners of war, 45
Proctor, Daisy, 182
Proctor, William, 181–2
Professional Classes Relief Council, 99
profiteers, 136–42, 146–7, 175, 196, 197,
    198, 199, 212, 226
propaganda, 6
    atrocity mongering, 63–7
    Belgian atrocities, 42–55
    'Bells of Antwerp,' 42–3
    'black legend,' 44–7, 49
    construction of Huns, 52, 57–63, 147
    corpse-rendering, 41–2
    Daily Mail, 47–63
    east coast destructions, 55–7
    government machinery, 207
    lies and half-truths, 40–4
    photographs, 51, 56, 61
    rumours, 63–7

volunteers and, 75
war function, 67–9
Prothero, Barbara, 104
Pwllhelli, 82

Quakers, 162, 181

racism
    See also anti-Germanism
    anti-Irishness, 242–4
    anti-semitism, 125, 155, 239–41,
        242, 270
    degeneracy, 242
    post-war, 270
    spread of hatred, 238–48
Raleigh, Walter, 212
Ramsay, Professor, 38–9
Ramsey, W. J., 109
rape, 50, 54, 62, 68
Rathbone, Eleanor, 17
rationing, 207, 215, 218
Ravenstonedale, 262
Raymond, Ernest, 268–9
Raynes, Will, 76
Read, Herbert, 275
Reading, Lord, 241
recruitment. See conscription; volunteers
Red Cross, 227
redemption, 266–71
Redmond, John, 25, 152
Reece, Ada, 34
Reeve, Alfred, 112–13
Reeve, Pemberton, 196
Reformation, 154
registration, 217
Reigate, 234
Reith, John, 83, 84–5
religion
    See also specific churches
    anti-clericalism, 184
    Christian socialism, 154, 160,
        165–7, 186
    Christian view of war, 4–5, 76
    conscientious objectors, 154–5
    Edwardian Britain, 158–60, 178–80
    historic peak, 184
    independence, 154
    just war theology, 183, 185
    laity and war, 177–86
    language of sacrifice, 156–7
    National Mission (1916), 162,
        165–73, 175
    nonconformists and the war, 173–7
    patriotism and, 7, 160–5
    poetic imagery and, 151

recruitment and, 79, 80, 88–9, 175–6
rhetoric, 152–8
teetotallers, 95–7
use of religious language, 179
Remarque, Eric Maria, 270
remembrance. *See* commemoration
rent control, 147
reparations, 295
Repington, Charles, 103, 104, 108
reprisals, 184
Rheims, 52, 57
Rhineland, 295
Rhondda, 223, 226
Rhondda, Lord, 218
Riddell, George, 21–2
right-wing politics
    anti-semitism, 239–41
    extreme politics, 246–8, 267
    groups, 234–5
    homophobia, 241–2
Rimmer, Mrs, 267
riots, 234, 235–8
Roberts, Lord, 96, 98
Roberts, Robert, 135, 194, 283–4, 298n2
Robinson, Frederick, 131, 209, 231–2
Rochdale, 243
Rogers, F. B., 64
Rogers, Hallewell, 128
Rosenberg, Alfred, 273, 274
Royal Artillery Commemoration Fund,
    261–2
Royal Naval Reserve, 82
Royal Patriotic Fund, 98, 264
Royal Scots, 82
Royal Welsh Fusilliers, 244
Royden, Maude, 173
Rubens, Paul, 73
Rubinstein, S., 306n10
Rubinstein, William, 240–1
rumours, 63–7
rural population
    casualties, 127–8
    farmers' military service, 117–22
    Military Service Tribunals, 122
    volunteers, 81, 91
Russell, Bertrand, 10, 27, 109
Russia, 19, 24, 207, 267
Russian Revolution (1917), 204, 213
Rwanda, 310n47
Rye, Walter, 117–18

sacrifice
    See also casualties
    civilians and soldiers, 131–6, 293–4
    discourse, 109, 142–51, 152, 187, 294

economy of sacrifice, 245, 257, 265
reciprocity, 222
religious imagery, 151, 156–7
uniformity, 255–6
value of blood, 112–13
volunteers, 108–11
war as sacrifice, 292
willingness to, 232–3
Sainsbury's, 138
St Albans, 259
St Andrews, 234
St Dunstan's, 265
St Mary's Newmarket, 21
Salford, 194, 282, 283–4
Salisbury, Lord, 225
Salvation Army, 85, 179
Sanderson, Lord, 304n110
Sandgrove, Thomas, 33
Sandon, 119
sanitation, 280
Sassoon, Siegfried, 3, 42, 64–5, 151, 165,
    170, 172, 271, 272, 294
Saunders, Robert, 133, 178, 209, 234,
    251–2, 277
Scarborough, 55–7, 60, 62, 223, 227
Schiller, Friedrich, 59
Schneider's, 289
Scotland
    casualties, 120–1, 127, 131
    church attendance, 180
    Clyde shipbuilding, 187, 188–91, 209
    infant mortality, 285
    riots, 237
    strikes, 203
    volunteers, 81–8
    war loans, 221–2, 227–9
Scott, C. P., 16, 37
Scouts, 263
sea warfare, 58–62
Seaman's Trade Union, 245
Sears, James Edmunds, 273–4
Second World War, 4–5, 295
Selby, E. M., 275–6
Selkirk, 120, 319n48
Sengennydd, 279, 280, 283
separation allowance, 286–7
Serbia, 22, 24, 150, 207
servants, 281, 289
Shakespeare, William, 73
Sheffield, 22, 88, 190, 200, 210, 223, 226
Sheffield, Gary, 272
Sheppard, Dick, 171, 173
Sheridan-Jones, Charles, 213
Shetland, 123, 222
Sibbick, W. G., 260

Sidebotham, R., 175
Sierra Leone, 340n32
Silbey, David, 32, 317n29
Simmons, William, 268
Simonides, 268
Singapore, fall of (1942), 4
Sinn Fein, 199, 240, 243
sites of mourning, 257–63
Smillie, Bob, 94
Smith, F. E., 241
socialism
    Christian socialism, 154, 160, 165–7, 186
    Jews and, 240
    London, August 1914, 15–16
    outbreak of war, 29
    pacifism, 84
    pre-war position, 22–3, 282
    principles, 37
    recruitment, 78–9
    war profiteers and, 137, 139
Socialist Church, 176
soldiers
    See also volunteers
    civilians and, 131–6, 293–4
    letters, 278
    pay and benefits, 136
    political myths, 293
    post-war mutinies, 283
    spiritual fate of dead soldiers, 157–8
    working-class experience, 282–3, 286–7
Soldiers' and Sailors' Family Association, 249
Soldiers and Sailors Help Society, 98
Somme, 4, 113, 116, 125, 127–8, 171, 283, 290
South Africa, 45
South Mymms, 229
South Wales Miners' Federation, 11–12, 140
Soviet Union, 5
spectators, 70–3, 76, 91–5
Spencer, Captain, 235
Spencer, Mrs, 260
spiritualism, 157–8, 185–6
sport, 71–2
Squire, J. C., 160
Srebenica, 310n47
Stalin, Joseph, 5
Standard Oil Company, 239
state repression, 206–8
Steele, Marshall, 65
Stenhouse, Helen, 211–12
Stephens, Martin, 272
Stockholm Conference, 245
Stocks, Mary, 25
Stoke Newington, 259
Stoke-on-Trent, 223, 226

Stoney Massey, 95
Strachey, Lytton, 109
Streeter, Canon, 170–1
strikes, 199, 202–11, 288
Stroud Brewery Company, 75
Stubley, Ernest, 148
stupidity of war, 3
submarines, 46, 58, 216, 236
Suffragettes, 23–4, 51, 99–100, 200
suicide, 253–4
Sunday schools, 179–80
Surbiton, 223, 226, 234
Swansea, 88
Swedenborg, Emmanuel, 158
Swindon, 28, 89, 194, 223

'Tank Bank', 220–33
Tanner, Duncan, 206
Tawney, R. H., 78, 187
Taylor, A. J. P., 298n2
Taylor, Philip, 41
Tayport, 98
Tearle, Godfrey, 73
technology, 60, 61
Teddington, 234
teetotallers, 95–8, 109–10, 196
Temple, William, 162–5, 166, 167, 170, 172, 173
Termonde, 57
Terraine, John, 272, 314n84
Tetbury, 119, 120, 131
textile industry, 140
theatre, 72–3
Thermopylae, 268
Thiepval, 123
Thom, D., 339n26
Thomas Firth, 191
Thompson, George, 139
Thompson, Paul, 179
Thomson, Basil, 202
Tillett, Ben, 15, 248
'Tipperary', 9, 73
Titanic, 40
Todmorden, 90, 129–30, 199, 215, 227, 244–5
Tomb of the Unknown Warrior, 254, 255
Tonypandy strike, 188
torture, 50
Tosh, J., 320n69
Towers, Winifred, 65–6
Town Hall Association, 99
Toynbee Hall, 160, 172
trade unions
    See also industrial relations
    Clyde shipbuilding, 188–91

conscription and, 110
defence, 199
militancy, 288
Military Service Tribunals and, 105
pre-war positions, 22
South Wales coal miners, 188
triple alliance, 195, 201
unemployment reports, 31
Tredegar, 223, 226
The Trench, 297n4
Trevelyan, C. P., 200
Truro, 223
tuberculosis, 286
Tull, Walter, 72
Tunbridge Wells, 223, 226, 237
Turkey, Armenian genocide, 168, 313n79
Turriff, 82, 90, 98, 120
Twain, Mark, 143
Tynan, Katherine, 169–70

Ulster Division, 123
Union of Democratic Control, 29, 38, 199
Unitarians, 175
United States
    atrocities in Philippines, 45
    Iraq War (2003), 296
    isolationism, 40, 43
university missions, 160
Upper Brae, 120
Urban II, Pope, 153
urban myths, 63–7

vegetarians, 80
Verdun, 2
Verhey, Jeffrey, 13
Versailles Treaty (1919), 295
Vickers, 196
Vietnam War, 266
Vigilante, 241
Vigilantes, 234–5
Vignes, Thea, 179
volunteers
    See also conscription; soldiers
    attestation, 72, 93, 94
    bribery, 74–5
    class and, 72, 78–80, 82, 244
    compulsion, 74, 77
    conscientious enlistment, 77, 176
    conscientious objection, 91
    double-think, 77
    economic distress, 74, 75
    enlistment, 7, 73–91
    ethnicity, 79–80
    gender, 99–100
    geographical disparities, 81–90

Ireland, 81, 91
Kitchener poster, 71
married men, 92–4
outbreak of war, 30–3
pals battalions, 78–9, 127, 227
posters, 71–2, 88
propaganda and, 75
recruitment meetings, 75–6, 151
refusal to volunteer, 91–5
religion and, 79, 80, 88–9, 175–6
rhetoric, 95
rural population, 81, 91
sacrifice, 108–11
Scotland, 81–8
social pressure, 77, 90
spectators, 70–3, 76
teetotallers, 95–8, 109–10
unfairness, 77
unfit men, 90–1
voluntary ethic, 95–100

wages, 190, 191, 195–6, 206, 209–10
Waites, Bernard, 193, 194, 198
Wakefield, 88
Wales
    August 1914, 11–13
    charitable giving, 227
    church attendance, 180
    Church disestablishment, 12, 159
    coal miners, 11–12, 187–8, 200, 202, 208
    nonconformists, 79, 174
    pacifism, 226, 234
    strikes, 203
    volunteers, 82, 85, 91, 175
    war loans, 226, 228
Wallace, William, 81, 85, 86
Walsall, 244
Walton-on-Thames, 237
war disabled, 263–6
war enthusiasm
    ambivalence and ambiguity, 33–6
    class, 25
    London, August 1914, 13–16
    myth of 1914, 6, 9–11
    outbreak of war, 25–30
    pre-war mood, 16–25
    reaction to war, 70–1
    recruitment, 30–3
    Wales, August 1914, 11–13
    war fever, 27
war experiences, 277–8
    middle classes, 289–91
    myths, 293–6
    women, 291–2
    working class, 278–80, 282–9

war graves, 255–6
war loans, 220–33
war memorials, 254, 257–63, 267–9, 272, 273–5
War Pensions Committee, 249
War Savings Associations, 221
Ware, Fabian, 255
waste, 144–5
Watford, 223, 227, 234
Watts, Hunter, 78
Weardale, Lord, 37
Webb, Beatrice, 142
Wellesley, G. V., 136–7
Wells, H. G., 5, 6, 142, 153, 157, 290
Welshpool, 234
Wemyss, Lord, 74
Wesleyans, 175
West Hartlepool, 223, 226, 227
Weymouth, 207–8
Whitcher, Mayor, 261
White, Arnold, 54, 238, 239, 241, 248, 300n35
White, Douglas, 170
White, Holt, 244
white feathers, 70, 73, 77
Wickes, Pembroke, 249
Wigan, 223, 226
Wigton, 262
Wilde, Oscar, 241
Wile, Frederick William, 62
Wilkinson, Eric, 135
Williams, Sarah, 153, 179
Williams, Valentine, 60
Williamson, Henry, 78, 271
Willis, Irene Cooper, 14
Wilson, Havelock, 245, 248
Wilson, Trevor, 67–8, 296
Wilson, Woodrow, 156
Winchcombe, 32
Winchester, 223, 237
Windermere, 119
Winnington-Ingram, Arthur, 168–70, 172, 183, 184, 185

Winter, Jay, 195, 236, 272–3
Wisbech, 223, 224
Wolverhampton, 223
women
  church attendance, 182–3
  Clyde shibuilding, 189
  emancipation, 2, 6, 291
  historiography, 6
  living standards, 194
  mortality rates, 286
  munition workers, 192
  National Mission, 169, 173
  volunteers, 98, 99–100
  war experiences, 291–2
Women's Co-operative Guild, 23
Women's Freedom League, 23
Women's Industrial Councils, 98
Women's Labour League, 23
Women's Social and Political Union, 23–4, 99, 199, 200
Women's War Service Bureau, 98
Woolwich arsenal, 192–3
Woolwich Crusade (1917), 171
Workers' Education Association, 201
working class
  diet, 279
  economic gains, 282–9
  housing, 279, 280
  infant mortality, 278, 279, 285–6
  living standards, 1–2, 280, 284
  pre-war experience, 278–80
Worksop, 223
World War II, 4–5, 295
World's Evangelical Alliance, 156
Worthing, 234

Yarmouth, 60
Yearsley, Macleod, 209, 239
York, 223
Ypres, 46, 60, 68, 123

Zeppelins, 46, 60, 62, 169
Zionism, 80
Zivilization, 58–9